Praise for Christopher Caldwell's

Reflections on the Revolution in Europe

"Caldwell compiles his arguments patiently . . . with lucidity and intellectual grace and even wit. . . . He is a vivid writer, and like an action-movie hero he walks calmly away from his own detonations while fire swirls behind him. . . . Mr. Caldwell's book is the most rigorous and plainspoken examination of Muslim immigration in Europe to date, a sobering book that walks right up to, if never quite crossing, the line between being alarming and being alarmist. . . . Well-researched, fervently argued and morally serious . . . it may serve as a wake-up call to many of Europe's liberal democracies."
—Dwight Garner, *The New York Times*

"This book is the best on its subject I have read."
—Theodore Dalrymple, *National Review*

"Four hundred pages of must-reading. . . . A truly rare combination of ground-truth reporting about—and historically and sociologically informed analysis of—the state of Europe today."
—*The Weekly Standard*

"Caldwell makes [his] arguments unusually well, in a book notable for its range, synthesis of the literature, analytical rigor and elegant tone." —Claire Berlinksi, *The Washington Post*

"Caldwell is a bracing, clear-eyed analyst of European pieties. . . . This book pulsates with ideas."
—David Goodhart, *The Observer* (London)

"Caldwell knows Europe, especially France, bet̲̲̲ most American and British commentat̲̲̲ t pinpointing denial and fligh̲̲̲ rpens a so far sluggish debate, pur-pose." —Martin̲̲̲ lon)

CHRISTOPHER CALDWELL

Reflections

on the Revolution

in Europe

Christopher Caldwell is a columnist for the
Financial Times, a contributing writer for *The
New York Times Magazine*, and a senior
editor at *The Weekly Standard*. He lives in
Washington, D.C.

CHRISTOPHER CALDWELL

Reflections
on the Revolution
in Europe

IMMIGRATION, ISLAM AND THE WEST

Anchor Books
A Division of Random House, Inc.
New York

FIRST ANCHOR BOOKS EDITION, JULY 2010

The Library of Congress has cataloged the Doubleday edition as follows:
Caldwell, Christopher.
Reflections on the revolution in Europe: immigration, Islam and the West /
Christopher Caldwell.
p. cm.
Includes bibliographical references and index.
(alk. paper)
1. Muslims—Europe. 2. Islam—Europe.
3. Europe—Emigration and immigration.
4. Islamic countries—Emigration and immigration.
5. Europe—Race relations—Religious aspects. .
6. Europe—Civilization—21st century.
7. Europe—Civilization—Islamic influences.
8. Culture conflict—Europe. 9. Multiculturalism—Europe. I. Title.
D1056.2.M87C35 2009
304.8088 297094—dc22
2008051563

Anchor ISBN: 978-0-307-27675-9

Author photograph © Brendan Hoffman/WpN

www.anchorbooks.com

Printed in the United States of America
10 9 8 7 6 5 4 3 2 1

to Zelda

Could he forget a child's ambition to be old
And institutions where it learned to wash and lie,
He'd tell the truth for which he thinks himself too young,

That everywhere on his horizon, all the sky,
Is now, as always, only waiting to be told
To be his father's house and speak his mother tongue.
                                        —W. H. Auden, "The Quest"

Contents

PART II

Islam

PART III

The West

PART I

Immigration

I

Rivers of blood

The rights and wrongs of Enoch Powell—How much immigration is there?—Muslim immigration—Europe's population problem—Civilization and decadence—Diversity is overrated—Can you have the same Europe with different people?

Western Europe became a multiethnic society in a fit of absence of mind. Mass immigration began—with little public debate, it would later be stressed—in the decade after the Second World War. Industries and government in Britain, France, Germany, the Low Countries, and Scandinavia set up programs to recruit manpower to their booming postwar economies. They invited immigrants. Some of the newcomers took positions, particularly in heavy industry, that now look enviably secure and well-paid. But others worked in the hardest, most thankless, and most dangerous occupations that European industry had to offer. Many had been loyal colonial subjects, and had even borne arms for European powers.

Europe became a destination for immigration as a result of consensus among its political and commercial elites. Those elites, to the extent they thought about the long-term consequences at all, made certain assumptions: Immigrants would be few in number. Since they were coming to fill short-term gaps in the labor force, most would stay in Europe only temporarily. Some might stay longer. No one assumed they would ever be eligible for welfare. That they would retain the habits and cultures of southern villages, clans, marketplaces, and mosques was a thought too bizarre to entertain.

3

Almost all of the assumptions with which mass immigration began proved false. As soon as they did, Europe's welcome to the world's poor was withdrawn—at first ambiguously, through the oratory of a few firebrand politicians in the 1960s, then explicitly through hard-line legislation against immigration in the 1970s. Decade in, decade out, the sentiment of Western European publics, as measured by opinion polls, has been resolutely opposed to mass immigration. But that is the beginning, not the end of our story. The revocation of Europe's invitation to immigrants, no matter how explicit it became, did little to stem their arrival. As the years passed, immigration to Europe accelerated. At no point were Europeans invited to assess its long-term costs and benefits

The rights and wrongs of Enoch Powell

On April 20, 1968, two weeks after the assassination of Martin Luther King Jr. and the race riots that it sparked in Washington and other U.S. cities, the British Tory parliamentarian Enoch Powell made a speech at the Midland Hotel in Birmingham that has haunted the European political imagination ever since. Powell was talking about the arrival, modest up to that point, of "coloured" former colonial subjects, primarily from the Indian subcontinent but also from the Caribbean. At the time, this migration had changed the face of only a very limited number of urban neighborhoods. Powell implied that the long-term consequence would be ghettoes like the ones in America that were burning as he spoke. "We must be mad," he said, "literally mad, as a nation, to be permitting the annual inflow of some 50,000 dependants, who are for the most part the material of the future growth of the immigrant-descended population. It is like watching a nation busily engaged in heaping up its own funeral pyre." Citing the poet Virgil, Powell warned, "I seem to see 'the River Tiber foaming with much blood.'"

Half a year later, in the course of an even more ominous speech to the Rotary Club of London, he warned that, should immigration proceed at the current pace, the urban part of whole towns and cities in Yorkshire, the Midlands and the Home Counties would be preponderantly or exclusively Afro-Asian in population. There would be several Washingtons in England. From those whole areas the indigenous population, the people of England, who fondly imagine that this is their country and these are their home-towns, would have been dislodged—I have deliberately chosen the most neutral word I could find. And here for the first time this morning I offer a subjective judgement . . . The people of England will not endure it.

All British discussion of immigration since then has been, essentially, an argument over whether Enoch Powell was right. It has been a sterile argument because those who engage in it tend to mix up two senses of the word *right*—the moral sense and the factual sense. To say the Emancipation Proclamation is right means something different than to say the Pythagorean theorem is right. Powell's remarks revealed a class-based split over which of these two kinds of rightness is the real business of politics. This split is a feature of all discussions of modern immigration in all countries.

Political elites focused on whether Powell was right morally. Even if most of the fears Powell appealed to were legitimate ones, and even if plenty of evidence can be mustered (such as his passion for India and for Indian languages) to show that Powell was not himself a racist, his speech can be defended against charges of bigotry only by splitting hairs. News coverage ran against him. Tory leader Ted Heath, Powell's archrival within the party, forced Powell to resign his position as shadow defense minister. Morally, Powell was not right.

Popular opinion, though, focused on whether he was right factually. And in this sense, right he was, beyond any shadow of a doubt. Although at the time Powell's demographic projections were much snickered at, they have turned out not just roughly accurate but as close to perfectly accurate as it is possible for any such projections to be: In his Rotary Club speech, Powell shocked his audience by stating that the nonwhite population of Britain, barely over a million at the time, would rise to 4.5 million by 2002. (According to the national census, the actual "ethnic minority" population of Britain in 2001 was 4,635,296.) At a speech during the 1970 election campaign, he told voters in Wolverhampton that between a fifth and a quarter of their city, of Birmingham, and of Inner London would consist of Commonwealth immigrants and their descendants. (According to the 2001 census, Wolverhampton is 22.2 percent, Birmingham 29.6 percent, and Inner London 34.4 percent nonwhite.)

Ordinary Britons loved Powell's Birmingham speech. He received literally vanloads of mail—100,000 letters in the ten days that followed, of which only 800 expressed disagreement. Yet if Powell was right that immigration would increase far beyond what an Englishman of 1968 would have considered tolerable, he was wrong to predict that Englishmen of the next generation would not tolerate it. Although blood has indeed flowed at times—a spate of racist murders of South Asians in the East End of London in the 1970s, a dozen major riots over the decades, and numerous terrorist plots, including the 7/7 transport bombings carried out by Islamist Englishmen of Pakistani descent in 2005—it has not made the rivers foam. What did Powell miss?

One thing he missed was shame. The dominant moral mood of postwar Europe was one of repentance for two historic misdeeds, colonialism and Nazism. It is true that Britain, uniquely among Western European countries, had no cause to feel penitence for having perpetrated, encouraged, or watched passively the outrages of fascism two and three decades before. Britain had, however, recently dissolved, or been chased from, the largest empire in the history of the world, which left most of its citizens feeling embarrassed and diffident. Powell was an exception. A lover of the old Empire, swept up in the romance of it, he had no ear for this dirge of repentance, and no sense that his contemporaries were hearing a different music.

When addressing Africans, Asians, and other would-be immigrants, postwar Europeans felt a sense of moral illegitimacy that deepened as the decades passed. The dominant mood was summed up in *The March*, a fictional movie that BBC 1 aired for "One World Week" in 1990. In it, a charismatic political leader called El-Mahdi leads a quarter of a million people out of a Sudanese refugee camp on a 3,000-mile march to Europe under the slogan "We are poor because you are rich"—a message the movie made little effort to contradict.

Even those who felt that such shame was misplaced were forced to admit its power. In *The Camp of the Saints*, the dark 1973 novel of the Frenchman Jean Raspail, a collection of philanthropists and activists incite a million underfed Indians to board a flotilla of rusty ships for Europe, with dire consequences, including the trampling to death of the well-wishers who rush to welcome the disembarking hordes. Raspail's vision captures more of the complexity of the modern world than *The March* does. Political clashes are provoked not just by simple inequalities but by accidents, the vanity of intellectual elites, and the snowball effect of the mass media. What the BBC's filmmakers saw as conscience, Raspail saw as a mix of cowardice and unintended consequences.

For Powell as for Raspail, mass migration into Europe was not a matter of individual migrants "looking for a better life," as the familiar phrase goes. It was a matter of organized masses *demanding* a better life, a desire with radically different political consequences. "It is much nearer to the truth," Powell said, "to think in terms of detachments from communities in the West Indies or India or Pakistan encamped in certain areas of England." Detachments, encampments—these are military metaphors. Powell is wrong to use them. But even if immigrants are not acting collectively, individual decisions to migrate can, in an age of globalization, produce massive collective effects. As the German poet and essayist Hans Magnus Enzensberger wrote in 1992:

The free movement of capital brings the free movement of labor in its wake. With the globalization of the world economy, which has been fully achieved only in the very recent past, migratory movements will take on a new quality, too. Government-organized colonial wars, campaigns of conquest, and expulsions will most likely be replaced by molecular mass migrations.

If one abandons the idea that Western Europeans are rapacious and exploitative by nature, and that Africans, Asians, and other would-be immigrants are inevitably their victims, then the fundamental difference between colonization and labor migration ceases to be obvious.

How much immigration is there?

Europe is now, for the first time in its modern history, a continent of migrants. Of the 375 million people in Western Europe, 40 million are living outside their countries of birth. In almost all Western European countries, the population of immigrants and their children approaches or surpasses 10 percent. Even the historically poor and backward countries of peripheral Catholic Europe, such as Ireland (14.1 percent immigrant) and Spain (11.1 percent), have become crossroads. Between 2000 and 2005, Ireland's foreign-born population was increasing at an average annual rate of 8.4 percent and Spain's at (what follows is not a typographical error) 21.6 percent a year.

But we must make a sharp distinction. Much of this movement—that part that involves Europeans moving to other European countries—is not really immigration at all. It is a program of increased labor and residential mobility explicitly agreed to, through treaties, by the more than two dozen states that are part of the European Union. The EU's members have pledged themselves to an "ever closer union." The so-called "Schengen agreements," ratified in the decade after 1985, permit free movement of residents across most of Europe's internal borders, with no checks or passport controls.

It is not such a big deal that a third (37 percent) of Luxembourg's residents were born abroad. Virtually all of them were born in the EU: Portugal, France, Belgium, Germany, and Italy are the most important sending countries. Luxembourg is a charter member of the European Union and one of the most loyal. And a Pole who moves to Ireland—as about 63,000 have done since the turn of the century, to the point where 2 percent of the island's population is Polish born—isn't just moving out of one country and into another. He is moving around *within* a federation.

The EU is not unanimously loved in Europe, and movement between EU countries is not popular—78 percent of Irish people, for instance, want to reimpose restrictions on Eastern European immigration. Such mobility erodes national cultures that have shaped and comforted people for centuries and it does so no matter who is doing the moving. For instance, the Swedish sociologist Åke Daun has often written about how Swedes "like being like each other." Most peoples do, and they have a harder time being so when their countries fill up with people from elsewhere. Preferences for cultural sameness are often about seemingly small matters—say, the pea soup that Swedes traditionally eat on Thursday or a national taciturnity so extreme that, in Sweden, according to Daun, "signaling in traffic is often considered an undesirable expression of aggression." If you are among those Swedes who feel a warm glow when eating pea soup on Thursday or a slight unease when signaling on turns, then immigration can make your life a little bit crummier, because it disrupts those patterns. And this is so even if the immigrants are perfectly upstanding citizens from a neighboring country.

But immigration from neighboring countries does not provoke the most worrisome immigration questions, such as "How well will they fit in?" "Is assimilation what they want?" and, most of all, "Where are their true loyalties?"—culminating in a troubled "Where is this all heading?" Describing intra-European movements as "immigration" can be a useful debating trick for those who wish to short-circuit discussion of the problems of *non*-European immigration. ("Why are Moroccan slums in Amsterdam a problem, but not German retirement communities in Ibiza?") In this sense, using the word *immigration* to describe intra-European movements makes only slightly more sense than describing a New Yorker as an "immigrant" to California. Movement between European countries does count as immigration for statistical purposes. But it is not what this book is about.

Muslim immigration

This book concerns a second type of immigration: immigration from non-European countries and cultures. To be more precise, it is about certain problems created by the desire of non-Europeans to settle in Europe for good: the problems of multiethnic and multicultural societies. There have always been Western European countries that contain multiple European peoples with distinct linguistic and cultural identities—Belgium, Britain, Finland, France, Spain, and

Switzerland in particular. Intercontinental immigration on the present scale, however, is unheard of. And it is unpopular. In no country in Europe does the bulk of the population aspire to live in a bazaar of world cultures. Yet all European countries are coming to the wrenching realization that they have somehow, without anyone's actively choosing it, turned into such bazaars.

In theory, any profoundly different culture could prove difficult to assimilate into European life. In practice, it is Islam that is posing the most acute problems. For 1,400 years, the Islamic and the Christian worlds have opposed one another, violently at times. We are living through one of those times. And yet, if immigration is somehow structurally or economically necessary to Europe—a proposition that will be examined more closely in the next chapter—it is from the overcrowded Muslim countries of Europe's southern and southeastern perimeter that it is likely to come. Of course, such immigration already has come and is continuing to come.

Net migration into Europe from elsewhere is at record levels, at around 1.7 million new arrivals a year. Europe's future peace and prosperity depend on how easily these newcomers (and their children and grandchildren) assimilate into European life. In the middle of the twentieth century, there were virtually no Muslims in Western Europe. At the turn of the twenty-first, there were between 15 and 17 million Muslims in Western Europe, including 5 million in France, 4 million in Germany, and 2 million in Britain.

The demographic "weight" of immigration in Europe is roughly what it is in the United States, making it tempting to compare Muslim immigration in Europe with Latin American immigration in the United States. Such a comparison obscures more than it illuminates. The cultural peculiarities of Latin American immigrants—aside from a different (European) first language, which they inevitably abandon for English by the second generation—are generally antiquated versions of American ones. Latinos have less money, higher labor-force participation, more authoritarian family structures, lower divorce rates, more frequent church attendance (still primarily Catholic, although with an impressive penetration of evangelical Protestantism), lousier diets, and higher rates of military enlistment than native-born Americans. In other words, Latino culture, in its broad outlines, is like the American working-class white culture of forty years ago. It is perfectly intelligible to any patient American who has ever had a conversation about the past with his parents. Mass Hispanic immigration can disrupt a few local habits, and the volume of the influx can cause logistical headaches for schools, hospitals, and local governments. But it requires no fundamental reform of American cultural practices or institutions. On balance, it may strengthen them.

Islam in Europe is different. Since its arrival half a century ago, Islam has broken—or required adjustments to, or rearguard defenses of—a good many of the European customs, received ideas, and state structures with which it has come in contact. Sometimes the adjustments are minor accommodations to Muslim tradition—businesses eliminating the tradition of drinks after work, women-only hours at swimming pools, or prayer rooms in office buildings, factories, and department stores. Sometimes new laws are felt necessary, such as the French one that has the effect of banning the veil in schools.

Occasionally what needs adjustment is the essence of Europe. A theme that runs through the later chapters of this book is that, on top of its economic costs, immigration exacts a steep price in freedom. The multiculturalism that has been Europe's main way of managing mass immigration requires the sacrifice of liberties that natives once thought of as rights. For instance, in most Western countries the surveillance of radical imams and mosques has been stepped up in the last decade. Such practices are easily (and sometimes cynically) criticized as putting people under surveillance just because they are Muslim. A regime of enhanced eavesdropping on *everyone* may become the path of least constitutional resistance. In countries where immigrant customs are held to repress women, intrusions into the domestic arrangements of *all* families have become more common. To take an example that we will return to in chapter 8, a Swedish cabinet minister has proposed national genital examinations of small girls as a means of combating the female circumcision common among a small minority of immigrants—the predominantly Muslim Somalis and other East Africans who began arriving in the 1990s.

European natives have become steadily less forthright, or more frightened, about expressing their opposition to immigration in public. But they express it in private, including to pollsters. It appears to be an objection not just to the arrival of new citizens but to multicultural society more generally. Only 19 percent of Europeans think immigration has been good for their countries. More than half (57 percent) say their countries have "too many foreigners." The more immigration a country has had, the higher the antipathy to immigration grows: 73 percent of French people think their country has too many immigrants, as do 69 percent of the British. The argument is not over how much immigration Europeans desire but over how much they will tolerate.

Misgivings about immigration in the abstract are as nothing next to the misgivings about Islam in particular. Since September 11, 2001, worries about immigrants and their children as a fifth column have percolated to the surface in all European countries. Even before September 11, though, the polls mentioned above showed that the French are three times as likely to complain of "too many Arabs" in the country than of too many of anything else. Mayor Alberto Ruiz-Gallardón of Madrid said in 2006, with reference to Islam that his city "is not—and does not wish to be—multicultural." The late Oriana Fallaci's tirade against European Islam (*The Rage and the Pride*) became the bestselling nonfiction book in the history of Italy in 2002, selling over a million copies. In 2004 the Princeton Islamic scholar Bernard Lewis scoffed when he was asked by a German newspaper to predict whether Europe would be a superpower by the end of this century. "Europe," he said, "will be part of the Arabic west, of the Maghreb."

Denmark has tightened immigration laws over the last decade largely because of alarming projections in the late 1990s that by 2020, 13.7 percent of Danes would have their roots in "authoritarian" countries and cultures. Since none of the countries in the EU is authoritarian, the word can be taken as a euphemism for non-European. That Europeans are most worried about immigrants of different races does not necessarily mean that racism is what motivates their worry. Their unease may come from a sense that ancestral grievances are easily reactivated, and nostalgia for clannish identities easily stoked. Such unease marks Europeans' views of the Basques, the Irish, and other European peoples, and there is no reason it should not mark their views of recent immigrants. Muslim residents of Denmark traveled the world in an effort to inflame hatred against their country during the Cartoon Crisis of 2006, and Muslim British citizens have now plotted and carried out attacks on civilians, not just in their own country but in Israel as well. Islam may prove assimilable within Europe over the long term, but there is nothing inevitable about it.

Europe's population problem

Whatever the mix in any individual country of European and non-European immigration, the second kind is growing, and is going to predominate. That is because Europeans are not having enough children. Whether due to prosperity, decadence, or some other factor of national morale, the birthrate of native Europeans has been plummeting for years, and is now at the lowest levels ever recorded in any major region of the world. The native-born population is dropping in virtually all of the EU states. In some of them, it is dropping precipitously.

Europeans commonly soft-pedal this difficulty. They say that demographers have been wrong in the past, and that one can know only roughly what the population of Europe is going to be twenty or thirty years from now. They are wrong. Europe could certainly experience a baby boom sooner or later, but over the short haul, demography is about as exact as a social science can be. There is not necessarily any end to this process of demographic shrinkage, particularly now that small families have become a cultural norm. In Austria and Germany, for instance, women aged twenty to thirty-four believe the "ideal" family has 1.7 children. As Wolfgang Lutz and colleagues have pointed out, this is very close to the level at which a country falls into a "low fertility trap" from which it is unlikely to emerge. For a society to remain the same size, the average woman has to have 2.1 children in a lifetime (the so-called "total fertility rate"). All European countries except Muslim Albania are well below it. There is a "safe zone" above 1.6 children per woman, where population declines are gradual and easily reversed. Below that, population tends to collapse rather than decline. A society that maintains a 1.8 total fertility rate will be 80 percent as large at the end of a century; a society with total fertility of 1.3 (Italy, Spain, Eastern Germany, and the Baltic nations are such societies) will fall to a quarter of its size. At current rates of decline, Italy's native population will be half its current size by the middle of this century, little more than a generation from now.

On top of not having children, Europeans are old. Already a quarter of them are over sixty. In the heavily North African Paris suburb of Montfermeil, the children from the housing projects refer to the zone of detached houses occupied mostly by French natives, which they cross every day on their way to school, as *la ville des vieux*—the old people's city. In many parts of Europe, young people tend to be of foreign descent. In Paris, when someone refers to a mugging by *une bande des jeunes*, a North African origin is often implied. Housing vacancies open up in places heavily populated with old people, and immigrants fill them, recapitulating at the level of European neighborhoods what is happening at the level of European civilization.

Since there is no European source of population growth, Europe can maintain its size and dynamism only by importing non-Europeans. In some European countries, the percentage of people who are either immigrants or the children of immigrants is bumping up towards a quarter. Of the 9 million people in Sweden, 1.5 million are either immigrants or their children. The same is true of 3 million of the 16 million Dutch—including two-thirds of the students in Amsterdam, Rotterdam, and The Hague. Projections are that by 2050, 29 percent of Dutch people will have at least one foreign parent. Some of these will be from other European countries but most— about 2.7 million, or close to a fifth of the Dutch population—will be of non-Western background. These figures may underestimate the number of people of non-European descent, because some will be the children of Dutch-born Dutch citizens.

In 2050, Britain will have 7 million "nonwhites" even if migration comes to an absolute halt, according to the Oxford demographer David Coleman, and 16 million if migration continues at a "high" level of 108,000 per year. (But even this high level may underestimate immigration pressures. In the middle of the first decade of the century,

Britain was receiving about 500,000 new immigrants—equivalent to 1 percent of its population—every year.) By midcentury, in most of the major European countries, foreign-origin populations will be between 20 and 32 percent.

Some of this increase has to do with new arrivals, but much has to do with the wide gap in birthrates between European natives and non-European immigrants, which can take generations to close. In Turin, the northern Italian city that has suddenly, since the 1990s, become about 10 percent immigrant, immigrants account for 0.2 percent of the deaths and 25 percent of the births. A fifth of the children in Copenhagen, a third of the children in Paris, and half of the children in London are born to foreign mothers. French-born women have 1.7 children apiece, but foreign-born women in France have 2.8 children. Tunisians, Turks, and Moroccans average between 3.3 and 3.4, more than their counterparts in their home countries.

Europeans assume the rapid population growth among immigrant groups will stop. They have tended to place an almost religious faith in theories of "demographic transition," which predict falling birthrates as peoples become more prosperous. According to such theories, when modern medicine, hygiene, and diet start arriving in a society, old people live longer and more young people survive to mating age—but long-standing habits of family formation are slower to change. The result is a massive surge in population for a generation or two. As modernity makes these societies more prosperous and better educated, however, and as a consumer society creates satisfactions that vie with those of child-rearing, a precipitous drop in fertility follows.

Sometimes this actually happens among immigrant groups. The "African Indians" who arrived in Britain from Kenya and Uganda in the late 1960s and early 1970s now have roughly the same birthrate as native-born Britons. But sometimes there is no such convergence. Pakistanis and Bangladeshis, groups that have been in Britain even longer than the African Indians, still have birthrates far above the national average.

There are reasons Europe's Third World immigrants, and particularly its Muslims, might not go through the same demographic transition that their Western hosts did. Muslim culture is unusually full of messages laying out the practical advantages of procreation. As the hadith saying has it: "Marry, for I will outnumber peoples by you" (Ibn Majah, 1:599). The late Yassir Arafat, considering the sevenfold increase in Palestinian population over one generation (from 450,000 in 1967 to 3.3 million in 2002), called the wombs of Palestinian women the "secret weapon" of his cause. Now, Arafat's hostility to Israel is not matched by European Muslims' hostility to Europe. But immigrants need not be the slightest bit hostile to the West, or its values, to question its squeamishness about child-bearing and -rearing. Along the road of European modernization (literacy, empowerment, individualism, and so on) lie the shopping mall, the pierced navel, online gambling, a 50 percent divorce rate, and a high rate of anomie and self-loathing. What makes us so certain that *that* Europeanization is a road that immigrants will want to travel?

Civilization and decadence

Much European discussion of immigration, reasonable and unreasonable, reveals a bottled-up panic over the state of native European civilization. Whether Europe can, for the first time in its history, successfully accommodate non-European minorities will depend on whether natives and newcomers perceive Europe as a thriving civilization or a decadent one.

For optimists, the availability of tortillas, Korans, and saris in the continent's major cities is evidence that Europe is thriving. It is a beacon to the world's poor. Newcomers bring exciting products and folkways because Europe is strong and self-confident enough to welcome such things. There are seven Polish-language newspapers in Dublin and six Chinese dailies in Hungary. Eggplant, mangoes, and baklava are easier to come by than they were. Even the record-setting traffic jams—which stretch for tens of kilometers every summer along highways in southern Spain, as North African workers from every country in Europe load their families into old cars and converge on the ferry crossings to Morocco—have their bright side. They show that immigrant Europe is on the move, active, vibrant, diverse, life loving.

But "advanced" cultures have a long track record of underestimating their vulnerability to "primitive" ones. Immigrants also bring a lot of disorder, penury, and crime. Turkish immigrants have been responsible for shootouts in schools in France and the Netherlands. Italy has Balkan "squeegee men" who shake down motorists the way panhandlers did in the Manhattan of the 1970s and '80s. And most countries in Europe have seen immigrant unrest, if not outright riots.

For pessimists, the vibrancy and energy of immigrant and ethnic communities come at the expense of European communities. Europeans know more about Arabic calligraphy and kente cloth because they know less about Montaigne and Goethe. If the spread of Pakistani cuisine is the single greatest improvement in British public life over the past half-century, it is also worth noting that the bombs used for the failed London transport attacks of July 21, 2005, were made from a mix of hydrogen peroxide and chapati flour. Immigration is not enhancing or validating European culture; it is supplanting it. Europe is not welcoming its newest residents but making way for them.

Both optimism and pessimism exist simultaneously in most Europeans' heads. Immigration is indeed an exhilarating, revivifying cultural opportunity. But it is also a test of strength between two cultures. The paltry mass immigrations between European countries in recent centuries—Jewish and Huguenot refugees, a few factory hands from Poland or Ireland or Italy—were big enough to enrich the lands of settlement but not so big as to threaten them. They are unlikely to be the template that the present wave follows. There are many other models for immigration, and not all of them end with the "absorption" of the newcomers into the host country: The arrival of a few hundred British adventurers in India in the eighteenth century was an immigration, and so was the settlement of ambitious ranchers in the early nineteenth century in New Spain (now Texas). Immigration enhances strong countries and cultures, but it can overwhelm weak ones.

Diversity is overrated

Journalists and government commentators often present immigrant Europe as a diverse phenomenon. It is hard to generalize about Europe, they say. In France, book after book presents the problems of immigration as a result of the problems of colonialism, or even as a continuation of colonialism by other means. But in Germany, one frequently hears that the problem in integrating Turkish newcomers is a *lack* of colonial experience, of the sort that, whatever damage it did, at least allowed countries such as France or England to greet their newest citizens as old acquaintances, with certain common cultural references to use as a starting point. Many French are skeptical about the assimilability of Arabs and more optimistic about the proud and independent Berber Kabyles of Algeria; the Dutch, however, try to explain away the high crime rates of their Moroccan population by saying that they are Berbers from the Rif, after all, and you can't expect them to assimilate as well as Arabs.

Another explanation that one hears from social scientists is that immigration problems are a clash between the "countryside" and the "big cities." As the Dutch historian Geert Mak wrote:

Around the 1970s, there was a great policy error made in the Netherlands, as elsewhere in Western Europe. Without sufficient selectivity, without good leadership, without programs to welcome all newcomers into Dutch society, a great wave of migration got underway from the Turkish and Moroccan countryside to the big cities of the Netherlands

What Europe confronts, in this view, is not a reenactment of, say, the Umayyad conquest of Spain but a reenactment of milkmaids and shepherds moving from villages in Normandy to factories in Boulogne-Billancourt. Mak, who considers himself a great defender of immigrants and has launched some of the most ferocious attacks on Ayaan Hirsi Ali, the Somali-Dutch feminist thinker and critic of Islam, sees that the Dutch project to integrate immigrants (at least its Muslim ones) has thus far failed. But he cannot admit the possibility that it may have failed because it is not a project with a high prospect of success in the first place.

Mak's reading of his country's woes is replicated by intellectuals in countries across Europe. Writers, academics, and politicians act as if it is only some quirk or accident or epiphenomenon—and never immigration itself—that has left their country with such intractable problems. Some political blunder or bit of red tape, or an unremarked peculiarity of its immigrant population, must be to blame—something that can be put right with some new program.

This is misguided. Europe's immigration situation is not particularly diverse, even if the peoples involved in it are. Leaving aside the economic crisis that began in 2008, coping with the fallout from immigration is the main problem in every country in Western Europe, and it is the same problem in all of them. If you understand how immigration, Islam, and native European culture interact in any Western European country, you can predict roughly how they will interact in any other—no matter what its national character, no matter whether it conquered an empire, no matter what its role in World War II, and no matter what the provenance of its Muslim immigrants.

All countries have the same shrinking populations. All countries make the same diagnoses of their immigration challenges, and put forward the same economic policies. When the Christian Democratic politician Rita Süßmuth published the conclusions of an independent immigration commission in 2001, saying that Germany would need 500,000 immigrants a year to maintain its age balance, the demographer Gunnar Heinsohn wrote sarcastically but correctly, "Now all the OECD states, and even the Slavic countries of Eastern Europe have their own Süßmuth reports. And all of them courageously declare, in ignorance of the others, their willingness to receive qualified and easily assimilable high-tech geniuses in ever greater numbers." All countries pursue roughly the same strategy for assimilating Islam, elevating Muslim pressure groups to pseudo-governmental status and declaring that doing so will produce an Islam that reflects the values of Europe rather than vice versa. This is the driving idea behind the Conseil français du culte musulman, the Italian Consulta, and the German Islamkonferenz (albeit to a lesser degree), and behind Britain's unnamed and unsuccessful attempt to win over the leadership of the Muslim Council of Britain to more moderate pronouncements. A reporter traveling from country to country can even hear the same immigration jokes and puns. French people are as impressed by their own wit in lamenting the import of radical imams from "Londonistan" as Italians are when they complain about disorder in their own city of "Cremonistan" (Cremona).

Why do European opinion leaders insist that there is a diversity of immigrations, a diversity of Islams? Perhaps to stave off discussing the possibility that the various, similar-looking immigrant problems in all Western European countries might merely be facets of a single larger clash. The Clash of Civilizations is associated with the late Harvard political scientist Samuel Huntington's book of that name. But the fear that globalization might exacerbate the tensions among peoples rather than allaying them is not just an idea that Huntington dreamed up in the 1990s.

In 1961 the French political philosopher Raymond Aron delivered a lecture in London called "The Dawn of Universal History." In it, he argued that "with humanity on the way to unification, inequality between peoples takes on the significance that inequality between classes once had. The condition of the masses differs more, from one continent to the next, and from one country to the next, than it ever has. Consciousness of inequality spreads, and resignation to poverty and fate disappears." Aron's remark remains mostly true in the age of the Internet. European countries are shrinking, aging, and short of workers. Their only obvious supply of rejuvenation and labor is in the Muslim cultures to the south and southeast, which have historically been either Europe's enemies, its overlords, or its underlings. Europe is wagering that attitudes handed down over the centuries, on both sides, have disappeared, or can be made to disappear. That is probably not a wise wager.

Can you have the same Europe with different people?

This is a book about Europe, and about how and why immigration and the multiethnic societies that result from it mark a rupture in its history. It is written with an eye to the difficulties immigration poses to European society. It is not a book about the difficulties faced by immigrants and ethnic minorities, about the injustices of the global economy, or about the imperatives of human rights, although these are all worthy subjects that will be touched on where necessary. This book aims to describe a particular European predicament, not to lecture Europeans about what their wishes and aims ought to be, or how their societies ought to work.

The predicament actually consists of two different problems that, because they overlap, are often mistaken for a single problem. There is the problem of Europe's ability to assimilate immigrants, and there is the problem of Europe's difficulties with Islam. Which of these problems is being addressed at any given time should be clear in context. The reader should be warned that, without a certain amount of shorthand and bluntness, nothing serious can be said. To hedge every point with *granted*s and *notwithstanding*s would have made this book a pain to write and a chore to read. Words are used in their vernacular, not their social-scientific or political sense. So for instance, the adjective *native* may be used to refer to the non-Muslim part of a European country. This does not mean the writer is unaware that Europe now has Muslim natives. The statement that European Muslims took a dim view of the decision of *Jyllands-Posten* to publish caricatures of Muhammad in September 2005 is to be understood generally. The author does not claim to have interviewed every last Muslim on the continent and found complete unanimity. Economy of expression, not stereotyping or exclusion, is the aim. This book will avoid alarmism and pointless provocation, but it will also avoid euphemism and the kind of preemptive groveling that characterizes most writing about matters touching on ethnicity.

There is no precedent for the mass immigration that Europe has seen over the last five decades and may see for years to come. Some of the moderate-sized migrations of the late nineteenth and early twentieth centuries ended well: the movement of Polish farm workers into Germany, for instance, or of Italian industrial workers into France. One ended catastrophically: the westward migration of Jews into Western European cities. The present immigration is many times larger than those, and involves far wider cultural differences. Its outcome is unclear.

Mass immigration may spur economies slowed by old habits, and breathe new life into societies demoralized by their twentieth-century mistakes and sins. But this doesn't look too likely. Europeans, as we will discuss in the next chapter, overestimated their need for immigrant labor. The economic benefits immigration brought were marginal and temporary. They now belong to the past. The social changes immigration brought, however, were massive and enduring. Accommodating more ethnic groups does not mean adding to what Europe already has. It means altering what Europe already has. Immigration is a poor fit with the welfare states that have been a cornerstone of European identity since the Second World War. It complicates efforts to build a European Union. The Islam professed by roughly half of Europe's new arrivals sits uneasily with European traditions of secularism. In the struggle between the two, it would be arrogant to assume secularism has the stronger hand. The spiritual tawdriness Islamic immigrants perceive in the modern West is not imaginary. It may be Europe's biggest liability in preserving its culture.

The rest of this book will ask whether you can have the same Europe with different people. The answer is no.

2

The Immigrant Economy

How postwar migration came about—The unprecedented scale of recent immigration—The capitalist argument: Rescuing moribund industries—Jobs nobody wants— The socialist argument: Rescuing the welfare state

From 1945 on, Europe was preoccupied with rebuilding what the war had destroyed—streets and railways, houses and offices, rituals and roles. The continent's labor force would have been inadequate to a task of that magnitude in any case, but the shortage of manpower was exacerbated by the loss of millions of working-age people in the war. The memory of World War II (in which the vanquished enemy was racist) and the gradual hardening of the Cold War (in which the West vied with the Communist bloc to flatter the masses of the non-European world) combined to mute the misgivings that would have arisen at any other point in European history about welcoming large numbers of people from other races and cultures.

How postwar migration came about

Countries that were decolonizing (France, Britain, the Netherlands) met their labor shortages partly by repatriating Europeans who were no longer welcome or content in their imperial outposts, and partly by recruiting former colonial "natives." In Britain, the first Jamaicans arrived in 1948 on the *Empire Windrush*, a passenger ship that now plays the role of the *Mayflower* in the foundational mythology of multicultural Britain. The newcomers worked in iron foundries, railroads, post offices, and hospitals, and as plumbers and electricians.

Their numbers exceeded anyone's expectations. The 1948 Nationalities Act had given citizenship to the subjects of Britain's former colonies, as a means of reassuring Canadians, Australians, and other traditional migrants to Britain that doors remained open to them, even as the Empire evolved into the Commonwealth. As for the King's tropical subjects, it was assumed that if they hadn't come before, why should they come now?

The Nationalities Act made immigration easy to launch and hard to stop, or even to slow, until citizenship laws were reformed in the 1960s. There were about 350 Africans, Asians, and West Indians in Bradford, Yorkshire, in 1953. But Indians and Pakistanis soon began arriving en masse, mostly as wool combers, transport workers, and restaurateurs. Within five years, the South Asian population of Bradford had increased ten times, and 15 percent of bus conductors in the city of Bradford were Indian or Pakistani. By the late 1950s, Britain had 55,000 Indians and Pakistanis and 125,000 West Indians, and immigration was accelerating. Using the most recent national census, Britain has 2,083,759 people of South Asian descent (Indians, Pakistanis, and Bengalis) and 1,148,738 "Black British," as the census calls them, among whom half are from the Caribbean.

Something similar happened in France. In a speech on March 3, 1945, Charles de Gaulle bemoaned France's lack of manpower as the "main obstacle to our recovery." It was estimated that at least 1.5 million workers were needed. France at first sought workers from Poland and the Netherlands, but those countries had their own manpower shortages and few migrants were forthcoming. It considered inviting interned Germans to stay, but public opinion would not permit it. Then it tried to recruit laborers from Northern Italy, but was outbid by businesses in Switzerland. Italian immigration to France wound up heavy anyway, but it came in an improvised and slapdash manner—tens of thousands of Sicilians immigrated to France in the decades after the war. The governor of Algeria suggested recruiting 100,000 Muslim workers, an offer that France rejected out of hand on the grounds of "health, social, and moral risks." Over the next three decades, France would get seven times that many Algerians, through less formal channels. No one arranged for their coming—they up and left, fleeing the violence of the Algerian revolution. For a period in 1962, they were arriving at the rate of 70,000 a week. By 2004, there were 4.3 million foreign-born people living in France, of whom about a third had acquired French nationality.

Countries without empires signed "guest worker" agreements with poorer nations. Sweden was a pioneer in such deals. Thanks to its neutrality in World War II, it emerged from the carnage with the only advanced European industrial base that had been neither destroyed by bombs nor looted by occupiers. Sweden was likely to be a main beneficiary of European reconstruction, as indeed it was—with 4 percent growth from the war until the oil crisis of the 1970s, including 7 percent for most of the 1960s. All Sweden lacked was sufficient people to man its factories. Finns, many of them Swedish-speaking, filled much of that need. But they were inadequate to fill all of it.

Hence guest worker programs, which were meant as a simple, short-term expedient. An industrial country would sign a bilateral agreement with a less developed country short on jobs or hard currency. Corporate recruiters, government officials, and doctors would be sent to choose teams of suitable young workers for short stints, usually of two years, at which point the laborer would return home. Sweden signed temporary labor agreements with foreign countries, starting with Italy and Hungary in 1947. But the labor resources of any given country were never quite adequate, and the guest worker program wound up spreading to more distant lands, until it reached Yugoslavia and Turkey two decades later. Thanks to guest worker agreements and an unusually large intake of political refugees, almost a sixth of the entire present-day population was either born outside of Sweden or had both parents born abroad.

West Germany's guest worker (*Gastarbeiter*) program turned into a European colossus. It began late, in 1955, as an orderly means of bringing in a modest amount of Italian farm labor. But Germany was in the midst of its postwar "economic miracle" and industry wanted labor, too. With lightning speed the program spread to new sectors of the economy, and Germany began to recruit all over southern Europe and North Africa—in Spain, Greece, Turkey, Morocco, Portugal, Tunisia, and Yugoslavia. The need for short-term labor grew even more acute after East Germany's Communists sealed their border with the West in 1961. Until then, the stagnant and exploited Communist east had provided the capitalist west with a reserve of millions of workers. There were 329,000 Gastarbeiter in 1960, a million by 1964, and 2.6 million in 1973. (East Germany, curiously, ran a Gastarbeiter program of its own, importing Vietnamese to work in Berlin's Narva lightbulb factory, among other places.)

Turks made up the biggest part of the migration to Germany. The Gastarbeiter program was a hard-currency bonanza for Turkey, and it has only recently been understood how aggressively the Turkish government petitioned for inclusion in it. Those who came first were largely single men, living in hostels (*Wohnheime*) and working in the mines and steel plants of the Rhine and Ruhr. They were diligent, upstanding, and a bargain, and were supposed to be rotated in and out, going back to their native countries once their two-year stints were up.

Three quarters of the 18.5 million who came to Germany between 1960 and 1973 did just that. But the gap between what natives understood the Gastarbeiter invitation to mean and what the workers themselves understood it to mean widened steadily. Few guest workers could earn as much back home as they could in Europe. Recruiting, vetting, and medically examining replacements was expensive. So corporations pressured the government to make Gastarbeiter contracts renewable, to let workers' families join them in Germany, and to permit those who had formed families to stay.

Virtually no one in Germany would have considered this an acceptable outcome at the time the Gastarbeiter program was launched. But any mass movement of labor—even a planned one, such as Germany's—develops momentum. The most important factor in migration is migration. It takes courage to be the first to strike out on your own and submit to the laws, customs, and whims of a society that doesn't care about you. But once your compatriots have set up a beachhead, migration becomes simple and routine. Networks reduce fear. They cure homesickness as reliably as penicillin cures strep. By the mid-1960s, moving to Germany did not even entail abandoning Turkish food for German, or (in the big cities) Muslim observance for Christianity or secularism.

Germany grew less mysterious and more convenient, further reducing the incentives for foreign workers to return home when their terms were up. And in the 1960s, the Turkish economy was lurching from crisis to crisis. Guest workers returned home en masse when they were laid off during the recession of 1966–67, but not during the more global recession of 1973–74, which drove up unemployment in their home countries. That second downturn brought the end of the Gastarbeiter program. By 2006, Germany had a "foreign population" of 7,289,149.

As Europe filled up with non-European migrants, a more savvy understanding of the European labor market spread to the migrants' home countries and, to some extent, to the entire Third World. That opened the way for freelancing. Denmark had no government Gastarbeiter program and no empire to speak of, but it did have an open labor market until 1973. Yugoslavs, Turks, Moroccans, and even people who had already migrated to other countries in Europe (such as Pakistanis working in Britain) became aware that there were lucrative jobs in Denmark and began to fill up the poorer neighborhoods in Copenhagen. Italy had no comprehensive national immigration laws until 1986. As foreign workers became less welcome in the "older" immigration countries, new immigrants began arriving, invited or not, in neighboring lands.

The unprecedented scale of recent immigration

Europeans are reluctant to admit how unprecedented all of this was. Intellectuals can be found in every Western European country who will claim that theirs has always been a "country of immigrants." One hears it even in Sweden, with a handful of Hanseatic trading outposts and reindeer-meat entrepôts in Lapland adduced as evidence. But mass immigration is something different from trade, and it is something different from individual migration. This has long been understood in the United States. On the eve of the enormous Irish influx of the 1840s that would forever alter—and, from the perspective of the natives of that time, destroy—the culture of Boston, Massachusetts, there were already immigrants speaking twenty-seven languages in the city. "These foreigners, however," wrote the historian Oscar Handlin, "were just strays; and the reasons for their coming derived from personal contingencies rather than from great social causes for mass emigration." This is an essential distinction. Pocahontas, the Fuegian Indians brought to Britain on the HMS *Beagle*, Alexander Pushkin's black grandfather, or three Chinese families running a laundry in a Roman backstreet do not a "country of immigrants" make. Today it is indeed true that every country in Western Europe is a "country of immigrants." But that was true of none of them (with the partial exception of France) a generation ago.

This distinction is lost on many recent historians. One book calls Britain the product of a "long and steady movement of people to these shores before the modern era." But this is false, and evidence that has emerged in the last decade makes it demonstrably so. Genetic studies of the population of the British Isles show that it has been remarkably stable for millennia. Aside from the invasions of Angles, Saxons, and Jutes that started in the fourth century AD—and which brought, at the very most, 250,000 new settlers to Britain over a period of several centuries—British "stock" has changed little. Only about 10,000 people arrived with the Norman Conquest. Tens of thousands more Huguenots came after the revocation of the Edict of Nantes in 1685. But, all told, three-quarters of the ancestors of contemporary Britons and Irish were already present in the British Isles 7,500 years ago. DNA from people who arrived after that makes up only 12 percent of the Irish gene pool. Describing the countries of Britain as nations of immigrants is absurd, unless you are describing processes that began not just before modernity but before civilization. That is what the *Guardian* did, presumably tongue in cheek, when it ran an article on recent paleontological discoveries below the headline "Britain's 700,000 years of immigrants: Ice ages defeated seven attempts at colonisation."

Migrations of one kind or another and tensions between in-groups and out-groups have always marked Europe, of course, as they have everyplace else. If you walk north across the piazza della Repubblica in Turin, you see, mutatis mutandis, what the Romans saw. To the east, two well-preserved Roman towers remain, and so do the walls built to separate citizens from barbarians. Today, in the space of about sixty seconds on foot, you pass from chic shops and wine bars through a lively multiethnic market into one of Europe's more menacing North African slums. Turin has always had religious and ethnic minorities. But until the past decade it never had masses of them. It was from the city's once-thriving Jewish community that the great chronicler of Auschwitz, Primo Levi, came. The city was also a stronghold of the ascetic proto-Protestant Waldensians, who flourished there for centuries until 1655, when they were, as Milton wrote:

> Slayn by the bloody *Piemontese* that roll'd
> Mother with Infant down the Rocks.

Turin saw heavy immigration in the 1930s to its Fiat factory in Lingotto. But these "immigrants" came from elsewhere in the Piemonte, from the nearby Veneto and from Sardinia, which was ruled, as was Turin, by the house of Savoy. And there weren't 100,000 of them.

Europe's path to *mass* immigration owes something to the intellectual habits of the statesmen and magnates who ran Europe's economy in World War II—on both the Allied and Axis sides. In scale, today's massive in-migration of "temporary" labor has only one precedent, and it is a recent one. At the height of the war, Nazi Germany impressed 10 million forced laborers from all over Europe to man its industries. Foreigners held a third of all jobs in Germany during the war, and more than half the jobs in the armaments industry. It should go without saying that no moral comparison is meant between the Nazis' press gangs and postwar European labor schemes. But they had one important economic point in common: the peacetime jobs for which the postwar guest workers were summoned wound up no more permanent than wartime ones that the Nazis forced the conquered peoples to do.

The manpower shortages that immigrants were brought in to solve were acute crises, not chronic problems. Many of the industries they propped up were on their last legs. Linen mills in the north of France were manned by Algerians only once it became clear, in the early 1960s, that those jobs would soon be eliminated. The same was true of textile mills in the British north.

That planners had exaggerated the need for long-term industrial labor did not become fully apparent until decades later. Between the 1970s and the early twenty-first century, European factories saw the same gains in productivity—and, as a consequence, the same massive layoffs—as the U.S. Rust Belt over that period. In Duisburg, the port city where the Rhine and Ruhr meet, 64,000 people, including tens of thousands of Turks over the years, used to work in just three steel plants, and tens of thousands more worked in the area's archipelago of mines. But today Germany's very last coal mines are closing, and there are only 20,000 industrial jobs left in the whole city of Duisburg, which is by some measures the most Turkish in Germany. Europe solved temporary economic problems through permanent demographic change.

Here, parallels between Europe's immigration and America's break down. The great wave of Latin American immigration began in the 1970s. The bulk of America's 35 million foreign born—including both high-skilled and menial workers—came in the last quarter-century, after the United States was well launched on its transition to a postindustrial economy. Postwar European labor immigration, by contrast, met the needs of the old economy rather than the new. If there are comparisons to be made with the United States, it is not to immigration but to the migratory component of the American race problem. As Nicholas Lemann and other historians have noted, it was the mechanization of southern agriculture in the early and mid-twentieth century that sparked a great migration of southern blacks into northern cities. By a cruel historical accident, they arrived at just the point when hiring in heavy industry was leveling off, and that accident is at least partly to blame for the burgeoning of a northern black underclass.

Something similar happened in Europe. The Turks, who throughout the 1960s and 1970s had a higher labor force participation than native Germans, are now, if not exactly an underclass, at least an economic problem, with unemployment reaching 40 percent in some cities (including Berlin), three times the national rate of welfare dependency, and an average retirement age of fifty. A difference between the European and American situations is that the Gastarbeiter were foreigners, with none of the claims on European society that southern blacks, as citizens, could make on the American north.

Labor immigration is always a mix of pluses and minuses. But in Europe, after a very few years, the context out of which the pluses arose no longer existed. "Temporary" workers had been welcomed as a short-term asset. Once it became apparent they were not going home, the rationale for the Gastarbeiter program shifted. Now mass immigration was presented as a route to economic advantages in some unspecified longer term. While Europe's citizens may once have accepted this quasi-official account it is evident they no longer do: 47 percent of Britons say the economic impact of immigration on their country has been negative, versus only 19 percent who say it has been positive. When social peace depends on people's ability to believe something they simply don't, doublethink becomes prevalent. A curious headline ran over a *Financial Times* article in 2006: "The uneasy cosmopolitan: how migrants are enriching an ever more anxious host."

The capitalist argument: Rescuing moribund industries

There are two basic ways to defend immigration on economic grounds: a capitalist way and a socialist way. There was long a consensus among political leaders that immigration strengthens the economy unproblematically, without doing much harm to productivity and without doing any harm to native wages. This view runs counter to classical economic theory and is being challenged with increasing rigor by economists. But it is still the argument most commonly encountered in newspapers, magazines, and popular books. A typical assessment is that of Philippe Legrain, who writes in *Immigrants: Your Country Needs Them*:

Sober-minded economists reckon that the potential gains from freer global migration are huge, and greatly exceed the benefits from freer world trade.... The World Bank reckons that if rich countries allowed their workforce to swell by a mere 3 per cent by letting in an extra 14 million workers from developing countries between 2001 and 2025, the world would be $356 billion a year better off, with the new migrants themselves gaining $162 billion a year, people who remain in poor countries $143 billion, and natives in rich countries $139 billion.

The argument that "a mere" 14 million more immigrants would add $139 billion to advanced economies smacks of either naiveté or mystification. It reminds one of the movie *Austin Powers*, in which Doctor Evil emerges from isolation to ominously demand "one *million dollars!*" for not blowing up the world. The aggregate gross domestic product of the advanced economies for the year 2008 is estimated by the International Monetary Fund at close to $40 trillion. In context, $139 billion is simply not that much money: It is 0.0035, or roughly one three-hundredth, of the advanced countries' output. It is about a sixth of the U.S. government's 2009 stimulus plan.

And that is reckoning without the "known unknowns"—the easily foreseeable externalities—that immigration produces. The income of a "diversity consultant," for instance, shows up in national statistics as part of that gain in economic output. But couldn't it just as well be deducted as a *cost* of managing diversity? The Oxford demographer David Coleman has urged that, when we tally up the economic impact of immigration, we also consider:

the total costs of the integration process, and of the associated immigration and race relations businesses, the costs of meeting the special education, health, and housing needs of immigrants, the net effects upon the education of ordinary children in immigrant areas, the permanent need to "regenerate" urban areas of immigrant settlement instead of demolishing them, issues of crime and public order, [and] the multiplier effect on future immigration.

Coleman is right that economic measures of immigration often ignore important costs. One could go even further and say that it is astonishing that champions of mass immigration place so much weight on fractions of a percentage point of GDP in the first place.

One gets the sense that the most serious part of the argument — the non-economic part—is being ducked. The social, spiritual, and political effects of immigration are huge and enduring, while the economic effects are puny and transitory. If, like certain Europeans, you are infuriated by polyglot markets and street signs written in

Polish, Urdu, and Arabic, sacrificing 0.0035 of your economy would be a pittance to pay for starting to get your country back. If, like other Europeans, you view immigration as a lifeline of excitement, worldliness, and palatable cuisine thrown to your drab and provincial country, then immigration would be a bargain even if it imposed a significant economic *cost*.

Assuming, for the sake of argument, a modest economic gain from immigration, these gains take place in a political context—democracy—that makes them fragile, and possibly unsustainable. Economics demands more immigrants than politics will tolerate. Questions arise about which members of society get the economic growth for which immigrants are responsible. Although today's labor markets are more fluid and harder to measure than they were in the age of nineteenth-century mill towns, the modern economy has not abolished the laws of economics. These laws say, according to one analyst, that immigration generates economic growth because it "raises the supply of labour, increases demand as migrants spend money, [and] boosts output while probably putting a downward pressure on inflation." Translated out of the language of academic economics, this means that immigration makes the economy more efficient because it drives down the wages of certain natives.

This is logical in theory, and evidence from both the large Polish migration into London and Hispanic migration into the United States show it to be true in practice. It may sometimes be the verdict of voters that downward pressure on wages is good for society as a whole. In many Western countries, in fact, the years of highest mass immigration coincided with the years when voters were becoming convinced that overaggressive trade unions could inflict grievous damage on an economy and on a society. An increase in the supply of labor, through immigration, helped render trade unions' wage demands economically unreasonable, and businesses more profitable, flexible, and competitive. It is society's right to use immigration this way, but the consensus on which such a policy rests is bound to be tacit, fragile, and temporary.

Much of the economic benefit of immigration goes to the immigrants themselves. One of the largest businesses in Kreuzberg, the Berlin neighborhood that is the capital of Turkish Germany, is the

Öger Türk-tur travel agency, owned by a Social Democratic member of the European parliament. Specializing in trips to Turkey, it is an excellent business by all accounts, and gets pointed out as an example of Kreuzberg's entrepreneurship and economic dynamism. But what does the native German get out of it? The need it fills is a consequence of immigration, not a cause. Similarly, it is good when Business Angel des Cités, a capital fund for businesses in the French *banlieues*, or suburbs, sets up companies in the community. But many seem to be companies exclusively *for* the community, too: Kool Halal, a halal fast-food chain in Mulhouse; Mecca Pasta; and Medina Shop, which sells Moroccan products. Starting in 2002, those who wanted to express their solidarity with the Palestinian cause by boycotting American products could buy a French-made Coke alternative called Mecca-Cola. It did a lot for anti-Israel solidarity. It didn't do much for the French economy.

In Spain, from the 1990s until the collapse of the construction market, building cranes—those great symbols of robust economic health—were visible everywhere. Immigrants made up many of the construction crews. Were they coming to the rescue of a country that needed this housing anyway? Probably not, since, by the time immigrants began arriving en masse in the 1990s, Spain's native population was on the verge of contracting. The total population of the country has grown by 4 million people (10 percent) since then, all of it due to immigration. Immigrants are more likely a cause than a symptom of the building boom. The houses the newcomers are building are their own.

Jobs nobody wants

Accounts of the benefits of immigration often describe the jobs immigrants take as jobs-no-European-wants. Of course, what is really meant is jobs no European wants to do at a particular wage. Recently, the immigration specialist Philip Martin of California–Davis and two colleagues drew parallels between today's migrations and the movement of would-be settlers to European colonies in the eighteenth century. Back then, migrants paid off the cost of their own resettlement through an indenture. They promised a given number of years of labor to the landowner who fronted their voyage. Perhaps today's immigrants pay an updated kind of indenture in the form of rights, living as they often do in an ambiguous legal status that condemns them to only the lowest jobs. If there really *are* jobs that Europeans won't do at any price, this indenture is a big part of what natives believe they are "getting" out of immigration.

Whether or not this indenture is fair depends on the context in which you view it. On one hand, the arrangement is corrosive. It creates two tiers of rights in the destination country. On the other hand, the immigrants are unlikely to complain. They are doing better than they would have done in their native countries, after all.

But there is a hitch. The benefits of this indenture accrue to immigrants' new countries only so long as immigrants are illegal and transitional. Immigrants don't stay that way forever. As soon as they are legally and socially assimilated in the way that society professes to want, they acquire all sorts of rights and expectations. They become Europeans who, by definition, won't do the jobs-no-European-wants. So the moment immigration is successful socially, the main economic reason society thinks it "needs" immigrants in the first place vanishes.

At that point, to ensure that those jobs-nobody-wants get done, society must recruit a new reserve army of foreign-born grunt workers, which sounds like the capitalism of Karl Marx's worst imaginings. The only alternative would be to maintain the precariousness of immigrants' legal status into the next generation by denying birthright citizenship, which sounds like a modern-day feudalism. Either way, the gains from immigration are all paid back in later generations—they are borrowed, not earned. The faster and more thoroughly immigrants adapt to your society, the more immigrants you need. Economies thus grow dependent on, or addicted to, immigrants, developing a momentum either towards further immigration or less assimilation.

There is no reason to assume high immigration is the continent's only long-term alternative. For many centuries Europe's economy did not require it. A real-life test of the proposition that high immigration is indispensable to a modern economy is taking place as this book is being written. Amendments to the Danish Aliens Act in 2002 and

Dutch legislation to restrict immigration, first crafted at the turn of the decade and considerably stiffened after the murder of the film-maker Theo van Gogh in 2004, have both led to a sharp decrease in immigration. If immigration were as economically necessary as many people say, one would expect to see Denmark and the Nether-lands underperforming other countries, as investors readjusted their assessments of long-term growth to reflect the dwindling supply of immigrants. There has been no hint of any such adjustment.

To speak of European countries "needing" immigrants is wrong. It is more accurate to say that certain European countries, or at least their business leaders, long preferred an immigrant economy to a non-immigrant one. There are rational grounds for this preference. While immigration is often described in terms of loss of control ("Britain is losing control of its borders"), it can just as often be a strategy to retain or regain control of an economy.

We can see this if we think about a basic aspect of immigration that all economists agree on: that it is a brake on productivity growth. There is less need for "labor saving" (i.e., for modern technology) when labor is cheap. Italy has lately received more than half a million immigrants a year from Africa and the Middle East, mostly to work in its farms, shops, and restaurants. The market price of certain kinds of Italian produce, so Italian farmers say, is in danger of falling below the cost of bringing it to market. Under conditions of globalization, Italy's real comparative advantage may lie elsewhere than in agricul-ture, in some high-tech economic model that is remunerative but not particularly "Italian." Italians may rebel against that.

Traditional ways of working the land may be viable only if there are immigrants there to work it. You can make similar arguments about traditional Italian restaurants, which in the present economy may be able to hold their own against soulless chains only with the help of low-paid immigrant labor. Ditto the country's lovely public parks, which have traditionally required dozens of gardeners, a level of manpower that the country's shrinking population cannot supply, except at a high price. Without labor from Algeria and Mali, those parks will either disappear or be "automated," as American parks are (through sprinklers and the replacement of elegant landscaping with grass). In many walks of life, Italy has a choice between keeping the population looking the way it did fifty years ago and keeping the landscape and the social structure looking the way they did fifty years ago. Through immigration, it is choosing the latter. Some natives may feel "swamped" by the demographic change, but immigration, though not ideal, may be the most practical way of keeping Italy looking like Italy. As the novelist Giuseppe di Lampedusa once wrote, "If we want everything to stay the same, everything must change."

Those familiar with the history of European labor immigration over the past half century might wager that Italians are going to lose a lot of their traditional economic structures anyway, immigrants or not. After all, when an industry is dying (such as linens in northern France), immigrants can delay its death for a few years, but not forever. When an industry is shedding jobs (such as steel in Germany), immigrants can delay restructuring for a few years, but not forever. The disillusionment with immigration that has set in in the older immigration countries comes from the disappearance of the tasks that immigrants were brought to do.

There remains only one European industry that citizens of every country still trust immigrants to save. This leads us naturally to the second, socialist, way of addressing the economics of immigration, because that industry is welfare.

The socialist argument: Rescuing the welfare state

The postwar Western European welfare states provided the most generous benefits ever given to workers anywhere. Germany's "social market economy" was the archetype. By the turn of this century, benefits for workers at certain large corporations included workweeks as short as thirty-two hours; seven-week vacations; full health coverage; free lunches; a compensation package that rose, in the case of unionized metal workers, to just under $50 an hour; and—most fatefully of all—retirement in one's fifties at just under peak career earnings. It is obvious the system had a built-in tendency to ratchet benefits up beyond the limits of sustainability. Indulgent arrangements with trade unions encouraged frequent striking and brinksmanship. Plum jobs for those who could find them were accompanied by disincentives—including generous unemployment benefits—to work in any other kind of job.

The social market economy was a model for the world well into the 1970s. But Thatcher and Reagan exposed its internal contradictions and the rise of the information economy dealt a blow to its prestige. Europeans had bestowed much of their investment capital and political passion on erecting, and then protecting, their welfare systems. Medium-sized and large corporations, along with government, were the most efficient means of delivering benefits and security. As a result, Europe had few of the small, flexible start-up companies that drove most of the innovation in recent decades. Apart from the Scandinavian cell phone industry, it did not participate fully in the late-twentieth-century information technology boom. Europe's entrepreneurial deficit got a lot of attention in the 1990s.

The social market economy had another problem. It froze the European labor market in place. In the first decade or two after the war, the relative poverty of the Italian Mezzogiorno was gradually being alleviated by migration to northern Italy and other European countries. But as the state grew increasingly generous, many preferred a life on social payments in Sicily, no matter how straitened the circumstances, to the loneliness and anonymity of industrial work in the snowy north. The European welfare state—although this was not the specific intent of those who designed it—wound up casting any line of work without access to the largesse of government and government-linked corporations as beneath the dignity of the meanest proletarian. Such unfavored jobs included agriculture, domestic help, cleaning, and food handling. Thanks to generous benefits, no proletarian had to take them. If the jobs were to get done at all, they had to be given to people outside of the system. That meant immigrants.

With millions of noncitizens and their children already on European soil, the continent's welfare states began to interact with demography in a disturbing way. European government pension systems operate on a pay-as-you-go basis: they pay present benefits out of present tax receipts, rather than letting individual workers "save" for their retirements. Polemicists and welfare economists have always noted the tendency of such systems, as they come under democratic pressure, to degenerate into Ponzi schemes. That is, politicians overpromise—

and cover those promises by roping in new investments (generally by borrowing against future tax receipts) to transfer more to current beneficiaries than the system can really afford.

In societies with growing populations, this is easy to do, because the welfare "support ratio"—the number of workers per retiree—grows, too. Politicians are tempted to loot, for present use, the entire surplus that comes from having a temporary bulge in workers, rather than investing it against the time when that bulge of workers becomes a bulge of dependent retirees. Europe's politicians did not resist this temptation. Today Europe's population is aging, its support ratio is shrinking, and, due to falling birthrates, there is no sufficiently large "next generation" of workers to restore it to balance. In the extremely short run, a baby bust such as Europe has undergone can enhance living standards, because it reduces the number of dependents per worker. But in the longer run a reckoning awaits, and the longer run has arrived.

As the European population receded (like a sea), a solution emerged (like an iceberg). The immigrant part of the European population was still relatively young, and relatively immune to Europe's falling birthrates. *They* would restore the support ratio! If only European publics could put away their prejudices for long enough to permit a massive rise in immigration, the argument ran, European welfare states could be put back on a sound actuarial footing. Immigrants, who were one of the symptoms of the European system's unacknowledged problems, suddenly found themselves cast in a new role as the deus ex machina of European luxury. They would emerge from the desiccated and starving hamlets of the Third World and ride to the rescue of the retirement checks and second homes, the wine tastings and snorkeling vacations, of the most pampered workforce in the history of the planet.

The idea is distant, to put it mildly, from the ideals on which the continental welfare states were founded. It is also unsound in cold economic terms. Although many people make the argument that immigration can save welfare, no informed person makes it. The United Nations Population Division calculates that replicating the age structure and support ratio of Europe would require 701 million immigrants, or considerably more than the continent's entire present-day population, by midcentury.

It is unrealistic to look to immigration for even modest alleviations in the welfare state's predicament. The Harvard economist Martin Feldstein has considered the case of Spain. Over the next fifty years, Spain's population will stay the same—around 44 million—but its ratio of workers to retirees will fall from 4.5:1 to below 2:1. Feldstein asked what the effect would be of taking in 2 million foreign workers—a 54 percent increase in the number of foreign born already there. We can assume the social effects would be huge, possibly disruptive, and expensive. But the fiscal effects of this influx, Feldstein shows, would be paltry. Those newcomers would constitute only a 10 percent increase in the workforce. And since immigrants tend to occupy the lower reaches of the economy, the increase to labor compensation—out of which the taxes that pay for the welfare state are drawn—would be well under that. Feldstein's estimate of the rise in labor compensation—"about 8 percent or less"—sounds generous. Out of that 8 percent or less, one must subtract the (high) cost of immigrant health care and education. Once you do that, the relief immigrants bring to the welfare state is unlikely to match their eventual claims on it.

Because immigrants are not immortal. They, too, age and retire, and the system must take care of them and their larger-than-average families. European leaders have faced this problem with little more than wishful thinking. "In the long term, migrants themselves will age and contribute to the increasing dependency ratio," stated a UK Home Office report in late 2007, "but only assuming that they remain in the UK during retirement." Goodness! What other assumption can be made? Are we to assume that migrants will give decades of their lives and tens of thousands of pounds of their earnings to fund an expensive and comprehensive welfare state for Europeans, and then obligingly slink back to the Third World to pass their retirement in poverty, at the very moment they are due to recoup their contribution?

For immigrants to help the welfare state, they and their descendants must pay more into welfare than they take out. They don't work or earn enough to do that. The evidence is that immigrants take more out of welfare than they pay in. In the Netherlands, for instance, 40 percent of immigrants get some form of government assistance. According to the Institute for the Future of Work, while native

Germans between the ages of twenty and sixty-five pay out more in taxes than they collect in services, Turks do that only between the ages of twenty-eight and fifty-seven.

One of the amazing statistics in the history of European immigration is that the number of foreign residents in Germany rose steadily between 1971 and 2000—from 3 million to about 7.5 million—but the number of employed foreigners in the work force did not budge. It stayed rock steady at roughly 2 million people. In 1973, 65 percent of German immigrants were in the workforce; in 1983, a decade later, only 38 percent were.

This evolution has been replicated across Europe. In 1994 in France, just 29 percent of all immigrants came for work purposes. (This does not mean the remaining 71 percent stayed unemployed, only that they were admitted for family reunification, an asylum application or some other noneconomic reason.) Those admitted for work included 70 percent of arrivals from other European countries, and 7 percent of those from North Africa. By 1997, only 12 percent of immigrants arriving in Britain from what used to be called the "New Commonwealth" (the nonwhite parts of the former British Empire) were coming for work. Just 45 percent of non-European immigrants in Denmark are in the workforce, a figure economists nonetheless consider impressively *high*, even the mark of an impressive work ethic, since almost half of them earn a monthly salary within €100 of what they could get on welfare. The economist Torben Andersen, who chaired a panel on financing the Danish welfare state in 2005, wrote that "increased immigration from low income countries would make matters worse since these groups on average have a labour force participation rate much below the standard in the Danish labour market." If immigration was made economically necessary by a labor shortage in the 1960s, why was it also necessary during a sustained period of double-digit unemployment, such as Europe underwent after the 1980s?

Europe now suffers from what Hans Magnus Enzensberger calls "demographic bulimia." It is gripped with the belief that it simultaneously has both too many people and too few. Welfare has a lot to do with this. The European welfare system has certainly made immigration more orderly than it is in the United States. In relative terms, there are few *illegal* immigrants—there are several hundred thousand in Britain, but only tens of thousands in the Scandinavian countries, as against 12 million in the United States. That is because the danger of deportation is low, and there are big financial incentives for an immigrant to let the state know he is there. The question is what he is there *for*.

3

Who Is Immigration For?

Good immigrants and bad—Is immigration for natives or
immigrants?—Welfare and white flight—Polish plumbers—
Barcelona or death—The duty of hospitality—Asylum and
human rights—Asylum and democracy

Several months before the French presidential elections of 2007, the
conservative candidate Nicolas Sarkozy found himself the butt of a
catchy satirical song by the West African reggae performer Zêdess. Sarkozy had given voice to a worry, increasingly common in France after
the national wave of riots in the autumn of 2005, that the quality of
France's immigrants was going downhill. Welfare dependency and
criminality were rising. Immigration was no longer represented in the
public mind by a diligent fellow manning a lathe for ten hours a day. It
was represented by the man Oriana Fallaci called "Mister I-Know-My-
Rights," and by the rioters, even if many were French born.

Proud of his own immigrant background (his father had fled Hungary after World War II), Sarkozy didn't oppose immigration. But he
thought France ought to be pickier. He called for an *immigration
choisie*, a selective immigration that would allow France to set standards for those with a claim on its social safety net. He distinguished
it from *immigration subie*, an immigration that is passively endured,
or undergone. "France," he said on a trip to Bamako, Mali, in May
2006, "cannot be the only country in the world forbidden to decide
who is welcome on its territory and who is not." One result of that
speech was the Zêdess song, which Sarkozy's political opponents
forwarded gleefully around the Internet:

His name is Nicolas Sarkozy
He invented *immigration choisie*
He is a son of Hungarian immigration,
Who wants to win himself a Gallic coronation.
    The muscular negro with his good set of teeth
      Is gone forever!
    Today, blacks have to have college degrees
      And be clever.
These are the standards of the new slave ship.
He had the nerve to say it on an African trip.
Nicolas Sarkozy!
Why did your father leave Hungary?

Good immigrants and bad

But really, the joke was on Zêdess. Not only did Sarkozy not "invent" *immigration choisie* (which became law in 2006 and 2007). By the time the video came out, France was, just as Sarkozy had claimed, one of the last places in the developed world where getting a better caliber of immigrant had not yet become a national priority. In every European country, there were calls for a more "Canadian" immigration policy. In recent years, Canada has admitted more immigrants per capita than any country in the world, if one excludes tiny tax shelters like Liechtenstein and the business hub of Switzerland. Almost a fifth (18.9 percent) of Canada's population is foreign born. But Canada lets immigrants in on a highly selective basis. Applicants for permanent residence get ranked on a 100-point scale that measures education (25 points), language skills (24 points), job experience (21 points), age (10 points), employment contacts (10 points), and "social adaptability" (10 points). There are additional financial, medical, security, and criminal background checks. It was Canada's selectivity, not the size of its immigrant flow, that was held up for emulation.

When European countries began looking carefully at their immigrants' qualifications, certain countries had a head start. By 2000, a third of the doctors in Britain (33.7 percent) were foreign born.

Ireland (35.3 percent) and Switzerland (28.1 percent) get a lot of foreign doctors, too. These percentages are rising as populations age. Britain passed a Highly Skilled Migrant Program in 2002, and added further inducements to educated immigrants three years later. The debate was also far along in Germany. Interior minister Wolfgang Schäuble noted that, unlike Spain, for instance, Germany didn't need low-skilled workers, since it had few national resources and was abandoning its extractive industries, such as coal. The sociologist Gunnar Heinsohn, confronted by the claim that Germany would need 700,000 immigrants in coming years, replied: "We need 700,000 *highly qualified* immigrants. We are getting people we don't need, while those we do need go to US or Canada."

He was right. Seven of the new additions to *Forbes*'s list of the four hundred wealthiest Americans in 2000 came from India alone, and all had made their money as high-tech entrepreneurs. The Consortium for Applied Research on International Migration, an EU-financed think tank in Florence, found that the United States and Canada got 54 percent of the world's academically qualified immigrants.

With a few exceptions, such as those British doctors, Europe has been unable to attract the kind of highly skilled immigrant workers who can juice up an economy. Germany tried its own version of *immigration choisie* early in the chancellorship of Gerhard Schröder. It launched a "green card" program for information technology workers from India and elsewhere, granting them up to five years' residence. It was a flop. Of the 20,000 green cards offered, more than half went unclaimed. Some people, including the immigrants themselves, blamed the narrowness of the program. Germany did not permit newcomers to bring families and didn't promise them a track to citizenship. Others blamed the messages of hostility that were rolled out along with the welcome mat. At the time, the Christian Democrat governor of North Rhine–Westphalia, Jürgen Rüttgers, made the memorable quip that what Germany needed was *"Kinder statt Inder"*—more children, not more Indians.

Immigration choisie contradicted the economic rationale for immigration that anxious Europeans had heard for decades—that there are certain jobs natives of rich countries "won't do." The protagonist of European immigration was no longer the illiterate Bengali janitress rolling her cleaning bucket through the hallways of a high-tech corporation after hours. The new protagonist was her compatriot, the physicist with a doctorate, working in an office down the hall. The immigration market had spoken, and what it had seemed to say was: "Janitors and busboys." Now governments were intervening to make it say: "Doctors and software engineers." Why was everyone so sure that an immigration managed according to government plans would be more efficient than an immigration managed according to the rough market that existed beforehand? *Immigration choisie* reflected a distrust of the efficiency of the global labor market—and the efficiency of the global labor market was the main economic justification for having immigration in the first place.

Is immigration for natives or immigrants?

The larger discomfort caused by *immigration choisie* was that it reopened the question of what and whom immigration was supposed to be *for*. Was it for natives or for immigrants? The more politicians said the former, the more they were suspected of thinking the latter. "They [the immigrants] are here because we were there," runs a familiar formula when Britons discuss Pakistanis or Dutch people Surinamese. Of course, the presence of, say, Sudanese in Norway or Bosnians in Ireland renders this well-meaning *bon mot* demonstrably false. But many Europeans and foreigners have tended to treat immigration to Europe as something immigrants are simply entitled to, part of an outstanding debt that Europe owes the rest of the world for centuries of economic exploitation.

So when the French government began discussing European co-operation to limit migration in 2006, prime minister Dominique de Villepin vowed to raise development aid by more than 50 percent over the coming three years. When EU leaders agreed on the outlines of a common immigration policy, to be implemented starting in 2010, seven heads of state from Mercosur, the South American economic treaty organization, assailed it as an expropriation of what was rightfully theirs. Bolivian premier Evo Morales warned Europeans: "Eating is a human right." This is a bizarre statement, coming from an elected head of state. If his citizens aren't eating, whose fault is that? Morales talks as if his representation of a constituency in the global economy is more important than his role as head of state.

Maybe it is. At any rate, politicians in emigrant countries have grown better and better at exploiting the confusion. In 2006, when Spanish authorities were trying to slow the arrival of African migrants to Europe by boat, the Gambian president, Yahya Jammeh, insisted that nothing could stop his citizens from making the passage. "This country only got its independence from Great Britain 41 years ago," he said. "To compensate for the exploitation to which our populations were subjected, our young people have the right to stay in Great Britain for the next 359 years."

If we leave aside the demagogy and focus on the economic aspirations, Jammeh had a point. Economically speaking, no model of development aid yet dreamed up has worked better than simply allowing migrants to set up a beachhead in an advanced economy and ship money home in the form of so-called "remittances." According to a World Bank internal document, a quarter of a trillion dollars in remittances were wired around the world in 2006; if you add unrecorded flows, they account for more funds than all the foreign direct investment in the world, and are more than double the level of international aid. Transfers to El Salvador, mostly from the United States but also from Spain, now make up a sixth of that country's economy, and Moroccans, mostly in Europe, sent €3.6bn home in 2003. In the spring of 2007, Western Union, once a telegraph company but now primarily a place where migrants wire money, opened its 300,000th agency—in India, where it has 36,000 already. Although remittances are likely drop along with the world economic downturn, they remain significant.

The economic effect of remittances is controversial. Do they mean that immigrant earnings are "lost" to the Western economies where they are earned? Or do they actually permit Third World countries to take control of their own capital development in a way that will benefit all countries in the global economy? *Immigration choisie* further complicates these questions. It takes something that many immigrant advocates consider a problem—the brain drain from poor countries—and subsidizes it. Economists differ on whether the migration of smart people from poor countries ultimately helps those countries (by relaying expertise) or hurts them (by sapping their brainpower). But in the short term, it hurts them. The migration of doctors to Britain mentioned above has caused desperate shortages in medical personnel in the Caribbean, Sierra Leone, Tanzania, Liberia, Malawi, and elsewhere. Is it generous of Europe to take so many foreign doctors or selfish?

When Zêdess implied there was something effectively racist about Nicolas Sarkozy's *immigration choisie*, he was, in the narrowest sense of the word, wrong. While the Sarkozy government set its standards high, it would not turn away any African who met them. Yet the song captured a certain reality: Sarkozy and others were declaring a return to the old understanding that there's immigration and then there's immigration. Sarkozy was replacing France's unconditional welcome of all the world's wanderers with a specific contract between France and certain qualified individuals. France would remain "open to immigrants," but only in the way it was when Émile Zola's father arrived from Venice: It would be open to immigrants who came pre-fitted to the economic needs and cultural preferences of the country. Economic needs and cultural preferences are sometimes hard to tell apart, and cultural preferences are often hard to distinguish from ethnic preferences. Zêdess was right to see that talking about immigration in terms of "training" and "social adaptability" did not make ethnic problems disappear. We will now turn to a few of them.

Welfare and white flight

One problem concerns welfare. Complex welfare economies such as those around which European economies have been organized for the past sixty years tend not to arise in multiethnic societies. The present wave of immigration will test whether multiethnic societies can even maintain them. Indications are that they cannot. The Harvard economists Alberto Alesina and Edward Glaeser have shown that roughly half of Americans' antipathy towards European-style socialism can be accounted for by the ethnic diversity of the United States. (The other half is a matter of political institutions.) This view is given strong support by the recent work of Harvard sociologist Robert Putnam, who has found that people living under conditions of ethnic diversity "hunker down." They trust their neighbors less and are less inclined to devote their money to common or social causes. The list of recent social science studies that arrive at the same conclusion is as long as your arm.

That welfare states tend to arise only in conditions of ethnic homogeneity is a new version of a very old problem. "A State cannot be constituted from any chance body of persons, or in any chance period of time," wrote Aristotle. "Most of the states which have admitted persons of another stock, either at the time of their foundation or later, have been troubled by sedition." What Aristotle calls sedition we, in a more relativistic age, would call dissent. Immigrants don't have the same prejudices as natives. They have what we would call fresh ways of doing things. That can make them valuable in a competitive modern society. But welfare is supposed to be a *refuge* from competitive modern society. It is a realm of society in which dissent, eccentricity, and doing one's own thing are not prized—as any American who remembers the uproar in the 1980s over "welfare queens" buying vodka with their food stamps will grant.

Once immigrants learn their way around the European welfare bureaucracy, they may have a different idea of the purpose of social security. Instead of using their benefits to pay for, say, food, they may use them to pay for, say, Islam. Two-thirds of French imams are on welfare. So are many British ones: Ghayasuddin Siddiqui, the head of Britain's "Muslim Parliament" told a conference in Birmingham in 2005, "Our mosques are largely tribal and controlled by old men on the dole with no understanding of the changing world around them." Most French and British citizens do not think of welfare checks as a do-it-yourself state subsidy for religion, nor would they support them through taxes if they did. If welfare recipients do not share the broader society's values, then the broader society will turn against welfare.

Another problem concerns mobility. It is assumed that immigration pits mobile newcomers against entrenched natives. It does, but only briefly. Natives are more mobile than they look. Migrations spark secondary migrations. The sociologist Rogers Brubaker, in a 1998 essay, called them "migrations of ethnic unmixing." For all the lip service paid to diversity, people tend to flee it. In the context of desegregation in the United States in the 1960s, such migrations were condemned as "white flight," and the secondary migrants were tarred as racists. But whites are not the only race that undertakes such migrations and race is only one possible cause for them. As mentioned earlier, the arrival of the Irish in Boston destroyed the Protestant culture of one of the most important cities in the history of Protestantism. The destruction occurred not only because the Irish arrived but also because New England Yankees chose not to live in an Irish-run city that was increasingly violent and corrupt. As Oscar Handlin noted, only half the descendants of the Bostonians of 1820 still lived in the city thirty years later. Immigration in general, and immigrant Islam in particular, has the potential to spark such flights in Europe.

Judging the impact and sustainability of immigration by looking at the "numerator" of new immigrants, people may neglect to look at the "denominator" of the native population. A falling denominator intensifies immigration's effect. Europe's native populations, as noted, are shrinking naturally, and this shrinkage is accelerated by emigration. Whereas 109,500 Germans left their country in 2001, 144,800 left in 2005, for Canada, Australia, the United States, Spain, and elsewhere, providing the occasion for a new television series called *Goodbye, Deutschland!*

These departures may be linked to immigration. Certainly the departure of Jews from France has been. In 2002, a year that saw hundreds of anti-Semitic attacks, most of them committed by North African immigrants and their offspring, more than 3,000 French Jews—about 0.5 percent of the population—moved to Israel, according to the Jewish Agency for Israel, which measures such relocations, and departures for Canada and the United States were high as well. Violence also unsettled the Dutch. In 2004, the radical filmmaker Theo van Gogh was brutally assassinated in broad daylight by a Dutch Islamist, after making a film that condemned Koranic passages on women. That year, the Netherlands recorded more emigrants than immigrants. A company that specializes in emigration paperwork got 13,000 hits on its website in the week after the Van Gogh killing, and the Canadian, Australian, and New Zealand embassies described themselves as swamped with inquiries about emigrating. In 2006, the former Tory cabinet minister George Walden wrote *Time to Emigrate?*, a semifictional letter to a son planning on leaving Britain for good; virtually all of the reasons he cited for emigrating involved consequences of *im*migration.

Judging by population statistics, there can be no doubt that white flight is happening. Birmingham's population, 77 percent white in the early 1990s, had fallen to 65.3 percent white by 2006, and whites were projected to constitute a minority there by 2026. Leicester was 70.1 percent white in 1991, but only 59.5 percent white in 2006. Whites will be a minority there in little more than a decade. The issue is not the race of a given city's residents but the cultural meaning of the ethnic shift. In the United States of the 1960s and '70s, white flight was an expression of danger, blight, and decay. Certain historic industrial cities, like Camden or Detroit, never recovered from it. The United States, a vast country with dozens of industrial cities, could easily absorb such losses. The stakes are somewhat higher in Europe, where a single city, such as Amsterdam, can be the repository of a great deal of a nation's heritage, culture, and literature. "The Netherlands is an art country," says Ayaan Hirsi Ali. "If the citizens of Amsterdam, 60 percent of whom will soon be of non-Western origin, are not made part of that, all of this will decay and be destroyed. When the municipality has to vote on whether funds go to preserve art or build a mosque, they may ask, 'Why should I pay for this stupid painting?'"

So the stakes of cultural compatibility are high. Canada, as we have seen, explicitly rewards immigrants for "adaptability." European countries are less forthright, but they are just as concerned. Consider Spain. Although it practically abuts North Africa, it gets only 20 percent of its immigrants from there; 38 percent come from Latin America. According to Bernabé López García, a professor of Mediterranean studies at the Universidad Autónoma in Madrid and a leading expert on Moroccan culture, this is not an accident. Spain has well-developed consular programs to recruit immigrants from Latin American countries (and the Philippines) that are not replicated in other poor countries. This, López believes, is a kind of "ethnic filtering," an effort to close the country's doors to Muslims.

Ethnic filtering is less sinister than it looks. It is a Canadian-style selectivity by a different means. Making a special effort to recruit Latin Americans is, by definition, discriminatory, but it is not racist. Spain is less concerned that its immigrants be white than that they have similarities of worldview with the people already established there, starting with knowing what the inside of a church looks like.

Polish plumbers

But that will not suffice to make an immigration problem-free. On Sundays in Paris, throngs of Polish immigrants overflow the seventeenth-century Jesuit-built church of Notre-Dame-de-l'Assomption, with its newly erected statue of John Paul II in front of the steps—a church that has not been full in decades. Yet the Polish immigration has been controversial. Cultural and economic factors interact in confusing ways, even when the immigrants come from a closely related culture.

When the European Union expanded from fifteen countries to twenty-five in 2004, eight of the ten new member states came from the old Soviet bloc. While some countries worried about being swamped by Slavs after EU enlargement, Europe's three most market-oriented countries—Britain, Ireland, and Sweden—left their borders open. Britain braced itself for an estimated 5,000 to 13,000 new arrivals. It got 627,000. The Republic of Ireland got so many immigrants after Polish accession in 2004 that, by the end of 2005, its 164,000 newcomers from the East bloc accounted for more than 4 percent of the country's population.

The economist Hans-Werner Sinn had long predicted such an influx, since the new accession countries were much poorer, relative to the EU, than predecessors such as Spain and Portugal. At the time of accession, laborers in such skills-rich places as Slovakia and Hungary were working at one-seventh the cost of the senescent and gripe-prone German work force. So EU expansion was mixed news for Western Europe. It meant downward pressure on wages; in 2005, the "Polish plumber" would become the great symbolic grievance of the successful French referendum campaign against a proposed European constitutional treaty. But it also raised hopes that Western

European labor needs could be filled by people who more or less *thought* like Europeans (say, maids from Hungary and machinists from Bulgaria) rather than people who did not (say, maids and machinists from Pakistan and Algeria). There seemed to be no limit to the pool of fellow Europeans ready to man service jobs.

But there was a limit. Except for Poland and Slovakia, every one of the new countries in the EU entered with a birthrate below the Western European average. The Baltic states in particular were due to lose 37.7 percent of their population by the middle of the twenty-first century. The eastward growth of the EU did not alleviate the EU's worker shortfall—it exacerbated it. Latvia is a case in point. In the eighteen months after Britain, Ireland, and Sweden opened their borders to migrants from the new EU countries, Latvia, a land with scarcely a million people, lost 100,000 of its youngest and most ambitious to emigration, a quarter of them to Ireland. The labor gap was severe enough for Latvian businessmen to consider filling it with workers from Ghana. Was Europe's eastern border moving eastward, following the pretensions of the continent's leaders? Or was the border moving *westward*, following the migration of Europe's actual population? "During the Cold War," one Latvian said, "we all dreamed of leaving, but the risk is that if everyone leaves, then the country will disappear." It is indeed a risk. Not every country, not every culture, not every language is going to survive this big latter-day *Völkerwanderung*.

In his poem "Going, Going" (1972), Philip Larkin wrote of over-development and environmental destruction in England, and of the way people knuckled under to its inevitability. Instead of challenging things they were uneasy about, people sought to "invent / Excuses that make them all needs." The economic need for mass immigration is that way. The justifications keep shifting: now growth, now welfare; now the benefit to the host society, now the benefit to the immigrants themselves. Immigration is a fait accompli for which people are scrambling to find a rationale.

Barcelona or death

Officially, Britain, France, and Germany had shut their gates to mass labor immigration by the late 1970s. They had reached a point of economic saturation. The advantages immigration brought (in theory) to a capitalist system were less apparent (in practice) to real voters, who understood more laborers to mean more unemployment. But the end to labor programs and the establishment of generously financed repatriation programs did nothing to stem immigration. Whether by design or by negligence the flow of immigrants continued untrammeled.

New excuses emerged to explain why immigration was a need. The main one was the duty to offer asylum to those threatened by violence, poverty, or political persecution. Labor immigration gave way to refugee immigration and to immigration aimed at reunifying (and forming) families. As natives began to doubt that mass immigration was to their economic advantage, they were informed that sometimes economic advantage had nothing to do with it. Admitting immigrants changed from an economic program to a moral duty. As such, it became less amenable to democratic decision-making. This change in emphasis actually increased the flow of immigrants at the very moment when politicians claimed to be shutting it down. Political differences deepened, with, on one side, a smoldering rage among working-class voters, and, on the other, an elite conventional wisdom that there was something "inevitable" about mass immigration.

How unmanageable immigration becomes when humanitarian considerations get mixed up with economic ones can be seen in Spain, which vies with Italy as the new century's top European destination for immigrants. Spain has two North African enclave cities, Ceuta and Melilla. These have been European since the fifteenth century, but never until the end of the twentieth were they magnets for immigration. Barbed wire was put up around Ceuta only in 1971, and then only to stem a cholera epidemic. Since 1999, there have been reception centers for immigrants and high-security fences in both places. The reception centers have been full ever since. The fences have been insufficient. For years, migrants from Central and West

Africa and elsewhere gathered near the perimeter, burrowing or vaulting through vulnerable spots onto European Union territory.

In September 2005, this migration underwent a quantum escalation. Moroccan police dispersed a group of four hundred migrants, largely Malians and Gambians, who had been living in the brush outside the perimeter of Melilla. Most were penniless and many had crossed the Sahara to get this far. Perhaps fearful that they would be sent far from the European border, the migrants, who numbered in the thousands altogether, gathered the following day to storm the barbed-wire fence en masse. Five hundred charged in the morning, some carrying ladders, others throwing stones and swinging clubs; 130 made it into Melilla, many with the skin ripped off their hands by the barbed wire. Hundreds more attacked the fence that night, and two hundred got over. To authorities' surprise, the Melilla-based migrants seemed to be in contact with those outside Ceuta, two hundred miles away, because similar attempts to storm the perimeter began there, too. All told, there were ten assaults in eleven days. Spain rushed three companies of its army to the two cities. The Moroccan border guard got involved. On September 29, they shot dead four people trying to rush the fence in Ceuta. A week later in Melilla, Moroccan forces killed six more people taking part in a four-hundred-man assault.

Many accounts describe the migrants' assaults as "desperate," and indeed they were. But there was more to it than desperation. Immigration is about ambitions as much as grievances. Just as impressive as the migrants' desperation was their confident resourcefulness, the level-headed tactical seriousness with which they sought to confound, outwit, and overwhelm the Spanish and Moroccan militaries. These were, albeit at a low level of technological sophistication, coordinated military operations.

The successful gate crashers, the survivors, applied for asylum status (for which the state of war that prevails in much of Africa provides a prima facie case) and were lodged in hospices set up by the Red Cross and other charities. Many were sent to peninsular Spain and released into the general public with "expulsion orders" that no one—either in Spain or among the immigrants—expected to be enforced. From there, thanks to the relaxation of border controls, they could travel unimpeded to most Western European countries. Today Ceuta and Melilla are secured with ditches and two rows of high-security fencing six meters high.

A few months later, motorized flotillas of long, banana-shaped West African fishing boats—called *lothios* in the Senegalese language of Wolof—began appearing off the resort beaches of Spain's Canary Islands. They carried thousands of Senegalese and other West African men and boys. These migrants, too, were recklessly brave. The Wolof motto that they recited to journalists back home in Dakar and emblazoned on their boats was *Barça mba barsakh*—"Barcelona or Death." Of course, Barça is the football club Barcelona, not the city, which may say something about the realism of these would-be immigrants' aspirations. Realistic or not, they were in earnest. Since the West African coast is where the Gulf Stream turns south and then rushes west, back across the Atlantic, routine engine failure could be fatal. Boats that drifted off course had been found months later, loaded with cadavers, as far away as Barbados. By the late summer of 2006, nearly 30,000 of these new "boat people" had landed in the Canaries. European commissioner Franco Frattini of Italy estimated that 3,000 people had died en route.

The Canaries had been a favored immigrant destination for decades—particularly for those making the sixty-mile hop from the Moroccan coastal villages of Tarfaya and Laayoune to the island of Fuerteventura. But this traffic had been a matter of a half-dozen or so North Africans arriving on skiffs and looking for short-term labor. The use of lothios, some of which could hold 150 men, signaled a leap in scale, an industrialization of the phenomenon. These and other big boats opened Europe up to populations that were ten days away by sea—and farther, because the attraction of the West African route into Europe, once it was shown to be reliable, was not limited to West Africans. A rusty freighter overloaded with Pakistanis was intercepted, and hundreds of Asians were picked up wandering in the desert between Morocco and Mauritania, thousands of miles from home.

Nor was the crisis confined to the Canaries. Boats launched from Libya, filled with Middle Eastern and Asian migrants, had been landing on the Italian islands of Lampedusa and Pantelleria. The scale was considerably smaller (10,000 boat people in the summer of 2006), the languages were different, but the scenes were otherwise similar. Some of the new immigrants were using speedboats and Jet Skis to break the chain of coastguard boats that ring the Italian and Greek islands, some were hiking into the EU through the hills surrounding the tiny Slovakian town of Ubla, where the EU borders Ukraine. Of course, these spectacular entries onto European territory were the exception rather than the rule. Most of Europe's illegal migrants enter legally, in airplanes, ferries, and automobiles, either as family members visiting with European citizens or as simple tourists. They *become* illegal by either overstaying their tourist visas or disappearing into the general population after rejection of an application for residence or asylum.

If the lothio invasion was a cause for worry, it was also a cause for pity. There was something shameful about turning away people who owned so little, who had risked so much, and who had shown such bravery. Smarter migrants had always known how to play off this bad conscience, and pretty soon the boat people did, too. That is why the actual landings in the Canaries were almost always peaceful and why few of the voyagers carried any scrap of identification of any kind. Under Spanish law, people of unknown nationality could not be deported, nor could they be detained longer than forty days. Those who remained silent under interrogation were almost automatically admitted into Spain and, in most cases, flown to the Iberian mainland, again with toothless "expulsion orders." The arrival of lothios in large groups swamped the Spanish authorities logistically and bureaucratically—as it was meant to. In cases where there *was* violence, the protocol differed surprisingly little. In April 2007, the Spanish patrol boat *Río Duero* approached a lothio carrying fifty-seven migrants off the coast of Mauritania and was met with a shower of Molotov cocktails. When the *Río Duero* sent crewmen to approach the lothio in an inflatable raft, the migrants tried to puncture it with pikes and sharp tools. The *Río Duero* escorted the boat to the Canary Island port of Arguineguín. The identifiable malefactors were sent back to Mauritania for trial. Many of the other passengers were released into Spain, and Europe.

At the height of the lothio crisis, Spain was pursuing a schizoid, two-track policy. On one hand, it was caring for the immigrants as brothers. It hastily refitted dozens of public buildings as temporary migrant housing: hotels and resorts, discotheques and prep schools, with circus tents thrown up, too, to handle the overflow. Military barracks, like the one at Las Raíces in the Canaries, made especially convenient refugee housing, since they had kitchens and recreational facilities. Since Spain, like other European countries, was shrinking its military, there were many such buildings lying idle. Arrangements were made to ensure that the newcomers could practice their religion—usually Islam—in the makeshift camps.

On the other hand, Spain was resisting the immigrants as invaders. Frontex, a transnational border guard that had been cobbled together out of the armed forces of European Union member states in 2005, got its first major deployment. The problem was that Frontex was something of a Potemkin agency, with a budget of only €15.8 million. Most of its work was done by the helicopters of Spain's Guardia Civil. The Italian and Portuguese navies made fitful contributions, but both Senegal and Mauritania refused to permit anything that looked like a Frontex warship in their waters. So the government of Spanish prime minister José Luís Rodríguez Zapatero—probably the least militarily inclined in Europe—considered stronger measures. At the height of the crisis its cabinet drew up plans to send a naval expedition to the African coast to cut off the migration at its source. The idea was rejected because defense minister José Antonio Alonso worried that the big ships might swamp the rickety lothios, creating an international human rights incident.

One can sympathize with Spain's ambivalence. What does "Barcelona or Death" mean? Does it mean "Help me in extremis" or "Cross me at your peril"? Obviously the Spanish government had no idea. Europeans in general could not figure out whether these immigrants were desperate wards, diligent workingmen, or ruthless invaders, and lacked the imagination to admit that they could be all of those things or none. What Europe needed under the circumstances was a moral code that would give answers about what it owed these people. It does not have one. A vague idea that Europe needs labor coexists with a lack of curiosity about whether migrants are indeed coming to work; a vague idea that migrants need to be cared for as refugees makes it seem impolite to count the cost of assuming responsibility for the world's poor. To roll out the welcome mat for all these people would be nuts; to turn them away would be racist. Unable to muster the will for either a heartfelt welcome or for earnest self-defense, they hope the world will mistake their paralysis for hospitality.

The duty of hospitality

Hospitality exists as a tradition and as a moral imperative in every culture. Modern readers of the *Odyssey* are sometimes surprised that, for days after Odysseus is welcomed as a stranger and guest into his own house, no one asks his name. It would have been a rude way to treat a guest. The same kind of hospitality is law in the Old Testament. (Leviticus 19:33–34: "And if a stranger sojourn with thee in your land, ye shall not vex him. But the stranger that dwelleth with you shall be unto you as one born among you, and thou shalt love him as thyself; for ye were strangers in the land of Egypt.") The New Testament (Matthew 25:31–46) repeats this imperative ("For I was an hungered, and ye gave me meat: I was thirsty, and ye gave me drink: I was a stranger, and ye took me in") and lays out the consequences of disobeying it. The severity of those consequences—damnation, to be precise—shows that hospitality is as central to the European or Christian tradition as it is to any other. The cliché that it is backward-looking and traditionalist to hinder immigration, and modern and open-minded to welcome it, is a mistake. In historically Christian countries, "pro-immigrant" politicians always draw on deep cultural reflexes, not to mention the support of most official church groups, and "anti-immigrant" politicians must always smash a few taboos before they can get anywhere.

There is a paradox about hospitality. Hans Magnus Enzensberger describes the paradox this way:

In order to avoid constant bloodbaths and to make possible a bare minimum of exchange and commerce between various clans, families and tribes, ancient societies set up the taboos and rituals of hospitality. But these precautions do not eliminate the status of "outsider." On the contrary, they set it in stone. The guest is sacred, but he may not tarry.

Hospitality is meant to protect travelers in hostile territory; it is not meant to give large groups of visitors—who may include militants, freeloaders, and opportunists—the run of the place. And yet, since hospitality is such an innate, deeply human inclination, canny people find it a particularly easy thing to exploit, much as advertisers exploit other deeply human drives, such as sex. That is why cultures establish all kinds of rules around hospitality. A guest who tarries becomes an interloper.

Hospitality is related to xenophobia. In fact, it is one of the faces of xenophobia. When Gothic tribes concluded a peace settlement with the troubled Roman Empire in 382, they were given *hospitalitas* (billeting on profitable lands) but not *connubium* (the right to marry Romans), and the accordance of the former privilege was linked to the denial of the latter. The most spectacular illustration history offers of the kinship of hospitality and mistrust is that of Captain Cook, who was feted, flattered, and worshipped for a month by the Hawaiian islanders in Kealakekua Bay in 1779. When he and his crew returned on an emergency visit to repair a broken mast, they were massacred.

The difference between hospitality and a full and permanent welcome has been widely remarked by Muslims who arrived in Denmark in the 1970s. Whether well disposed or ill disposed towards Danish culture, they tend to describe their reception back then as almost dreamlike in its generosity, at both the governmental and interpersonal level. But sometime in the 1990s, the climate changed with incredible suddenness to one of suspicion and even hostility. The temptation is to look for some precipitating event, some act of bad faith on someone's part. Liberal Danes often cite the rise of the Danish People's Party after 1995, as if it were possible in a democracy to manufacture society-wide anti-immigrant discontent out of thin air. The late imam Ahmed Abu Laban, a Palestinian firebrand who spent the last years of his life in Denmark, tried to explain the shift as a matter of religious intolerance. Danes, he said, "did not react to [immigrants] as Muslims. After a short period, Danes recognized that Muslims are committed, that Muslims are not going to give up Islam."

What happened in Denmark was more inevitable than that. The welcome immigrants received in their first months or years was not the permanent natural order of things. It was the reflexive courtesy accorded guests. Immigrants stayed long enough to lose their ritualized role as "guests," and, with it, their claim on Danes' hospitality. (This does not mean they lost their claim on decent treatment, only their claim on the specific form of decent treatment that is hospitality.) Once immigrants lost that role, what were they? Danes like any others, with well-defined constitutional responsibilities and unspoken cultural ones? Danes with special privileges *relieving* them of those responsibilities? Workers, requiring a new contractual relationship? Or interlopers, requiring resistance?

The problem in Denmark, as in Spain and the rest of Europe, is that no consensus answer to those questions has arisen. It is often noted with shock how long it took for European natives to realize that immigrants had settled in Europe to stay. Europeans went on thinking that immigrants would simply "go home" until at least the 1970s, when France first established programs to pay immigrants to repatriate themselves, and in some cases well into the 1980s. Today, however, Europeans often make the opposite mistake. They *exaggerate* how well established immigrants are in Europe. In high-immigration countries like Spain and Italy, the overwhelming majority of immigrants are first generation, and even in the oldest immigration countries, the immigrant population is much less rooted than it appears. In 2000, 60 percent of Germany's vast foreign population had arrived after 1985. Plenty of immigrants are full members of the society of their new homeland, with full claims on it. Just as many are not.

Asylum and human rights

Political asylum is the modern, bureaucratized version of the ancient duty of hospitality. As Enzensberger notes, the "'noble' asylum-seeker" was a staple of nineteenth-century literature. But the experience of the twentieth century caused an erosion of the distinction between people who come for refuge and people who come to stay. The willingness of a state to vouch for the migrants living in it often meant the difference between life and death—as it did for Jews in Nazi-occupied France and those Poles who were "repatriated" from Western Europe to the Communist-occupied east after World War II, to name just two of many instances. The West, anxious not to repeat these mistakes, became understandably absolutist in its reluctance to abandon refugees. Those who fled Communist and other tyrannies that arose after the war often had an automatic claim on the hospitality of the free world. The American welcome to refugees from Cuba was duplicated in Europe when it came to refugees from former colonies. Influential voices, from across the political spectrum, arose in anger if that welcome was withheld. When Britain passed its 1968 Immigration Act, which aimed to close the country's gates to ethnic Indians driven out of Kenya by "Africanization," the conservative journalist Auberon Waugh called it "one of the most immoral pieces of legislation ever to have emerged from any British parliament." The *Times* wrote: "The Labour Party has a new ideology. It does not any longer profess to believe in the equality of man. It does not even believe in the equality of British citizens. It believes in the equality of white British citizens."

Despite occasional legislation (such as the 1968 act) aimed at limiting the claims of foreigners to refugee status, an understanding spread that the welcome due to refugees was practically unconditional. Europe's refugee population began to grow, forming, as the Swedish economist Torsten Persson put it, "a ringlike pattern of political crises." To consider just the flow into Scandinavia, Polish Jews fleeing state anti-Semitism and Greeks fleeing the dictatorship of the "colonels" began arriving in the late 1960s. There followed pro-Allende Chileans in the 1970s, Vietnamese boat people somewhat later, and, in the 1980s, Kurdish nationalists from Turkey and refugees from both sides of the Iran–Iraq war. It was enough to be from a war-torn area—Eastern Turkey, for instance, or Algeria—to get settled in Europe at government expense while authorities adjudicated one's case. Some countries, the Netherlands most conspicuously, codified principles placing the burden of proof on those who would deny asylum to refugees. Even when the government decided against the petitioners and their families, it often maintained support for them if they chose not to return to their native countries. It seemed a violation of the higher law of hospitality to order them back.

By the early 1990s, when the warlord-induced famine in Somalia and ethnic warfare in the Balkans arose almost simultaneously, an easily game-able system was in place that made admission automatic to prospective immigrants who understood it. Various immigrant-advocacy NGOs in Europe made sure they understood it. Many evolved out of religious charitable organizations, such as the influential VluchtelingenWerk in the Netherlands. Anti-racist groups often played this role in France, and the Red Cross served as informal immigration lawyer to the African boat people who arrived in Europe after 2006. The right to settle one's relatives in the asylum country was an inevitable sequel to humanitarian immigration. In the quarter century after 1980, according to the Organization for Economic Cooperation and Development, half of all residence permits granted in Sweden—almost 400,000—went to reunite families from various geopolitical disaster areas.

European countries wound up so overburdened by asylum applicants that it was almost a joke. In 2006, the British home secretary John Reid announced a goal—not necessarily an attainable one—of working through the "legacy backlog" of asylum applications within five years. Germany received almost half a million applications for asylum, largely from the former Yugoslavia, in 1992 alone. Enormous though these numbers were, Germany may not have been the country most heavily burdened. That same year in Sweden, a country of only 9 million, asylum applications were reaching a peak of 84,000 a year. This wave came at the wrong time. Between 1990 and 1994, squeezed between an expanding state sector and increasing global competition for its industries, Sweden was undergoing the worst economic slump that any Western European economy went through between the Second World War and the financial crisis of 2008. GNP shrunk by 6 percent, and employment levels declined by 12 percent. Since the vast majority of asylum seekers were accepted, Sweden was adding almost 1 percent a year to its population. And that was before "family reunification" was factored in. An explicitly xenophobic party, New

Democracy, founded on the eve of Sweden's elections, stormed into parliament with 6 percent of the vote.

Refugees are not a random assortment of humanity. They are, by definition, products of societies marked by violence, corruption, or both—and no humanitarian principle permits one to choose only the most honorable among those taking flight. For Europe, the biggest nearby humanitarian catastrophes and the bloodiest nearby wars were either in the Muslim world (Iran, Iraq, Somalia, Eastern Turkey) or on its borders (the former Yugoslavia). One result, for Sweden, was a Muslim population of between 200,000 and 400,000 by the turn of the century, a figure that was topped up, after 2003, by tens of thousands of Iraqis fleeing the aftermath of the US-led invasion.

The refugee and asylum system has been tightened across Europe in recent years, in the face of popular opposition. A report in 2006 by the UN High Commission on Refugees showed only 9.2 million refugees and asylum seekers worldwide—the lowest level in a quarter century, and probably indicative of nothing more than tougher European screening procedures. Denmark, which approved a majority of asylum applicants in 2001, was approving only a tenth three years later. Even the once-liberal Netherlands changed its laws in 2001, limiting possibilities of appeal that could drag on for years and provide a pretext for de facto residency. By 2006, only a sixth of asylum applicants in the Netherlands were getting "A" status, that is, the right to an immediate transfer to subsidized municipal housing, along with integration activities and Dutch lessons. (Rejected applicants do, however, get the right to send their children to Dutch schools, and no one monitors whether they leave the country or not.)

"You have to have a hell of a good story," said one Dutch immigration official in 2005. But the best stories were easily counterfeited. They became well known through an incredibly efficient grapevine of immigrant information. The asylum system will always be somewhat manipulable. As of early 2006, women from countries that practice female circumcision could stay in the Netherlands on a five-year permit. People fleeing Iran usually had to prove they had been tortured or otherwise targeted by the regime—except for male homosexuals, who were admitted automatically. Pregnant women who had fallen afoul of China's "one-child policy" were well viewed. Unsurprisingly,

Chinese and East African women and Persian gays have made up a larger proportion of those seeking asylum in recent years.

There were very specific responsibilities under international law regarding migrant children. Very few teenage migrants give their age as eighteen or over, and many deny having living parents. European countries have differed on whether to permit forensic procedures (wrist-bone X-rays, dental tests) to determine age. Migrants knew the best countries to claim to come from—since Ivory Coast was at war in 2006, many of the boat people arriving in Spain claimed to be from there, despite speaking Senegalese languages and no Ivorian ones. They also knew the best countries to go to: At a visit to a Dutch immigrant hostel in 2005, one could hear the immigrants' own rankings of the easiest countries for migrants to get into. At the time, these were: 1) Ireland, 2) Belgium, 3) "England" (meaning Britain), 4) Sweden (which had recently become easy again after a temporary crackdown), and 5) France. The list is certainly different today. It does not necessarily show that any country is a perennial "soft touch" (although some are), only the incredible sensitivity of prospective migrants to shifts in immigration law, and to countries' "mood" towards immigrants.

Asylum and democracy

To those Europeans who believe their continent has an immigration problem, asylum policy is at the red-hot core of it. This marks a contrast with the United States, where the main distinction drawn is between legal immigrants and illegal ones, and asylum seekers provoke no particular outrage. In Europe, all candidates for asylum go through an orderly legal process, after extensive government vetting. Europeans' big distinction is between "real" asylum seekers, who have the right to stay, and "bogus" ones (to use the British tabloid term), who do not. A majority of asylum seekers fall under the heading of bogus, in the sense that they are not under a specific threat in their countries of origin, other than the threat of poverty. Weeks after the assaults on Ceuta and Melilla mentioned above, 3,000 Sudanese camped in front of the office of the UN High Commissioner for

Refugees in Cairo to seek refugee status. What was bizarre is that many of them already *had* refugee status in Egypt. So these were bogus petitioners in the sense that what they were really seeking was passage to some country more prosperous than Egypt. The sad ending to the story, though, shows that the line between "real" and "bogus" calls for help is not always easy to draw: In the last days of 2005, Egyptian riot police attacked the encampment, killing twenty-three.

In very few parts of Europe are active steps taken to send rejected asylum seekers home. The number of rejected applicants who stay may run as high as 80 percent. Asked by the BBC in 2003 how many foreigners were living illegally in Britain, home secretary David Blunkett replied, "I haven't got a clue, is the answer. I suppose that's a lovely headline that my advisers will be horrified with, but I haven't and nor has any other person in government." A common populist assumption is that elites favor liberal asylum policies not as an end but as a means—to more labor immigration. There may be something to this. One often hears that limiting asylum applications by sending back those who don't make the cut would be too cruel, or too costly. The "futility thesis" (to use Albert O. Hirschman's term) is frequently invoked. The £4.7 billion it would cost to deport Britain's illegal overstayers, according to the Institute of Public Policy Research, consigns it to what *Guardian* columnist Madeleine Bunting calls "make-believe policy land." This may be true, but not necessarily because voters think that spending £4.7 billion to make their immigration policy more ruthlessly efficient would be a waste of the Treasury's money.

The way asylum is discussed in Europe does not calm but rather radicalizes the political debate. Since rights to asylum are based on universal values, on civilized norms, they are insulated from the democratic processes that have curtailed other kinds of immigration in recent years. It ensures that those who *still* object to Europe's level of immigration and wish to tighten asylum admissions further must now take aim at the civilized norms themselves. Populist anti-immigrant politicians—starting with Pia Kjaersgaard of the Danish People's Party and continuing with the talk-show host Robert Kilroy-Silk, who led the eccentric UK Independence Party to a surprising third-place finish in European elections in 2004—have called for their respective countries to withdraw from the 1951 Geneva Convention on the Status of Refugees, which lays out what its signatories owe to refugees and asylum seekers. In the summer of 2006, British prime minister Tony Blair and home secretary John Reid hinted they might reexamine Britain's participation in the Convention, too. While Gordon Brown has been more muted on the subject, he has not rallied the public to the cause of European rights legislation, either. Leading parliamentarians in Kjaersgaard's party openly proclaim their distrust of "left-wing intellectuals" and of the "expert" values that govern the adjudication of asylum decisions. They use "expert" as a synonym for anti-democratic, and they have a point. The idea that democratic electorates are untrustworthy custodians of civilized norms is implicit in much political discussion of immigration, in Europe and elsewhere.

The administration of asylum policies and the question of whether asylum seekers are bogus or truly desperate have less to do with public outrage than first meets the eye. Asylum upsets voters because it is a different bargain than they were promised when mass immigration began. Problems come, as the late sociologist Abdelmalek Sayad put it, "when immigration stops being exclusively work immigration— that is, an immigration of workers alone—and turns into family integration (or into an immigration of settlement)." These new immigrants who come as relatives and refugees aren't coming to *do*, they're coming to *be*.

It was often said in the aftermath of the Gastarbeiter program that Europe had sought factors of production and realized only later that it was importing human beings. Refugee applicants come unambiguously as human beings—they present themselves in suffering humanity's name. They are seldom thought of as "factors of production." So while offering fewer quantifiable benefits to the land of arrival, they lay a much larger claim on it than the old labor immigrants ever did. This transformation was inevitable once mass immigration got under way. To native Europeans it felt like part of a larger change— from a *passive* population of immigrants to a *willful* population of immigrants. This was something that European values, as they had evolved in the decades since the Second World War, were totally unprepared for.

4

Fear Masquerading as Tolerance

Neutrality and political correctness—The criminalization of opinion—Grievance groups—Diversity and self-loathing—Second-class citizens

A central problem in welcoming people from poor countries is that Europeans have lost faith in parts of the civilization to which migrants were drawn in the first place. "Europeans would like to exit from history, from *la grande histoire*, from the history that is written in letters of blood," wrote the French political scientist Raymond Aron in the 1970s. "Others, by their hundreds of millions, wish to enter it." It is hard to follow Europe's rules and embrace Europe's values, as newcomers are sometimes told they must, when Europeans themselves are rewriting those rules and reassessing those values.

Some kind of ethnic conflict simmers in every country where there has been mass immigration. Understanding why requires looking back at the intellectual and moral climate of Europe over the last six decades. The Europe into which immigrants began arriving in the 1950s was reeling in horror from World War II and preoccupied with building the institutions to forestall any repetition of it. NATO was the most important of these institutions. The European Union, then in embryo, was the most ambitious. The war supplied European thinkers with all their moral categories and benchmarks, whether the issue at hand was the progress of civilization, criteria for ethical statesmanship, or rationales for military intervention. Avoiding another European explosion meant, above all, purging Europe's individual countries of nationalism, with "nationalism" understood to

68

include all vestiges of racism, militarism, and cultural chauvinism—but also patriotism, pride, and unseemly competitiveness. The singing of national anthems and the waving of national flags became, in some countries, the province only of skinheads and soccer hooligans.

Prompted by the United States, which was addressing its own race problem at the time, and with the threat of Communism concentrating their minds, Europeans began to articulate a code of "European values" such as individualism, democracy, freedom, and human rights. These values were never defined with much precision. Yet they seemed to permit social cohesion, and their embrace coincided with sixty years of peace. Whether credit for that peace belongs to European values or U.S. military power is a trickier question.

The end result of these efforts was the European Union, which by the first decade of the twenty-first century had grown to twenty-seven countries. It was an elite project, designed by statesmen and diplomats—and a moralistic one. Those who dissented from it stood accused not of poor judgment but of corrupt morals, of wishing to send the continent back to the horrors of the twentieth century. In a speech at the Theresienstadt concentration camp in May 2005, on the eve of a Europe-wide series of referenda on the EU, Sweden's European commissioner, Margot Wallström, warned that any hesitation in surrendering national sovereignty to Europe-wide bodies such as the EU would risk another Holocaust.

Architects and supporters of the "European project" did not hide their virtues under a bushel. "The European Dream is a beacon of light in a troubled world," wrote Jeremy Rifkin, an American-born author who advised Romano Prodi when Prodi was European Commission president. "It beckons us to a new age of inclusivity, diversity, quality of life, deep play, sustainability, universal human rights, the rights of nature, and peace on Earth." The New Labour strategist Mark Leonard describes Europe as superior to its rivals in its "ability to attract others and through that to set the rules for the global economy."

But attraction and admiration are not synonyms. There are lots of reasons immigrants might come to Europe besides a desire to live by its rules. In a barroom at 2 a.m., a pretty woman has an "ability to attract" quite independent of her values. The Ottoman Empire and China both had a power of attraction for Westerners in the nineteenth century. But it was not out of any admiration for their systems of government or their ideals of human rights that Europeans signed treaties with, settled in, and disrupted the national lives of those two countries. It was because they were rich places too weak and disorganized to look out for themselves.

Neutrality and political correctness

The "European project" was not dreamt up with immigrants in mind, but it wound up setting the rules under which they were welcomed. Postwar Europe was built on an intolerance of intolerance—a mindset that has been praised as anti-racism and anti-fascism, and ridiculed as political correctness. Our interest here is neither to defend it as common sense nor to reject it as claptrap. It is to understand, first, what Europe was thinking when it welcomed immigrants in such numbers—since this is something it would not have done at any previous moment in its history—and, second, what grounds Europe had for dealing with newcomers in the often naive and overindulgent way it did.

Postwar Europeans behaved as if no one's culture was better than anyone else's. In 1996, the Dutch cabinet held that "the debate over multi-culturality must be conducted starting from the principle that cultures"—presumably all of them—"are of equal value." Native cultures would not be favored over those of newcomers. The state would confront matters of immigration and ethnicity with a scrupulous neutrality, aided only by a set of "universal values" supposedly common to all cultures. It seemed inappropriate to force—or even to persuade—immigrants to assimilate into the old nationalistic loyalties that Europeans themselves were abandoning. "We're not going to bother Turkish children with the Occupation, are we?" asked one Dutch administrator during a discussion about multicultural education. During a debate over immigration in Catalonia in 2006, one Socialist leader asked mockingly whether immigrants would be tested on their knowledge of the "Virolai," Jacint Verdaguer's hymn to Our Lady of Montserrat.

Just because they were migrating to Europe did not mean immigrants accepted, understood, or even noticed the European project to leave behind "the history written in letters of blood." On the contrary, many immigrants, and many children and grandchildren of immigrants, considered it a duty to shout from the rooftops their wish for a Palestinian state or a Kurdish homeland or an Islamist Algeria. They kept alive dreams of cultural, national, and even racial glory that were beyond the reach of Europeans' universalism because they were beyond the reach of Europeans' understanding. The misunderstanding was mutual.

In the name of universalism, many of the laws and customs that had held European societies together were thrown out the window. Tolerance became a higher priority than any of the traditional preoccupations of state and society—order, liberty, fairness, and intelligibility—and came to be pursued at their expense. Around the turn of the century, Europe's ideology of neutrality buckled under the weight of mass immigration, and became a source not of strength but of what Alsana, the bitchy Bengali housewife in Zadie Smith's *White Teeth*, called "hosh-kosh nonsense." Looking around her diverse and bien-pensant London neighborhood, Alsana thinks: "No one was more liberal than anyone else anywhere anyway. It was only that here, in Willesden, there was just not enough of any one thing to gang up against any other thing and send it running to the cellars while windows were smashed."

The term "political correctness" was borrowed from American debates to describe the contortions of logic that European universalism required. No one has ever been quite satisfied with the expression. Maybe it is an unduly harsh way to described the well-intentioned white lies, wishful thinking, and petty misstatements of the sort that used to be called "talking out of one's hat." The musician Billy Bragg, for instance, declared at a forum on British identity, "When Churchill talked of 'their finest hour,' he meant 500 million men and women of different languages and cultures, all coming together on our small island to fight fascism." (*No, he didn't*, someone should have replied.) France's minister for equal opportunity, Azouz Begag, after nationwide riots in France in the autumn of 2005, called for the collection of data by race, asserting, "Diversity is not about charity, it's about profitability." (*No, it isn't.*)

Political correctness is often ridiculous. There was a campaign waged by the Dutch Honor and Reparation society against Zwarte Piet, the soot-colored sidekick of Saint Nicholas, who, according to centuries-old holiday-season folklore, takes bad children to Spain in a sack—a variant of the German-American legend that Santa Claus will put coal in the Christmas stockings of children who misbehave. "If you want to create a multicultural society," complained the leader of Dutch Honor and Reparation, "you can't have holidays every year that remind blacks of the slavery era." In the British Midlands, the town of Dudley banned certain toys and images from its municipal offices after a Muslim employee complained about a colleague's keeping a picture of Piglet (the Winnie-the-Pooh character) on her desk. For similar fear of giving offense to Muslims, authorities in Derby decided against restoring the statue of a Florentine boar that had stood in the city's arboretum since 1840 and had been damaged in World War II. (They reversed their decision after a petition drive.) In late 2007, the British schoolteacher Gillian Gibbons was arrested and threatened with whipping in Sudan, for having presided over a class of seven-year-olds that voted to name their teddy bear "Mohammed." Even when political correctness showed a tendency to authoritarian excess, its self-important perpetrators resembled Gilbert and Sullivan characters more than Stalinist henchmen.

Yet these were serious matters. A new, uncompromising ideology was advancing under cover of its own ridiculousness—not as the Big Lie of legend, perhaps, but as something similarly ominous that might be called the Big Joke. As anyone could see, its advance was also accompanied by intimidation and fear. The European Union and the Dutch lower house held anguished debates on how words such as *jihad* and *terrorism* should be used, if at all. In 2008, the British home secretary, Jacqui Smith, stopped using the phrase "Islamic terrorism" and began calling it "anti-Islamic activity" instead. Two years before, Britain had passed its Law Against Incitement to Religious Hatred, which as originally drafted had aimed (but, after emendation, failed) to criminalize criticism of Islam. The columnist Melanie Phillips was right when she said, "The term 'politically correct' does not do justice to this sinister, totalitarian project."

By the turn of the century, immigration was an area where even mild dissent against the status quo could be met with sharp condemnations. In a seldom-remarked passage of his 1968 "Rivers of Blood" speech, Enoch Powell paused from his rant against immigration to address the question of freedom of expression:

In the hundreds upon hundreds of letters I received when I last spoke on this subject two or three months ago, there was one striking feature which was largely new and which I find ominous. All Members of Parliament are used to the typical anonymous correspondent; but what surprised and alarmed me was the high proportion of ordinary, decent, sensible people, writing a rational and often well-educated letter, who believed that they had to omit their address because it was dangerous to have committed themselves to paper to a Member of Parliament agreeing with the views I had expressed, and that they would risk either penalties or reprisals if they were known to have done so.

The range of opinions expression on immigration and ethnicity was, beyond any doubt, narrowing dramatically. Was this narrowing something European publics had assented to or submitted to? Had they been convinced or coerced? Were they acquiring manners or losing liberties? This is always a hard line to draw. As Tocqueville remarked of the collapse of Christianity at the end of the Ancien Régime, "Those who kept the old faith worried they would be the last to remain faithful. Fearing isolation more than error, they joined the crowd without thinking like it. The sentiments of what was still only a part of the nation therefore seemed the opinion of all, and appeared irresistible to the very people who had given it this false appearance."

The criminalization of opinion

Over time, the ideology of tolerance changed in two ways. First, it broadened. The classes of people entitled to protection from intolerance grew, and what constituted an offense against tolerance became arbitrary and ad hoc. In the "Macpherson inquiry," ordered by the British Home Office into the grisly, unsolved 1993 murder of the black Londoner Stephen Lawrence, a racist incident was defined as "any incident which is perceived to be racist by the victim or any other person." This definition of racism—that it was whatever anyone said it was—became the working norm in many European countries. There was a new "expanded list of the rights of man," in Pierre-André Taguieff's phrase.

Second, the ideology hardened. It developed real powers of enforcement, partly because it was codified into law, and partly because non-governmental groups acted as freelance enforcers. Offenses against the ideology of tolerance now brought not just criticism and ostracism but the possibility of lost livelihoods and encounters with public authorities.

Where these two tendencies—the broadening and the hardening—interacted, the result was severe punishment for conduct that had been until quite recently considered normal. Gay rights is the most extreme example of this process. By 2006, a British husband-and-wife team of Christian evangelists in Britain had been interrogated for eighty minutes by police on the suspicion that the literature they were distributing showed "potentially homophobic attitudes"; a sixty-three-year-old Lutheran preacher in Sweden had been condemned to a month of prison for citing the Bible's disapproval of homosexuality; and Christian Vanneste, a member of the French National Assembly who had said he found "heterosexuality superior to homosexuality on the moral level," had become the first Frenchman convicted of homophobia. What had been a consensus opinion of humanity, from the dawn of civilization until the tail end of the twentieth century, was suddenly, at the beginning of the twenty-first, a crime punishable by imprisonment.

On matters of race and immigration, rules were renegotiated almost as quickly. In 1984, Ray Honeyford, a popular head teacher at an ethnically mixed school in Bradford, England, published an article in the *Salisbury Review* in which he attacked certain remedies of what he called the "race-relations lobby." He argued—much as Daniel Patrick Moynihan had done in his 1965 report *The Negro Family*—that activist government policies could harm the minorities they were intended to help. Neglect, indifference, and hostility did not explain all the failures of Pakistani and West Indian students, Honeyford wrote. Since they needed to acculturate themselves to British styles of learning, programs urging them to take pride in their native cultures and in British ghetto culture—what we would today call "multi-culturalism"—could hinder them in school, and further segregate them from society at large. Honeyford turned out to be right. The mixed student body he described a quarter century ago is mixed no more—or at least it has very few children of English ancestry in it—and the school has been renamed the Iqra School, following the wishes of the overwhelmingly Muslim community it serves. But being right, not to mention well liked among students of all backgrounds, did not save Honeyford from being fired.

In 1990, France's National Assembly crossed a new frontier. In the interest of repressing "all racist, anti-Semitic or xenophobic acts," it passed a law, sponsored by the Communist deputy Jean-Claude Gayssot, that rolled back certain guarantees of the 109-year-old Law on the Liberty of the Press. The Gayssot law criminalized not just an act but an attitude or a belief, specifically the denial of the Nazi Holocaust. Germany and Switzerland soon followed suit, and then other countries, so that denying (or minimizing the seriousness of) the Holocaust became an offense in Austria, Belgium, the Czech Republic, Lithuania, Poland, Slovakia, and Switzerland. It was under such laws that the British historian David Irving was sentenced to three years' imprisonment in Austria in 2006. (He served less than a year.)

France had been embarrassed by a number of fringe intellectuals and ex–Vichy politicians claiming the Holocaust had never happened. The law may have seemed like a reasonable tool for imposing decency on the public. It was not. The late historian Madeleine Rebérioux, a biographer of the great Dreyfusard socialist Jean Jaurès, warned against the Gayssot law as soon as it was passed. It should go without saying that neither Rebérioux (who came from a celebrated family of *résistants* and concentration-camp deportees) nor any of the many other historians who opposed the Gayssot law claimed there was the slightest *scholarly* value to letting people pretend the Holocaust hadn't happened. The problem, rather, was political. "The USSR paid a high enough price for its behavior in such matters that France should not wish to follow in its footsteps," Rebérioux later wrote. "One day, [the law] is going to lead into other areas besides the genocide against the Jews—other genocides and other assaults on what will be called 'historical truth.' "

She was right. In 1995, a French court condemned the Anglo-American historian Bernard Lewis—the West's preeminent authority on twentieth-century Turkey—for failing to apply the term *genocide* to Turks' massacres of Armenians on the eve of the Kemalist revolution. A law declaring those massacres a "genocide" passed in 2001; five years later, the National Assembly voted to subject anyone who denied that definition to a year's imprisonment and €45,000 in fines (although this bill did not become law). Another 2001 law defined the slave trade as a "crime against humanity"; in 2005, as a sop to those nostalgic for colonialism, legislation mandated that teachers stress the "positive role" of the French presence in North Africa.

Once the Gayssot law passed, it became hard to make a strong case against an endless criminalization of opinion, as Rebérioux had warned it would. The episodes upon which grievance groups sought to impose an official truth—the massacres of Armenians, the horrors of colonialism, the slave trade—were every bit as real as the Holocaust. If France really wished to stamp out all racism, xenophobia, and anti-Semitism, why the focus on the Holocaust? One could counter that, since Holocaust denial generally arises from anti-Semitism, and since anti-Semitism has such a clear record of corrupting Western political systems, France had a special stake in preventing it from rearing its head. One could also note that nobody actually *did* deny that slavery or colonialism took place.

But various ethnic lobbies read the Gayssot law as a challenge to "rank" their own sufferings alongside those of the Jews. One association of "Sons and Daughters of the African Deported" created a Hebrew-sounding word for historic slave transports that might better vie with the resonant *Shoah*, as the Holocaust is known in France. They took to calling slave runs the "Yovodah." In 2005, the most eminent French historian of slavery, Olivier Pétré-Grenouilleau, criticized the 2001 slave-trade law in an interview. A pressure group of "descendants of slaves" took him to court for "disputing a crime against humanity." Many claimed, following the American black Muslim preacher Louis Farrakhan, that Jews were responsible for the entire Western slave trade. The radical comedian Dieudonné Mbala-

Mbala, leader of an Afro-French agitation group called Les Indigènes de la République, said, "Africans are forbidden to look in their archives, as Palestinians are forbidden to return to their lands."

The Gayssot law was set up to defeat a straw man. It addressed tendencies of the 1930s (populism, nationalism, fascism) that, by the turn of the century, were long discredited and confined to a few isolated cranks. The problems of the twenty-first century (immigration, Islamism, bankruptcy of welfare states, financial panic, and the every-man-for-himself feeling that people got living in a consumer society) were different. There was a new cast of extremists. Many of them—like those anti-Semitic "descendants of slaves"—were adept at serving their own ends by gaming a legal system focused on the ills of seventy-five years ago. Each new officialization of remembrance summoned into being more "moral lobbies," as they came to be known in France, which pressed their claims with ever more insistence and clout, in ever more central areas of political life. Serious threats to freedom could arise while Europe was keeping under surveillance a collection of aging "fascist" buffoons. Arise they did.

Grievance groups

In the three decades that preceded the financial crisis of 2008, for reasons that have to do with globalization and technological change, authority migrated away from government and towards private interest groups. This drift, whether or not it persists, has been part of the spirit of the age. It has proceeded under governments of all ideological colorations, in domains ranging from diplomacy (consider the influence on aid to Africa exercised by the singer Bono) to residential zoning (consider the spread, in all Western countries, of "gated communities" with highly elaborated codes of private law). In the business of tolerance and race relations, too, non-governmental groups have taken over important state functions, and have proliferated to the point where, in French, they are called simply *les associations*.

The Communist-inspired Movement against Racism and for Friendship among the Peoples (MRAP), founded in France in 1949 to fight racism and anti-Semitism, came in later decades to play a different role. In 2002, the journalist Oriana Fallaci wrote an incendiary response to the attacks on the World Trade Center in the pages of the Milan-based daily *Corriere della Sera*. When republished in book form as *The Rage and the Pride*, it became one of the bestselling nonfiction books in postwar Europe. MRAP sued her under laws against incitement to racial hatred and sought to block publication.

There *was* racism in Fallaci's book. "Thank God," she wrote in a notorious footnote, "I've never had anything to do with an Arab man. In my opinion, there is something about Arab men that is disgusting to women of good taste." And there was other language that, while not racist, seemed to be written with maximum possible uncouthness to give maximum possible offense, as when she described pious Muslims as "the gentlemen who, instead of contributing to the progress of humanity, spend their time with their behinds in the air, praying five times a day." Still other language had a racist "ring" to it without being racist in any strict sense, as when Fallaci wrote that the disciples of Islamic fundamentalism were "multiplying like protozoa."

But *The Rage and the Pride* was not just a racist tract, and Fallaci was assailed for far more (i.e., for far less) than racism. One of the opinions that offended MRAP, for instance, was: "Any theologian can tell you that the Koran authorizes lies, calumny and hypocrisy in defense of the faith." Another was that radical Muslims are "everywhere, and the most hardened of them are living among us." While open to discussion, these were absolutely defensible points. Many scholars of Islam, not to mention Islamic theologians, do indeed say that there is a role for so-called *taqqiya* dissimulation in defending the faith. Few Islamologists can have had a deeper love of Muslim culture than the late Marshall G. S. Hodgson of the University of Chicago, and here is what he writes about *taqqiya* in his magnum opus, *The Venture of Islam*:

Many of the Shi'is who also had to accommodate themselves to authority which they could not in conscience accept, had developed the notion of *taqiyyah*, pious dissimulation of one's true opinions. It was not only to protect oneself but also to protect the community of which one was a member that a Shi'i was urged to practice *taqiyyah* dissimulation over against Sunni majorities or Sunni governments: at the least, not to press on their attention the Shi'i belief that the established Islam and the established government were illegitimate and should, in principle, be overthrown in the name of the imam.

Fallaci's point about dangerous radicals in the West, meanwhile, was made around the time that the Syrian-born radical Omar Bakri, who would be barred from England shortly after the terrorist attacks of July 7, 2005, told the London Arabic daily *Al-Hayat*, "Allah willing, we will transform the West into Dar Al-Islam by means of invasion from without. If an Islamic state arises and invades, we will be its army and its soldiers from within."

MRAP's suit was launched as part of a campaign against "Islamophobia"—a neologism often heard in the months after the September 11 attack. It threatened to erase the distinction between the criticism of minorities on intolerant grounds and the criticism of any minority on any grounds. It threatened to extend the de facto censorship that already existed on matters of race to matters of religion and beyond—to political acts done in religion's name. Islamism was getting the best of both worlds. While government officials refused to link the words *Islamic* and *terrorism*, the fact that the terrorists claimed a religious motivation gave them a measure of immunity from criticism. Fallaci was placed in the position where she had to demonstrate her "reasonableness" before warning Europeans about a dangerous and violent political movement in their midst. Although MRAP's suit failed, it opened the question of whether there was *any* language in which one could criticize Islamist violence without finding oneself in a courtroom. Islamophobia was an accusation that could be—and was—leveled at those who expressed worry over suicide terrorism in the Middle East or anti-Semitic attacks by Arab youths in Paris. Europe's toleration laws were beginning to work to the advantage of the intolerant.

The "Finkielkraut affair," which raged in France in the days after the nationwide ghetto riots of 2005, was another landmark. It showed that, to incur the wrath of the "anti-racist" establishment, it was not necessary to show even a hint of racism. The philosopher Alain

Finkielkraut gave an interview to the Israeli newspaper *Ha'aretz* in which he dissented from the prevailing view that the riots had been a "rebellion" against social conditions. Finkielkraut noted that that was not the way the rioters themselves described it. In their rap lyrics and their slogans against France and Frenchness, many had cast their deeds in ethno-religious terms. "Imagine for a moment that they were whites, like in Rostock in Germany," he added. "Right away, everyone would have said: 'Fascism won't be tolerated.'" Finkielkraut also questioned the logic behind the argument, put forward by other French intellectuals, that the modern exclusion of immigrants was a mere continuation of colonial conditions. "Okay," he said, "but one mustn't forget that the integration of Arab workers in France during the time of colonial rule was much easier."

Finkielkraut is mild-mannered and moderate, much less prone to egotistical media "interventions" than most of his philosophical contemporaries, who has spent much of his career unraveling the ethical and metaphysical problems that arise from totalitarian violence. When *Le Monde* reported on the interview and excerpted from it, though, he was subjected to a campaign of vilification. The *Nouvel Observateur* magazine called him a "neo-reactionary." A letter to the daily *Libération* attacked him as "belonging to that very French tradition of writers who, sunk in deep despair, abandon humanistic ideals." Another compared Finkielkraut to a functionary of Jean-Marie Le Pen's fascistic National Front. That is all a normal, if scurrilous, part of French public debate. What made the affair so sinister was its legal aspect. MRAP announced its intentions to sue Finkielkraut, along with Hélène Carrère d'Encausse, a member of the Académie Française who had made some rather rash statements that the riots were linked to the practice of polygamy among Muslim immigrants, for incitement to racial hatred.

That MRAP dropped its threat to sue just days after issuing it indicates that it did not have much of a case. But that is small consolation. No one believed that would stop the routine judicial harassment of any intellectual (or ordinary citizen) with the temerity to put forward a dissenting explanation of France's worst social problem. The "minority rights" in the name of which people could be sued consisted, first and foremost, of the right of banlieue rioters not to be made uncomfortable by the right of free speech. Here was another instance in which institutions established to promote tolerance had begun to work against the tolerance they proclaimed.

The policing of tolerance had no inbuilt limits and no obvious logic. Why was "ethnic pride" a virtue and "nationalism" a sickness? Why was an identity like "Sinti/Roma" legitimate but an identity like "white" out of bounds? Why had it suddenly become criminal to ask questions today that it was considered a citizen's duty to ask ten years ago? Erudite philosophers of tolerance such as Jürgen Habermas might possibly have been able to untangle such questions and draw the proper distinctions. Political elites could resolve them by fiat. But they left the person of average intellect and social status feeling confused and disempowered. A democracy cannot long tolerate a system that makes an advanced degree in sociology or a high government position a prerequisite for expressing the slightest worry about the way one's country is going.

The virtues of the multicultural era were elite virtues. The British political scientist Geoff Dench suspected, with good reason, that favoring elites was a large part of the point of multiculturalism. Conflicts in a striving meritocracy, he noted:

> can probably be managed much more easily where there are groups whose membership of the nation is ambiguous, who are very dependent on elite sponsorship, and whose presence flushes out ethnocentric responses among the masses which can then be held against them. A society tied to the notion of meritocracy may therefore have a particular need for minorities.

As the main way this need for minorities was supplied, immigration became a pivot point of all European politics, not just immigration politics. That was a big difference between Europe's challenges and similar American ones. In the United States, there was a "race problem" and there was an "immigration problem," and the two did not always have much to do with one another. Even if they were sometimes confused, they could generally be disentangled by people of good faith. In Europe, the immigration problem *was* the race problem. So declaring immigration a success and an "enrichment" became the only acceptable opinion to hold. To hold immigration a failure was to reveal oneself a racist; to express misgivings about immigration was to confess racist inclinations. The philosopher Pierre-André Taguieff coined the term *immigrationisme* to describe the regnant ideology that immigration is always "both inevitable and good." People still talked about immigration and its consequences, but only along pre-approved lines. Real discussions—about the increasing "diversity" of European society and whether it was a good or a bad thing—were all but shut down.

Diversity and self-loathing

Diversity described both a sociological reality (there were more foreign-looking people around) and an ideology (there ought to be more foreign-looking people around). The ideology was perfectly in tune with the neutrality among cultures espoused by the builders of the European ideal. Diversity, though, could never really be a stable or neutral ideal because Europeans did not know enough about other cultures to make it one. Diversity meant rooting out traditions that excluded people and trammeled the liberties of newcomers. All cultures have many such traditions. But while Europeans could easily dismantle their own prejudices, the prejudices of other ethnic groups were, quite naturally, invisible to them. At the heart of European universalism was European provincialism.

Europeans who considered churches houses of stupidity, sexism, and superstition didn't know enough about mosques or ashrams to form a judgment, and left them unmolested. They abolished the old and much-mocked nationalistic school lessons about the virtues of *nos ancêtres les gaulois*, but absorbed the new lessons about the virtues of other cultures, and the justice and nobility of exotic political causes, with a childish credulity. Immigrants could indulge certain comforting prejudices, myths and traditions that natives would be disciplined, chastised, ostracized, or jailed for indulging. Effectively, diversity meant taking old hierarchies and inverting them.

The European obsession with Third World "causes" was a function of Europe's new, guilt-based moral order. Immigrants and their children were at liberty to express politically their wishes *as a people*, in a way that European natives were not. Grim-faced censure was always at the ready for Europeans who indulged in the merest nostalgic buffoonery, like that of the UK Independence Party, which favored nothing more radical than pulling Britain out the European Union. The only national claims that could be made without provoking accusations of nationalism, racism, or xenophobia were those of foreigners. With their own nationalisms off limits, many Europeans were tempted to embrace vicariously the nationalisms of others—particularly Palestinian nationalism, which, in its most radical versions, allowed Europeans to reconnect with a discredited strand of European nationalism, anti-Semitism.

Where it interacted with immigration, there was an illogic at the heart of diversity. If diversity "enriched" and "strengthened" nations as much as everyone claimed, why would any nation ever want its immigrants to integrate into the broader society? That would be *drawing down* the nation's valuable fund of diversity. In this regard Ethiopians are for serving Ethiopian food, and helping substantiate the boasts of suburban school administrators that "our students speak 170 languages in the home"—not for taking jobs as marketing managers and dental hygienists. Or was the supply of diversity meant to remain—via immigration—permanently on tap? No European public wanted that. So European leaders defended large-scale immigration in one breath by saying it would make their countries different (through diversity), and in the next by saying it would leave them the same (through integration).

Diversity won its most heartfelt assent at the level of consumerism—primarily cuisine and fashion. In the 1950s and 1960s, before immigrants had changed European culture in any significant way, Europeans were immensely grateful for the novelties they brought—from samba to hashish to baba ghanoush. But from the 1960s on, immigration became less and less about curiosities that shoppers could take or leave, and more and more about the core structures of society — the welfare system, the prosperity of important industries, the resources various European economies brought to world trade, the principles of rights that governed transactions between individuals. Bizarrely, as immigration began to change Europe at its economic and cultural core, the political vocabulary remained the same as when immigration had been a fringe phenomenon. People kept talking about restaurants.

In essence, diversity was mere exoticism, an exoticism that declared itself sober and reasonable and kind rather than frivolous and exploitative and colonialist. The influence of young ethnics on fashion was extreme. In the poorest neighborhoods in France, young people's spending on fashion averaged €200 per month and outlays of €600 were not uncommon. Every country had a name for fashions that had started off as the uniform of ghetto youth and had become the mode of a big part of the young native-born mainstream. In France it was *le look banlieue*; in Britain, kids who flaunted designer clothing were called "chavs"; in Holland and elsewhere, a British company called Lonsdale made a killing dressing up thuggish teenagers in rap-style pseudo-athletic clothing.

Non-European immigrants may not have been enviable in a socio-economic way, but they were enviable in an existential way. They were cooler. They were aristocrats of identity. This was the message of a fascinating newspaper, *Gringo*, that was founded in the heavily immigrant suburbs of Stockholm. The ghettoized *svartkalle*—"black head," in the Swedish slang—was stereotypically downtrodden and excluded. But the pages of *Gringo* were full of braggadocio trying to pass itself off as self-deprecation. Ethnic Swedes were patronizingly called Svennar, the "Svens," much as American ghetto slang used to refer to white people as "Chuck." Native Swedes were clueless people who probably didn't know how to dance. Every issue carried the motto *Sveriges svenskaste tidning* ("Sweden's Most Swedish Paper"). The magazine's editor, Zanyar Adami, sometimes said that *Gringo*'s project was to create a new Swedish national identity. This meant, one assumes, getting rid of the dead weight of the old one.

Second-class citizens

Mass immigration, and the demographic revolution it brought, had long been defended as a means of giving the continent a much-needed transfusion of youth. But how much youth did Europe need? And what did Europe need it *for*? Was it for measurable efficiencies? Or was it simply to provide a rush of dynamism to a society too old and tired to provide such things for itself? Corinne Hofmann's erotic autobiography *The White Masai*—which describes how, on a holiday trip to Kenya, she cast her eyes on the bejeweled body of a young tribesman and, enchanted, decided to abandon her life in Switzerland—did not just reflect Hofmann's own tastes, but the entire German-speaking world's. The book sold 4 million copies and spent *years* on German-language bestseller lists. As Kingsley Amis wrote in a similar context, one can understand why Europeans like this sort of thing; the question is why they like it *so much*.

Europeans began to feel contemptible and small, ugly and asexual. They viewed themselves much as their nineteenth-century forebears had viewed the "savage" peoples in their empires. The brilliant novels of Michel Houellebecq, which minutely dissected such worries, sold millions of copies in France and all over Europe. The hero of *Atomised* (1998), for instance, describes the cultural anguish and sexual insecurity he feels while teaching Proust and the French classics to a largely immigrant-descended high-school class outside Paris. No one is interested in Proust, and the girl he has a crush on fawns over a macho African student ("this baboon," in the narrator's description) who holds him in contempt. Houellebecq's teacher comes to suspect the high European culture he is peddling might be worthless:

What was a banker, a minister, an executive compared to a movie actor or a rock star? Financially, sexually and in every respect a loser. The strategies of distinction so subtly described by Proust no longer made the slightest sense. . . . Proust remained radically European. He was, along with Thomas Mann, one of the last Europeans. What he wrote no longer had any relation to reality whatsoever.

In 2005 the novelist Matthias Politycki wrote an essay called "White Man, What Now?" It conveyed a message similar to Houellebecq's about who *really* feels inferior when Europeans confront non-Europeans. While researching a novel set in Cuba, Politycki writes, he came to look at the vitality of poor, dark people not just with fear but also with a kind of envy. Politycki stressed that he was using skin color "only in a metaphorical sense"—but, of course, cultural discussions of skin color are always metaphorical. He wrote:

The brutality of the raw life that took no heed of the moral or esthetic standards of an Old European, the unbridled wildness of will that frequently expressed itself as outright violence . . . Was I supposed to sneer at this as a lack of culture? Or must I marvel at it as a surplus of vitality, in the face of which I was a loser from the get-go. . . . Sometimes I was so completely humiliated by these eruptions of physical force that I tried to persuade myself that I carried in my white skin the whole epochal exhaustion of the Old World. But dressing up my weakness in the face of reality as the superiority of a refined reason didn't help at all.

Variants of this experience haunt Politycki everywhere he goes in the Third World. In Burundi, he has the vague sense of a lurking physical threat. But he and his scared Western traveling companions would not have wanted a weapon to use in self-defense, he confesses, because they would have lacked the will to use it. In the Far East, Politycki is shocked by the hard-working inhabitants' "unbridled energy, which provokes not any particular ethical reflections so much as a basic feeling of impotence." In the Arab world, he is unnerved by the sexual energy of—in particular—Moroccans. "What is troubling about these travel experiences," he writes, "is less the shame in the face of an unbridled virility but the bitter feeling we get at the weakness of our culture—or, better, of our worldview."

The word Politycki most often uses to describe poor people is "unbridled"; his word for Westerners is "camouflaged." Reason and enlightenment and "individualism," he comes to believe, sap Europeans' vital energy without extinguishing their admiration for vital energy. So making extravagant claims for the European way requires an ever-ramifying system of lies and rationalizations. "Whether a completely enlightened (read: godless) society has anything of value to set against a semi-enlightened one," he writes, "is a basic problem that has accompanied many advanced cultures to their doom."

In the hands of Politycki and other Europeans, multiculturalism became almost (if one will pardon the expression) a self-directed xenophobia. This tendency was visible throughout society, as the poet Hans Magnus Enzensberger was among the first to note. "The defense of immigrants is always carried off with a moralizing flourish and a maximum of self-righteousness," wrote Enzensberger. "Slogans like

'Foreigners, don't leave us alone with the Germans!' and 'Germany—never again' testify to a pharisaical reversal. It is the photographic negative of a racist cliché."

Ordinary people have a hard time consulting principles before acting. They repair to "friend-or-foe" heuristics and rules of thumb. By now it is almost second nature for Westerners to assume that anything familiar, traditional, and Western is to be opposed; and anything discomfort-inducing and foreign is to be protected. So in 2006, Nadia Eweida, a British Airways stewardess and an Egyptian Christian, was suspended from work without pay for wearing the cross, although the airline permits its Muslim employees to wear hijabs and headscarves. (After several days of tabloid outrage, the airline backed down and rehired her.) The BBC forced a Christian woman to remove her cross in the office, although it, too, allows headscarves. Europeans were coming to despise their own cultures, much as the bigots among their forebears had despised the cultures of other peoples.

The German jurist Udo di Fabio warned in 2005 that the language of multiculturalism and diversity "opens the gates to a new Middle Ages, in which the model is not the human individual but the harmonious ordering of groups." And the way the groups were ordered often left natives feeling like second-class citizens in their own countries. According to a report of the British government's Office of Communities and Local Government in 2008, "White people are less likely to feel they can influence decisions at the local level than people from minority ethnic groups (37 percent compared to 45 percent). White people are also less likely to feel they can influence decisions affecting Great Britain (19 percent compared to 31 percent)." Whites' relative pessimism about exercising their rights is supposed to strike us as puzzling, or surprising, but of course it is not. It reflects a belief that their aspirations are not the real subject matter of Britain's politics.

The message that majorities have needs, too, is often unwelcome. Bassam Tibi, a Syrian-born sociologist in Germany, suggested that German culture be understood as the main, or leading, culture (*Leitkultur*) in Germany's pluricultural society. Tibi was pilloried for the suggestion that Beethoven and Thomas Mann might deserve a larger role in shaping the national consciousness than foreign voices, as was Friedrich Merz, the Christian Democratic politician who tried to popularize the idea. Europe was a place of aspiration for immigrants, and of deference and restraint for the native born.

The values that were supposed to liberate Europeans had left them paralyzed, until Europeans' very standing to demand that immigrants adapt to European ways was put in question. "We no longer consider any human action legitimate, or even intelligible," wrote the philosopher Pierre Manent, "unless it can be shown to be subject to some universal rule of law, or to some universal ethical principle." This universal ethics had one uncomfortable similarity to religious fundamentalism and the other exclusionary cultures to which it was supposed to be the antidote. For universalism as for religious fundamentalism, Manent noted, "the only truly unforgivable human action is what one used to call *conversion*. There is no longer any legitimate grounds for change because there is no longer any legitimate grounds for preference."

Before immigrants could live by European rules, Europeans had to figure out what those rules were. Gordon Brown, in the years before he became Britain's prime minister, suggested that his countrymen be more explicit about the values and customs that everyone in society ought to respect, no matter what their background. But that was thin gruel, and it was late to make such a suggestion. The old religion-based cultures of Europe performed just the function Brown described until they were questioned in the 1960s and '70s, in the name of personal liberation and individual autonomy, and then repudiated in the 1980s and '90s, in the name of making Europe more friendly to minorities. How could Brown now expect immigrants and their children to help revive a culture that natives and their children had done little but snicker at? Especially since there was an alternative source of values that appeared, to many European immigrants, more legitimate, more coherent, and more alive than Europe's discredited national cultures.

That was, of course, Islam.

PART II

Islam

5

Ethnic Colonies

Europe's historic understanding of Islam—Muslim populations, present and future—Rejuvenation of run-down neighborhoods—Architecture and segregation—Lawless zones—Segregation or self-segregation?—Spaces of sharia —Violence, crime, and rioting—The banlieue riots and Islam—Tribalism, ideology, and escalation

Had Europeans realized, when immigration from Turkey, Morocco, Algeria, and elsewhere began in the 1950s and 1960s, that there would be thousands of mosques across Europe half a century later, they would never have permitted it. European tolerance of other cultures was sincere, particularly among elites, but not even they anticipated that such tolerance would mean the establishment, entrenchment, and steady spread of a foreign religion on European soil. In exchange for minor economic returns of extremely short duration, Europe replanted the seeds of a threat that had taken centuries of patience and violence to overcome—interreligious discord, both domestic and international.

Europe's historic understanding of Islam

It can fairly be said that, until its steep military decline in the nineteenth and twentieth centuries, Islam was the arch-enemy of European civilization. For virtually all of Europe's history since the Dark Ages it had been a mortal threat. Between the seventh and ninth centuries, militarized Islam conquered half of the fragmented Roman Empire. "It very nearly destroyed us," wrote Hilaire Belloc in 1938. At the time, Belloc thought it dangerous that Westerners

have forgotten all about Islam. They have never come in contact with it. They take for granted that it is decaying, and that, anyway, it is just a foreign religion which will not concern them. It is, as a fact, the most formidable and persistent enemy which our civilization has had, and may at any moment become as large a menace in the future as it has been in the past. . . . It has always seemed to me possible, and even probable, that there would be a resurrection of Islam and that our sons or our grandsons would see the renewal of that tremendous struggle between the Christian culture and what has been for more than a thousand years its greatest opponent.

Belloc's language was blunt even for the time. He referred to Western culture as "white civilization." He was an especially ardent defender of the Crusades, which he called the "one supreme attempt to relieve that [Islamic] pressure upon the Christian West." But his general thoughts on Islam were only those of most Europeans in most eras.

According to the Belgian historian Henri Pirenne, the Islamic conquests *created* Europe—at least Europe as it has existed since the end of the Roman Empire. Unlike the invasions of Rome by Germanic barbarians in the first centuries after Christ, which were easily absorbed into existing institutions, the Islamic invasions changed everything. Islam's advance broke the ancient world because it broke the unity of the Mediterranean. Cut off from the Christian capital (and the emperor's fleet) at Constantinople, Europeans abandoned the Mediterranean to Muslim navies and Saracen pirates. "The West was bottled up and forced to live by its own means, in a vacuum," Pirenne wrote. "For the first time ever, the center of life was pushed back from the Mediterranean, towards the north." Europe's heart moved away from its southern littoral to somewhere between the Seine and the Rhine. "Now on the coasts of *Mare Nostrum*," Pirenne wrote, "stretched two different and hostile civilizations."

There have always been European exceptions to the prevailing distrust of Islam. Goethe and Carlyle, both admirers of Muslim civilization, were inclined to stress its achievements. This line of thinking, a minority one in past generations, is a majority one in our own, to the extent that one often encounters the suggestion that Europe ought to be *grateful* for Islam's historic hostility. Bassam Tibi, Pirenne's most tendentious reader in the present generation, writes: "Without the challenge of Islam, the Christian West of Charlemagne would never have existed. What Pirenne means is this: Both powers—Europe as the West and Islam as a civilization—arose together historically and constitute a challenge for one another." This will not be the last time we see the word *challenge* used to mean *problem*, although the euphemisms vary. The Cambridge anthropologist Jack Goody, for instance, sees the centuries of hostility less as a series of battles than as a series of "encounters." He is as interested in Muslim influence on European pharmacology and troubadour poetry, in the Muslim custodianship of many works of Greek philosophy through the Dark Ages, as he is in the conquest and bloodshed.

These Muslim achievements were real, and are increasingly well documented. But Europeans, up until the present generation, have not seen Islamic civilization as particularly impressive. Typical was the French polymath Ernest Renan, who wrote in 1883:

Those liberals who defend Islam do not know Islam. Islam is the seamless union of the spiritual and the temporal, it is the reign of dogma, it is the heaviest chain mankind has ever borne. In the early Middle Ages, Islam tolerated philosophy, because it could not stop it. It could not stop it because it was as yet disorganized, and poorly armed for terror. . . . But as soon as Islam had a mass of ardent believers at its disposal, it destroyed everything in its path. Religious terror and hypocrisy were the order of the day. Islam has been liberal when weak, and violent when strong. Let us not give it credit for what it was merely unable to suppress.

Both Renan and Belloc complained of complacency among their contemporaries. That is nothing new. But neither of them lived at a time of mass Muslim immigration. It will surely puzzle future generations why Europeans did not worry more about the religion of those guest workers who began arriving from South Asia, North Africa, and Turkey in the 1950s and 1960s. Why, between World War II and September 11, 2001, did Europeans seem unanimously to embrace Tibi and Goody's tolerant (or Panglossian) view of Islam rather than Belloc and Renan's intolerant (or bigoted) one?

Part of the answer is that the European masses did come to accept the views of European opinion leaders. The wounds of racism and fascism were still open, and popular misgivings about Islam were easily quashed by official doctrine and intellectual fashion. For a few decades, Europeans felt they had more to fear from native, secular fanaticism than from foreign, religious fanaticism. And they mistook the Cold War, in which political conflicts tended to revolve around the economic and materialistic ideologies of the industrial age, for the permanent order of things.

This mistake should not surprise Americans. It certainly did not occur to anyone in the United States in the 1970s that importing migrant farm labor from Mexico might strengthen the hand of traditional Roman Catholicism (as well it might have, considering the political battles over feminism, liberalized abortion rights, and reform of other traditional folkways in the years of maximum immigration). Religion was simply not on anyone's list of political fears at the time. It was scarcely on anyone's list of identities. That America's immigrants proved more compatible with the majority culture than Europe's did is often taken by Americans as a proof of either a superior economy or a superior tolerance. Maybe, but it also reflects that America drew its manual workers from Latin American Catholicism, while Europe drew most of its bottom-rung labor from Mediterranean Islam. Europe's failure and America's success are in part an accident of geography.

They are also an accident of history. In the 1950s, Arab nationalism, of the sort practiced by Gamal Abdel Nasser in Egypt and the Ba'athist leaders of Syria and Iraq, was the main political force coming out of the Muslim world. It was driven largely by people who wanted to break theology's stranglehold on Muslim societies. Even if Arab nationalism was a threat, a young man ready to leave his nation to work in a mill in Belgium was unlikely to embody it. Europe's Arab and other Muslim newcomers could be assumed the most secular and modern of their countrymen, with a vocation to act as Europeans. Indeed, photos of groups of Moroccans and Turks newly arrived on Rotterdam's docks or in Rhineland train stations show clean-shaven men in conservative jackets and ties.

But right around the time immigrants began arriving in Europe en masse, a global resurgence of political Islam was beginning. It is now in full swing. Islam once again ranks high among the problems Europeans are most worried about. In 2004, France's National Consulting Committee on Human Rights (CNCDH) asked people's basic feelings about major religions. More than half of respondents (52 percent) had a "positive" view of Christianity, versus 13 percent who were "negative." Europeans were 30 percent positive and 20 percent negative about Judaism. About Islam, they were 23 percent positive and 66 percent negative. In Germany, a 2007 poll asked, "When you hear the word 'Islam,' what do you think of?" Ninety-three percent said, "oppression of women," 83 percent "terrorism," and 82 percent "radicalism." The first European generations in 1,300 years that did not see Islam as a threat turned out to be the last ones.

Muslim populations, present and future

While political Islam grew abroad, another problem was growing inside Europe itself. The new, mostly Muslim immigration was less manageable and less soluble than any that had come before it. This was partly a matter of size. The postwar waves of immigration were larger by orders of magnitude than the old ones. By the turn of the century, fully a sixth (16.9 percent) of French residents under eighteen had immigrant parents, and that was true of 40 percent of children in Paris. There were dozens of cities and towns where the *majority* of children had parents born abroad. But the immigrants were not only more numerous, they were also more foreign. France, for instance, had had enclaves of Italians, Spaniards, and Poles for much of the twentieth century, but there is a difference between immigrants who speak cognate languages and worship in local churches, and those starting from cultural scratch.

France's most heavily immigrant places a generation ago were mining communes in the Moselle, heavily inhabited by Italians. In Behren-lès-Forbach in 1968, for instance, 72 percent of young people had immigrant parents; 43 percent were Italian. Behren-lès-Forbach remains heavily immigrant (although thirty-five communes have passed it in concentration), but today only 7 percent of the kids have Italian parents; 41 percent have North African ones. This process is going on all over the country. France's population of sub-Saharan African immigrants rose by 45 percent between 1999 and 2004. In the department of Seine Saint-Denis, the heavily North and West African area where the riots of 2005 began, the number of children of French-born parents has fallen by 41 percent, while the number of children of immigrants increased two and a half times. Many parts of the country are marked by what the demographer Michelle Tribalat calls a "process of substitution."

There are about 20 million Muslims on the continent, if you count the millions of native Muslims in the Balkans. As noted earlier, there are around 5 million Muslims in France, 4 million in Germany, and 2 million in Britain. Pakistanis and Bengalis predominate in England, Arabs in France, Belgium, and Spain, and Turks in Germany; but Islam in all Western European countries is to some extent a mix of people from all over the Islamic world. The heavy concentration of these populations has the potential to multiply their influence. A million Muslims now live in London, where they make up an eighth of the population. In Amsterdam, Muslims account for more than a third of religious believers, outnumbering Catholics, as well as all the Protestant orders combined.

Muslims now either dominate or vie for domination of certain important European cities. A partial list of them would include Amsterdam and Rotterdam in Holland; Strasbourg and Marseille (and many of the Paris suburbs) in France; Duisburg, Cologne, and the Berlin neighborhoods of Kreuzberg and Neukölln in Germany; and Blackburn, Bradford, Dewsbury, Leicester, East London, and the periphery of Manchester in England. Such places may, as immigration continues and the voting power and political savvy of the Muslims already there increases, take on an increasingly Muslim character.

Most of Europe's leaders, in the first years of this century, embraced the view laid out (and disputed) in Chapter 2 that Europe "needs" immigration for economic reasons. If this is true, then the demographic pressure of Islam on Europe is only in its very earliest stages—because the economically backward, overcrowded lands of Islam are Europe's nearest neighbors across the Mediterranean. The U.S.

National Intelligence Council expects the Muslim population of Europe to double, continent-wide, by 2025.

Immigration is not the only thing causing the weight of Islam in Europe to grow. The gap in fertility between immigrants and natives is at its widest for Muslim immigrants. Religion, or religiosity, is the strongest predictor of fertility. Looking at Britain, the sociologist Eric Kaufmann found that Caribbean and Eastern European immigrants rapidly picked up the ambient secularism (and low birthrates) of British society, but that there was virtually no change at all in the religiosity (and fecundity) of Bangladeshi and Pakistani Muslims between the first and second generations. In Birmingham, Pakistanis made up 7.1 percent of the population in 1991, a figure that will nearly triple, to 21 percent, by 2026. Britain's Barrow Cadbury Trust, which gathered the data, noted that "this increase is likely to be driven by existing demographics of Birmingham's youthful Pakistani population, rather than migration."

Austria is a good country in which to study the variance in population growth between natives and newcomers. Its immigration has been heavily non-European and it is one of the few countries that includes religion in its census. There, the total fertility rate of Catholics is 1.32 children per woman. It is 1.21 for Protestants and 0.86 for the nonreligious. The total fertility rate for Muslims is 2.34. This divergence may sound unspectacular—after all, American women had higher total fertility rates than that as recently as the Baby Boom—but the effects of such a divergence increase rapidly. According to four demographers from the Vienna Institute of Demography, Islam could be the majority religion among Austrians under fifteen by midcentury; it is probable that Austria as a whole, which was 90 percent Catholic in the twentieth century, will be under 50 percent Catholic by the middle of the twenty-first.

In Belgium, the relatively well-established Moroccan-Belgian community has a birthrate two and a half times higher than the native Belgian one. In Brussels, where a quarter of the residents are foreign citizens, the seven most common given boy's names were Mohamed, Adam, Rayan, Ayoub, Mehdi, Amine, and Hamza.

Rejuvenation of run-down neighborhoods

One of the things that immigrants are supposed to do, in the popular mythology of immigration, is to "regenerate" or "bring new life to" areas that have lost their magic for natives. That is exactly what has happened in many cases across Europe, even if natives have sometimes been slow to admit it. The Turks who came in droves to the Berlin neighborhood of Kreuzberg were often accused of turning it into a ghetto, but it would be more accurate to say that they rescued it from being one. The building of the Berlin Wall in 1961 had transformed Kreuzberg into an urban cloaca in the shadow of East German sharpshooters. The working class moved out. A grotesque tower block full of welfare flats went up in 1974. "Commuters came no more," as a display in the Kreuzberg Museum bluntly puts it. In the late 1960s and early 1970s, hippies and Turks moved into this neighborhood's rotting flats for the same reason: cheap rent. The hippies brought rock music, panhandling, skid-row alcoholism, prostitution, drugs, and city-sponsored coin-operated hypodermic-needle-dispensing machines. The Turks brought (along with their warehouse mosques) families, sewing circles, sweet shops, sports clubs, and streets that, while decidedly rough, grew safer by the year. The parents among them even organized groups to collect discarded drug paraphernalia from the streets.

In Turin, the literary scholar and novelist Younis Tawfik turned a crummy bathhouse, built in 1958 for migrants from the Italian south and abandoned for more than a decade, into the beautiful Centro culturale Italo-arabo, with a *hammam* (or Turkish bath), a restaurant, and an interfaith library. In the Rhineland port of Duisburg, after industrial jobs disappeared and the central city atrophied, immigrants preserved the life of working-class neighborhoods such as Marxloh and Wanheimerort. When they gathered the funding to build the largest mosque in Germany, which opened at the end of 2008, they devoted a substantial part of it to a community center open to all faiths. In London, the inviting, restaurant-filled neighborhoods around Whitechapel and Bethnal Green (dominated by Bengalis) were in places so tightly entangled with the neighborhoods around Liverpool Street (dominated by headquarters of high finance) that it was hard to tell where one left off and the other picked up.

This was the picture immigration that European elites, who increasingly inhabited their countries as international tourists à l'intérieur, saw most often. It was misleading. Most Muslims lived apart, in places that were terra incognita to the vast majority of Europeans. In conditions of isolation, many Muslim neighborhoods turned into ghettoes, with customs, rules, and institutions of their own. It was not always easy to tell whether it was the natives who desired this or the immigrants themselves. But the sense that the Muslim part of Europe's immigrant population was shearing off and forming a parallel society has been at the heart of European worries of Islam since well before September 11, 2001. To understand European unease about these parallel societies, it is necessary to make a detour into urban planning and segregation.

Architecture and segregation

In the 1950s and 1960s, vast housing projects were built for low-income earners in most European countries, just as they were in the United States, and with the same goal: to remove the poor from the filth and stale air of the slums. There was a price for this "progress," and it was too high. The new grands ensembles, as they were called in France, were without variety. They were often isolated from job markets. And while organic neighborhoods can be woven into rich communities, vast, soulless landscapes of residence pods usually cannot be.

Such housing projects were a European idea. It was the Swiss planner Le Corbusier who inspired the tracts of HLMs (habitations à loyer modéré) that ring Paris and other European cities. His theory was that human beings are pretty much like plants—aside from nourishment, what they mostly need is sunlight and air. In the United States, it is now acknowledged that high-rise housing projects built according to the Corbusier philosophy—the Robert Taylor Homes in Chicago and Pruitt-Igoe in St. Louis, to name two of the most notorious—were traps of violence and poverty for the mostly black people who got stuck there. As long as Europe had a large industrial proletariat—regulated by inherited political habits and disciplined by employment—the consequences of such architecture were not as catastrophic there as they were in the United States. But people hated these places, and as the European economy boomed in the postwar years, they made this hatred plain by moving out. At that point, architecture began to interact with migration in unforeseen ways.

The most dramatic transformations came in Sweden, possibly because it was there that the subsidized housing stock increased most dramatically. Facing a shortage of housing units in the early 1960s, the government undertook an ambitious plan to build a million of them—this in a country of only 7 million people. It came to be known as the Million Program. The apartments that resulted compare well with other European subsidized housing, but Swedish culture is not built around apartments, and native Swedes were unwilling to stay in them once they could afford their own houses. Over the decades, the perfectly serviceable apartments of the Million Program emptied out. When immigrants began arriving en masse—and particularly when Kurds, Bosnians, and Somalis fleeing simultaneous wars in the early 1990s overwhelmed the country's refugee system—there was an obvious place to stick them.

Consider Bergsjön, a planned community outside of Gothenburg, which, with its Volvo plant and some of the world's biggest shipyards, used to be an industrial powerhouse. Bergsjön was built between 1967 and 1972 to reward the city's workers. Only a tram ride away from Gothenburg's factories, it resembles the places Swedes of all classes retreat to in midsummer—quiet, pristine, speckled with lakes, and smelling of evergreen trees. The central "campus" of the housing project has no cars. Its 14,500 people live in apartments set on grassy hills within a lasso-shaped ring road.

But in the 1980s and the 1990s, Sweden's shipyards collapsed. The Swedish industrial workers Bergsjön was planned for no longer live there. By 2006 it was inhabited by immigrants of a hundred nationalities, many of them refugees. Seventy percent of the residents were either born abroad or had parents who were. The same goes for 93 percent of the schoolchildren. You can see Somali women walking the paths in hijabs and long wraps, and graffiti reading "Bosna i Hercegovina 4-Ever."

Lacking indoor space and places where lots of noise can be made, and hard to keep under surveillance by responsible adults, housing projects have always been bad environments for raising children. Awkward even for the working-class people for whom they were designed, they are even less well suited to immigrants, with their vast families and their astronomical unemployment rates. Neighborhoods built to keep Swedish families of the 1960s close to nature served four decades later to keep the foreign-born unemployed far from the job market. Assar Lindbeck, the dean of Sweden's welfare-state economists, pointed out that to send newcomers to areas where there were empty apartments meant sending them to places that were "by definition in an area of high unemployment."

As of 2006, 40 percent of the families in Bergsjön were on welfare outright, and many of the rest collect various equivalents of welfare that differ only in name. Far below half the population is employed. The mayor of Gothenburg declared earlier this decade, "The prospects of turning Bergsjön into a normal Swedish neighborhood are almost nil." And there are neighborhoods like it all over Sweden— the Stockholm suburbs of Rinkeby and Tensta, hundreds of miles to the northeast, are little different. Immigrants and their children make up 85 percent of residents in both places, with dependence at levels comparable to those in Bergsjön. In Tensta, for instance, a fifth of the women in their late forties collect disability benefits. So fully have immigrants become associated with the Million Program that the *Gringo*, the Stockholm immigrant newspaper mentioned in the last chapter, coined the term *miljonsvenskar*, or "Million Swedes," to describe them.

This substitution of immigrant populations for working-class ones was replicated in almost every European country. One could say of public housing and immigrants what the American movie *Field of Dreams* said of ballparks and ballplayers: "Build it and they will come." France, too, began to warehouse immigrants in the places against which its own citizens had voted with their feet. More than half of the country's North Africans live in HLMs today, versus only a sixth (17.6 percent) of French natives. The movement of old residents away from HLMs has accelerated over the years. The whites who could not afford to leave have been the mainstay of right-wing parties, including Jean-Marie Le Pen's National Front. In industrial Turin, too, state-financed apartments built in the 1960s to accommodate short-term factory immigrants from Sicily, were by the turn of the century heavily North African. The notorious high-rises of De Bijlmer in southeastern Amsterdam were completed only in 1975, but were soon heavily immigrant. Large parts of the Bijlmer projects have already been demolished and much of the rest is under reconstruction.

Lawless zones

On top of that, Europe's housing projects, like those in the United States, were perfectly fitted to the needs of criminals and hoodlums. Anyone who could control the elevator bank (and, when that became too terrifying to use, the graffiti-covered stairwells) could hold a dozen families (or several dozen, if the building were high enough) for ransom. Anyone who could control the long access roads could block traffic in and out of the projects and harass (and even repel) the police. On several occasions in the summer of 2004, transit authorities stopped bus traffic to Tensta because of attacks on passengers. Firemen and emergency medical technicians were attacked in the suburbs of Malmö. In France, areas where the police would not go—more from reluctance to provoke unrest than from fear or indifference— were plentiful at the turn of the century. They came to be known as *zones de non-droit*, or "lawless zones." Local youths set up informal neighborhood-watch-groups-in-reverse, not to warn police of active criminals but to warn criminals of approaching police.

Pierre Cardo, the popular longtime mayor of Chanteloup-les-Vignes, twenty miles west of Paris, referred to much of the infrastructure of his city as *architecture criminogène*, or crime-generating architecture. Chanteloup was one of the most spectacular failures in the history of French state planning. Since it sits in the middle of rich gypsum deposits and was near several automobile plants, plans were drawn up in 1966 to expand a pretty rural village of 2,000 into a bedroom community of 20,000 overnight. When it was half built, the investigative weekly *Le Canard enchaîné* revealed that Chanteloup's expansion rested on one of the largest kickback schemes (it came to be known as the Aranda affair) in French postwar history. Construction was halted by court order. The developers, annoyed, covered up the utility and water grids that were already built and destroyed the records of where they could be found. In the early 1970s, president Valéry Giscard d'Estaing opened the unwanted apartments to immigrants. The three-, four-, and five-story HLMs that made up two-thirds of the housing in Chanteloup were named after poets and educators, but everyone knew them by more gladiatorial sobriquets the local kids had given them, like "the Bestiary" and "the Hippodrome."

By 1995, two-thirds of Chanteloup's residents were of foreign origin. That year, director Matthieu Kassovitz released *La Haine* ("Hatred"), a drama of suburban violence and police brutality filmed in Chanteloup. It was considered such a grittily realistic exposé of the lives of trapped French teenagers that then prime minister Alain Juppé ordered his entire cabinet to see it. Today, certain of its details appear quaint to the point of sentimentality. Its depiction of a Jewish and a North African teenager chumming it up together as members of the same street gang is particularly implausible in today's suburban France. In the days before *La Haine*, youths would wade across the locks that separate Chanteloup from the nearby town of Andrésy to atack rival gangs with iron bars and baseball bats. (A bemusing aspect of rough neighborhoods in Europe is the prevalence of baseball bats in countries where baseball is not played.)

A decade later, the violence of Chanteloup had become more ambitious and audacious still, and had broken out of the confines of the housing development. Marauding gangs from Chanteloup often wreaked havoc at La Défense, on the edge of Paris, and Cergy Pontoise, several train stops away. In 2006, when a twenty-four-year-old from the town was shot dead after taking a hostage during the armed robbery of a Paris outlet of the Gap, sixty hooded and armed youths launched a coordinated assault on Chanteloup's police station. Next to that, *La Haine* looked naive. It bore the same relationship to the violence of twenty-first-century France that *West Side Story* had to American riots in the late 1960s.

Segregation or self-segregation?

In 2005, Trevor Phillips, the chairman of the Commission for Racial Equality, warned that Britain was "sleepwalking its way toward segregation." Isolation was particularly severe among ethnic Pakistanis and Bangladeshis. Phillips noted that the number of Britons of Pakistani descent living in outright "ghettos"—places where at least two-thirds of the residents belonged to a specific ethnic group—had tripled in the course of the 1990s. In certain British cities, such as Bradford and Leicester, almost 15 percent of those surveyed were in ghettos, a figure roughly comparable to that of blacks in Miami and Chicago, neither of which is considered a model city for race relations. "Some minorities are moving into middle-class, less ethnically concentrated areas," Phillips said, "but what is left behind is hardening in its separateness."

Some scoffed at Phillips's pessimism. London mayor Ken Livingstone claimed that British society was becoming *less* segregated, since the number of "mixed neighbourhoods" had risen from 864 to 1,070 in the course of the 1990s. He also claimed that "inter-ethnic couples and children of mixed ethnic parentage have risen 20 percent in 10 years." But the research Livingstone cited, sponsored by a multiculturalist lobby, did not so much disprove segregation as define it away. Its argument was that, since "thousands of areas that are 95% White are not called segregated," calling a neighborhood segregated just because very few whites lived there was a "colour-laden value on which many other discriminatory claims are made." This is wrong. A neighborhood with no native English people can be *diverse*, but it cannot be *integrated*—assuming that it is, in fact, England into which the study's authors wish the immigrants to integrate.

Nothing did more to radicalize native opinion about immigration than this manner of addressing it—using statistics generated more by ideology than by social science to bully people into disbelieving what they were seeing with their own eyes. If you define your terms so that any neighborhood with a large number of minorities in it can be called "mixed," then any increase in minority population (or immigration) will result in an increase in mixed neighborhoods, which can be presented as a boon for social harmony, no matter whether the newcomers integrate or not. So it was in Britain. Those vaunted mixed marriages were mostly *among* immigrants, not between young people descended from immigrants and young people descended from natives, the study's authors acknowledged. "White Christians," as English people of English descent were described, tended not to intermarry.

British immigrants often complained that they never met native Europeans. A British government report, issued after days of violent clashes between whites and Asians in several northern cities in 2001, quoted one Briton of Pakistani descent as saying, "When I leave this meeting with you I will go home and not see another white face until I come back here next week." But the increasingly voluble complaints of many immigrants that they were being systematically excluded from European life were not always heard, and were even dismissed as unreasonable. Europeans tended to meet immigrants as retail or restaurant or other service employees—all jobs in which complaisance can be purchased even where it is not sincerely felt. *How can you say you're excluded*, Europeans wondered, *when I'm always saying how delicious your baklava are?*

The Europeans most alarmed at the isolation of immigrants were those who, like Phillips, had worked hardest for racial harmony. Whose fault was this isolation? Was it *imposed* or *chosen*? Was it segregation or self-segregation? Were the natives racist and cold? Or were the newcomers idle and violent?

There was certainly measurable discrimination in the European job and housing markets, although it was mild alongside what one might have found in the United States four decades ago. Studies in Sweden found that Swedish-raised children adopted from other lands, who often look different, did worse when looking for jobs than similarly situated ethnic Swedes, and that apartments "open" for a Swede were somehow "taken" when non-Europeans showed up. Laws mandating that the résumés of job candidates be made color-blind were proposed in several European countries, including in France in the weeks after Nicolas Sarkozy's election in 2007. Studies similar to the Swedish ones had been carried out in France—this time involving résumés with Muslim-sounding surnames—and they seemed to show a particular reluctance to hire, or rent to, Muslims. And while immigrants' poor career prospects might be evidence of prejudice, success need not be evidence of its absence. The children of Muslim immigrants often repeat the experience of Jewish Americans in the industrial age, who made an end run around prejudice by focusing on professional credentialing. From Arab cab drivers and Kurdish kebab vendors, one hears a lot of *My son the doctor* and *My daughter the attorney*. Arabs are now heavily represented in French medical and law schools, and some of the most prominent doctors in the country are children of immigrants.

Which side was held to blame for segregation may have mattered morally, but it did not matter that much practically. A vicious circle was at work. Noting the way third-generation minorities in Germany were retreating into their own "parallel worlds," the journalist Giovanni Di Lorenzo wrote: "A lack of job qualifications is readily excused by alleged discrimination on the part of Germans—and the result is a growing aggressiveness from, say, young Turks, which then leads to rejection in fact." Once minority communities harden into ethnic islands, the process is hard to reverse, even if the majority population has the will and the money to do so (which it seldom does). There is an excellent distinction made in French public policy discussions between *mixité* (people of different hues and religions living alongside each other) and genuine *sociabilité* (deeper contacts, even intimacy, between people of different cultures). The former is easy enough to produce, but how to get the latter is a mystery. When a neighborhood in eastern Helsinki, one of the European capitals least touched by immigration, filled up with so many Somalis that it got the nickname "Mogadishu Avenue," city government proposed high-income housing for the area. But even the presence of rich people did little to break the isolation and unemployment of the Somalis. It replaced segregation *between* neighborhoods with segregation *within* neighborhoods. Americans learned the idleness of this exercise in the later stages of desegregation—the stage marked by such fruitlessly divisive programs as forced busing of high-school students.

Americans seeking to understand the impasse in Europe's integration of its ethnic minorities, particularly its Muslim ones, should look at their own history of race relations as well as their own history of immigration. American immigration has involved—and still does—a fairly predictable process of economic advancement and social assimilation, in which old-country customs gradually disappear. Differences between natives and the children of immigrants are often superficial and situational, even when they appear to be profound and cultural. There is occasional friction because there is much contact. The American race problem, on the other hand, grew out of lack of contact between blacks and whites. The position of Latino immigrants in the United States has nothing in common with it. The position of Muslims in Europe has more in common with the American race problem, as we will discuss later.

The segregation of Europe's neighborhoods is not merely a consequence of migration patterns, of poverty meeting plenty, of the Third World meeting the First. The difficulties presented to Europe by its first generation of mass migrants were actually negligible compared to those presented to the United States by the violent and crime-prone Irish who arrived in the nineteenth century. The difficulties presented by Europe to its migrants, in the form of prejudice, were also small, relative to those the nineteenth-century newcomers to America faced. Europe's problems came later. The European-born children of the guest workers and refugees wound up viewed with considerably more suspicion than their parents, who had arrived as illiterate villagers from eastern Anatolia, say, or the Atlas Mountains. Why was this so?

In the summer of 2006, just months after the nationwide riots in France, a European minister gave a despairing off-the-record diagnosis to a congress of migration experts meeting in Italy. He had spoken of the prospects for integration with one of his counterparts from a country with a somewhat longer history of mass immigration. "He was very pessimistic," the minister said of his colleague. "His experience with difficult neighborhoods is that the second generation is worse than the first generation and the third is worse than the second." If Italy did not yet face these second-generation problems, the minister worried, it was because its second generation was as yet only in grade school. If Italy was like other European countries, it would evolve in the opposite direction from the American model. As the generations passed, the children of immigrants would found more, not fewer, foreign establishments; develop more, not fewer, separatist sentiments; and demand more, not fewer, concessions from the country at large. That is where Islam came in.

Spaces of sharia

The problem of parallel societies was more deep-seated in Muslim than in other communities that arose from immigration. In 2004, France's Renseignements Généraux, the country's domestic intelligence agency, surveyed several hundred neighborhoods with large Muslim populations and found half of them ghettoized on religious lines. Whether Islam was the *cause* of this separation or just an extremely serious complicating factor, Europeans—including the Muslims among them—had begun to think of Islam as the religion of the continent's ghettos.

Even before September 11, 2001, Islam's pretensions to global domination made European television news on many nights. So many European natives looked at segregation not as a fate endured by immigrants but as a project hatched by them. As soon as it became obvious that certain immigrants proposed to establish foreign cultures on European lands, immigration—and Muslim immigration a fortiori—appeared in a different light. It appeared in the light of a project to claim territory. The establishment of Muslim institutions was worrisome, no matter how innocent their ends or how peaceful their ethos. In 2005, the English journalist Rod Liddle saw the first outlines of a Muslim state in Europe. He wrote that there was already "a string of towns and cities, from Rennes in the south, through Lille, Brussels, Antwerp, Zeebrugge, Rotterdam, Bremen to Aarhus in Denmark in the far north, where the Muslim population approaches or exceeds 20 per cent (and in some cases constitutes a majority)."

It was not just that young Muslims were assimilating too slowly into European culture as the generations passed. It was that they were *dis*-assimilating. In 2002, an imam in Roubaix, France, refused to meet Martine Aubry, the mayor of Lille and the former minister of labor, in his neighborhood, saying that it was Muslim territory and that it would be *haram* (unclean) to welcome her there. In Aubervilliers, a suburb just north of the Paris *périphérique* that has become so heavily North African and so devoutly Muslim that many children take Fridays off from school to prepare for prayers, the city council voted to offer swimming hours at public pools segregated by sex, for fear of offending Muslim women's modesty. In the Norman city of Dreux, and also in Denmark, there were protests over the serving of non-halal meat in school cafeterias. It was alarming how quickly the culture of a place such as Rosengård, a Swedish housing estate just outside of Malmö, could diverge from that of the mainstream. Ninety percent of the women went veiled (including many who had not worn the veil before arriving in the country), as did their Swedish-born daughters. Rosengård was not dangerous criminally, in the sense of high drug and crime rates—at least not at first. But immigration there has always been unsettling politically, in the sense that it has turned Rosengård into a wholly un-Swedish place. Clashes with authorities eventually arose. In December 2008, there were several nights of serious anti-police riots, with Molotov cocktails and homemade bombs.

Across Europe, people saw the growth not just of parallel societies but of "ethnic colonies," in the words of the Turkish-German ethnographer Rauf Ceylan. The children of immigrants did not always find European culture—with its atomization, its consumerism, its sexual wantonness—self-evidently superior to their parents' cultures. And thanks to television and airplanes, ancestral cultures are now, for the first time in the history of transcontinental migration, generally available for all immigrants and their descendants to fall back on. Half a century into the Turkish immigration to Germany, Ceylan found, Turkish was still the language of the cafés, mosques, and hairdressers of Neufeld, near Duisburg—even for German-born young people. The men's establishments were sharply divided by political leanings—and the politics that divided them was the politics of Turkey, not Germany.

That is why native Europeans began to get upset over developments that would seem in an American context—and used to seem in a European context—like normal immigrant behavior. A Pakistani teahouse in an area that is hostile to outsiders (say, a segregated street in Oldham) has a different cultural meaning than a Pakistani teahouse in a multicultural setting (say, Liverpool Street Station). Once a community is closed off to outsiders, only the residents of that community "get" something out of it. Their neighborhood now looks like a seizure of territory rather than a multicultural enrichment. And if the community is increasingly religious (as most immigrant communities are), then it looks like a space not just of separatism but of sharia, a subject we shall take up in chapter 8. When a halal Franprix that sold no alcohol opened in the relatively well-off banlieue of Évry, south of Paris, it was forced to close due to public pressure.

Mosque building was particularly alarming to Europeans. There was not much ambiguity about what *that* meant over the long term. This was not a provisional foothold for the next generation, which would inevitably be Europeanized. No, it was a declaration that people intended—at least in one realm of life, and perhaps the most important—to live henceforth as they had in the old country from time immemorial.

The establishment of religious institutions is a familiar and predictable stage of immigrant life, but the native residents of west Amsterdam, Munich, and Cologne—all of which saw pitched battles over mosque construction—did not see things that way. The mosque complex in Duisburg/Marxloh, the largest in Germany, met resistance, too, even though it was the very model of a modern religious establishment, with its upper-middle-class membership and its millions of euros in funding from the European Union and local government. The mosque's request for a thirty-four-meter-high minaret was approved, but a muezzin (or call to prayer) once a week was rejected out of hand. The ZDF television network aired sensational claims that Germans now had to speak Turkish to go about their daily business in Marxloh. The big, modern mosque, meant to move Duisburg's Turkish Muslim community into the modern age, provoked more public alarm than Duisburg's forty-four other mosques ever had, even though those had been located in garages and basements and back alleys, and some of them had been run by Muslim hard-liners. And the reason was obvious: The great mosque meant that Islam had arrived in Germany to stay.

Violence, crime, and rioting

The relative violence of Muslim neighborhoods is a main obstacle to social mixing and integration. Immigrants and their children commit much of the crime in all European countries, and most of the crime in some of them. Citizens of other countries make up 26 percent of Swedish prison inmates. Among those serving sentences longer than five years—which in Sweden are given out for only serious crimes like major drug dealing, murder, and rape—about half are foreign citizens, and these figures exclude the foreign born who have become Swedes. Among immigrants, Muslims are especially prone to get in trouble. According to the sociologist Farhad Khosrokhavar, Islam is now "probably the first prison religion of France." Although precise numbers are hard to come by, Muslims make up 50 percent of the population in many French jails, and up to 80 percent in certain prisons near the banlieues. A prison official estimates that forty-five percent of inmates in the jails in Turin are foreigners (Moroccans, Tunisians, Algerians, and Albanians occupy the top four slots) and that rate of foreign inmates is *below* Italy's national rate (47 percent). A huge influx of Romanians over the past decade has been the focus of political controversy, but in private conversation North Africans are more often singled out. When a crime is committed in Italy, a journalist said in 2006, "you often hear '*Sarà stato un marocchino.*'" ("It was probably a Moroccan.")

Violence has kept native Europeans out of certain immigrant neighborhoods as effectively as an electric fence. Such places are ethnic colonies in a more literal sense of Ceylan's term. While still European territory de jure, they are places where Europeans sense they have lost their right of way. "Silently, squeamishly, the natives are disengaging," wrote the former Tory minister George Walden in 2006, "and the lines of ethnic mini-states are forming around us."

The riots that began in the banlieues of Paris in October 2005 were the worst and most widespread civilian violence Western Europe had seen in decades. On October 27, two teenage boys in Clichy-sous-Bois, Zyed Benna and Bouna Traoré, believing (erroneously) that they were being pursued by the police, broke into a fenced-off area that held a power transformer and were electrocuted. Dozens of cars were burned in protest that night. In the days that followed, sympathy protests broke out in immigrant and ethnic neighborhoods all over the country, and even in other European countries. It was a two-week rampage of burned cars, smashed buildings, and (for benefit of the television cameras) menacing gestures copied off of hip-hop videos. It touched every major and medium-sized city in France. Eight thousand cars were burned and 2,900 people arrested. It was an explosion that many—in fact, most—observers of the banlieues had predicted.

Historically, France had been less touched by race rioting than, say, Britain, where there was a decades-long history of ethnically based mob violence, starting with white attacks on West Indian settlers in Notting Hill in the late 1950s. Since then, Britain had seen at least a dozen race riots launched by ethnic minorities. In the 1980s, there were serious episodes of unrest in Bradford, Bristol, Brixton, and Broadwater Farm.

Although France had had fewer explosions, its banlieues had always been cauldrons of discontent, too. There had been riots unleashed by *beurs*, as young French Arabs were called, in the suburbs of Lyon in 1981 and 1990. In Strasbourg, rampaging vandals burned dozens of cars every New Year's eve, in what had become a tradition of sorts. By coincidence, the day before the deaths of Benna and Traoré that unleashed the riots, interior minister Nicolas Sarkozy announced that nine thousand police cars—an average of twenty to thirty per day—had been burned or otherwise destroyed already that year. There were riots of a more isolated kind somewhere in France on two hundred different nights in 2005.

Who were these rioters? Were they admirers of France's majority culture, frustrated at not being able to join it on equal terms? Or did they simply aspire to burn to the ground a society they despised, whether for its exclusivity, its hypocrisy, or its weakness? Unlike the American race riots of the 1960s, and unlike France's student riots of 1968, for that matter, this steady but occasionally surging violence produced no leaders, no social movement, no body of thinking that outside observers could either accept or deplore, and no demands that could be productively answered. Years after the events, there was still no consensus in French public opinion over what the riots were even "about."

At the level of political and media discussion, people seized on the first explanation at hand: official racism, or some form of exclusion, to which the uprisings in poor neighborhoods were merely a response. But how this putative racism worked was not obvious. There were two basic explanations. The first was that French authorities were neglecting the banlieues—an improbable accusation for a country that was plowing an extraordinary 1.9 percent of its GNP into low-income housing. The second explanation was police brutality. That was even less likely. Hundreds of video cameras were present in the banlieues throughout the 2005 riots, and revealed very few instances of excessive zeal, let alone brutality. Not a single rioter was killed during tens of thousands of man-hours policing widespread violence and destruction.

There was something formulaic about the accusation of police brutality. The liberal magistrate Jean de Maillard warned, after another round of rioting in December 2007, that certain banlieues had become *zones de non-droit* not because the police were out-gunned, but because the residents would resist any policing, no matter how mild. Those who held out hope that softer policing might help calm the ghettos were deluding themselves, de Maillard wrote:

You can't graft local police on to a society that is so sick and broken, and whose members are in open rebellion against society. The police are a means, not an end. . . . Police are no longer considered legitimate in these banlieues . . . and can no longer exercise the slightest control without provoking a mini-riot and, obviously, getting called racists.

While it was improbable that France's policing had become tougher, it was unquestionable that the country's streets had become meaner. By 2002, European Union statistics showed that France had 4,244 crimes per 100,000 residents annually, making it a higher-crime society than even the long-belittled United States. Again, much, if not most, of that crime was committed by immigrant minorities and their children. It was probably not a coincidence that 2002 was also the year that the fascistic National Front of Jean-Marie Le Pen succeeded in reaching the final round of the presidential elections, ousting the Socialists as France's second party at the ballot box.

That triumph of fearmongering reactionaries was attributed less often to crime than to *l'insécurité*, a new official euphemism. In France and elsewhere, politicians spoke of "insecurity" more than they did of crime. "Insecurity" meant the *perception* of crime. The implication was that people perceived more crime than there actually was. The crime to which statistics attested loud and clear was held to be a figment of the pampered upper-middle-class imagination. If "insecurity," not crime, was the problem, the blame for it lay not with the people committing it but the people reporting it — the general public. In the years before and after the riots, French bookshops were full of titles that brought up worries about crime only to pooh-pooh them, such as *Violence and Insecurity: Fantasy and Reality in the French Debate*, or *Punishing the Poor: Governing by Social Insecurity*.

A similar reflex was at work in the outrage over the rhetoric of interior minister Nicolas Sarkozy. While he was visiting Aulnay-sous-Bois at the height of the riots, on October 31, 2005, a mother pled with him from a window to do something about the "riff-raff" (*racaille*) who were burning down the neighborhood and he promised her he would, using the word *racaille* in turn. Many banlieue youth, interviewed on television, cited Sarkozy's rhetoric as one of their primary grievances, until one could almost forget that the country's ghettoes had been burning for four days by the time he spoke. English-language newspapers around the world further confused matters by translating the word as "scum," although neither Larousse nor Robert gives that translation for *racaille*, an old French word that is cognate with our own word "rascal." The "scum" translation made Sarkozy's pronouncement sound dehumanizing, even Nazi.

There was a desire, verging on desperation, to explain the riots as due to some misconduct of the majority society. Because if the riots could not be explained by the misconduct of the majority society, then they could be explained only as part of the agenda of the rioters. And to raise the agenda of the rioters was to raise, once again, the subject of Islam.

The banlieue riots and Islam

Given the North African origin of much of France's immigrant population, the West's military engagement in Iraq and Afghanistan, and
worries over jihadist terrorism in all Western countries, it was natural
to ask whether the rioters were radicalizing along Islamic lines. In
1995, France had suffered a banlieue-based wave of Islamist killings:
Khaled Kelkal, a young sympathizer of Algeria's Armed Islamic
Group from the Lyon suburb of Vaulx-en-Velin, had bombed a train
in Paris and a Jewish school in Lyon. At the time of the 2005 riots,
other Lyonnais were detained under suspicion of al-Qaeda-linked
terrorism in Guantánamo. Islam seemed important to the rioters. On
October 31, just as the violence seemed to be dying down, it was
given a second wind by the firing of a teargas grenade near a mosque
in Clichy, which was decried as a desecration. Police deferred to
Muslim leaders to help keep order, even withdrawing from neighborhoods at the request of local imams. In Clichy there were shouts of
"Allah akbar!"

Most observers sought an explanation for the riots that did not
involve Islam: That the riots were committed by Muslims, they
argued, did not make them Muslim riots. Maybe the rioters were not
angry Muslims but angry poor people who happened to be Muslim.
The International Crisis Group (ICG), while admitting that the riots
had a strong Islamic element, nonetheless claimed that the more
Islamic the riots looked, the less Islamic they actually were. "Paradoxically," the ICG opined, "it is the exhaustion of political Islam
more than its radicalization that explains this predominantly Muslim
violence, and it is the depoliticization of young Muslims much more
than their alleged re-organization along radical lines, that ought to
make us uneasy."

This was unconvincing. The ICG conclusions rested on biased
definitions. What the ICG meant by "political Islam" was *official*
political Islam, as defined by bureaucrats in France: old-line local
imams of long standing, the Muslim Brotherhood–linked Union of
Islamic Organizations of France (UOIF), government-sponsored anti-
racist groups, and various organizations that had participated in the

French Council on the Muslim Faith (CFCM) started by Nicolas Sarkozy in his early years as interior minister. These, it is true, managed neither to win the allegiance of ghetto youths nor to control them in the course of the riots, because the youths had drifted towards other identities.

But the identities to which the ghetto youths *had* drifted—anomic, modern, individualistic identities that they had learned on TV—were exactly the identities that most French people thought of when they heard the expression "political Islam." The youths sympathized with jihad, the report admitted. They were furious partisans of the Arab cause in Iraq, Afghanistan, and Palestine. They embraced an auto-didactic version of fundamentalism that the report's authors called "shaykhist salafism." The three urgent recommendations the ICG made to French authorities—stop police repression, increase Muslim political participation, and address the rioters' discontent about Palestine and Iraq—did not leave the impression that political Islam played no role in the uprising.

Perhaps the ICG was looking for a *religious* rationale for the riots, as opposed to a sociological one. But theology is not the whole of religion, and theological disputation was not something these sneaker-obsessed gangstas of the banlieues were particularly interested in. A religion can cast a shadow of group allegiance that has nothing superficially to do with religious doctrine. Maybe the rioters were not attacking enemies of the Muslim religion. But they were attacking enemies (as they saw it) of the Muslim people. Even if they did not believe in Islam, they believed in Team Islam.

This effect should not surprise Westerners. It is not unique to Islam. As the philosopher Alain Finkielkraut explained in the weeks after the riot, "Religion plays a part—not as religion, but as an anchor of identity. Religion as it appears on the Internet, on the Arab television stations, serves as an anchor of identity for some of these youths." Finkielkraut was looking at the same evidence as the International Crisis Group. The difference was that he chose to see the rioters as historical actors rather than as victims of a callous society. He argued that the rioters were burning schools and institutions of the state not because they had been thwarted by an uncaring society but because they wanted to attack schools and institutions of the state. "Instead of hearing what they're saying—*Fuck your mother! Fuck the state! Fuck the police!*—we hear them out," Finkielkraut said. "That is, we translate their appeals to hatred into cries for help, and their vandalism of schools into demands for education."

The distinction between sedition and protest is often blurry. In early 2007, Angelo Hoekelet, a thirty-two-year-old Congo-born immigrant with a long criminal record and no fixed address, attacked two agents who had stopped him in the Gare du Nord in Paris for traveling without a ticket. When Hoekelet hollered for help, dozens—and eventually hundreds—of youths gathered, chanting, howling, and riled up by wild rumors passed over their mobile phones. A small uprising ensued, and lasted until the wee hours of the next day—with fires, looting, and various windows and advertisements smashed by youths wielding metal bars. The rioters understood their attack as aimed at France and its symbols: "From the moment policemen or agents stop someone," said one leader of a police trade union after the Gare du Nord riots, "the crowd doesn't try to understand what is going on—it turns on the uniform." As Hoekelet was arrested, some in the crowd began shouting, as has become normal in such circumstances, "*Nique la France!*" ("Fuck France!")

Ought these people, assuming they are noncitizens, be put on the next plane out of the country? That depends on what "Fuck France!" means. It may be a constitutionally protected gripe, spoken with less than optimal decorum. It may also be a rallying cry against France itself. It can mean disappointment or enmity.

Tribalism, ideology, and escalation

Finkielkraut's assessment of the riots' causes was accurate. It was also, as things turned out, brave, because his opinions proved intolerable to certain guardians of French public opinion. He discussed the riots as a product of ghetto kids' aspirations rather than their grievances—as an ideology generated in the ghetto itself, rather than as a reaction to oppression. To do so was to question the premise that ethnic violence is always the result of social unfairness or native racism. Similar uprisings had taken place where white people were altogether absent, and where European racism was therefore an implausible culprit. Just days before the French banlieue riots, there had been two nights of murderous violence in the Lozells neighborhood of Birmingham, where tensions had long simmered between South Asian Muslims and Caribbean blacks. Pakistani shop owners had broken an unwritten neighborhood rule by selling products that appealed to West Indian customers, harming business for West Indian proprietors.

A rumor began to spread on black radio stations and websites—without a scrap of evidence ever presented to back it up—that a fourteen-year-old West Indian girl had been caught shoplifting in a Pakistani-owned cosmetics shop. As punishment, the tale continued, she had been gang-raped by nineteen Pakistani men. This, too, was untrue, although that did not stop the *Voice*, the leading national black newspaper in Britain, from running a page-one headline that read, "Gang of 19 rape teen." Mobs of armed men began assembling in the streets and a young West Indian was stabbed to death by Pakistanis. It is exceedingly unlikely that many of them were motivated by racism, unless we water that term down to the point of meaninglessness. If one could have polled Birmingham's blacks and Asians on whether they wanted a Britain where skin color determined what people could do and be, both would almost certainly have voted no in a landslide. What there was was a clash of interests among mistrustful tribes.

Rioting tends to escalate. Millions of middle-class Frenchmen who had been laissez-faire about inner-city policies until 2005 came to support emergency powers for the governments thereafter. Hundreds of kids who, on the eve of the French ghetto uprisings, did not know how to make Molotov cocktails emerged as tested paramilitary leaders. In the last days of 2007 in Villiers-le-Bel, one of the communities that had remained relatively calm two years earlier, a fifteen-year-old Moroccan named Moushin Souhelli and his sixteen-year-old Senegalese friend Larami Samoura, traveling seventy kilometers an hour on a mini-motorbike, hit a police car and were killed. This time, the violence reached maximum seriousness in less than forty-eight hours. In one night alone, 138 cars were burned and eighty-two policemen were wounded, many by shotgun blasts. It took a deployment of a thousand heavily armed police the following day to calm the neighborhood down. "There are entire populations here who no longer feel they are part of this country," warned Malek Boutih, the French Socialist secretary for social affairs and former president of the government-linked public-service group SOS Racisme. He added that violence was "rising, and will continue to rise."

What was new and unsettling about the riots in Villiers-le-Bel was that its residents were ready for a confrontation with authorities *before* the two kids crashed their dirt bike. Gasoline had been stockpiled, rioters used walkie-talkies to communicate information about the movements of police to one another, and one woman told *Le Monde* that, with the police, "It's war." While there is no evidence that the two boys had been looking for trouble, it is clear they considered themselves in a state of cold war with the authorities. It turned out that one of them, Larami, the Senegalese, had kept a blog, on which he had posted, shortly before his death: "I'd happily die, just not killed by a cop." The two teenagers, both of them French citizens, were sent to Morocco and Senegal, respectively, for burial.

A phrase that was coined to describe the allegiances of the rioters was *nationalisme de quartier*: "neighborhood nationalism." The expression was also invoked to explain the traditions of *omertà* that were developing in Europe's Muslim neighborhoods. The implication was that the solidarity that led boys to wreak destruction in the streets was just a particularly passionate kind of old-fashioned neighborliness, consisting mostly of a sentimental attachment to the kids with whom one had shared one's childhood. But this made absolutely no sense. It did not explain why an episode in Clichy should provoke uprisings in Brittany and even Brussels. If there was such a thing as *nationalisme de quartier*, it was 99 percent *nationalisme* and 1 percent *quartier*. Larger identities were involved—political identities or, to put it more sharply, tribal identities. But what identities? Who, exactly, did European Muslims think they were?

6

An Adversary Culture

Jus soli *and* jus sanguinis, *assimilation and integration—
The illusion of diversity—Islam as a hyper-identity—Dual
loyalty —Humiliation and Islamophobia —Muslims and
U.S. blacks*

People's loyalties do not necessarily shift along with their citizenships—or even with their outward behavior. "The immigration population was not rooted in this country," Enoch Powell insisted in 1968.
"It still belonged to the communities back home, both west and
east ... For the vast majority [of immigrants] it has literally been
transportation within a community settling across the globe into—it
happens to have been Britain. It might have been anywhere else." For
Powell, the mass movement of foreigners into Europe was more like
a colonization than an immigration. His view was not admissible in
polite company by the 1990s. At that point, the former Tory party
chairman Norman Tebbit suggested a milder, more easygoing way of
judging the allegiances of newcomers: how they behaved, or how
they felt in their hearts, when their ancestral country's team played
England in cricket. "Which side do they cheer for?" Tebbit asked.
"It's an interesting test. Are you still harking back to where you came
from, or where you are? And I think we've got real problems in that
regard."

Tebbit's mischievous remark drew accusations of unreasonable-
ness that made his point. The problem with the "Tebbit test" was
that so many immigrants—and even children of immigrants—failed
it. In the Dutch town of Osdorp, heavily settled by Moroccans, a

crowd of locals subjected a bartender to "howls of abuse" when he tried to set the television to the Dutch-Czech World Cup qualifying match rather than the Moroccan-Tunisian one. On October 6, 2001, a month after the attacks on the World Trade Center, the French and Algerian national soccer teams met in a "friendship match" at the Stade de France, north of Paris. Thousands of French Arab youths whistled the French team and the "Marseillaise," the French national anthem. Hundreds stormed the field, forcing the stoppage of the game. "Hooting the Marseillaise isn't a crime, or even a misdemeanor," one journalist at the daily *Libération* wrote preemptively. "To hold it against the French and French-Algerian immigrant youths would be to question their full status as citizens." Under the prevailing political understanding, the Tebbit test asked too much of immigrants.

Jus soli *and* jus sanguinis, *assimilation and integration*

For much of the period after the Second World War, it had been relatively easy to become a European citizen. Britain, to the fury of Powell and other opponents of immigration, dissolved an entire empire of more than half a billion people without enunciating clear citizenship criteria. The Nationality Act of 1948 *sought* to do this, by creating a category of noncitizen subjects, but a loophole allowed entry to the British mainland for all those "who hold a UK passport or a passport issued by the Government of the United Kingdom." Since colonial passports had been issued by the UK, too, the law opened the gates to Britain for those who understood how to manipulate it.

There were two basic regimes of citizenship in Europe. Under jus soli ("right of soil") which was favored in France, not to mention the United States, all those born on national territory were automatically citizens, no matter where their parents came from. Under jus sanguinis ("right of blood"), traditional to Germany, they were not. You got citizenship if—and in most cases only if—your parents were Germans. So those born to Algerians in France could call themselves French, but the German-born children of Turks were not German by law.

Jus sanguinis was not as illiberal as it looked; it had had its origins in the geographical scattering and semi-feudal political organization of the German lands until the nineteenth century, not in any modern racial doctrines. In yesterday's Germany, jus sanguinis had been *more* liberal—it meant that you were first and foremost the child of your parents, not the property of the prince on whose domains you happened to have been born. But in postwar Europe, jus sanguinis was a butt of liberal scorn. Notoriously, in 1998, Germany sought to deport Muhlis Ari, a serially violent fourteen-year-old noncitizen (he was called "Mehmet" in the interest of protecting his anonymity) back to Turkey. When Ari's lawyers and relatives were able to show he knew little of Turkey or Turkish, it was inevitable he would be allowed to stay. Jus sanguinis was on its way out.

The arguments for replacing jus sanguinis with jus soli were not just principled. They were also practical, and even cynical. For some champions of jus soli, minimizing obstacles to valuable EU citizenships was a good in itself. For many immigrants, the equal rights obtained under jus soli were a route to the special privileges of jus sanguinis. They were able to pick and choose between the two regimes. On the formal, legalistic, and impersonal "modern" grounds of having been long resident, or born, on a given country's soil, an immigrant, or child of immigrants, was accorded citizenship. Then, on the solemn, mystical, clannish, premodern grounds of "blood," he could petition for rights of residence (to be followed, eventually, by citizenship) for his foreign relatives.

One of the first measures passed by the government of Gerhard Schröder after it came to power in 1998 was a citizenship reform that largely converted German law to jus soli. It established that, starting in 2009, German-born children of foreigners could (and must) decide at age eighteen whether they wished to be citizens of Germany or of their countries of origin. Having millions of "foreigners" on national territory was both a bureaucratic headache and a political liability. Reclassifying foreigners as natives looked like a simple way to "solve" a number of problems, assuming voters didn't notice. But, of course, they noticed. Within weeks of the passing of the new citizenship law, Schröder's Social Democratic party suffered a string of crippling losses in Bundesrat elections, all of them centered on the citizenship issue, from which (as of this writing, a decade later) it has never fully recovered.

The largest wholesale grant of citizenship in recent history—Spanish prime minister Zapatero's massive amnesty to 700,000 illegal immigrants in 2005—left a similar aftermath. In the Spanish case, the hostility was directed not at the government but at its beneficiaries. A year after the amnesty, polls showed that Spanish Muslims had a relatively high opinion of their relations with non-Muslim Westerners. Almost half of Muslims (49 percent) were happy about how they got along with native Spaniards, versus 23 percent who were not. That was a rosier attitude than Muslims held towards their non-Muslim fellow citizens in Britain (23 percent positive, 62 percent negative), Germany (29–60), or France (41–58). But Spanish *non*-Muslims were suddenly more hostile than other European natives to their country's Muslims. Only 23 percent of Spaniards thought they and their Muslim neighbors got on well, and 83 percent associated Islam with fanaticism.

The tension between jus soli and jus sanguinis arose only at times of heavy immigration. Otherwise, the regime under which foreigners became citizens was no big deal. A person born on, say, French soil got French citizenship. He would live his life as "frenchly" as someone who was French by ancestry. He would assimilate into France and into French culture and become French. What else was he going to do? Before the age of mass immigration, assimilation was an imperative, because not assimilating meant ostracism, loneliness, and non-participation in the economy. If the need to assimilate was never spelled out legally, it is only because it was too obvious to have to be.

Just as there were two models for becoming European according to the letter of the law (i.e., citizenship), there were two models of becoming European according to the spirit of the law (i.e., assimilation). There was a French model of assimilation, which held that immigrants should become French in their cultural loyalties. And there was a more multicultural British model, which held that one could keep one's culture as long as one obeyed the law of the land. In the age of massive, heavily Muslim migration, neither had a particularly good record of keeping the peace or producing jobs for ethnic minorities. Whether the French or the British model was in vogue among policymakers depended on which country had suffered rioting less recently. Eventually, decisive evidence emerged—in the form of terrorism, gang violence, and mass mobilizations against free speech—that Britain had the direst problem assimilating immigrants of any country in Europe. But by that time, Britain's model, which had the advantage of requiring the least investment of effort by its political leaders, had mostly triumphed. Increasingly, naturalized immigrants were asserting the right to "integrate"—basically, to live in Europe as foreigners—rather than to assimilate.

Politicians acquiesced in this understanding, even the most reputedly right-wing and intolerant among them, as if integration were a new, improved version of assimilation. That the word *integration* had been borrowed from the U.S. civil rights struggle in the first place is another indication that Europe was dealing with an intractable problem (like race in America) rather than managing a process of transition (like immigration in America). Göran Johansson, an old-school Swedish labor leader who had become mayor of Gothenburg, was known for shooting from the hip about how immigration was transforming his city. But even he said, "I don't like assimilation; I like integration. Both Sweden and immigrants must change." Asked to clarify what he meant by integration, Johansson said: "I don't care if you respect our culture. You just have to obey the law."

But of course you have to obey the law! That's what makes it the law. To demand that immigrants must obey the law is to demand exactly nothing from them. The result was that Europe filled up with excellent, virtuous, law-abiding people whose ideas of excellence and virtue had nothing at all to do with Europe. Sarfraz Manzoor, an English columnist of Pakistani background, writes,

My generation and the generation after me are still wrestling with the question of where our allegiance lies, and this is after a lifetime of having lived immersed in British culture. The men who dream of moving from Lahore to Leicester, the women who pray that an arranged marriage will transport them from Bangladesh to Brick Lane, are not coming because they have any affinity with what might loosely be described as British values. They seek to come for the simple reason that it is better to live here than where they came from. That is an entirely honorable and understand-able reason. But it is ludicrous to suggest that the only impact this has on our country is economic.

The idea that nothing, not even loyalty, would be required of immi-grants, so long as they didn't subvert the laws of the country, came up constantly in one form or another—again, even among so-called hard-liners. Jürgen Rüttgers, the minister-president of North Rhine–Westphalia, had earned the reputation as one of Europe's arch-xenophobes for remarks like the one about Indians mentioned in chapter 3, and warned that there was no evidence of multicultural societies' ever having worked anywhere in the world. Yet he, too, said, "Integration is not assimilation. You don't have to give up your religion, but you must obey our basic values."

Rita Verdonk, the former Dutch minister of immigration, who in the years since the 2004 killing of Theo van Gogh has been thought the most implacably anti-immigrant cabinet-level politician in Europe, was particularly insistent that integration, not assimilation, was the Dutch way. "Assimilation means you lose the identity of your country of origin," she said. "Our policy is: You must learn the Dutch language, follow our norms and values and obey the law." Only one prominent mainstream politician of the past decade has dissented publicly from this view: the conservative ex-leftist German interior minister Otto Schily, who said, "The best form of integration is assimilation."

The illusion of diversity

Whenever Europeans worried about the long-term assimilability of immigrants, it was Muslims they worried about most. Sometimes it was Muslims they worried about exclusively. In Denmark, where the right-wing Danish People's Party (DF) had frightened the ruling coalition into passing Europe's strictest laws against immigration, the DF leadership was at pains to convey that it did not consider *all* immigrants problematic. "They are no problem—totally integrated," said the priest and DF parliamentarian Jesper Langballe of the many Tamils who had settled in his own parish in Jutland. "The problem is, you can't integrate large numbers of Muslims in a country that has a cultural base that is Christian." Rikke Hvilshøj, the country's integration minister at the time, said that this was not an unusual view. Denmark had received large immigrant flows from Hungary in 1956 and Poland in 1968, not to mention an unusually big contingent of Vietnamese boat people in the late 1970s and early 1980s. "When Danes speak of immigrants today," she said, "it is not Hungarians or Vietnamese they are talking about."

The view of the European man-in-the-street (of 88 percent of Germans, for instance) was that Muslims "want to remain distinct"—but nowhere was that opinion reflected in government policy. The official view was that Muslims were much the same as any other immigrant group, and while Muslims had admittedly shown a reluctance to embrace European culture thus far, inexorable historical processes were at work. Over the long term, Muslims could no more constitute a culture apart than immigrants in previous centuries had, according to political leaders, and the reason was Muslim diversity. Not only is Islam a varied spectrum of beliefs and cultures—Arab and non-Arab, Sunni and Shia, traditional and modern—but that spectrum is further refracted by Islam's sudden entry into Europe. In what sense do English-speaking Pakistanis share a culture with Italian-speaking Moroccans or German-speaking Turks? To speak of "the Muslims" was an ignorant stereotype, an optical illusion. It was what the French would call an *amalgame*.

Certainly diversity among Muslims is greater than it looks. Neighborhoods that outsiders perceive as "Pakistani" may be Pakistani and Bengali, and the Pakistanis in it may be divided between people who think of themselves as Punjabis and others who are Mirpuris. A single Parisian neighborhood made up of Algerians who emigrated in the 1960s (Ménilmontant, for example) might be divided between Arabs and Berbers. A Rhineland neighborhood made up of Turks who arrived in the 1960s (Marxloh, for instance) will almost certainly be split between religious Sunnis and Alevites, as well as between ethnic Turks and Kurds. Knowledgeable about this diversity, many Muslims grow impatient with being lumped together as an undifferentiated mass. "What do you mean, 'Islam'?" one German social worker asked a journalist at *Der Stern*. "There's no such thing as single, unique

Islam." The French sociologist Dounia Bouzar wrote a book called *"Mister Islam" Doesn't Exist*. But for all its pleasing glibness, this harping on diversity is misguided. It is like saying that, because a Volvo is different from a Volkswagen, there's no such thing as a car. While diversity certainly exists among Muslim groups, its importance has been overstated.

There is a reason that diversity became such a treasured myth among well-meaning Europeans: A utopia could be built on it. If Islam can exist in so many forms, they asked, why not a European form, which would graft onto the religion not just a loyalty to Muslims' new countries of citizenship but also a respect for constitutional rights known to be anathema in almost every part of the Muslim world? The late French scholar of Islam Jacques Berque first raised the idea of replacing Islam *in* France with an Islam *of* France in the late 1980s, and since then the idea, along with the catchphrase, has become popular among bureaucrats and intellectuals throughout Europe. Stefano Allievi, probably the leading Italian sociologist of Islam, wrote of younger generations in which "Islam in Italy is becoming Italian Islam." Creating a "German Islam" out of a bunch of German Muslims is the explicit goal of the Islamkonferenz launched by interior minister Wolfgang Schäuble in 2006.

What has actually happened in most countries in Europe is the opposite—a partial embrace of the national identity of the new country has been followed by a withdrawal to the religious identity of the old. This shift is more pronounced among younger generations. In Berque's own France, the country that has devoted the most resources to domesticating Islam, young people of Muslim descent think of themselves as Muslim before they think of themselves as French. Asked what element characterizes them best, about a third of Muslim students answered that it was their religion, versus fewer than 5 percent of native French children who said the same. The leftist journalist Alain Gresh notes that the expression "second generation" was never used for previous generations of young French people whose parents happened to be Italian and Polish. This could be a failure of the French traditions of *citoyenneté*—it is more likely a sign that, however strong those traditions may be, the attachment of this generation to its ancestral traditions is stronger.

The situation is similar in Britain. In early 2007, the think tank Policy Exchange released a troubling study. It found that nearly a third (31 percent) of British Muslims thought they had more in common with Muslims in other countries than with their fellow citizens. Only half referred to Britain as "my country." The sense of belonging to Britain was *higher* among those over 45 (55 percent) than among those 18 to 24 (45 percent). Military enlistment offers another clue to how "British" young British Muslims feel. In February 2007, British authorities uncovered a plot hatched by local Muslims in Birmingham to kidnap a British Muslim soldier and torture him to death on a video to be disseminated over the Internet. It emerged that the targeted soldier was one of only 330 Muslims in the British armed forces, a number that not even dogged recruiting efforts have sufficed to raise. Britain's Muslims were joining the military at roughly one-twentieth the rate of other Britons.

In theory, Germany has a better chance of forming the kind of national Islam that European governments claim to want, not because of any particular wisdom in its policies but because of the orientation of the Turkish culture out of which most of its immigrants came. "People look with pride on their own history of modernization since Atatürk," wrote the journalist Jörg Lau, "and see themselves, for the most part, as already part of Europe and the West." This is not an indication that Turks are more willing to adapt to Germany than other immigrant groups are to their respective new countries, only that they have less need to adapt.

One way to get a sense of German Turks' deepest allegiances is to look at their choices about burial. All Muslim organizations in Germany have burial funds (*Bestattungsfonds*) to which community members subscribe. Muslim burial has generally meant burial in the subscriber's country of origin. According to a study by the Center for Turkey Studies in 2000, only 5 percent of Turks could see themselves being buried in Germany. The fact that 68 percent favor the establishment of Muslim cemeteries in Europe—which would allow burial in shrouds rather than coffins, among other adjustments—may be an optimistic sign. But it indicates that the price of a more "European" Islam will be a more Islamic Europe. When asked whether there is "a special, German form of Islam," 68 percent of German Turks say there is not. They are evenly split on the question of whether the laws of Islam are even compatible with the rules of German society—52 percent say they are, while 46 percent say they are not.

Certainly, European-ness would enter the cultural lives of Muslims who live there. How could it not? Any people who have been in a given country for fifty years will show certain cultural signs of their sojourn. These signs can be the reflection of something profound, or they can be mere superficialities. That most British imperialists could tell you what *pukka* and *sahib* meant did not make them Indian. Here, as in their insistence that immigrants "obey the law," Europeans are taking something they assume to be inevitable and framing it as the fulfillment of a demand. The official bodies out of which a national Islam was supposed to be built—from France's CFCM to Britain's quasi-autonomous Muslim Association of Britain—were misconceived. Certainly they could accept national funds. But they could not create national Islams. *Islam de France, deutscher Islam, islam italiano* . . . these were slogans, answers to a question that Islam does not ask.

Islam as a hyper-identity

Islam has ever been understood as a mighty identity, shaping every aspect of a believer's life and reducing lesser allegiances to unimportance. Ernest Renan wrote in 1883 that certain habits inculcated by the Muslim faith "are so strong that all differences of race and nationality disappear before the fact of conversion to Islam. The Berber, the Sudanese, the Circassian, the Malay, the Egyptian, the Nubian, once they have become Muslim, are no longer Berbers, Sudanese, Egyptians, etc.—they are Muslims." This, indeed, is the view not just of Islam's detractors but of its adherents, especially when they are trying to present Islam as a source of brotherhood that can serve as an antidote to Western racism or nationalism. Malcolm X, on his pilgrimage to Mecca in 1964, wrote:

For the past week, I have been utterly speechless and spellbound by the graciousness I see displayed all around me by people of *all colors*. . . . America needs to understand Islam, because this is the one religion that erases from its society the race problem. Throughout my travels in the Muslim world, I have met, talked to, and even eaten with people who in America would have been considered "white"—but the "white" attitude was removed from their minds by the religion of Islam. I have never before seen *sincere* and *true* brotherhood practiced by all colors together, irrespective of their color. . . . Perhaps if white Americans could accept the Oneness of God, then perhaps, too, they could accept *in reality* the Oneness of Man—and cease to measure, and hinder, and harm others in terms of their "differences" in color.

Inayat Bunglawala, a prominent activist with the Muslim Council of Britain, gave a repentant—but dishearteningly vivid—account of his joining a Muslim rally in Hyde Park in 1989, in support of the Ayatollah Khomeini's fatwa calling for the murder of British novelist Salman Rushdie:

It was an amazing day. There was an increasing realisation that by giving greater importance to our Islamic identity we could transcend and overcome the divides among us. We may have Pakistani, Bengali, Gujarati, Arab, Turkish backgrounds, but this was less important than what brought us together: we were British Muslims. And so Rushdie's novel became, unwittingly no doubt, the catalyst for the forging of a more confident Islamic identity.

As for the fatwa itself, Bunglawala recalls that it left him "elated."

Whether or not Renan, Malcolm X, and the young Inayat Bunglawala are right that Islam trumps all social, cultural, and national differences, conditions are ripe for the various Muslim communities of Europe to coalesce in a unified identity. The United States offers the best example of how, in an age of mass immigration, sub-identities get melded into larger ones. "Hispanic" identity was largely a fictional category when federal census takers invented it in the 1970s. "Hispanic" was a linguistic, not a sociological, term. It was useful as a proxy for northbound immigration flows, but there was no such thing as a "Hispanic" person. Spanish speakers themselves complained that the "Hispanic" category did not respect the difference between, say, a white Cuban pianist and an Indian cowboy from Mexico. But affirmative action and Spanish-language marketing and television combined to turn this abstract identity into a real one. Today there really is such a thing as a Hispanic (or Latino) identity, made up of Chilean-Americans and Mexican-Americans competing for the same bilingual marketing jobs at corporations in New York, of Puerto Ricans and Bolivians watching the same shows on Univisión, and of new migrants working in industries—such as landscaping and restaurants—where Spanish is a lingua franca.

In Europe, formerly distinct communities' interests have started to converge into a larger Muslim culture. In most immigrant housing projects, satellite dishes run up the buildings like buttons, picking up the news from home. This would seem to throw into reverse television's historic role as an engine of immigrant assimilation, keeping open lines of communication from the old country. But in other ways, television does indeed assimilate immigrants. It is just that it assimilates them into something other than traditional European culture. It assimilates them into globalized Islam. The Muslim scholar Yusuf Qaradawi's weekly fatwa show on al-Jazeera, for instance, is watched all over Europe.

Just because Europe is a main audience of this new, online Islamic culture does not mean that that culture will be pro-European. It may mean the opposite. Muslim websites are no less marked by slapdash verification and an incendiary political idiom than their counterparts in the non-Muslim world. One of the paradoxes of the Internet is that this most modern of media has brought new power to premodern habits of discourse: rumor, gossip, urban myths, old wives' tales. A lot of young Palestinians in Denmark, most of them refugees from the civil war in Lebanon, believe the welfare payments they accept in Denmark put them in no position of indebtedness towards the Danish state, because the money has been effectively stolen from families like their own. "They say, 'The money comes from the United Nations,'" recalls one integration expert in Copenhagen. "'They send it to Denmark, and Denmark takes half. That's why I'll never be loyal to the Danes.'" More than half (56 percent) of British Muslims do not believe Arabs committed the atrocities of September 11, 2001, versus 17 percent who do.

European Muslims often wind up locked in the ancient and present-day grievances of their homelands—and other people's homelands.

Extremists who recruit volunteers for jihad abroad have often done so by using videos, with stirring musical accompaniment, that show Muslims mistreated, humiliated, wounded, and killed in various trouble spots; one friend of the four 7/7 suicide bombers told the *Wall Street Journal*, "They were aware that we Muslims are suffering the most in the world, be it Iraq, Afghanistan or Palestine."

That Muslims suffer the most is the focal point of an increasing number of European Muslims' identity. The day after the unspeakable violence in the London Underground in July 2005, Imran Waheed of the radical group Hizb ut-Tahrir insisted, "We have far greater experience as victims of terror than as perpetrators of terror." Who is the "we" that he is referring to here? It is not, by any stretch of the imagination, Britons. He added that the British Muslim community's reaction to Britain's participation in wars in Afghanistan and the Middle East had until then been "remarkably restrained."

Dual loyalty

Empathy among Muslims creates a big potential problem that does not exist with other immigrations. Imagine that the West, at the height of the Cold War, had received a mass inflow of immigrants from Communist countries who were ambivalent about which side they supported. Something similar is taking place now. European countries have lately been at war with Muslim forces in Iraq, Afghanistan, the Balkans, and Africa; and this is leaving aside countries of European culture, such as the United States and Israel, that are fighting similar battles. The late Harvard political scientist Samuel Huntington devoted much of his 1996 book *The Clash of Civilizations* to Islam's "bloody borders." This may be a controversial observation, but it is an observation—it is not something Huntington dreamed up. As of this writing, Muslim countries or groups are either at war or in a hostile truce with every civilization that Islam abuts, from Nigeria to Xinjiang.

The problem that European Muslims' solidarity creates, at least potentially, is dual loyalty. Two years into the Iraq war, French authorities had already identified seven French Muslims killed fighting for the insurgency there, a "British brigade" of 150 anti-British Britons was also in the field, and there were recruitment networks set up in Belgium to send further soldiers.

In the case of Omar Khan Sharif and Asif Mohammed Hanif, dual loyalty was not just a potential problem but a clear and present danger. Sharif was born in Derby, grew up there in a red-brick semi-detached house, spent two years at a £10,000-a-year preparatory school, and studied at Kingston University. Hanif, while Pakistani-born, was no less rooted in English life. Yet the two absorbed a lot of Islamic fundamentalism from their TV sets and computer screens. In 2003, they traveled to a Tel Aviv discotheque in their very British pressed shirts and chinos and murdered several people with suicide bombs. Their Britishness, or at least their British passports, were essential to their crimes. The pair entered Israel from Jordan at a crossing point where Europeans face laxer scrutiny than visitors from the Muslim world.

One student who met Hanif and Sharif in Damascus speculated that they hoped to escape "the soulless wastelands of modernity." There is nothing un-British or un-European about that. A strain of adventure tourism that seeks and wreaks violence in the service of ideologies both noble and sadistic runs through European history from the Crusades to the Spanish Civil War. These travelers have fulfilled an impulse that Lord Byron described in the "Stanzas" he wrote in November 1820, shortly before his own departure to fight against the Ottoman Empire in Greece:

> When a man hath no freedom to fight for at home,
> Let him combat for that of his neighbours;
> Let him think of the glories of Greece and of Rome,
> And get knock'd on the head for his labours,
>
> To do good to mankind is the chivalrous plan,
> And is always as nobly requited;
> Then battle for freedom wherever you can,
> And, if not shot or hang'd, you'll get knighted.

Omar Abdullah, spokesman for the radical group al-Muhajiroun, said much the same thing in his own hard-line way. He excused the Derby suicide bombers by saying: "British men go off to join the Israeli army and when they die nobody makes anything of it."

Abdullah has a point in theory. Loyalty to two countries is always potentially problematic. Britons who joined an Israeli militia during Israel's war for independence in British-mandate Palestine would rightly have had their loyalty questioned. But as far as today's world is concerned, Abdullah's point is a disingenuous one. British men do not join the Israeli army for the purpose of killing foreign civilians or making war on Britain, and those are precisely the reasons for which certain Muslim radicals fight abroad. "I know people who went to Iraq to fight off the aggression," a Syrian-trained exile from Birmingham told a British reporter. "I support them because Iraq is a Muslim country that is being violated by America and Britain." That is what separates today's adventure-seeking European Islamists from their Byronic forebears.

But where terrorism is not involved, dual loyalty can be a vague, dangerous, and constitutionally corrosive thing to allege. Are radical political opinions enough to justify a charge of disloyalty? Surely not. How about allegiance to some radical group? Depends on the group and its aims.

Such questions are complicated by subventions that the mostly conservative Gulf states pay to build up the institutions of European Islam, often with the complicity of European countries. Saudi Arabia, where conservative Wahhabism predominates, pays vast sums for building mosques and other institutions. The Saudis have contributed £100 million to a controversial project to build the largest mosque in Europe in East London in time for the 2012 Olympics. In France, the UOIF, an umbrella group of doctrinaire Muslim youth organizations, gets a quarter of its annual budget from Saudi Arabia, the United Arab Emirates, and Kuwait, and other foreign donors. Stockholm's Great Mosque was long financed by a sheikh from the United Arab Emirates.

Europeans face a trade-off. On the one hand, the Gulf states' brand of Islam can be seen as anti-Western, as contributing to the radicalization of European Muslim populations. French Islamologists say that the extent of Saudi support in Europe is greatly under-estimated, since a lot of the other governments that putatively support French mosques—such as Algeria, which funds the Great Mosque of

Paris—use money passed through from the Saudis. But foreign funding is not a bad thing in every respect. In both Spain and the Netherlands, some dogged foes of fundamentalism *support* foreign subventions on the grounds that it is easier to pressure, say, the king of Morocco, than a charismatic underground imam who draws his support from unknown sources, whether criminal gangs or religious fanatics.

More complicated cases arise with nonstate organizations that explicitly indoctrinate their members against any loyalty other than that towards the organization itself. Hizb ut-Tahrir, the radical off-shoot of the Muslim Brotherhood founded in Jordan in 1953, aims at the restoration of the Muslim caliphate, which was abolished along with the Ottoman Empire in 1924. Its members take a solemn oath to "carry out even those decisions of the party leaders that I find objectionable." Yet, since Hizb ut-Tahrir does not explicitly authorize assaults on European states, European countries have differed on how to address it, just as they differed on how to address membership in the Communist Party half a century ago. Russia and Germany ban Hizb ut-Tahrir (both due to alleged anti-Semitism); the Netherlands, Denmark, and Britain have discussed banning it; but most permit it to operate legally.

Hizb ut-Tahrir is not the only group that remains inside the letter of the Western law while straying far outside its spirit. The Salafist (fundamentalist) as-Soennah mosque in The Hague, under the influence of the Syrian-born imam Fawaz Jneid, does not promote violence, but it does promote a distance between its members and Western institutions. Several women of the Hofstad network, the group out of which Theo van Gogh's killer came, asked the imam if they had his permission to testify in a Dutch court of law in the Hofstad case. (He granted it.)

Humiliation and Islamophobia

Europeans asserted that they were bending over backwards to accommodate Islam, and they were. For the first time in modern history, European societies were taking pains to allow residents—and, increasingly, *citizens*—to lead their entire lives in a foreign culture. Mostly this separation was achieved through private initiatives. An

Arab immigrant to Germany, for instance, could "assimilate" into the "Arab part" of his new, multicultural country, into the "ethnic colonies" Rauf Ceylan wrote of. At the Saudi-sponsored King Fahd Academy in Bonn, students' weekly curriculum consisted of twelve hours of religion, six hours of Arabic, and one hour of German.

But public authorities approved—and even funded—similarly separatist facilities. Mohammed Bouyeri, Theo van Gogh's killer, demanded shuttle-bus service to his publicly funded youth clubhouse. He insisted that municipal authorities renovate his parents' flat in line with Islamic custom. Just months before he killed van Gogh, Bouyeri had slashed a policeman's neck with a knife—and received a twelve-week sentence for it. The largesse, nonjudgmentalism, and leniency of European governments bred contempt, and a temptation, wrote the journalist Ian Buruma, to "milk the state."

Yet despite this private and public largesse, accusations have multiplied that Europe is biased and prejudiced against Muslims, and even "Islamophobic." Immigrants often proclaimed their disappointment with Europe, and even a sense that they had been "had." Reckoning integration in Sweden "a complete failure," Massoud Kamali, an influential Iranian-born professor of ethnic studies at Uppsala, talked in 2005 of the high hopes many immigrants had brought: "Many of us saw Sweden as the homeland of tolerance, solidarity and democracy, based on the image of Sweden abroad." Yet, he said, the foreign-born found that the longer they lived in Sweden, the more foreign they felt.

As Hans Magnus Enzensberger has noted, this rise in rancor is part of a paradox of liberal progress. The fairer, the more egalitarian, the less racist society becomes, the more humiliating failure in it is felt to be. People become more "disappointable," more desperate for scapegoats and all-encompassing alibis. This happens in small ways (when egos get damaged) and in large (when cultures lose prestige). And as more Europeans began to question multiculturalism, another kind of disappointment rose up among immigrants. Europe's welcome to them felt like a bait-and-switch, a bargain broken. Part of the attractiveness of settling in Europe in the first place had been the understanding that Europeans would accept foreigners as they were. And Europe had done just that. But *if* foreigners remained as they were, if they kept their non-European identity, they would get only halting access to the economy, the civilization, the institutions that they had come to Europe for in the first place.

The transition from an industrial to a service economy, which has "humanized" the workplace for many people, has also created new opportunities for humiliation, envy, and ethnic resentment. It was often lamented in the past that factory jobs were unfulfilling or, to use the Marxist term, alienating. But for that reason, an industrial economy—and perhaps *only* an industrial economy—could absorb people from different cultures without automatically provoking dangerous cultural conflict. What was essentially human about a factory worker was simply not at stake in the workplace. If you were a Muslim and your co-worker was a Christian, it didn't matter— both of you turned lathes the same way. Today's Western service economy, by contrast, involves a lot of self-expression, bought servility, and even intimacy; it is organized around sensual and other pleasures. An immigrant family living in Germany in 1975 would have been proud to have its daughter working at a big international corporation like Siemens. Would the same family be proud, decades later, to have a granddaughter working at a big international corporation like Hooters?

If we return to Huntington's observation about the frictions between Islam and every single culture with which it is in contact, or if we consider the penury, servitude, violence, and mediocrity of Muslim societies worldwide . . . how do we explain it? Either there is a major problem with Islam that must be addressed by Muslims themselves, or a wide variety of non-Muslim cultures has, by incredible coincidence, developed exactly the same unfair malevolence towards Islam. Naturally, this last is attractive to activist immigrants and their defenders. It is what they are referring to when they speak of Islamophobia.

It is tempting to look at Islamophobia as a translation into the European idiom of American-style political correctness. In this view, Islam is simply the latest category, after gender, sexual preference, age, and so forth, added to the prim way that Americans invented to talk about their race problem during the civil rights era. But *Islamophobia* is a more labile term than that. It encompasses misconduct towards Muslims, racism, fear of Muslim radicalism, and political opposition to certain Islamist political tendencies. Those who accuse others of Islamophobia often want to have their cake and eat it. Any European reluctance to embrace Islamic immigration gets called Islamophobia. So does any suggestion that immigrants or their children adapt to European ways.

Some Europeans condescendingly assume that those who embrace their Islamic identity are just seeking consolation for their poor education or low job status, but that is wrong. "On the contrary," found a German study released in 2007, "Muslims living in areas with a lower unemployment rate seem to display a higher sense of identity." Nor was the problem that immigrant Muslims were reluctant to "give up" their traditions. Muslim traditions exercised a strong pull even on the European-born children whose families had *already* given them up. Something drew ethnic Muslims to return to their cultural origins—even those whose families had been in Europe so long that their "origins" might be little more than a parody, a hobby, an affectation, a romantic dream.

The old identities didn't seem to go away. They were always ready to be tapped into at any time by second- or third-generation Muslims somehow discontent with European culture. Europe was full of Muslim "community leaders" who, while of Muslim background, had learned their Arabic not over the kitchen table but at university. On one hand, it seemed shameful to view their acquisition of a foreign language with any more suspicion than one would direct towards any other European doing the same. On the other hand, it was hard not to wonder whether they were learning that foreign language in hopes of becoming something other than European. Mohammed Sidique Khan, the mastermind of the 7/7 bomb plot, spoke in a thick accent typical of his part of Yorkshire and played soccer with a lot of native English "mates" who called him "Sid." His problem was not that he had "failed to assimilate"—it was that he had chosen to *dis*-assimilate.

Khan was making an individual choice to seek his "roots." But a sense of alienation from wider European culture does not always arise this way. In some families, the sense of belonging not to one's country but to one's religion is inculcated early. One investigation of schools by the French ministry of education found:

Many French and even second-generation French students of North African origin, who make up the majority in certain schools, live as if they are foreign to the national community. They reply to anything you say to them with two categories: "the French" and "us." Where once they claimed an Arab identity (which is not, by the way, always self-evident for North Africans), today they increasingly claim a "Muslim" identity. This is an indoctrination that begins as early as primary school, certain teachers claim. Many schoolchildren, if you ask them what their nationality is, will reply, "Muslim." If you inform them that they are French, as we did in a junior high school in the Paris suburbs, they reply that that is impossible, because they're Muslims!

Thus did Muslim immigration diverge from earlier immigrations. Newly acquired national allegiances were negotiable, revocable, provisional. Whether this was due to the timeless nature of Islam or to the changing world of the twenty-first century, Europe was not dealing with an ordinary immigration problem at all, but with an adversary culture.

Muslims and U.S. blacks

We have already remarked that the European experience of Muslim immigration has less in common with the American experience of immigration (largely a success) than with the American experience of race (an enduring problem, with all successes attained only at very steep costs). It is not so much that the living conditions of Muslims resemble those of inner-city U.S. blacks in the late twentieth century—although they sometimes do, with drugs, crime, rioting, and dead-end school systems creating problems that look insoluble. It is also that their cultural self-understanding has more in common with American blacks than with immigrants. Black culture could be called an "adversary culture"—a culture built on distrust towards the dominant one, and tending to hold oppositional views on almost all political questions.

An adversary culture is not necessarily a "sick" or a "failed" culture, as some critics would have it. In fact, American black culture is a gloriously *robust* culture by two important measures. First, it has remained intact through the cyclone of globalization, even surviving its own enrichment (in contrast to, say, the culture of contemporary Ireland, whose natives abandoned their traditions as soon as they could buy their way out of them). Second, its cultural products have swept the world.

Nowhere has U.S. black culture evoked more emulation and empathy than among European Muslims. One Turkish rapper, a fan of Dr. Dre, Eminem, and 50 Cent, said he felt "a certain commonality" with black Americans. "In America it's called slavery," he said. "Here it's called *Gastarbeiter*." By the time of the French riots in 2005, in which arsonists in €200 basketball shoes and sideways New York Yankees caps communicated with the television cameras in gestures copied off of rap videos, these gestures and this garb had become part of what the American cultural historian Mark Lilla called "a universal culture of the wretched of the earth."

But for all its remarkable internal coherence and its vast cultural influence, black America remains the poorest of America's subcultures, and has been subordinated for centuries. Blacks have been a cultural problem for the United States, but not a cultural threat to it. Before the days of the Internet, it was natural to view European Muslims, in each individual country, as a subculture even *less* influential than American blacks—exiled, rootless, divided amongst itself, and infinitesimally small. Today they are none of those things. A fast-shrinking population of several hundred million Europeans lives north of the Mediterranean, while a fast-growing population of several hundred million lives south of it, with a desire to take up residence in Europe that seems unslakeable. What is more, a certain part of it is dedicated to Europe's destruction by armed violence. This part may be small, but the London and Madrid bombings show that it is very difficult to determine satisfactorily *how* small. In an age of global communications Islam does not look like a "sub"-culture in any sense of the word. There are 1.2 billion Muslims, bound together by the Internet in a global ummah, or nation of believers. In most cases this is a pro forma kind of belonging, but in some it involves a fervid kind of loyalty.

Since Muslims make up roughly half of the "new European" population, they could come to constitute a dominant culture among immigrants as a whole, even those who do not profess the Muslim faith. They could be a *Leitkultur*, to use the German idea of a "leading culture" in a different context. Latin Americans provided a similar *Leitkultur* to American protest marchers in the 1980s. Whether they were protesting the Ku Klux Klan or nuclear power, they would chant, "*¡El pueblo! / ¡Unido! / ¡Jamás será vencido!*"—in a language borrowed from another cause, understood neither by the marchers nor the people they were defending nor the people they were addressing.

From a similar fascination with ghettoized Muslim communities, there has developed an idiom useful for rallying the disgruntled. One can see it in the successes of Islamist proselytizers among non-Muslim convicts. One can also see it at the level of gangs. Almost the entire wave of attacks on Jews that began in France in 2002 was instigated by *beurs* (French Muslims of North African descent)—but in many cases African and Caribbean neighbors of the organizers joined them as accomplices. The Muslim-led gang of two dozen self-described "barbarians" who used acid, knives, and lighter fluid to torture to death the Jewish cell-phone salesman Ilan Halimi over three weeks in 2006 was a multicultural mix of recent immigrants from Africa and Asia, as well as several French-born minorities. What is developing resembles a system of *cujus regio ejus religio* ("Whose rule, his religion") at the level of a cell block or street gang or elevator bank.

7

Europe's Crisis of Faith

Religious resurgence—Islam and European believers—Islam and European unbelievers—Benedict XVI: New ideas about belief and unbelief—Western sympathy with, and conversion to, Islam—The European model of managing religion—Organizing religious bodies—Freedom of religion = Freedom of Islam—The Danish cartoon crisis

Islam has not turned out to be the vestige most Europeans assumed it would become when immigrants started arriving in the 1950s, '60s, and '70s. It is a force to be reckoned with. Commentators and politicians are fond of voicing the cliché, as if they are making a generous concession, that Islam is now "the second religion of Europe." Some even say this exaggerates Islam's impact. "We have a public debate as if religious Muslim immigrants constituted 30 percent of the population," says the Danish religion writer Anders Jerichow. "The religious part is probably 1 percent."

But to describe Islam as the second religion of Europe is actually to sell it short. If you measure Islam by the intensity of its followers' convictions, by its importance in political debates, by the privileges it enjoys under the laws of many European countries, or by its capacity to intimidate potential detractors, then Islam is not the second religion of Europe but the first. In some Western European countries, the absolute numbers of church and mosque attendees are similar. In all countries, the rates of mosque attendance are higher. Europeans are not wrong to feel nervous about what remains, after all, a minority religion. Maybe Europe will not turn into an outpost of the Arab world, as Bernard Lewis warned. But it does have a "nation of Islam" within it, small but growing inexorably.

Religious resurgence

In most Muslim communities in Europe—rich or poor, fresh off the plane or two generations from the dock—the importance and prestige of Islam are on the rise. In the Muslim middle class, it is not embarrassing to admit that one's parents are religious, as it would be among middle-class Europeans of Christian background. In France, 85 percent of Muslim students describe their religious beliefs as "very important," versus 35 percent of non-Muslims. In Germany, too, religiosity is more widespread among Muslim immigrants than among natives: 81 percent of Turks come from a religious background, versus 23 percent of Germans. But, equally important, religious beliefs are more passionately and confidently held among Muslims: 68 percent of Turks think their religion is the only true one, versus just 6 percent of Germans. Seventy percent of European Muslims fast during Ramadan.

Islam has become an alternative deliverer of social services to poor people, sometimes a more effective one than the state. Mosque groups frequently feed the hungry (as the Muslim pillar of *zakat* enjoins), and the record of "faith-based" programs in getting troubled housing-project kids off of drugs is particularly excellent. When drug pushers began to make inroads into Beeston, in Leeds, Mohammad Sidique Khan—later the ringleader in the July 2005 London transport bombings—set up a group called the "Mullah Boys" along with fifteen or twenty other second-generation Pakistanis. It was a sort of street gang organized for social work. When they had identified a drug-addicted neighbor, Khan and the Mullah Boys would obtain the permission of his parents to kidnap him, and would then detain him while he detoxed in an apartment near the local Wahhabi mosque.

This does not necessarily mean that kids would be turning less to Islam if they lived in richer, less drug-ridden neighborhoods. As noted in the last chapter, there is a tendency among Europeans to assume that the fervent embrace of Islam among ethnic youth must be a result of some nonreligious factor, like poverty or social exclusion. It is not. Religion is not a consolation prize. Islam's sudden high visibility is part of a global shift. For decades European Muslims, like virtually every other people in the world except European Christians, have been gravitating (back) towards religion. The American evangelical movement is part of the same trend.

The demographic and cultural weight of Islam in the world continues to grow, and Europe is the place it is growing fastest. There is something bizarre about this. Islam may have 1.3 billion adherents, but Europe's own religion, Christianity, has 2 billion. Christianity is growing faster than Islam and, indeed, faster than any major religion in the world. There were 9 million Christians of all denominations in Africa in 1900; by 2005 there were 393 million. One key factor in halting the spread of militant Islam through Africa has been a growing Christianity that is sometimes equally militant (a phenomenon that is not without its own problems). There exists little evidence of such growth in Europe, and no such counterforce.

The ideology under which the Muslim aspirations advance can be arbitrary. The return of Islam is not just the resurgence of a doctrine but the resurgence of a *people*. Muslim armies (including terrorist ones) are increasingly assertive. On a number of issues, particularly those involving condemnation of the West, the rhetoric of today's Arab "religious fanatics" is indistinguishable from that of yesterday's Arab "godless nationalists." The idea that more young people are calling themselves Muslims because Islam has somehow been humiliated is wrong. Whatever their reasons for calling themselves Muslims, Islam appears to have the wind in its sails.

Islam and European believers

Much of the work of assimilating Islam has been done through interreligious dialogue. In 1970, at the Breeplein church in the working-class Rotterdam neighborhood of Feyenoord, the pioneering Dutch Reform pastor Pleun Reedijk noticed that the Muslims who had moved into his neighborhood would kneel in prayer on the street in the middle of winter. They had, naturally enough, no mosques of their own. Reedijk decided to open up his own crowded church to them, and let them worship there *in their own faith*.

Whether his act was generous or vain, courageous or naive, was a question that fed the sensationalist press for weeks and split Reedijk's own congregation in two. Looking back on the episode from his Rotterdam apartment in 2005, he was not so sure of his judgment. "Was it good to give Muslims the church?" he asked. "It is 50–50." On one hand, the sort of parishioners who were against the immigrants are now better disposed towards them, he said. Acts like these, where they have happened, have won Christians a lot of goodwill from Muslims. Although polls, as we have noted, show that European Muslims have misgivings about the broader European society in general, they show an overwhelming approval for Christians in particular. In France, 91 percent of Muslims have a positive attitude towards Christians, and the figures in Spain (82 percent), Britain (71 percent), and Germany (69 percent) are also high.

On the other hand, there are now only 250 parishioners in Reedijk's old church, as against 2,000 four decades ago, when it made its big-hearted offer from a position of strength. The Breeplein church no longer negotiates with *anyone* from a position of strength, especially now that its neighborhood has become heavily Moroccan and Turkish. In the tense days after the killing of Theo van Gogh, somebody threw a firebomb into the church's offices.

Interreligious dialogue was based largely on a Christian misunderstanding, or perhaps delusion would be a better word for it. Since natives know their countries' institutions better, and since they still hold commanding positions in the economy, in the job market, and in high and low culture, Christian groups often entered into dialogue with Muslims as if they were the stronger partner, issuing a magnanimous invitation to foreigners to *join* their culture. But the currency in religious dialogue, as opposed to dialogue between religious communities and the state, is not money or jobs or cultural influence. It is religious belief. The gains from interreligious dialogue go to religious people. Those who no longer believe get nothing out of it.

What Europeans saw as volunteerism and magnanimity was actually just a shift in religious power, away from Christians and towards Muslims. The German interior minister Wolfgang Schäuble is fond of quoting a formula of the eighteenth-century Prussian ruler Frederick the Great: "If the Turks came and wanted to settle the land, we would build them mosques." To the journalist Georg-Paul Hefty, though, such words sounded like north-German provincialism. "Those who lived further south in the German-speaking lands," Hefty wrote, "especially east of Vienna, knew back then that when the Turks wanted to settle a country, they didn't ask Christian rulers' permission to build their mosques."

Today, one of the major topics of interreligious dialogue concerns the protocols for the purchase of churches by Muslim groups, who then reconsecrate them as mosques. A document issued in 2006 by the EKD, the central authority of German Protestants, provoked controversy among the Central Council of Muslims because it evinced a certain reluctance (or perhaps just nostalgia) on the part of Christians:

The loss of a church is always hard to explain to a congregation, because many people have an emotional bond to their church. The rededication of a church as a mosque is felt by many Christians not just as a private loss, but also, and more seriously, as a public irritation. The outer symbolic value of the church remains intact, while inside another religion is being practiced. The public gets the impression either that Christians are retreating in the face of Islam, or that Islam and Christianity are, in the last analysis, interchangeable religions.

The hangdog, sad-sack, our-day-is-done tone of such communiqués is reflected in interreligious dialogue, which is generally built around discussing how Christians can make life easier for Muslims. At the publicly funded Hamara Centre in Leeds, local Muslims and Christians promote fellow feeling partly, as the *Wall Street Journal* put it, "by emphasizing their opposition to globalization, the war in Iraq and, in some cases, Israel's policies in the Palestinian territories." That is not cross-cultural communication. That is rallying Christians behind a Muslim agenda.

In Spain, the ongoing attempts of Muslims to get the Cordoba cathedral rededicated for Muslim prayer have had a similar outcome. Eight hundred years ago, Cordoba was under Islamic rule and the cathedral was a mosque. On the other hand, the mosque itself had been built on top of a Visigoth church. The cathedral has not been used as a mosque since Christians reconquered it from the Moors in 1236—although the aging dictator Francisco Franco did permit Saddam Hussein to pray in the old Byzantine *mihrab*, or shrine, after the two had a meal in Cordoba in 1974. "It would never occur to us to go to Mecca to say an Our Father," said a local Catholic leader who opposes sharing the cathedral.

He touches on an explosive point. As a religious matter, dialogue with Muslims is not taking place on an equal footing. Italian conservatives have been particularly sensitive on this matter. They argue that the guiding principle of interreligious dialogue must be *reciprocità*. It is not right, they argue, to permit the largest mosque in Europe to be built in Rome with Saudi money, while Saudi Arabia persecutes Christians and other Muslim countries forbid the construction of churches and missions. "Dialogue without *reciprocità* is empty talk," said the Italian cardinal Mario Pompedda, a few months before his death in 2006. It is essential to interreligious harmony, he continued, that Westerners "demand that the rights we ensure in Italy also be ensured in the Arab countries. In other words, if we open up an Islamic school or provide Muslim students with instruction in their faith, the same must be guaranteed in our own schools in Islamic lands." Pompedda, like many Muslims, believed that the relevant arena for discussions between Christians and Muslims is not any European nation-state but the globe. His demand was just, but unlikely to have any practical effect. The problem is not just that Saudis do not permit Christianity in their country; it is also that Europeans are less interested in evangelizing there than Saudis are in proselytizing in Europe. As long as Muslim believers are more passionate than Christian ones, and as long as the Christian world is more free than the Muslim one, *reciprocità* is a nostalgic wish, rather than a demand.

Islam and European unbelievers

"For a century and a half, secularists have been announcing the end of religion as pious Jews announce the coming of the Messiah," says the Islamologist Hans Jansen. Sometime after the Second World War, though, this secularist Messiah arrived in Europe. Among natives, at least, religion shows signs of being a thing of the past. A poll by *Le Figaro* found that 45 percent of self-described Catholics in France are unable to say what Easter celebrates. In 2003, a Lutheran pastor north of Copenhagen was suspended from his job for mentioning in an interview, "I don't believe in God the Creator." In the ensuing controversy, a survey carried out by a Christian daily newspaper found that fewer than two-thirds of Denmark's 2,100 pastors thought such remarks placed one outside the "framework of the church." It is not just religion that has disappeared from Europe—so has the memory of what a religiously ordered, or even a religiously in-clined, society was like. A good definition of religion for most modern Europeans might be "an irrational opinion, strongly held."

When a deeply religious foreign subculture irrupts into a less religious one, native responses are generally of two kinds. The first is straightforward and reactionary: Natives turn back to their ethnicity and their traditions. They tend to see the abandonment of their religious and other traditions as a mistake—and perhaps what left them vulnerable to getting swamped by foreigners in the first place. The second response is haughtiness or snobbery. The native society views its distance from religion not as a cultural loss but as a cultural attainment. It proclaims its postreligious universalism more loudly, haughtily, snobbishly.

Generally societies respond in both ways simultaneously. The group consciousness of the Irish Catholic masses who arrived in Boston in the nineteenth century goaded native Bostonians to stress (and in many cases to fabricate) an identity as Anglo-Saxons. They migrated from congregationalism to Episcopalianism (American Anglicanism) "not so much out of doctrinal differences as out of the desire for an affiliation that gave greater emphasis to authority, order, ritual, and to ties with England," the historian Oscar Handlin wrote. But more often the natives damned the newcomers on the grounds that Irish Catholicism was, *in its essence*, "alien to the spirit of progress" that animated nineteenth-century New Englanders. For Bostonians, it was proof of Irish backwardness that the newcomers would have no truck with "the bright and beautiful sisterhood" of philanthropic reform movements that obsessed the city, from temperance to abolitionism to women's rights.

Twenty-first-century Europeans do something similar with Islam. Many have come to see religious skepticism as part of the essence of European-ness. When newcomers, in the name of revealed religion, reject the European civilization built around bureaucratized rationalism, Europeans are bound to feel either insulted or shown up. Religious belief, no matter what its wellspring, is seen as a kind of treachery.

Marcello Pera, who as president of the Italian Senate worried greatly about the erosion of Italian culture, uses a convoluted logical formula to show that the cultures of Europe are superior to the cultures of those who migrate there: "If the members of culture B freely demonstrate their preference for culture A and not vice versa—if, for example, migration flows move from Islamic countries to Western countries and not vice versa—then there is indeed reason to believe that A is better than B." This gives the speaker a warm sense of satisfaction as long as he assumes A means "Western countries" and B "Muslim countries." But Pera's rankings will not be obvious to anyone who doesn't *already* consider the West superior to the non-West. If you called A "Beethoven's symphonies" and B "Internet pornography," the statement would be equally true. Judging merit by following the herd works for economists, but not for cultural historians.

Pera is not a believing Christian himself, and most intellectuals who proclaim the West's superiority do not mean that Christianity is better than Islam. They mean that transcending religion—in the name of rationality, neutrality, and other ideals of the Enlightenment—is better than practicing it. But Europe is becoming less confident about its godlessness. There have never been so many Bibles sold in either Dutch or Danish as in 2004 and 2005, when fresh translations in both languages were published. In the Netherlands, there has been much talk of *ietsisme*. A growing number of nonreligious people say that, while they don't believe in God, exactly, they do believe in "something" (*iets*).

Books calling, vaguely, for a spiritual revival are growing more and more popular. A book by the television pundit Peter Hahne, urging Germans to get serious about their crisis in "values" after September 11, lingered at the top of bestseller lists for months. This could reflect a taste for hortatory fluff, or it could be the first sign of a return to traditional religion. When the mushy motivational fable *Jonathan Livingston Seagull* spent thirty-eight weeks as the bestselling book in the United States in the early 1970s, no one considered it a harbinger of a nationwide religious revival, although, in retrospect, that is probably what it was.

The Dutch historian Joshua Livestro notes a rise in youth churches in the Netherlands, from forty-five (with 10,000 members) in 2003 to eighty-eight (with 20,000 members) two years later. Church attendance for those under twenty rose from 9 to 14 percent between 2003 and 2004. Crucifixes have been reintroduced into Dutch Catholic schools. The immigration of unjaded Third World Christians is a major factor in this revival, Livestro thinks.

But Islam may play a role, too, if only indirectly. Elsewhere in Europe, proximity to Islam spurs religiosity among *non*-Muslims. In British neighborhoods with high Muslim populations, the sociologist Eric Kaufmann has found, the percentage of white Britons who call themselves "Christian" (rather than "no religion") is considerably higher than in similar, less mixed, neighborhoods, even after one reckons in income and other complicating factors. Whether they are deepening their Christian beliefs or simply professing a tribal allegiance to Team Christianity is hard to say.

Everywhere Islam has asserted itself in recent years, it has provoked reflection among Christians. In 2005, two years into the Iraq war, General Sir Richard Dannatt, the much-decorated head of the British general staff, unwittingly launched a nationwide discussion on faith. Dannatt warned that British military operations in Iraq, if not scaled back or rethought, would "break" the British army. Before the controversy over his remarks subsided, newspapers became interested in Dannatt for a very different reason. A devout Christian, he made clear that his misgivings about the conduct of the Iraq war did not mean he was indifferent to radical Islam. On the contrary. It was just that the dangers, as he saw them, were more spiritual than military, and they were more domestic than foreign: "When I see the Islamist threat," he said, "I hope it doesn't make undue progress, because there is a moral and spiritual vacuum in our country. Our society has always been embedded in Christian values; once you pull the anchor up there is a danger that our society moves with the prevailing wind." Something is going to fill Europe's spiritual void, General Dannatt believes, and that something could be Islam.

Benedict XVI: New ideas about belief and unbelief

Europeans sense that they have a big problem somewhere in the area of religious faith, but no one has been able to identify it with precision. Is the problem the decline of religion in general? The decline of the specific religion of Christianity? An excessive sentimentality or lack of courage in defending "Enlightenment values" *against* Christianity?

Western thinking on these questions has changed a great deal in the past decade, among both believers and nonbelievers. One of the most intellectually adventurous of the revisionists has been Pope Benedict XVI. Benedict's predecessor, John Paul II, looked at the essential cleavage in the world as being between religion and unbelief. Devout Christians, Muslims, and Buddhists had more in common with each other than with atheists. John Paul sought dialogue with leaders of other faiths, visited mosques, and apologized for the Crusades.

Benedict does not agree. He thinks that, within societies, believers and unbelievers exist in symbiosis. Secular westerners, he implies, have a lot in common with their religious fellows. It is not by accident that secular ideologies such as human rights and democratic socialism have flourished primarily in the Christian West—they have their roots in Christian ethics. Secular intellectuals should be in sympathy with the church, Benedict's thinking goes, even if they are not in communion with it. He notes, for instance, that in the times of Jesus, the Jewish Diaspora was filled with "God-fearers" who reported in varying degrees to the synagogue and who, in different ways, lived the spiritual treasure of the faith of Israel. Only a few of them wished to enter fully into the community of Israel, through circumcision, but for them it was a reference point that indicated the way to life.

So while he attempts to convince secular-minded people to join the flock, he is following another track, trying to convince them that they are, in a way, in it already. There is no *rational* requirement that we should care about human rights, for example; anyone who does so is taking Judaism and Christianity as "the reference points that indicate the way to life." That is why Benedict has devoted so much time to public dialogue with such prominent secular philosophers as the Italian Paolo Flores d'Arcais and the German Jürgen Habermas, who, though he continues to profess atheism, holds that "Christianity, and nothing else, is the ultimate foundation of liberty, conscience, human rights, and democracy, the benchmarks of Western civilization. To this day, we have no other options. We continue to nourish ourselves from this source. Everything else is postmodern chatter." Both Habermas and the pope are right about that. If we focus on what this acknowledgment means for the relationship of the church and Western unbelievers, the Benedict/Habermas position looks modern, tolerant, ecumenical and touchy-feely. But if we broaden our horizons to Christianity's encounters with other faiths, it looks harder-edged.

In November 2006, the Pope delivered a speech at his alma mater, the Bavarian Catholic university at Regensburg. Benedict cited a four-teenth-century dialogue in which the Byzantine emperor Manuel II Palaeologos inquired of a learned Persian what was new in Islam besides the commandment to spread faith by the sword. Manuel II's Christian argument against converting people through violence is this: "Not to act rationally is against the nature of God." Benedict endorsed this argument, noting that things are different in Islam, under which "God is absolutely transcendent. His will is not bound to any other category, not even to rationality." Whether or not this was fair to Islam (some Catholics would make similar objections to Calvinism), it sent Muslims in Europe and elsewhere into an uproar.

Morocco recalled its ambassador to the Vatican, six churches were burned in Palestine, and an Italian nun was shot dead in Somalia.

The Muslim backlash was an overreaction, but it was not an ignorant overreaction. The pope was saying, in essence, that *reasoning* people—modern people, enlightened people—had a natural home in Christianity. By implication, Christians can speak from a position of authority in Europe's rationally constructed secular order, even if that order has less room for God than most Christians would like. Whether Muslims have any role to play in secular Europe was left hanging. We know that Benedict has his doubts on the matter. Not only has he questioned publicly whether Islam can be accommodated in a pluralistic society. He also demoted one of John Paul II's leading advisers on the Islamic world and tempered his support for a program of interreligious dialogue run by Franciscan monks at Assisi.

Benedict, however, is not among those who see Islam's resurgence as a function simply of all the money Saudi princes and foundations are flinging around. For him, Islam's strength comes mainly from "people's conviction that Islam can provide a valid spiritual foundation to their lives." There is a grudging compliment in the Pope's fascination with Islam, and in the fact that he was reduced at Regensburg to arguing for his religion's superiority in the first place. An astute Muslim convert, Audalla Conget, a former Cistercian monk from Saragossa who had become secretary of the Islamic League in Spain, sent an open letter to the Pope in which he wrote:

You are criticizing us in order to hide your deep admiration for our faith, for our intense and persevering worship. An unshakeable faith that leads you to ask, without finding any convincing answer: Why are there so few Muslims who convert to Christianity? And why are there so many of us who, having been active Christians, have come to recognize in Islam our place in the universe? If one is a Christian, it is painful to look, every Friday, upon the mosques packed with men and women of all ages, with their foreheads pressed to the ground in the sincerest gesture of acceptance of the will of God.

Western sympathy with, and conversion to, Islam

Where does a spokesman for Islam get off condescending to the pope? The Islamic world is an economic and intellectual basket case, the part of the potentially civilized world most left behind by progress, as the annual Arab Human Development Reports published by the United Nations make plain, year after year. The Arab countries—which don't make up all of the Muslim world but do make up the heart of it—have 5 percent of the world's population but only 0.5 percent of its Internet users. Spain translates more foreign books in a year than all the Arabic-speaking countries have translated since the reign of Caliph Mamoun in the ninth century. Half of Arab youths polled want to emigrate from their countries. Outside of fossil fuels, the entire Arab world exports less than Finland does. Islam's prestige is low among non-Muslims. An Ifop (Institut français d'opinion publique) poll taken in France in late 2001 asked Muslims and non-Muslims to describe Islam in three words. The Muslims chose *justice, liberty,* and *democracy.* The native French chose *fanaticism, submission,* and *rejection of Western values.* So why do people like Conget want anything to do with Islam, let alone sing its praises unreservedly?

Islam may be quantifiably backward, but it is backward at a time when progress has acquired a bad name. To say that controversial Muslim figures "come straight out of the Middle Ages"—whether they be holy men like Yusuf Qaradawi, for instance, or terrorists like Osama bin Laden—does nothing to blunt their appeal. The Middle Ages is their selling point. One need not be a fundamentalist or a fanatic to worry that it is in the West's nature to advance too far, too fast. The Green and anti-globalist movements share such worries. So do an increasing number of thinkers and statesmen. "In some areas—decency, respect, loyalty, care for one's wife—Islam could actually have a positive influence on our culture," says the influential Dutch philosopher Andreas Kinneging. German interior minister Wolfgang Schäuble has been optimistic that Islam can revivify certain admirable traits that he considers quintessentially German, including "the importance of family; respect for elders; a confidence and pride at contemplating one's own history, culture, religion and traditions; and the daily living-out of one's faith."

One could extend Kinneging's and Schäuble's point. Western intellectuals, through their dug-in hostility to traditional metaphysical answers, have drowned out the most important metaphysical questions. And it should be hard for *anyone* to withhold a measure of gratitude to Islam for having made those questions audible again. This most recent encounter with Islam, however painful and violent, has been an infusion of oxygen into the drab, nitpicking, materialistic intellectual life of the West. It is a liberation to be able to talk about God once more, even if in someone else's language.

If Europeans need what Muslims are bringing—basically, more religion—then did Europeans take a wrong turn when they got rid of these traditions in the first place? If so, where was the wrong turn made? In the 1960s? In the 1760s? And if Europeans are beginning to feel the tug of religion again, why should we expect them to prefer a diffident, mocked, and un-chic faith like European Christianity over a dynamic, confident and streetwise one like European Islam? The answer is, we should not.

It is hard to get reliable statistics about how many Europeans are converting to Islam. The German Islam Archive recently estimated that Germans were converting at the rate of 4,000 a year, although those numbers have been questioned. Francesca Paci, a leading Italian journalist on Muslim matters, says there are roughly 50,000 Italian converts to Islam. These include two prominent diplomats —former ambassador to the UN Mario Scialoja and former ambassador to Saudi Arabia Torquato Cardilli—and Hamza Piccardo, a former leader in the left-wing labor group Autonomia Operaia who became head of the Muslim umbrella group Ucoii.

Whatever the appeal to Westerners of Muslim theology, many of the prominent converts get deeply involved in the politics of it. Yvonne Ridley, a British journalist who was kidnapped by the Taliban in Afghanistan in 2001, converted to Islam two years later. Within a few years she had become a prominent spokesman for the Respect Party, which grew out of British opposition to the Iraq war, and was calling on Muslims to stop cooperating with the police. Since politics is more newsworthy than prayer, published accounts of gung-ho converts are not necessarily representative. One hears less about converts who practice their faith in tranquility—even famous ones, such as the English-born musician Yusuf Islam (Cat Stevens)—than one does about converts for whom Islam is a route into politics.

There is a significant subset of converts for whom conversion is a route not just to politics but to radicalism, and even terrorism. The working-class Belgian Catholic Lionel Dumont, from a devout family of eight brothers and sisters, came to detest his Francophone fellow citizens, whom he called "spoiled children." He converted to Islam and fought in Bosnia, attended an extremist mosque in Roubaix, in northern France, and was jailed for a bloody series of terrorist shootouts with police near Lille in 1996. The story of Muriel Degauque, also a devout Belgian Catholic from a run-down coal-mining town, is even better known. She drifted into drugs and motor-cycles, and seems to have escaped that world thanks in part to Islam, to which she was introduced by a boyfriend. In December 2005, she blew herself up in the middle of an American military patrol in Baquba, Iraq, wounding one soldier. The most destructive of Western converts to Islam was Germaine Lindsay, a formidably brainy young man who was raised in Huddersfield of an evangelical Jamaican family, embraced Islam in his teens, and blew himself up on London's Piccadilly line in July 2005, murdering twenty-six others in the process. All three of these violent people seemed to have been seeking something that Christianity failed to provide them. Whether or not Dumont, Degauque, and Lindsay are representative, the zeal of the convert can be the explicit goal of conversion to Islam, not just an accidental by-product.

Perhaps Islam is a better match than Christianity with a society that has spent half a century dismantling its institutions in the interests of rendering life more direct and "real," less formal and "hypo-critical." "Sincerity, in all senses," wrote Thomas Carlyle a century and a half ago, "seems to me the merit of the Koran; what had rendered it precious to the wild Arab men." That Islam lacks the mediation of a hierarchical clergy makes it attractive to people who believe there is something phony about all authority and all official roles. That Islamic theology relies very little on miracles makes it attractive to the kind of people—modern people—who are impatient with the Christian style of revelation. As the French Catholic poly-math Alain Besançon has noted, Islam combines the appeals of natural and revealed religion. It is, in his sparkling formulation, *la religion naturelle du Dieu révélé*.

In London in May 1840, Carlyle gave a lecture on Muhammad, one passage of which led John Stuart Mill, who was present in the audience, to leap to his feet and angrily shout his disagreement. Carlyle argued that, unlike modern, utilitarian Europeans, Muhammad had grasped the deadly earnest of all that we do on earth, and had thus taught a lesson that men forget at their peril. This earnest, said Carlyle:

is the first of all truths. It is venerable under all embodiments. What is the chief end of man here below? Mahomet has answered this question, in a way that might put some of *us* to shame! He does not, like a Bentham, a Paley, take Right and Wrong, and calculate the profit and loss, ultimate pleasure of the one and of the other; and summing all up by addition and subtraction into a net result, ask you, Whether on the whole the Right does not preponderate considerably? . . . Benthamee Utility, virtue by Profit and Loss; reducing this God's-world to a dead brute Steam-engine, the infinite celestial Soul of Man to a kind of Hay-balance for weighting hay and thistles on, pleasures and pains on:—If you ask me which gives, Mahomet or they, the beggarlier and falser view of Man and his Destinies in this Universe, I will answer, It is not Mahomet!

The European model of managing religion

Western Europe's system of separation of church and state does not encourage pronouncements about which ideas of truth are better and which are, in Carlyle's words, "beggarlier." It deals with the place of religion in society rather than scrutinizing religious doctrines from the inside. This modesty has been a great strength. As long as battles about religion concerned bickering between Christian faiths, or the status of unbelievers in Christian communities, the system worked remarkably well. But it is inadequate to address Islam.

One sign of its inadequacy is that politicians are increasingly given to pronouncing on what is and is not Islam. Those who make such pronouncements are usually trying to exonerate Islam from the charge that it is a violent or intolerant religion, as George W. Bush famously did in the days after September 11, 2001, by pronouncing that "Islam is peace." One hears non-Arabic-speaking statesmen holding forth on what the Koran does and doesn't say about the duties of veiling. One reads about "poorly trained, mostly foreign imams" who incite young men to terrorism or "poorly educated judges" on sharia courts. The blame never falls on Islam itself but always on something aberrant, adventitious, exogenous, atypical, something imposed on it by an unrepresentative handful of nutcases, misinterpreters, Svengalis, and secret agents. The public is generally unconvinced. It asks what kind of religion requires expertise—even "training"—to keep it from being dangerous in the hands of its practitioners. Surely most Christian ministers in the United States are "poorly trained," and most new priests in Ireland (where only a handful a year are now ordained) are "foreign." But they don't scare people. And if they did, few would argue that their scariness had nothing to do with "real" Christianity.

Europe's system of religious pluralism varies in its specifics from country to country. Some countries, such as Denmark and Britain, have state churches, but these are vestigial and largely ceremonial— state religions have no precedence over others. Germany levies a church tax and uses religious organizations as a means of distributing health and other social services. Ireland mentions the Holy Trinity in its constitution. France's system, known as *laïcité*, is the most highly elaborated. It strictly separates religion from politics and assumes that religious communities will appoint representatives as interlocutors with the government. But the basic outlines of all these regimes, and the rock-bottom freedoms they guarantee, are the same. They constitute a single system, which we can call European secularism.

The *history* of secularism is at odds with the *theory* of secularism, at least as that theory is put forward today. All European regimes for regulating religion were designed to constrain not religion in the abstract but Christianity in particular. In European secularism, there is always a tacit balance between Christianity and Enlightenment skepticism, and sometimes the balance is explicit. In the Netherlands, so-called "Article 23" schools—which permit religious communities to establish their own schools—have become controversial since mass immigration began. In theory, they allow Muslims to teach things that Dutch people find repugnant, starting with the inequality of the sexes. But such schools cannot simply be abolished. They are seen as the quid pro quo offered a century ago to the strong Dutch Reformed community, in return for its renouncing demands for a wider Christianization of Dutch culture. The traditional Roman Catholic "hour of religion" in Italian public schools was an explicit concession made to the Catholic Church at the time of Italy's unification.

Even where concessions to religion were not enshrined specifically in a constitution, the religious character of society was assumed. All European cultures depend for their stability on certain ethical survivals of Christianity, and would have a difficult time defending their "values" without them. Shortly after the murder of Theo van Gogh, the Dutch novelist Leon de Winter lamented the way the "counterbalancing forces" on which his country's tolerance rests were undermined by the pressures of mass immigration. "Under the effusive 'anything goes' exterior, the majority of Dutch people held on to their disciplined Calvinist values," de Winter wrote. "In the longer term, we must somehow stimulate young Muslims to identify with the Calvinist values of the majority."

But as Benedict XVI would predict, there is no obvious way to turn Muslims into Calvinists, even in the absence of what de Winter calls an anything-goes culture. Calvin was not a mere ethicist or a purveyor of "leadership secrets"—he was a religious leader. Calvinist values are not freestanding. They arise from a certain interpretation of Christian doctrine and from centuries of living it out. One is reminded of an observation of the philosopher Rémi Brague. "Faith produces its effects only so long as it remains faith and not calculation," Brague wrote in the 1990s. "We owe European civilization to people who believed in Christ, not to people who believed in Christianity."

European secularism is a system set up with Christians in mind. The conflicts that arise out of Muslim communities are not identical to the ones that used to arise out of Christian communities and still arise out of post-Christian ones. In recent decades, the key issues in relations between Christianity and the state have tended to involve education and sexuality. They come up in conflicts between Islam and the state too, of course, but there are also conflicts over dress, interpersonal relations and foreign policy. These are trickier and no consensus exists yet on how to answer them. Does a woman have the right, on religious grounds, to refuse treatment from a male doctor when making use of the national health service? (*No* is the French verdict.) Can a police officer wear a turban? (*Yes* is the English decision.) Is it all right for a citizen to declare his support for the enemy in wartime? (Effectively, *yes*, given the privileged position the British Muslim Council of Bradford retained as an interlocutor with government, even after it voted unanimously to back Iraq in the first Gulf War in 1991.)

There has been a deep change since the Second World War in people's idea of what "tolerance" means in the first place. Under several influences—war guilt, modern ideas of human rights, globalized media, and non-governmental organizations—leaders came to see secularism not as a way of managing relations between religious communities but of transforming religion's role from a public into a private one. Traditions are no longer presumed to be right just because they are traditions.

Take the annual *Moros y cristianos* festivals held to celebrate the expulsion of Islam from Spain in roughly 400 communities across Valencia, Alicante, Murcia, and Albacete. The climax of these events often involves taking a big wooden effigy called a "Muhammad" and either pushing it off a tower or blowing up its head with firecrackers. Until a decade ago, these gatherings were big tourist draws, but they have come under fire from left-wing and Muslim groups, not to mention the post–Vatican II Catholic Church, partly for their exclusion of women and partly for their triumphalism. The fact that such processions have been celebrated in largely the same way for centuries (the one in Lleida dates from AD 1150) is not considered a convincing argument for their preservation. Almost all of them have been radically reformed over the past decade.

Arguments over the privileged place of Western religious tradition grew heated in the half decade of negotiations over the drafting of the European Union's constitutional treaty after 2000. The main division concerned whether to include in the document a mention of God, or of Europe's Christian heritage. One argument *for* such a mention was that, as we have discussed, the very values the EU meant to enshrine—democracy, individualism, freedom of conscience, and speech—arose out of Christianity. But only three countries made this argument: Ireland, Italy, and Poland. Nobody else bought it. All the other countries argued, instead, that invocations of God are judgmental and exclusionary. A scent of the old, pre-EU culture of nationalism lingers about them. Talking about God risked alienating the Islamic cultures that are the EU's neighbors and the homelands of many of its citizens.

The God-in-the-constitution forces countered that Europe's secularists were taking two very different words—*secular* and *atheistic*—and mistaking them for synonyms. And they have a point. In 2004, Rocco Buttiglione, a devout and scholarly Catholic nominated as European minister of justice was rejected, not for his political stances—he promised to uphold the European constitution—but for answers he gave when interrogated on his *personal* views of Catholic religious doctrine.

As the Islamologist Olivier Roy put it, "We need to make clear what the problem is for our *laïcité*—is it such-and-such a religion, or is it *all* religion?" Europeans have given no clear answer. On one hand, there is historical secularism, which reins in Christianity while taking it as a sociological given. On the other there is ideological secularism, which aims to break every link between religion and public life, shepherding people out of religion altogether. If Europeans were confused by this, imagine how Muslim immigrants and their children and grandchildren felt. Which version of secularism were they supposed to respect?

Organizing religious bodies

When Islam became Europe's main religious problem, almost nobody dared to say so. Instead, across Europe, policies were designed to trammel Islam while pretending to trammel all religions indifferently. The classic example of this was the so-called Stasi Commission set up by French president Jacques Chirac in 2003 to address a growing tendency of young Muslim students to attend school veiled, a practice that had provoked national outrage for fourteen years. The Stasi Commission made believe it was addressing general threats to *laïcité*, rather than a specific symbol of Islam on the rise. In the interest of this pretend neutrality, it also banned yarmulkes and "large crosses" (whatever they are) from public schools. Following the same tactic, it proposed creating a new national holiday of Eid al-Adha, and balancing that off by making Yom Kippur a holiday, too. (This recommendation was rejected.)

While disingenuous on an intellectual level, this approach was an undreamt-of success on a political level. The veil was eliminated from schools with a minimum of protest. Since then, other countries have taken up this system of conferring and revoking religious rights according to a "neutral" system of trade-offs. In Italy and certain German states where the veil controversy has also raged, the "price" for getting veils out of public schools has been the removal of crosses from classroom walls where they have hung for centuries.

Governments hewed to this phony neutrality even in matters of public safety. Weeks after the July 7 transport bombings in London, Tony Blair outlined an anti-terrorism legislative packet that aimed at balancing two things: a harder line on terrorism and a respect for constitutional freedoms. Both were admirable goals, but constitutional freedoms were deemed to be infringed by *anything* that had a disproportionate effect on Muslims. Closing radical mosques, for instance, a centerpiece of the plan, was quickly dropped as unworkable. No doubt it could have been arranged if the government had been able to find a few churches radical enough to close, too.

In the interest of negotiating neutral principles like these, European governments have begun to organize Muslims into official bodies. One of the achievements Nicolas Sarkozy bragged about most in his campaign for president of France in 2007 is that, as interior minister, he had succeeded, where a handful of his predecessors had failed, in establishing the French Council of the Muslim Faith (CFCM), which organizes the country's Muslims as a religious minority. The CFCM provides a channel through which the state can discuss with Muslims how best to regulate community matters—getting non-pork dishes into school cafeterias, arranging for Muslim burials in municipal cemeteries, and mediating between the (generally ethnic) communities that need mosques and the (generally European) neighborhoods that object wherever they are proposed. Catholic and Jewish organizations operate this way, although the best analogy is to France's "confederation" of varied Protestant churches.

But the Muslim body has become much more important than its Catholic, Protestant, or Jewish equivalents. One difference is that the matters within the CFCM's remit are more contentious, and less easily limited to purely religious matters. At times of ethnic violence, the government, in desperate need of interlocutors, has encouraged the CFCM and other Muslim leaders whose function is supposed to be strictly spiritual to take on an explicitly political role. During the French banlieue riots, the Socialist mayor of Nantes, Jean-Marc Ayrault, complained that Sarkozy had "promoted religious organizations to a role as mediators in the daily life of the housing projects."

The CFCM has also become a more strident organization than anticipated. Sarkozy managed to get his Council set up only by giving a leading role to the radical Union of Islamic Organizations of France (UOIF), heavily influenced by the Muslim Brotherhood. Roughly half the country's Muslims polled considered the CFCM's original leader, Dalil Boubakeur, rector of the grand mosque of Paris, an "Uncle Tom" (French Muslims actually use this term), and pledged their loyalty only to the UOIF. The UOIF's fortunes have waxed and waned, but it has at times commanded twelve of the twenty-five regional councils that control the arcane bureaucracy of the CFCM. Italy's fledgling Consulta Islamica was organized on the same basis. It, too, has faced the problem, common to all political structures, that the best organized groups tend to be neither the most representative nor the most moderate.

This is the problem, more generally, with organizing Muslims into any state-sponsored regime of religious freedom. Christianity's role in the modern national life of Western countries was determined by the whole of society in an anticlerical era. Islam's role is being determined by Muslims in a multicultural era—and, indeed, by the subset of Muslims devout enough, or politicized enough, to join Muslim organizations in the first place.

Freedom of religion = Freedom of Islam

Universalistic secularism is grandiose in its conception, but in execution it has turned out to have no more authority than its traditional adversary, crusading Christianity. As a means of regulating Islam it has been inadequate. Rules designed for unworldly churches work less well when applied to organizations with the kind of worldly dynamism Islam has: networks, foreign financial backers in Saudi Arabia and elsewhere, a political agenda, a clear sense of who its friends and enemies are, and a willingness to play hardball with dissidents inside the faith and skeptics outside it. This dynamism leads to what the New York University legal philosopher Thomas Nagel calls the "unequal impact of formally neutral laws." Since atheists, agnostics, and Christians don't *use* freedom of religion in Europe nowadays, freedom of religion comes to mean freedom of Islam.

That the course of Western history will be imitated, or at least submitted to, by everyone else is an article of faith for a lot of Western liberals. It can be a pathetic spectacle to watch them waiting around for Islam to "modernize"—or to become less all-consuming in the lives of its practitioners—in the way that Christianity did from the sixteenth century on. They make a fundamental mistake. We tend to learn about the Reformation and the Enlightenment as episodes in intellectual history, so we think of European secularism as having been a matter of soul searching. It was, in part—but Europe's religious authorities were also *forced* to change by the hostility, often the armed hostility, of their adversaries. One of the reasons Europeans are waiting for Islam to crumble from within is that their regime of tolerance has erected a wall around Islam that protects it from all the external pressures that beset Christianity between the sixteenth and nineteenth centuries.

A main weapon in the eighteenth-century Enlightenment's attacks on Christianity was ridicule. But while hoping that Muslims will learn the lessons of Voltaire, Europeans have gone to great lengths to insulate Islam from Voltaire's methods. Ridiculing Islam has been confused with xenophobia and racism. Those with questions about Islam are expected to content themselves with kicking the dead horse of Christianity in hopes that Muslims will, by inductive reasoning, come to see that the general laws so established apply to their religion, too. The spate of book-length tracts against "religion" in general, by Richard Dawkins, Michael Onfray, Christopher Hitchens, and others, surely owe a lot of their popularity to a timid public's unease at expressing misgivings about Islam specifically.

The reasonableness of Christianity was attacked over the centuries, and continues to be attacked, with utter ruthlessness. No socially acceptable way has yet emerged for attacking the reasonableness of Islam in any way at all. In fact, Islam increasingly receives legal protection against criticism. In January 2009, the politician Geert Wilders was indicted by a Dutch court on charges of incitement to violence for *Fitna*, a film in which he called the Koran a violent book and likened it to *Mein Kampf*. The following month, the British home secretary denied Wilders permission to enter the country although he had been invited to give a showing of *Fitna* in the House of Lords. Wilders's criticism was clumsy and off-target, but it was a protest against violence, not an incitement to it.

In 2006, the Blair government brought to a vote a long-planned "law against incitement to religious hatred." Formally, the new law protects people of all religions, but it was urged only by Muslims, starting with the U.K. Action Committee on Islamic Affairs, a group formed in 1989 to protest Salman Rushdie's portrayal of the prophet Muhammad in *The Satanic Verses*. When such protests were brought to the attention of the Ayatollah Khomeini, he issued a fatwa calling for the murder of Rushdie. That fatwa has never been revoked and was even renewed by the Iranian legislature, the Majlis, on its twentieth anniversary in 2009. One Labour MP, Khalid Mahmood of Birmingham, supported the law against religious hatred on the grounds that, had it existed back in the 1980s, it would have allowed authorities to "edit" Rushdie. No other faith in modern times has ever demanded anything remotely similar of the British government. The real goal of the law was to protect Islam's tenets from public criticism. The law's proponents—prominent among them the sometime British home secretary David Blunkett—often admitted as much. Anglicans, as worshippers in an established church, were already protected from certain insults under law, they said, while Jews and Sikhs were protected from others by antiracism laws. Muslims had no such protections.

But this is a dangerous analogy. Protecting people from criticism of features they cannot control—skin color, sex, ethnicity—is different than protecting them from criticism of their beliefs. And the law against incitement to religious hatred was unprecedented in its scope. As drafted, it would have made it difficult to criticize anything that advanced itself in the name of religious belief or practice, since the law permitted prosecution of anybody who was "reckless as to whether religious hatred would be stirred up" by things he said or wrote. On the insistence of the House of Lords, and over the objections of the government, language was included that would specifically protect "discussion, criticism or expressions of antipathy, dislike, ridicule, insult or abuse of particular religions or the beliefs or practices of their adherents." So the legislation, which went into effect in 2007, wound up something less than a postmodern blasphemy law.

There is, however, already a de facto blasphemy law benefiting Muslims. It arises from the proven willingness of religious fanatics—whether in Western societies or in the governments of Muslim countries—to commit violence against anyone, even private citizens in the West, who addresses Islam in a way they do not approve of. The threats start with the fatwa against Salman Rushdie and run through the murder of Rushdie's Japanese translator and his Norwegian editor, the murder of Theo van Gogh in the Netherlands in 2004, the standing death threats posted on the Internet against the Dutch politician Wilders, the violent demonstrations in the wake of the Danish cartoon crisis, and the list goes on and on. The climate of fear is made evident in less spectacular ways. All translators of the work of Somali-Dutch feminist Ayaan Hirsi Ali have insisted on anonymity. The French schoolteacher Robert Redeker received a death threat that sent him into hiding in 2006 after he wrote an op-ed in *Le Figaro* that described Mohammad as a "master of hate." There is clearly a kind of standing fatwa against Islam's harshest and most pointed critics. It is sufficient to render discussion of Islam, as a practical matter, less than free at every level of society.

Geert Mak, in seeking the causes of terrorism, has explained that "humiliation, whether on a national or an individual level, appears to be one of the greatest risk factors" for terrorism. True enough! But since humiliation is in the eye of the sufferer, since no two religious fanatics are alike, and since some of them are hypersensitive to the point of paranoia, no citizen knows precisely *what* he can say about Islam. If you translate Mak's observation into a rule for behavior, it would be that to write about Muslims in any way is to court retribution. Who can tell where the line will be drawn? Could one say of the Muslim household the things that Betty Friedan said of the American suburban household in *The Feminine Mystique*? Certainly not without fear of reprisal. In the autumn of 2008, the London home of publisher Martin Rynja was firebombed after he announced he would publish a novel that concerned a wife of the prophet Muhammad.

Since society has plenty of other problems that need talking about, writers, artists, and political commentators can still feel they are doing their job even if they don't touch the topic of Islam. In Europe, this tendency to shy away from Muslim topics is most glaring among those "subversive" and "transgressive" artists hailed for assailing bourgeois norms and flouting political correctness. The management of the Deutsche Oper considered it not worth the risk to stage a performance of *Idomeneo* that included a scene in which the decapitated heads of Jesus, Muhammad, and the Buddha appeared. Presumably it was not Jesus's head that made them lose their nerve. Grayson Perry, a cross-dressing pottery maker from England whose works mocked Western religious beliefs (one showed the Virgin Mary being born out of a penis) made a point of never mocking Islam, and was forthright enough to say why. "The reason I haven't gone all out attacking Islamism in my art," he explained, "is because I feel real fear that someone will slit my throat."

The Danish cartoon crisis

When anti-religious artists like Grayson Perry criticize seven-eighths of all religion, making an exception for Islam, they are not producing art that is seven-eighths free or seven-eighths countercultural. They are producing art that is objectively Islamist. That they do this out of fear rather than conviction does not change the nature of the art. That, and not cowardice or lack of imagination, is why "transgression" and "subversion" of the modern sort have never been a preoccupation of most serious artists. There is too much chance that servility and conformism will enter through the side door. When Flemming Rose, the combative cultural editor of the Danish daily *Jyllands-Posten*, decided to use a publicity stunt to expose this truth, the result was explosive.

A Danish writer of children's books had announced he could find no artists willing to illustrate his biography of the prophet Muhammad—for the usual reasons. The biography was to be a friendly one, written in the spirit of multiculturalism. But Islam disfavors images of Muhammad, and the artists feared violence. In hopes of clearing the air of self-censorship, Rose commissioned a dozen cartoons of Muhammad from as many cartoonists. They were published in September 2005. Some were mere doodles with gags. Others (including one of a generic Arab with a bomb in his turban) were insulting. They caused resentment in Denmark and outrage in Pakistan, where the radical Jamaat-i-Islami party put a price on the head of (oddly enough) the biographer. The reaction was lamentable, but probably containable.

Over the ensuing weeks, though, two imams living in Denmark sent emissaries to the Middle East to show the cartoons to a variety of influential hotheads. Bizarrely, the Danish imams added *pornographic* anti-Muslim drawings that had never been published in *Jyllands-Posten* or any other paper. In the last days of January, a Saudi preacher with an international following broadcast a sermon on the subject.

The Muslim world flew into an anti-Danish rage. Syria, Kuwait, Saudi Arabia, and Libya withdrew their ambassadors from Copenhagen. *Jyllands-Posten* was evacuated twice for bomb threats. The Danish embassy was attacked in Jakarta. In Gaza, Palestinian terrorists threatened visitors from Denmark, France, and Norway (where the cartoons had been reprinted) as well as Swedes, for whatever reason. Gunmen took over a European Union office in Gaza and a German couple was kidnapped. The Catholic priest Andrea Santoro was shot dead in the Turkish city of Trabzon. Fifteen people were killed in Benghazi a few weeks later, when Libyan troops opened fire on a crowd protesting reports than an Italian minister had worn a T-shirt with the caricatures on it.

Boycotts were launched across the Muslim world against Danish companies such as Lego, Bang & Olufsen, and Arla Foods—which announced it was losing $2.4 million a day. The reaction of the European business world was abject and sycophantic. The French retailer Carrefour posted signs in its stores reading: "We express solidarity with the Islamic and Egyptian community"—and then, in red letters: "Carrefour doesn't carry Danish products."

The most alarming aspect of the affair was that Muslims in Europe tended to side with protesters abroad, rather than with their fellow citizens. There were amazing scenes in Westminster, where young radicals marched with signs reading, "Behead Those Who Insult Islam," "Massacre Those Who Insult Islam," and "Europe, You'll Come Crawling When Mujahideen Come Roaring." Death threats pursued all of the participants in the cartoon crisis for years. In February 2008, two Tunisians and a naturalized Dane were arrested in Aarhus, where *Jyllands-Posten* is headquartered, for plotting to murder seventy-three-year-old Kurt Westergaard, who had drawn one of the cartoons.

European Muslim sympathy for the anti-cartoon protests was not limited to a fringe of violent, radical, or unhinged individuals. It was deep. Asked whether the controversy was over Muslim intolerance or Western disrespect, Western Europeans choose the former, by a multiple (67–28 in France, 59–19 in Britain). But Western Muslims blame "disrespect" for the prophet by margins that are little different than those in the Muslim world: 79–19 in France, 73–9 in Britain, 80–5 in Spain. "*Jyllands-Posten* didn't create any new realities with the cartoons," Rose would later say. "The cartoons only brought attention to a reality that already existed." The reality was an abyss of mutual incomprehension between European Muslims and non-Muslims that might remind Americans of the racial divide over the O.J. Simpson trial.

This gap was not easily bridgeable. There were no overt Muslim "demands." No demonstrator anywhere in the world objected to any demeaning "message" in the cartoons. They objected to the sacrilege of depicting Muhammad at all. So the protests were not a demand for respect or fair treatment or a rightful place for Islam among the cultures of the world. They were something new: a warning that non-Muslims, wherever they may be, cross Muslim religious taboos at their peril. The idea, widespread in Europe up to that point, that you can fully respect both free speech and the dignity of religion turned out to be an optical illusion. The two had seemed compatible only because no one in Europe had seen fit to press the case for the dignity of religion in any urgent way for about half a century. Once Muslim immigrants arrived and did so, the easy coexistence of religious and expressive freedoms was a thing of the past. A choice was now necessary.

Most journalists and politicians tried to pretend that the terms of debate had not been altered by the rise of activist Islam in Europe. Wrapping the episode into Europe's historic duty to fight anti-Semitism, and dealing with Muslims as analogous to European Jews before World War II, was one rhetorical strategy. "The issue at stake here is not 'self-censorship,'" Edgar Bronfman of the World Jewish Congress wrote in the *Times*. "It is whether respect for other religious beliefs, traditions and practices really applies to everybody, including Muslims." Bill Clinton, the former U.S. president, also likened the cartoons to historical anti-Semitism.

Another approach was to take the obsession with "neutrality" in all matters of government religious policy and impose it on individual citizens as a requirement in their private utterances. It would henceforth be okay to attack "religion" in the abstract (a rather meaningless right) but not Islam in particular. "This all would have been very well," the Danish social scientist Jytte Klausen wrote of the cartoon crisis, "if the paper had a long tradition of standing up for fearless artistic expression. But it so happens that three years ago, *Jyllands-Posten* refused to publish cartoons portraying Jesus, on the grounds that they would offend readers." The French satirical newspaper *Charlie Hébdo* was put on trial for defamation after it reprinted the cartoons. Its lawyer sought to defend it on the grounds that "*Charlie* has [also] been very tough on the Catholic religion."

Putting criticism of Islam on the same level as anti-Semitism and demanding intellectual "neutrality" as a precondition for participating in debate were both ways of saying that Europe needed more respect for religion and less for a no-holds-barred "right to offend." Had it been stated forthrightly—and outside the context of violent intimidation—this would have been a defensible position. But it was not stated forthrightly. It was an attempt to disguise a submission as a concession.

Rose engaged in no such beating around the bush. Unlike most political/journalistic provocateurs, he was a well-traveled and cultured man, an anti-Communist who had been a correspondent in Moscow, spoke Russian like a native, and knew the historical boundaries of free-speech debates. Those who attacked his paper reminded him, he said shortly before the riots began, of the ideology department of the Soviet Central Committee. Soviet censors often claimed to be open to any speech that could show itself to be part of a legitimate public debate—and then defined legitimate public debate with extreme narrowness. "Law professors say there has to be an intention to what you're doing," Rose said, and paused before adding, "*No, there doesn't.*" Rose's point was that freedom of speech does not mean just freedom of speech-the-authorities-deem-reasonable. All governments—the worst twentieth-century totalitarianisms decidedly included—have *that* kind of freedom of speech. The price for managing Islam would be paid in rights.

8

Rules for Sex

Sexual freedom as a non-negotiable European demand—
Virginity and violence—Islam or custom?—The appeal of
sharia—Arranged marriages—The Danish marriage law—
Controversies over the headscarf—The French veil law—
Compulsory liberation

Muslims in Europe arrive from (or are reared by parents from) cultures where women are strictly subordinated to their husbands and, more generally, to men. Sometimes this subordination is justified religiously, sometimes not, but in the Muslim world it is a near-universal sociological fact. Newcomers to Europe land in a society intent on proclaiming the equality of the sexes. That is a shock. To many Muslim males it is also a fraud. They claim that European society actually oppresses *them*, and they have a point. European bosses and bouncers, teachers and police, are petrified of Muslim men, whom they associate with delinquency, crime, and bad school grades. Women find it easier to enter the corporate world, hang around in public spaces, and gain admission to nightclubs. Educational discrepancies are big and growing. In the Netherlands, there are slightly more native women than men studying law; among non-Western immigrants and their offspring, however, women outnumber men in law schools almost two to one. Marriages in which the wife works as executive secretary to the owner of a law firm or assistant to a top surgeon, while the husband drives a cab or collects unemployment, are not uncommon.

Sexual freedom as a non-negotiable European demand

Most European leaders, like most American leaders, proclaim that the sexes are equal and identical. But there is a difference. The United States is considerably more tolerant of women who choose not to work, or who want to live in domestic arrangements of the kind that were commonplace fifty years ago. In much of Europe, certainly in the minds of the northern European ruling class, such wiggle room is associated with backsliding and cultural surrender. The occupation of housewife exists neither as an aspiration nor even as an intellectual category. In Sweden in 2005, the feminist essayist Nina Björk sparked a national debate when she had the temerity to suggest, in an op-ed in the national newspaper *Dagens Nyheter*, that children might be better off being raised by their own parents than in state-subsidized, one-size-fits-all child care. The Dutch film that instructs immigrant would-be citizens on their responsibilities insists that: "In the Netherlands, the aim is that everyone works, both men and women, so each has his or her income. This applies to women with children, too." The two-income household is not an option, as it would be the United States—it is an *aim*.

Adapting to European styles of sexuality and gender relations is the only non-negotiable demand that Europe makes of its immigrants. So tightly are ideas about feminism bound to assimilation that Sweden has a cabinet member (Burundi-born Nyamko Sabuni, at the time of this writing) who serves as "minister of integration and gender equality," as if those two briefs were just different names for the same thing. Europeans may be reluctant to proclaim any preference for their own high culture and cuisine over foreign ones, eager to give way on freedom of speech when it hurts Muslim sensibilities, and willing to tar as extremist or fascist anyone who holds that Islam poses an especial danger of terrorism. Sex is different. It is the litmus test according to which assimilation—and even membership in the national community—is judged. It is the one area where Europeans retain both a deep suspicion of Muslim ways and a confidence in their own institutions that is free of self-doubt.

What is more, the suspicion falls directly and uneuphemistically on Islam the religion, and not any epiphenomenon, such as "poverty" or "segregation" or "tradition." In Great Britain—the European country where the attitudes of Muslims and non-Muslims towards women are closest—60 percent of natives consider Muslims "disrespectful" to women. The mistrust is mutual in all countries. If you ask Spanish non-Muslims whether Muslims are "respectful of women," they reply "no," by 83 percent to 12. If you ask Spanish Muslims whether non-Muslims respect women, they reply "no," by nearly identical measures (82 percent to 13). Of the traditionalist Muslim view that women who wear revealing clothing are inviting sexual aggression, the Egyptian-Dutch feminist Nahed Selim writes: "A great number of Dutch Muslims are probably in full agreement with this sentiment, even if, for understandable reasons, they would never say so in public."

The collision of feminism and Muslim immigration creates a man problem. To many Muslim men, it is not obvious that the Western system of rights for women is superior on its merits. Humiliated by a reversal of the traditional economic relations between men and women, panicked to see their women free of their control in a rich and hedonistic society, they are liable to look nostalgically on the traditions of the old country, where sexual conduct is more closely monitored by communities. This does not go just for immigrant men but for their European-born sons, who may blame Western feminism for the low status, the gelding, of their fathers. Men take refuge in spaces that they can control: housing projects, social clubs, and especially mosques. Mosques are male institutions in most places in the world, just as churches tend to be female ones. Among Algerians in France, for instance, about 15 percent of men attend services, versus 6 percent of women. As Muslim institutions proliferate—however moderate or public spirited they may be—an alternative model of gender relations proliferates with them.

Virginity and violence

Alongside each culture's rhetoric of women's rights is an idea that the rival culture's values are a threat to young women's virtue. For many immigrants, virtue takes the traditional form of chastity; for many Westerners, it takes the newer form of sexual autonomy. The two are often incompatible. "Female circumcision" (mutilation or removal of the clitoris in childhood) and infibulation (stitching the vagina shut) are customs common in East African Muslim countries such as Somalia, Sudan, and, to a lesser extent, Egypt. Although the practices are generally justified with reference to Muslim ideas of purity, most scholars don't believe there is anything specific to the Koran or sharia that requires them. Certainly genital mutilation is rare in most of the Muslim world.

Whatever their justification in their countries of origin, they can have no place in a sexual culture built on autonomy. You might assume that one of those models—either the chastity model or the autonomy model—would have to go. Not necessarily. European history is full of instances where public sexual mores coexist with very different private ones. A study by Amsterdam's Free University found that among some East African immigrant groups, genital mutilation is widespread—although it is usually carried out on visits to the old country, in order to avoid criminal prosecution. Such practices are defended ferociously. The Antwerp senator Mimount Bousakla has received threats of violence for her own attempts to stamp out genital mutilation in Belgium.

The course of the genital-mutilation controversy in Sweden shows that integrating big populations from markedly different cultures can mean trading rights to get social peace. Nyamko Sabuni, understandably alarmed over reports of genital mutilation, called for nationally supervised gynecological inspections of little girls. It was rejected by Muslims and non-Muslims alike as an invasion of privacy. Which, of course, it was. One can applaud the seriousness with which she takes the problem, but one must also recognize the damage that her approach does to the country's constitutional order. Fifty years ago, if a politician had suggested that parents be required to subject their young daughters to an intimate, government-monitored strip search, the public would have reeled in horror. Today, the emergency of genital mutilation makes such practices seem defensible, if not yet feasible.

Middle Eastern mores, stringently applied, are incompatible with Western ones, whether Christian or secular. But they are famously compatible with Western science and technology. Strategically, this mix has given us the hybrid ideology of Islamist terrorism. Economically, it has given us the shopping mall culture of the Gulf states. Culturally, it has turned many of Europe's housing projects into jazzed-up, Internet-savvy versions of traditional Muslim villages, where a girl's virginity is her most prized asset. Muslim parents sometimes request "certifications of virginity" from their daughters' gynecologists. In Holland, repair of broken hymens was often covered by national insurance until the ministry of health blocked it in May 2004. A small scandal erupted in Britain in 2007 upon the discovery that the National Health Service had paid for dozens of "hymen replacement operations" over the previous two years. Britain's *Daily Mail* interviewed one doctor who specialized in such operations, including pre-wedding ones in which "a membrane is constructed, sometimes including a capsule of an artificial blood-like substance." This hybrid culture, this technologically advanced Puritanism, really is something alternative and new. It is in the most literal sense an advance for "diversity," although you are unlikely to hear it extolled as such.

There is a lot to be said for placing a high value on chastity and virginity. It can further dignity, responsibility, and self-respect. What is outrageous about surgeries meant to "restore" virginity is not that they are prudish. It is that they are unpleasant, hypocritical, and sometimes paid for with public funds. Beyond that, provided they are freely elected, it is hard to say why they should offend us more than a vasectomy does. Or more than the various lifts, grafts, tucks, and piercings that Westerners undergo in order to live up to their own society's reasonable or unreasonable sexual expectations, or (what amounts to the same thing) to fend off their own reasonable or unreasonable self-loathing.

Still, you don't have to be a feminist or a libertine to understand that, on an anthropological level, an obsession with virginity can do something less pleasant. The most frequent criticism is that, human drives being what they are, it is hard in practice for people to remain celibate until marriage and that, when the flesh is weak, it is women, not men, who are held culpable. But in a sexist subculture, that is only one of a woman's worries. Male-dominated societies lay down codes of virginity not *although* they are hard to live up to but *because* they are hard to live up to. Such codes create a category of "sluts"— women who can be used sexually with a clear conscience because they have trespassed society's laws and thereby forfeited society's respect. And where families, police, and other social institutions are weak, what results is a sexual reign of terror.

Samira Bellil, an Algerian-born resident of the really tough Paris suburb of Seine-St-Denis, spent her short life (she died of cancer in 2004) bringing to public attention the practice of *tournantes*, or gang rapes, carried out in a number of French housing projects. Bellil had been raped several times, starting at the age of fourteen, by gangs led by a single particularly enterprising local youth. When several of Bellil's friends told her that he had victimized them, too, she made the decision to go to the police and press charges against him. At that point, her parents disowned her.

The vaguer and the more arbitrary the sexual code being enforced, the better it suits predatory men. In 2002, Sohane Benziane, a young Berber woman living near Paris, was taken by a gang to an abandoned basement where a local *caïd* (or gang leader) named Jamal Derrar, who had hoped to have sex with her but wasn't having much luck, poured gasoline on her and burned her alive. Derrar, who described Benziane as his "fiancée," convinced himself that she had embarrassed the community through some breach of propriety that existed mostly in his own head. This was the episode that led the Algerian-French anti-racist activist Fadela Amara (later France's secretary of state for urban affairs) to found the grassroots organization Ni Putes Ni Soumises ("Neither whores nor submissives").

So-called "honor killings," the most serious form of sexual intimidation, are concentrated in Kurdish and, to a lesser extent, Pakistani communities. Brothers murder their sisters (or fathers their daughters) for some trespass against sexual propriety—usually either wearing

Western clothing or dating Western men. There were forty-five such murders in Germany alone in the first half of the decade, according to a 2005 study by the Federal Criminal Investigation Agency. In Berlin, Hatun Sürücü "dishonored" her family by dating a German and raising a child on her own. Her spectacular killing by several of her brothers in broad daylight in early 2005 was one of a half-dozen honor killings that year in Berlin alone.

Fadime Sahindal, a Kurdish immigrant to Sweden, created a national outrage when she spoke in the Riksdag in 2001 about how she had been stalked across the country by her father and brothers when it was discovered she had fallen in love with a Swedish boy:

All of a sudden, I had been transformed from a nice Kurdish girl into a slut. I decided to break with my family and move to Sundsvall. My brother found me and threatened me. The situation got worse and worse. The reason that my brother came was that he was a minor and wouldn't be punished as severely by the law.

Using minors for enforcement is a common pattern in honor-related violence, including Hatun Sürücü's murder. Kurdish families may be too confused by Western culture to grant their women autonomy, Sahindal implied, but they are quite savvy enough to understand that Western penal codes give juveniles virtual impunity even for crimes as serious as attempted murder. A restraining order was placed on Sahindal's father. But eight weeks later he ambushed her on a visit to her mother in Uppsala and shot her dead.

Islam or custom?

In sharp contrast to, say, urban rioting or anti-American or anti-Israeli demonstrations, Muslim violence against women elicits no calls for an "understanding" of the circumstances that give rise to it. Roger Cohen, a sensitive and nuanced writer about European immigration, writes of honor killings: "An authentic culture is one thing, trampling on fundamental human rights like the equality of men and women quite another." That Kurdish culture can be violent and sexist does not make it inauthentic. Nor is the equality of men and women "fundamental"—in fact, in a global perspective, it is rather peculiar. It is the attainment of one strand of Western social thought that begins in the nineteenth century.

It takes very few acts of violence to threaten that attainment for an entire community of Muslim women. It will be many years before the murder of Fadime Sahindal is not in the back of the mind of a lot of Kurdish women in Sweden. Acts such as the burning of Sohane Benziane do more than terrorize and kill. Such acts *make law*. They assert sovereignty over a certain part of European territory for a different sexual regime. What is the nature of that regime? Is it, in fact, Islam that is being promulgated when women are shot, burned, and mutilated? Or is that just an after-the-fact excuse for thuggery?

The question is hard to answer. The subordination of women is certainly a part of most Islamic cultures. Female circumcision and the disciplinary violence of honor killing both arise out of specific traditions in East Africa and eastern Anatolia that are Muslim. Yet we should not confuse the misogyny and lawbreaking of certain Muslims with conservative Islam as a whole, still less with radical Islam. Conservative Muslims in the West have often taken the lead in rooting out cultural practices that secular Westerners find most abhorrent. Hassan Moussa of the Swedish Imam Council has been in the forefront of efforts to prevent female circumcision. In Duisburg, a campaign against traditional Turkish cousin marriage was led by Yasemin Yadigaroglu, a devout, hijab-wearing Muslim, who called it "a misrepresentation of Islam."

The most politicized Muslims, the radicals or Islamists, do not always have a predictable relationship to gender relations — they can be either traditional or modern, either egalitarian or sexist. The young women of the Hofstad network, the group out of which Theo van Gogh's killer came, told the Dutch investigative journalist Janny Groen that radicalism for them was an escape from tradition. "They are going to lessons in mosques where they are taught about the 'pure' Islam of 1400 years ago," Groen writes. "Men and women are biologically different, they are told, but were equal in those times. They learn, in a frank way, about their sexual rights. For those girls 'pure Islam' seems to liberate them from oppressive partners." They have even found a loophole in Islamic law that allows them to partake, however casuistically, of the ambient promiscuity of Dutch society—informally polygamous "marriages" that last from five days to a couple of months.

The British journalist Shiv Malik found the same thing among British radicals. "One of the biggest factors that has helped the growth of British Islamic radicalism is marriage," he wrote. "Islamism's most important tenet is that Muslims should not be divided by race or nationalism—that all Muslims are one. It therefore can offer an Islamic route out of having to marry your cousin." Western hedonism is an object of scorn for a lot of Muslim radicals — but a desire to escape traditional households and have more sex can in some cases be an *incentive* for young Muslims to radicalize.

The appeal of sharia

"Taken one by one," writes the French Islam expert Olivier Roy, "the elements (the veil, halal) that seem incompatible between Islam and the West actually are not, even on the woman question." But taken one by one, the pieces of a gun are harmless. Europeans sense that the special dangers to assimilation that Islam poses have something to do with the way everything fits together—with the comprehensiveness of Islam's alternative system, the collection of holy laws known as sharia. Even if people can be liberated from oppressive moral conventions, they cannot be liberated from their need for moral conventions altogether. "Individual conscience" most often means the freedom to choose among such conventions, combined with the integrity to choose well. It is human nature to gravitate towards conventions that are confidently asserted and tested by time.

Sharia meets that description. It is, of course, a variable thing. For Europeans, sharia is a frightening tabloid specter: lopping off people's hands for theft, as occurs in Saudi Arabia; stoning adulteresses to death, as has been the practice in Iran since the Khomeini revolution of 1979. Sharia is that, of course. But it is also a pedestrian, and frequently admirable, European reality. There are halal butchers across the continent. There are sharia-conforming stock funds (such as those offered by Deutsche Bank) for Muslims who don't want to invest in alcohol, tobacco, pork, or gambling. (Many of these outperformed the market in 2008.) There are imams and scholars who arbitrate divorce proceedings. The crucial question is whether sharia will continue to be a private and voluntary matter (in the way of, say, kosher practices) or whether it will receive some kind of recognition from the state.

Europe is tending in the latter direction. In 2008, the archbishop of Canterbury, Rowan Williams, gave a talk about religion and British law before the Royal Courts of Justice. In an interview about the speech, he noted, "We already have in this country a number of situations in which the internal law of religious communities is recognised by the law of the land." He was talking, on the one hand, about conscientious objection and, on the other, about the recourse Orthodox Jews have to rabbinical courts in adjudicating marriages and divorces. So in his lecture he suggested, gingerly, "a delegation of certain legal functions to the religious courts of a community."

A predictable drama ensued. Stage one: there was an uproar in the tabloids over the idea that the archbishop had backed sharia. ("Victory for Terrorism," "Arch Enemy," and "Bish Bosh: What a Load of Tosh" were some of the headlines that ran in the *Sun*.) Stage two: an equally strident defense of the archbishop was made by activist Muslims who now inferred that Jews were favored—or at least treated better than Muslims were—under British law. Stage three: Archbishop Williams and the "thoughtful" part of the press argued that the archbishop's subtle points had been misunderstood and distorted by a coarse public.

But in this case, the tabloids were more clear-eyed than the archbishop's defenders. In fact, those rabbinical courts, Battei Din ("houses of justice"), which have existed in Britain since the eighteenth century, are recognized only as a form of binding arbitration, of the sort that companies can submit to in business dealings. The decisions they ratify are *not* part of the "law of the land," except to the extent that they involve contracts. Similar arrangements are available to Muslims if they wish them. That being the case, what new accommodations for Muslims could Williams be arguing for at such length? He did, in fact, seem to be arguing for community jurisdiction over believers (albeit with the state as a decider of last resort), and not simply for any individual's right to enter into contracts of binding arbitration.

The tabloid-reading public is not off-base to fear the introduction of sharia law—as law—in certain European communities. In Britain, 37 percent of Muslims between sixteen and twenty-four want the introduction of sharia law, and 37 percent favor executing Muslims who renounce Islam. In Ireland, a majority of young Muslims (57 percent) wish for Ireland to become an Islamic state. These attitudes are consistent with a dislocated people taking refuge in nostalgia. They are also consistent with a people patiently conquering Europe's cities, street by street. In late 2006, the Dutch justice minister, Piet-Hein Donner, said in an interview, "If two thirds of all Dutch people should want to introduce sharia tomorrow, then surely that would be possible? Surely there could be no objection under the law? And it would be a shame to say: 'You can't do that.' The majority is what counts. That is the very essence of democracy." He is right of course. It is not the essence of liberalism, but it is the essence of democracy. It is unlikely that two-thirds of Dutch people will want sharia any time soon. But it is probable that two thirds of certain smaller, heavily immigrant communities want it now. There is a liberal case to be made against these communities, but there is not a democratic case against them.

Some aspects of sharia that touch on sex are hard to regulate, once democracy has opted for sexual liberation. Maybe this seems paradoxical but it is not. The acceptance of polygamy, for instance, would seem to be a logical consequence of the attack on "morals" legislation carried out over the last half century, from the overturning of the British ban on *Lady Chatterley's Lover* in 1960 to France's PACS and other civil-union laws enacted after the 1990s. What all such reforms have in common is that they make sexual morality a matter of individual conscience. The right they give people is the right to organize their interpersonal affairs on a contractual basis, with no intervention from the state, and no recognition of time-honored social norms. Once the state can no longer insist that marriage involve a commitment to a member of the opposite sex, there is no grounds (other than superstition) for insisting that marriage be limited to one person rather than several.

Polygamy, traditional in some Muslim cultures, has seldom been a flashpoint of public opinion. Not even the potential cost of caring, through the welfare state, for extra foreign-born spouses has riled Europeans particularly. In 1991, the Dutch liberal politician Frits Bolkestein made a speech in Groningen in which he tried to establish the principle that there could be no family reunification immigration on the basis of polygamous marriage. He was rebuked by the JOVD, the youth organization of his own party, and attacked by others for fomenting "anti-Islamism." In February 2008, the British Department for Work and Pensions issued guidelines giving recognition (and some benefits) to additional spouses. "Where there is a valid polygamous marriage the claimant and one spouse will be paid the couple rate," the guidelines ran. "The amount payable for each additional spouse is presently £33.65."

Where polygamy has become contentious, it has been over issues other than sexual morality and money. Most observers believe there are tens of thousands of polygamous families in France, many of them of West African origin. In the wake of the riots in the country's banlieues in November 2005, two French politicians of the ruling UMP party, labor minister Gérard Larcher and party leader Bernard Accoyer, sought to blame polygamy. But just *how* polygamy was supposed to be at fault was unclear—it had something to do with cramped living spaces. One got the impression there was an ulterior goal in bringing marriage into the discussion, and there was.

Arranged marriages

In a lot of European countries, marriage is not just an aspect of the immigration problem; it *is* the immigration problem. When Germany's guest worker program was abruptly halted during the economic crisis of 1973, large-scale immigration from Turkey scarcely abated. For years, political asylum was easy for Turks to obtain, owing to political assassinations, military coups, and the violent Kurdish nationalist movement in eastern Anatolia. Since getting overwhelmed by refugees during the Balkan wars of the 1990s, Germany, like most of its neighbors, has steadily tightened its criteria for political asylum.

But one avenue into Europe has remained wide open—because it cannot be closed without compromising the rights of natives. Half of ethnically Turkish German citizens seek their spouses in Turkey, according to the interior ministry. For years, about 25,000 people a year, two-thirds of them women, have successfully applied at consulates in Turkey to form families in Germany. That means, since the mid-1980s, half a million imported spouses—fresh nuclei around whom brothers, sisters, parents, and children can later make their own legal claims to immigrate under family reunification criteria. "Chain migration," as it is called, ensures exponential growth of minority populations, even if the borders are completely closed to illegal immigrants. The Turkish population in Germany multiplies not once in a life cycle but twice—at childbirth *and* at marriage.

The situation is similar in every country in Europe. In France, the number of foreign spouses rose from 23,000 in 1990 to more than 60,000 in 2004 and family-related immigration now accounts for 78 percent of permanent legal immigration. In Denmark, the vast majority of first-, second-, and third-generation Turks and Pakistanis take their spouses from the home country; some studies have shown the rate for Turks to be over 90 percent. In the Bradford District Race Review, published after Britain was hit by a wave of race riots in the summer of 2001, Sir Herman (later Lord) Ouseley warned that "50% of the marriages that take place in the Asian community result in an intake of new residents who are unable to communicate in the English language, which limits their participation in mainstream social and educational activities." Fully 60 percent of Pakistani and Bangladeshi marriages are to spouses born abroad, a major factor in the roughly 50 percent growth of the Pakistani population of Manchester, Birmingham, and Bradford over the 1990s. Six decades into the mass immigration from the Indian subcontinent, three-quarters of Bengali children aged 0–4 have mothers born in Bangladesh.

Why should large numbers of marriage migrants be a problem? If the migrants were assimilating, they wouldn't be. But the marriages themselves are evidence of a collective choice *against* assimilation. As the demographers David Coleman and Sergei Scherbov note, marriage migration in Britain "has increased *pro rata* with the growth of the young age-groups of the Asian ethnic minority populations." That a preference for marrying foreigners should increase the longer an ethnic group is in a European country is a dismal surprise. It indicates that an "ethnic minority" is waiting patiently not until it is welcome enough to assimilate, but until it is strong enough to separate.

One can well ask whether this choice for separation is being made by immigrants or by natives. In 2000, the German Youth Institute reported that 53 percent of Turkish women ages 16 to 29 would not consider marrying a German "under any circumstances." But the feeling is mutual. A survey taken in the late 1990s found a majority of Germans agreeing it would be "unpleasant" to have a Turkish relative. Among UK Muslims, it appears to be the newcomers who are taking the lead in advancing segregation. The researchers Tariq Modood and Richard Berthoud have shown that only 1 percent of British Bangladeshis and Pakistanis have white partners, versus 20 percent of Afro-Caribbeans.

Marriages among traditional Muslims are seldom Western-style love matches. The Turkish ones in Germany are often arranged by parents. A 2003 study by Germany's Federal Ministry of Family Affairs found that a quarter of Turkish women in Germany hadn't even known their partners before they married. The rural Anatolian practice of marrying relatives, usually first cousins, is frequent. It accounts, according to the Center for Turkey Studies at the University of Duisburg-Essen, for between a sixth and a quarter of binational pairings.

These marriages bring Anatolian practices, many of which Europeans hold in contempt, into the heart of Germany. Domestic intimidation—wife beating—is prevalent in a lot of Muslim cultures. Its causes can be questioned, but not its extent. Gülgün Teyhani, who works at a battered women's shelter in Duisburg, reckoned that of the eighty-six women her house took in in 2006, sixty had a migrant background, and fifty-one of them spoke Turkish. Doctors in Northern England have seen a high number of Pakistani women admitted to hospitals with faces permanently marred by "chip-pan accidents." Some of these women don't have a chip pan (what Americans would call a deep-fat fryer) in the house. Scotland Yard suspects they have been punished for some trespass against sexual morality or spousal authority.

A more difficult question is whether these marriages are freely chosen or contracted under compulsion. A 2002 Berlin Senate report documented hundreds of complaints of "forced" marriage. But what constitutes a forced marriage is really in the eye of the beholder. In Turkish culture, for instance, people tend to discuss liberty in terms of the family rather than in terms of the individual. Most Western cultures were sympathetic to this idea of liberty until a very few decades ago. If you embrace this idea of liberty, then Turkish-style betrothals are merely the kind of consultation you would expect in a close family. They don't involve matchmakers or extra-familial institutions.

Obviously there are culture clashes among immigrant generations. A village-oriented father may settle on some Anatolian village elder as the right match for an Italian-born daughter who is in grad school in Ireland. But not all daughters object to arranged marriages. Nor, necessarily, should they. The track record of these family-arranged marriages in creating durable relationships compares quite favorably—even in Europe—with the record of more individualistic European marriages. The closer one gets to European culture, the farther one gets from family and its raison d'être, children. In North Rhine–Westphalia, Germany's most populous state, 80 percent of Turks aged twenty-five to thirty-four are married; their average marriage age is twenty-one for women and twenty-four for men. Among non-Turks, only 32 percent of twenty-five- to thirty-four-year-olds are married; the average marriage age is twenty-nine for women and thirty-two for men. Germans have one of the lowest fertility rates in the history of the world—1.36 children per woman, according to 2004 figures. While it is hard to find precise figures for Turks in Germany, the rate is widely agreed to be higher. The rate in Turkey itself is almost twice as high, at 2.4 children per woman. If a good chance of middle-aged childlessness and elderly solitude is the price of assimilation, it is for many Turks an exorbitant one.

German interior minister Wolfgang Schäuble is not inclined to see coercion in these arrangements. "Forced marriages are illegal," he said in 2007. "They're assaults on human rights. They don't meet the minimum demands of a free society. But arranged marriage—that's a complicated area." Schäuble admits, though, that the tendency of

Turks to bring spouses from abroad is a "main reason why integration isn't improving with the passing generations." The hundreds of thousands of new families that have formed through immigration are families in which the children's first language is more likely to be Turkish than German. You frequently hear stories from school-teachers about a child of guest workers who was a star pupil in the 1970s but whose own children, although born in Germany, struggle to learn German in grade school. After half a century of immigration, every new generation of Turks is still, to a large extent, a first generation.

The Danish marriage law

Naturally, Europeans see arranged marriage not just as a demographic problem but as a slap in the face, an expression of contempt. Muslims, after having been welcomed into European societies, now turn around and assert that there is no one in their new country worthy of committing to and making a life with. It is not only the European natives who are found wanting—so are the Muslims contaminated with Western habits. To find a "real" man or woman, one must travel to Diyarbakir or Tetuan. According to a study done by the Center for Turkey Studies, young Turkish women and men brought up in Germany view their fellow Turkish Germans of the opposite sex as "distant from their own culture, or 'degenerate.'" Where traditional young women start families and assimilated ones have trouble finding mates, the next generation is brought up—almost by definition—by those who are least assimilated themselves.

Now let us recall Marcello Pera's insistence that any migration from Place A to Place B implies the superiority of the latter's culture, and consider what an empty platitude it is. The marital behavior of immigrants and their children (not to mention the entire history of colonization) shows that you can migrate to a place while being hostile to it, or at least while holding it in no special regard. Yes, immigrants "just want a better life," as the cliché goes. But they don't necessarily want a European life. They may want a Third World life at a European standard of living. They may want to use the cosmopolitanism made possible by the Western rule of law to secure citizenship for their nonfeminist brides and their pre-Enlightenment ways. These marriages are no weaker than European ones, and may indeed be stronger. They could, for that very reason, corrode European social institutions. Virtually every shade of native European opinion, from feminist to nationalist, wishes that they be stopped. But in a society with the rule of law, where even the German interior minister admits that these are marriage compacts entered into freely, how can that be done?

Certain countries in Europe have managed to place sharp restrictions on those who marry foreigners. In each case, it has meant damage to the country's constitution and has exacted a high price from natives, in the form of both rights and convenience. In the wake of the Van Gogh killings in 2004, the Netherlands imposed mandatory civics examinations and language tests on those seeking to marry Dutch citizens. Both parties to a marriage involving a non-EU citizen had to be over twenty-one. (Studies show that the lower the age of marriage, the greater the tendency to have an arranged marriage.) The German government has followed suit: In 2007, it raised the minimum age of foreign-born spouses to eighteen.

But it was Denmark that went furthest. Under the terms of its Aliens Act, extended and made more stringent under the influence of the anti-immigrant Danish People's Party (DF) over the last two decades, Denmark's marriage regime requires a combination of testing, waiting, and exclusion, strictly enforced. Citizens under the age of twenty-four who marry non-EU spouses are not allowed, except in special cases, even to reside in the country. The Danish experiment has been, on its own narrow terms, a stunning success. In 2002, 62.7 percent of marriages by Danes of non-Western background were to foreigners; by 2005, that figure had fallen to 37.9 percent.

What makes the measure defensible against EU human rights laws is that it is race-, religion-, and ethnicity-blind. It achieves this race blindness by stripping rights wantonly from all citizens, rather than targeting the problem it seeks to address. "It has had bizarre consequences for people who would never expect to clash with immigration authorities," says Tøger Seidenfaden, editor of the daily *Politiken*, which ran a long campaign against the legislation. "The legislation is the same for a Dane as for a foreigner," boasts integration minister Rikke Hvilshøj. It does, however, make one constitutional innovation that affects different ethnic groups differently: the *tillknytningskrav*, a measure of one's "connection" to Denmark. Citizens can override the measure once they have 28 years of "connection" (which basically means citizenship) to Denmark. A native-born twenty-two-year-old will be able to bring his foreign-born wife to live in Copenhagen in three years, because by then she will have three years of citizenship and he will have twenty-five. But a twenty-year-old who only became a Danish citizen two years ago will have to wait a good long time before he and his wife are welcome. And once that principle has been established, a lot of the sentimental talk about immigration is revealed as either a polite fiction or a cynical imposture. It turns out that, all cant to the contrary, newly naturalized twenty-year-old Mohammed is *not* "just as Danish as you and I." He may be eventually. But for now he and his Danish passport are on watch. "We just have to say: It's necessary," says Hvilshøj. "I hope someday we don't need it."

Denmark has managed to stem the implantation of Muslim culture on its territory by making believe that its worries are over rash marriages in early youth, not over Islam or immigration. European publics are beginning not just to accept but to demand that their governments shade the truth, or at least conceal the intent of the laws they pass. Something similar happened when Europeans grew desperate to stop the spreading use of the Muslim headscarf.

Controversies over the headscarf

Since modesty is enjoined on women in the Koran and Sunna, all Muslim cultures have historically had some form of "veil," or head covering. This can be a loose scarf, of the sort worn in Turkey. More conservative women wear the *hijab*, which covers all the hair. The *niqab*, which reveals only the eyes, is what you see on women in Saudi Arabia, along with the big, black *abaya*, to cover the body. The notorious *burqa*, common in Afghanistan when the Taliban were in power, covers absolutely everything.

We have noted that Europeans didn't think much about the religion of immigrants in the first years after their arrival. As far as women were concerned, they had no reason to. Most daughters of even devout immigrants—in fact, most immigrants—were quickly "emancipated" into a less restraining style of dress. But once Muslims began to feel at home in Europe, this assimilation went into reverse. In the 1980s, women of Muslim background, including ones from non-veil-wearing cultures and families, began to take up the veil. France saw a wave of headscarf controversies starting in 1989, when two girls returned from a summer visit to relatives in Morocco insistent on wearing their headscarves to school in the Paris suburb of Creil. Throughout the 1990s in France, the issue kept getting opened, settled, and reopened through a series of bans, rules, waivers, overturnings, and decrees.

Who adjudicates such matters, and on what basis? In 1985, when Muslim schoolgirls refused to remove their headscarves in the Dutch town of Alphen aan de Rijn, a civil servant asked the late Jan Brugman, an Arabic professor at Leiden University, whether the Koran explicitly commanded that girls wear cover. He answered—defensibly enough—no. But he was not asked about other sources of religious law, and no one's answer can settle what is basically a political debate. Most Muslims, even those who oppose the headscarf, consider it a religious expression, and are unlikely to be dissuaded from this view by a Koranic scholar.

Westerners, by contrast, have been happy to sound off giddily on what the Koran does and does not say about the veil and other Muslim religious behavior, and on what Muslims need and need not do. Even Bel Mooney, the agony aunt of the *Times* of London, resorted to scriptural exegesis when she got a letter from a divorcée who had converted to Islam and was wondering how far things were going to go with her new friend, a guy named Hassan. "If he was simply biding his time to be sure of his feelings," Mooney advised, "he would be acting in a manner approved by the Koran—which does not encourage leading ladies on: 'Do not make troth with them secretly unless you speak honourable words.'"

Eventually the veil turned from a nuisance into a menace. In the aftermath of the second intifada in Israel in 2000, and of the attacks on the World Trade Center the following year, French people began to notice that their secondary schools—at least those in Arab areas—

had become hotbeds of anti-Semitism and other intimidation and violence. In 2002, Emmanuel Brenner (a pseudonym of the historian Georges Bensoussan) assembled a two-hundred-page book, *The Lost Territories of the Republic*, recounting dozens of incidents in which students directed ethnic slurs at their teachers and poured loud ridicule on lectures about the Holocaust. The book reportedly made a deep impression on French president Jacques Chirac. That these incidents coincided with the rise of veil wearing in schools made the veil, at least in European eyes, a symbol not just of Muslim identity but also of truculent Islamism.

European natives understood the veil as a banner of solidarity with a violent international political movement. They sought a way to stop young women from wearing it. But in free societies that permit free expression, there are no neutral grounds for banning a particular scrap of clothing. Other grounds had to be found. One promising avenue was to point to the security hazards of letting people go around with their heads covered. There is some precedent for this. For centuries, Italy has had laws against the wearing of masks and disguises (*travisamento*) in public, and they had been invoked as recently as the 1970s in prosecuting the leftist Red Brigades. Spain, for similar reasons, forbids motorcycle messengers from entering certain offices with their helmets on. Both countries invoked their disguise laws in controversies over the veil. It was not an outlandish thing to worry about. In 2006, Mustaf Jama, the most wanted criminal in Britain at the time, who had been accused of killing a policewoman in the course of a robbery, was able to escape from the country on a commercial flight to Somalia by disguising himself in his sister's niqab. (In late 2007 he was arrested in Africa and deported back to Britain.)

But generally, when they complained about the "dangers" of veiling, politicians were talking about dangers to something more abstract: Europe's feminist order. They heard the stories of sexual violence in Muslim-controlled housing projects. They looked at places like Rosengård in Sweden, where even the women from non-veil-wearing cultures take up the veil. This looked like a contagion of either intimidation or peer pressure, although it could just as easily be viewed as a matter of privacy. Since equality of women is such a bedrock, non-negotiable principle of modern European societies, the veil was most often interpreted as a political challenge, a symbolic rejection of Western ways.

In England, a 2007 study showed that slightly more than half of Muslims in Britain (53 percent) would prefer that women wear the veil. But that number disguises an overwhelming turn towards tradition on the part of younger generations. Only 28 percent of those over fifty-five prefer the veil, while 74 percent of those aged eighteen to twenty-four do. Most UK polling about religious practice reveals a similar hardening of views among younger respondents. Almost a third of British Muslims believe that converting to another religion "is forbidden and punishable by death." But that breaks down to 19 percent of those over fifty-five and 36 percent of those eighteen to twenty-four.

Those numbers were recorded shortly after a young woman named Aishah Azmi was fired from her position as a schoolteacher in Dewsbury for insisting on teaching in her niqab. Although a local court backed her firing, it ordered the school to pay her £1,100 damages for the hostile environment it had created. British prime minister Tony Blair backed the school's ouster of Azmi. "It is a mark of separation," he said of niqab wearing, "and that is why it makes other people from outside the community feel uncomfortable. No one wants to say that people don't have the right to do it." Actually Blair was wrong on both counts—98 percent of Britons, if the rampaging tabloid the *Daily Express* was to be believed, *did* think the niqab ought to be banned. And what, specifically, was wrong with a "mark of separation"? It would not have been out of place for devout Muslims to ask what the prime minister thought the periwigs people wore in the House of Lords were.

Jack Straw, who at that point had just left his post as Britain's foreign secretary, also warned that the veil was becoming a "visible statement of separation and difference." That was an alarming reversal. Straw had built his political career in the increasingly Muslim and increasingly segregated city of Blackburn, where U.S. national security adviser Condoleezza Rice was met with such hostility on a visit there in 2006 that the public appearances she was scheduled to make with Straw had to be canceled. Throughout his political career,

Straw had been an optimistic and enthusiastic promoter of multiculturalism.

Now, in the twilight of his political career, he granted that, well, yes, there were reasons to worry. This was a pattern in matters concerning Islam—politicians seemed to express their true feelings only on the verge of retirement, or afterwards. The outspoken former cabinet member George Walden wrote that he, too, would keep his counsel under today's circumstances:

I'd be so alarmed by the situation I'd do everything possible to suggest it was under control. It's up to politicians to play mood music in a crisis, and up to the people to understand that there's little else governments can do. The last thing they can say is that we face a threat to which we can see no end because it's based on a fundamental clash of cultures. On the IRA we told the truth; on the Islamic problem, we lie.

Britain's leaders were not asserting values. They were fighting a disquieting social development with ad hoc measures, and then casting about for values after the fact. The real basis for acting against the veil was that British society was becoming slightly more Muslim every day, and did not want to be. No one could say this. Every argument had to be made from neutral principles. Trevor Phillips, the head of British Council on Racial Equality, complained, at the height of the controversy over the veil, "What should have been a proper conversation between all kinds of British people seems to have turned into a trial of one particular community, and that cannot be right." So what was Britain, supposed to do, then? Have a discussion based on the false premise that *all* its citizens had fallen into the habit of wearing separatist religious garb?

Apparently. That is what France did.

The French veil law

To return to a matter discussed in the last chapter, France was the only country that made a coherent constitutional case against the veil. It succeeded only because France has a constitution unique in Europe for its enmity towards—or, to put things mildly, its distrust of—

religion. In 1905 laws were passed to discipline the Catholic Church, which at the time controlled primary schools, influenced politics through its assets, and had recently exposed France to international disgrace through the role it played in the Dreyfus Affair, in which a Jewish army captain was framed on espionage charges. Church and state were separated by means of *laïcité*, which is difficult to translate. It differs from the Anglo-American tradition in that it seeks less to neutralize public authorities in matters of religion than to neutralize religious bodies in matters of public life.

In December 2003 a twenty-member commission headed by a politician and immigration expert, Bernard Stasi, completed a five-month study hailed by President Chirac as a way of bringing *laïcité* up to date in a multicultural society. The commission recommended banning conspicuous religious symbols—not just headscarves but also yarmulkes and large crosses—from public schools and other institutions. In the interests of neutrality, it seemed, every infringement that disproportionately affected Muslim practice had to be balanced by some compensatory restrictions on the majority culture—even if those restrictions were bogus and pro forma. The ban on yarmulkes and "large crosses" was meant only to disguise the singling out of Islam. Most people understood this. The social scientist Farhad Khosrokhavar correctly wrote on the morrow of the report: "It is common knowledge that what is aimed at is Islam, especially the headscarf. The rest is trivia."

Again: over the long term, the price of managing immigration is paid by the broader society in the form of rights. Jews attending violent public schools may have considered the loss of the right to wear a yarmulke a small price to pay for some sign of state action against the Islamization of institutions. As for Christians, they were largely unaffected, since the crosses they wear on necklaces are generally small. (No one, in fact, could ever figure out what was meant by a "large cross.") The non-Muslim public understood that this was the best deal it was likely to get.

The French veil laws were as disingenuous as the Danish marriage laws, and they worked for the same reason: huge majorities of the non-Muslim society insisted on them. As the headscarf ban was being debated at Christmas 2003, thousands of veiled women marched in

Paris, and Muslim leaders—from the activist writer and scholar Tariq Ramadan to the anti-Semitic Alsatian rabble-rouser Mohammed Ennacer Latrèche—warned of worse to come, once it went into effect. But once France's resolve became clear, the marches fizzled out, and they were attended by only a handful of cranks. On the first day of school in the autumn of 2005, only 12 students arrived veiled, as compared to 639 the previous fall. Chirac ordered that the hundredth anniversary of the 1905 *laïcité* law be celebrated as quietly as possible.

Compulsory liberation

It would be easier to share Straw's view that there is something illegitimate per se about a woman's separating herself from the gaze of the public if the alternative model of comportment were not so often based on racy advertisements, reality TV, and (at least in this decade) a vogue for exposed navels and jeans that cinch halfway down the bum crack. More eloquently than any other Westerner, Ayaan Hirsi Ali has made the case for the superiority of the Western conception of women's rights over the Muslim one. It is not lost on Muslims, however, that she has done so from Amsterdam, a city that, whatever its other glories, is known to the world as a place where young women sit naked in shop windows waiting for men to pay them for sex. Whether an anything-goes sex industry is caused by feminism or simply correlated with it, it has traditionally been considered a more serious kind of exploitation than choosing to wear—or even than being made to wear—a scrap of cloth. "Liberation" can place its own constraints on women's freedom.

Today, very few non-Muslim politicians in Europe see the matter this way. Some policymakers are uneasy about signs of family breakdown—the 43 percent nationwide illegitimacy rate in Britain, for instance—but those who connect their unease to misgivings about sexual liberation (Christine Boutin in France, Ann Widdecombe in England, to name two examples) are more often ridiculed than rallied behind. Public approval of sexual liberation appears almost compulsory. Europeans can conceive of no reason why any individual might want to preserve his chastity or modesty. Consider the pitiless remark of Jacques Chirac, at the height of the veil debate, that "nothing can justify a patient's refusing on principle to be treated by a doctor of the opposite sex."

Or consider the informational video Dutch authorities show to would-be citizens. Most European citizenship instruction seeks to ensure that newcomers know enough of the language to get by and enough of the political system to exercise their rights—Germany's, for instance, requires 600 hours of language training and 30 hours of history. But the Dutch naturalization packet also insists that immigrants be able to handle the country's *moral* peculiarities. It is centered on a video that includes gays expressing affection in public and bare-breasted women at the beach. (An expurgated version is offered for those applicants who live in countries where possession of the video would violate the law.) Wolfgang Schäuble, Germany's interior minister, has defended the Dutch film and would not mind having something similar for his own country. "Someone who doesn't want to see these kinds of things shouldn't move to a country where they're reality," he says.

To Muslims, the Western unwillingness to even hear the case for bodily modesty could be a radicalizing force. Tahar Ben Jelloun, a Moroccan-French novelist whose views on such matters are moderate, sees Europe's relative hedonism as a cause of veiling. In an article called "Moroccans and the Reasons for the Veil," he wrote: "Some Islamism has entered Morocco via emigrants from Belgium and Holland. For fear of losing their daughters, fathers make them cover themselves." A Turkish-born Dane who works at a hard-line fundamentalist school in Copenhagen recalls that, before he turned to devout Islam, his main interest was disco. That interest had a lot to do with his desire to live in Europe in the first place. "I read a novel about a man from Switzerland," he says. "I wanted to be like him. He had so much appetite."

Beneath its bold assertions of liberation, Europe is badly divided. Its relationship to its own post-religious morality is ambivalent. As in a television beer advertisement, the product (in this case "European values") gets so tangled up with hedonic promises that you can't see where the product lets off and your titillation picks up. Michel Houellebecq, in some ways the most libertine of modern novelists, argues in *Whatever* (1994) that a world in which sexual pleasure is made a preeminent good is not a world in which people are brought closer together. It is a world in which the gap between haves and have-nots is magnified along a new dimension. Because it is attentive to such pitfalls, Islam—especially in its preachiest and most conservative form—can appear like a real enrichment, and not just to Muslims.

The British parliamentarian Denis MacShane warns that the Islamist intellectual Tariq Ramadan "repudiates core European principles that developed from Galileo to gay marriages." But it does no good to label brand-new gender and sexual arrangements as "core European principles." They may be core principles *someday*, when they have stood the test of time. Right now they are innovations, carefully sheltered from parliamentary accountability by human rights laws. What secular Europeans call "Islam" is a set of values that Dante and Erasmus would recognize as theirs; the collection of three-year-old rights they call "core European principles" is a set of values that would leave Dante and Erasmus bewildered.

When Europeans assert their "values" against Islam, what are they asserting—a religious heritage? A philosophical heritage? A morality? A lifestyle? Clearly they do not know. In one of her more rabid tirades against Islam, the late Italian polemicist Oriana Fallaci threatened war against any Islamic terrorist who harmed a list of Florentine landmarks starting with the cathedral of Santa Maria del Fiore and the Baptistery that stands nearby. Is she defending cathedrals as tourist attractions? (If so, she has a very weak hand to play against a 1,300-year-old religion.) Or is she defending them as houses of worship? (If so, she has broken with most of the Europeans who worry about Islam, because what is at stake for them is Islam's threat to liberation from religion.)

It is not even clear that the beneficiaries of sexual liberation will fight in its defense. The journalist Henryk Broder of *Der Spiegel* notes the behavior of participations in the various erotic parades and sex festivals that have become a mark of contemporary Germany. At the Carnival of Cultures in Berlin, the marchers are happy to accuse Joachim Meisner, the cardinal of Cologne, of being an inquisitor, or to depict German chancellor Angela Merkel being buggered by George W. Bush. But they stress their sensitivity to Muslim concerns about the parade, and there are no sex jokes about leaders who have been considerably less hospitable to sexual liberation, such as Iran's Mahmoud Ahmadinejad.

Islam is not a particularly prudish religion; in fact, most religions are less prudish than Europe's traditional Christianity, both Catholic and Protestant. As the demographer David Coleman notes, the easy-going sexual order that is part of the "second demographic transition" is a late European development, but it is not late to other cultures. "Divorce and easy re-marriage (for men) is traditional in some polygamous African societies," Coleman has written, "[as well as] in Islam and in traditional Japan, while cohabitation and extramarital birth were institutionalised in Latin America and the Caribbean, and to some extent among US blacks, for a century before the 'first' demographic transition arose."

There are grounds for believing that Muslims are closer to assimilating into post-religious European sexual and family life than we thought. In the Netherlands in the first half of this decade, divorces increased by 46 percent among Moroccans and by 42 percent among Turks. There are Muslim feminists and Muslim gays, of course, and even conservative Muslims often live cheek by jowl with the most modern sexual stuff Europe has to offer. The hard-line mosque in Munich is across the street from a lap-dancing establishment. Many heavily gay neighborhoods are also heavily Muslim neighborhoods. "Gays are attracted to cultural diversity. There is a good local culture of tolerance," says Ilda Corti of The Gate, an urban regeneration project in Turin's heavily Muslim Porta Palazzo neighborhood. Sankt Georg in Hamburg is a neighborhood with a similar mix.

Maybe. But gay–Muslim comity is more likely transitional and illusory. Both gays and Muslims inhabit those neighborhoods as sub-cultures—as a result of their relationship to the dominant culture, not as a result of their relationship to each other. A *New York Times* report on a Turkish nightclub in Kreuzberg that has a monthly gay night did not exactly reveal a confident community. One twenty-two-year-old Turk demanded anonymity "out of fear that he would be ostracized or worse if his family found out about his sexual orientation." A twenty-one-year-old Arab would not give his name on the grounds that "my brothers would kill me." There are still yawning gaps between Muslim and non-Muslim sentiment on gays. In France, Muslims are twice as likely to disapprove of homosexuality as non-Muslims.

Like the system of separation of church and state, our present sexual morality was forged in opposition to Christianity, not in opposition to religion in general. The West's new, "loose" sexual morality is ordered more around male prerogatives than around female ones. It may fit traditional Muslim thinking better than it fits traditional Western thinking. If the besetting sexual failure of Christianity is prudery, the besetting sexual failure of Islam is sexism. Traditional Islam is only *partially* at odds with present-day sexual practice, not totally at odds, the way Christianity is.

PART III

The West

9

Tolerance and Impunity

Political self-assertion as a turning point—Intimidation and self-defense—The politics of terror—Anti-Semitism and anti-Zionism—"The Communism of the twenty-first century"

Controversies over the veil in France were resolved to the satisfaction of the majority, and without provoking unrest among Muslims. But there was something ominous about the resolution. The mufti of Egypt warned Jacques Chirac that the anti-veil law would "destroy the social peace of French society." The Muslim Brotherhood in Egypt called it "an interference in the realm of Muslims' personal and religious liberty." And Mohamed Hussein Fadlallah, spiritual leader of the Lebanese radical group Hezbollah, wrote an angry letter to Chirac that complained of a "stripping of liberties from Muslims, even when they have not disobeyed the law."

Such warnings were a shock. They came less than a year after France had won the gratitude of the Muslim world by opposing the U.S.-led invasion of Iraq. France flattered itself that it was a privileged interlocutor with Islam. Now it turned out that the world's Muslim leaders thought they had a privileged role in France. And they did. Nicolas Sarkozy, then the interior minister, cut short a vacation to visit Mohamed Sayyed Tantawi, an influential imam at the al-Azhar theological institute in Egypt. On his return, Sarkozy announced that Tantawi had said France had the right to ban the veil.

So here was a domestic political initiative that the French government felt it required a *nihil obstat* from some foreign Muslim cleric to pass. Questions naturally arose about whether the Muslim world had a similar veto power over France's foreign policy, and about how heavily it had weighed in Chirac's Iraq war deliberations. It was certainly a bigger factor than in 1991, when president François Mitterrand was able to bring France into the Gulf War coalition without showing the slightest curiosity about Muslim sentiment. If Chirac had chosen to back the United States in Iraq in 2003, would France have seen its explosion in the banlieues two years earlier than it did? Was Islam becoming part of France or was France becoming part of the Islamic world?

Political self-assertion as a turning point

In all mass immigrations, there is a turning point when immigrants—or their native-born children—end up not just inhabiting but also shaping their country of arrival. Natives expect immigrants to become like natives themselves before they start throwing their political weight around. That happens—but the process is never complete before immigrants begin asserting themselves. The moment when natives discover they must share power with the semi-foreigners living among them is as fraught with tension as the moment of arrival. According to Oscar Handlin, there was a period of calm after the Irish first arrived in Boston. They were nearly invisible, and had no effect on politics or the economy. Massachusetts, then probably the most advanced democratic society in the West, saw itself as enlightened and humanitarian. The first generation of Boston Irish were made as welcome as a mass influx of violent and destitute illiterates could possibly be. As Handlin wrote:

Nativist fears failed to develop more significantly because the Irish before 1845 presented no danger to the stability of the old society. They were in a distinct minority and, above all, were politically impotent ... Their opinions were still a matter of private judgment, with no influence upon the policies of the community.... The dominant group took no step to limit social and political rights or privileges until the ideals of the newcomers threatened to replace those of the old society.

By the time it entered the minds of Bostonians that the newcomers might someday have claims to power, a point of no return had been passed. Before the Irish had gained even a foothold in any of Boston's democratic institutions, their eventual dominance of all of them was certain. It was at this point, in the 1850s, that natives began to voice intolerant opinions, to mutter openly about the newcomers' higher birthrates, to form radical and secret political parties, and to take active steps to exclude the Irish from their institutions. The xeno-phobic "Know-Nothing" party, so named for its secrecy rather than its obscurantism, won every major office in the state in the mid-1850s. But Know-Nothingism was not a political program; it was a death rattle. When the Irish became numerous enough to dominate Massa-chusetts politics decades later, they turned it into a weapon for the disempowerment and expropriation of the Massachusetts establish-ment. Later generations of Irish-Americans would remember that establishment as the reactionaries of the second, Know-Nothing stage of immigration, not as the Good Samaritans of the first.

Europe's situation has been similar in its general contours to the early part of Boston's. France started passing anti-immigrant laws in the late 1960s, when immigrants first began protesting and striking for rights. Germany abruptly ended its guest worker program in 1973. The economic downturn brought by the oil crisis was certainly part of the explanation, but so was the first participation of immigrants in industrial strikes.

Now, decades later, a second wave of unease has come, as Muslims have become active in European democracies. They have long been, by the standards of American minority politics, disengaged, apolitical, and excluded. As of 2009, none of the 577 deputies in France's National Assembly is Muslim, even though at least 10 percent of residents are. Britain is further along in some ways, worse off in others. Its elaborate system of local government, although much weakened since the premiership of Margaret Thatcher, is still ample enough that anywhere an immigrant population settles, a class of immigrant political leaders grows. This is particularly so in places like Leicester, Blackburn, and Bradford, where natives will soon con-stitute a minority. There are many Muslims in Parliament and even several in the House of Lords. But there is no country in Europe where the political opinions of Muslims diverge more widely from those of non-Muslims.

The problems that European politics addresses lag behind the continent's demographic reality. Well into the twenty-first century, certainly until voters' minds got focused by the financial collapse of late 2008, the pressing political issues in most European countries were still largely the ones that Europeans had been debating in the wake of the Cold War. They revolved around "non-Muslim" issues, from the integration and enlargement of the European Union to benefit levels for the old-fashioned state-employee pensions that Muslims arrived too late to partake of. Newcomers maintained their "own," old-country preoccupations, simply superimposing them on European politics as best they could. For instance, one of the reasons Turks for many years gravitated less to the German Greens than to Social Democrats, despite the Greens' assiduous (and unique) recruitment of Turkish politicians, is that the Greens were in the forefront of attacking the Turkish government's human rights record.

The Muslim vote is nonetheless already influential. Only a few hundred thousand Turkish-Germans vote, but their monolithic support for Gerhard Schröder accounted for the razor-thin margin by which he was reelected chancellor in 2002. Muslims—all immigrants, in fact—have tended to vote heavily on the center left in all countries, since it was Labor, Social Democratic, and Green parties that were quickest to pick up on the American left's ideas of racial and cultural equality—or, more to the point, the tactics of organizing ethnic voting blocs that went with them. But such loyalties are changing. Muslims are pledging their votes based on the issues that have been brought to the fore by September 11, 2001, and its aftermath. Many Muslims abandoned Britain's Labour Party in the May 2005 elections over its participation in the Iraq war—although polling shows that British participation in the U.S.-led war in Afghanistan would have sufficed to alienate Muslims even had the Iraq war never happened.

The question for the future is not whether the Muslim vote will shift the electoral balance on today's contentious issues, but whether it will change the issues themselves, reopening aspects of European society that are today considered settled. In the two months after riots broke out in the Paris suburb of Clichy-sous-Bois, the number of registered voters there almost tripled. One assumes most of the new registrants were not preoccupied with tax rates, depreciation schedules, or infrastructure projects. What issues *did* make them want to make their voices heard?

Intimidation and self-defense

Muslim opinion is hard to read because Muslim political claims can be made in two ways. There is the way of reason and the way of intimidation. In general, Muslims participate with extreme decorum in the established political systems of the countries they have settled in. In no country is there a shortage of reasonable, nonviolent, and patriotic interlocutors. But matters touching Islam directly are outside the purview of politicians, and they are often governed by intimidation. It gets felt among families, through honor killings and violence against women; among young men through the activity of gangs. The native born hardly see it. Paradoxically, the more Muslims have integrated, the more this intimidation has spread.

The Ayatollah Khomeini's fatwa against novelist Salman Rushdie was a turning point in two ways. First, it disputed, for the first time in centuries, Europe's claims to sovereignty over all its citizens. Rushdie might *call* himself an Englishman, was the assumption behind the fatwa, but he was a Muslim first. He was accountable to Islam for the apostasy of which *The Satanic Verses* was evidence. This was a serious claim. The Koran declares the penalty for apostasy to be death. Nowhere in the West do a majority of Muslims believe that this penalty should be enforced. The highest level of support for such draconian justice is found among young British Muslims, 36 percent of whom favor death for apostasy. But it does not take a majority to murder somebody.

One reason that Europeans have not paid much attention to the political leanings of ethnic minorities is a faith in democratic decision making that verges on superstition. Even if people are worried about what will happen when ethnic minorities make up 50.1 percent of the population in certain cities, they seem not to consider that anything could possibly go wrong until that moment arrives. Of course, minorities can shape countries. They can conquer countries. There were probably fewer Bolsheviks in Russia in 1917 than there are Islamists in Europe today.

As long as a few influential imams and freelance crackpots believe in enforcing their theological understandings through intimidation, no Muslim or ex-Muslim, however well assimilated, can write or speak without the sense that someone dangerous is looking over his shoulder. When the Dutch magazine *HP/De Tijd* published a feature on Islamic converts to Christianity, most of those who spoke to the magazine insisted on anonymity. Shortly before he was baptized a Catholic in early 2008, the Egyptian-born Italian Muslim commentator Magdi Allam asserted that there were in Italy thousands of "secret Christians"—Muslims who have become Catholic or Protestant but hide their belief out of fear for their lives.

The Rushdie fatwa did not just send a message to European Muslims. It also caused the claims of Islam to lap up against the lives of non-Muslim Europeans. Up until this point, enmity to free expression was a parochial thing. It could be understood as enforcing—in however benighted and violent a way—the internal norms of a community. That understanding broke down. The death sentence on Rushdie was not an Iranian idea—it had been called for by Muslims in the heavily Pakistani city of Bradford. But Rushdie was not a member of Bradford's Muslim community. He was an Indian-born member of London's literary establishment. If a death sentence could be declared on *him*, not to mention all his publishers and translators, then the mores of immigrant communities now held partial sway over British public life.

In 2005, the twenty-year-old Moroccan-Dutch columnist Hasna El Maroudi stopped her column on a youth website of the national newspaper *NRC Handelsblad* when she started receiving death threats over things she had written about tensions between Arabs and Berbers. Was that a matter of intra-immigrant relations or a threat to press freedom at one of Holland's establishment newspapers? It was both, of course, but those too scared to do anything about it could dismiss it as exclusively the former.

Immigrant communities had become too big to quarantine. But the problem was more than one of size. It also came from the successes of integration, not just internationally (in the form of globalization) but also nationally. There had not been any Salman Rushdies or Hasna El Maroudis at the heart of Europe's literary establishments a generation earlier. Suddenly, immigrant communities weren't just *in* Europe; they *were* Europe.

Europe—meaning its Muslim and non-Muslim citizens alike—was subject to intimidation by Muslim clerics and their followers. European natives sensed their position—as measured by both demography and will—was weakening. In early 2006, a member of the Italian parliament received police protection after she was declared an "enemy of Islam" by Iranian clerics. In academia the early years of this decade witnessed the "Luxenberg Affair," in which a German Arabic scholar, publishing under the pseudonym, Christoph Luxenberg, argued that the Koran, rather than being a "pure" Arabic, was heavily influenced by other tongues and literary influences. This is obvious to most scholars, but it was hard to talk about in the academy. "The very first sura of the Koran contains [in verse 5] a Latin word," one Arabic professor said. "When I teach Arabic, I have to explain that the alphabet is an invention of two centuries after the Prophet. The Koran cannot have contained those dots. Muslims can't accept that. They insist on the dogma that the Koran is pure Arabic. So the dean of faculty leans on me not to explain this. He says we should not teach things that chase away Muslim students."

These are not high points or worst cases but a mere sampling of the "chilling effect" that spread through newspapers, legislatures, and people's conversational habits when the subject touched on Islam. The category of prohibitions kept expanding, and so did the class of people to whom it applied, through a clear series of stages:

1. Muslims must respect Muslim law.
2. Members of the Muslim "community," even if they are nonbelievers or if their allegiances lie with the larger national culture, must respect Muslim law.
3. Non-Muslims must respect Muslim law.
4. Non-Muslims must be above even the suspicion of not respecting Muslim law.

It took fifty years of mass immigration for Europeans to grow frightened of their minorities. When people start doing out of fear what they previously did out of conviction or generosity, they often do not notice the transition.

The politics of terror

For years, Europeans have been visibly nervous about the "real" political attitudes of the Muslims among them. September 11, 2001, a plot hatched in part in Hamburg, Duisburg, and other European cities, confirmed unspoken fears. It was a day of joy in much of the Muslim world, including parts of Muslim Europe. Celebrations were reported in Belgium and in the West Yorkshire city of Halifax, and there was cheering on the streets in the Dutch city of Ede. A poll by the magazine *Contrast* found just under half of Dutch Muslims were "in complete sympathy" with the attacks. A quarter of French Muslims opposed helping the United States find the terrorists. Large numbers of Muslims are ambivalent about which side to back in the battle between the West and radical Islam.

The ambivalence is most visible in the United Kingdom—the very European country where Muslims appear to be best integrated into politics and the working world. Nine days after the bombings in the London Underground in 2005, prime minister Tony Blair denounced the "evil ideology" that motivated Muslim radicals. "They demand the elimination of Israel," Blair said, "the withdrawal of all Westerners from Muslim countries ... the establishment of effectively Taliban states and Shariah law in the Arab world en route to one caliphate of all Muslim nations. We don't have to wonder what type of country those states would be." British Muslims were not unanimous in their opposition to all these things. Taji Mustafa, a representative of Hizb ut-Tahrir, an organization that promotes the reestablishment of the caliphate, said: "My challenge is, Go to Whitechapel and ask: Do you question the state of Israel? Do you believe in Shariah law?" And Hassan Butt, a twenty-five-year-old aspiring jihadist and spokesman for the radical group al-Muhajiroun, went further. He said later that summer, "The majority of Muslims in this country care about neither moderate nor radical Islam; they care about living their day-to-day life. They're happy with that. But of those people who are practicing, the majority of them hold my views. The difference is that some people come out publicly and others keep quiet." (Butt has since renounced his own jihadist views.)

In virtually all polls, British Muslims stand out as significantly more radical than all other European Muslim populations. In fact, they are more radical than the Muslims in a good number of Muslim countries. A sixth of British Muslims believe that suicide attacks on military targets in the United Kingdom are justified. Almost two-thirds (63 percent) consider westerners "arrogant"—a higher level of mistrust than is registered in Nigeria, Indonesia, and Turkey.

It is partly trends in foreign Islam that are causing this shift. Since most British Muslims are Pakistani, Bengali, or Indian, probably the majority of Britain's 1,500 or so mosques have their roots in the Sufism of central Asia and the Indian subcontinent. But the Sufism that most aged Pakistanis practice in England has become a remnant in its country of origin, like the French that is spoken in Quebec. Since immigrants began arriving en masse to Britain more than half a century ago, this softer Islam has lost ground in South Asia to more worldly and strident tendencies. The Deobandi school, which was founded in India in the nineteenth century, has grown more conservative, more distrustful of non-Islamic cultures, under the influence of Saudi Wahhabism (and money). Since the Afghan war in the 1980s, hard-line Deobandi madrassas have spread throughout Pakistan. Jamaat-i-Islami, the sectarian and highly politicized movement started by the journalist Abu A'la Maududi in 1941, has grown by leaps and bounds since the 1960s, and is an influential current in the largest British Muslim group, the Muslim Council of Britain (MCB). The MCB has no official government status, but it does claim to speak for much of the Muslim population. "Mainstream" and "moderate" are not necessarily synonyms in Britain.

A Draft Report on Young Muslims and Extremism leaked from the Home Office in 2004 found that a main source of anger among youth was "a perception of 'double standards' in British foreign policy, where democracy is preached but oppression of the 'Ummah' (the one nation of believers) is practiced or tolerated, e.g. in Palestine,

Iraq, Afghanistan, Kashmir, Chechnya." By overwhelming numbers, British Muslims oppose *all* intervention in the Arab and Muslim world. Somewhere between 64 and 80 percent, depending on the poll you consult, opposed Britain's participation in the Afghan war.

Europeans were not, however, in a strong position to call these views disloyal, and many were not inclined to grumble about them. When Muslims marched in antiwar demonstrations, after all, their secular and Christian fellow citizens marched alongside them. As one German parliamentarian put it, "Young people who are left-wing are proud to be German because there are no soldiers in Iraq." By this he meant all young people, not just Muslim ones. Why should Muslims be punished for professing opinions that many Europeans wear as a badge of honor?

That question sowed confusion all over Europe. In Turin in the wake of September 11, the Moroccan radical Bouriki Bouchta set fire to an Italian flag, slandered Israel, and spoke out in favor of Osama bin Laden. Although Bouchta changed his views and his tone after the Madrid bombings of 2004, he was deported to his native Morocco in late 2005. At that point he hired lawyers and made strenuous efforts to be readmitted. Part of his defense was that none of his behavior would have been unusual for a member of the Italian radical left. "In a sense," recalls the Italian journalist and Islam expert Francesca Paci, who covered his case, "he behaved too much like an Italian."

On one hand, opposition is a right. On the other hand, it is a right that was granted to certain Muslim immigrants too early—before they had become citizens and before they had learned the difference between dissent and subversion. That was how Europe suddenly found itself facing a grave problem, and maybe the very last problem it would have expected at the beginning of the twenty-first century— the resurgence of anti-Semitism.

Anti-Semitism and anti-Zionism

The most sustained episode of anti-Semitic violence and vandalism in Europe since the Second World War began in the autumn of 2000, at the same time as the Palestinian insurrection known as the al-Aqsa intifada. Eighteen months later, Jews were being harassed and assaulted on French streets at the rate of a half dozen incidents a day. Molotov cocktails were thrown at Jewish schools and Jewish-owned businesses, synagogues were burned to the ground, and pro-Palestinian marchers demonstrated waving swastikas and wearing suicide-bomb belts.

Facing international criticism for not responding more forcefully, foreign minister Hubert Védrine said, "There is no anti-Semitism in France," and president Jacques Chirac echoed his sentiments. They were sincere. In their view, no country in Europe exercised more vigilance against anti-Semitism than France—and they were right. But the anti-Semitism that French authorities and French society had been trained to combat was the mostly Catholic Church–based bigotry of the nineteenth-century Dreyfus affair and of Vichy France in the 1940s. Both those societies were easily differentiable from our own. They were hostile to "diversity."

Today's threat to European Jews comes from diversity itself. Among Muslim immigrants, dislike (to put it mildly) of Jews is endemic. One French government report noted that, in heavily immi-grant schools, anything that was crummy, corrupt, broken, dirty, or undesirable was described as *feuj*, a slang word for Jewish. Moreover,

there is a rise in insults, threats, and attacks . . . towards students who are Jewish or assumed to be, both inside and outside of school. These attacks are generally carried out by North African fellow students. In the testimony we have gathered, events in the Middle East and suras from the Koran are often invoked by the students to legitimize their words and their attacks. Praise for the Nazis and Hitler is not unusual: it is everywhere present in graffiti, notably of swastikas, and even in remarks made openly to teachers, professors, and administrators.

Most of the street attacks, meanwhile, had been carried out by bands of loosely organized youths of Arab background. France, with its enormous Muslim population, was hit worst by anti-Semitism, but this was part of a Europe-wide pattern. Graves were desecrated in Jewish cemeteries in London and Manchester, youths threw eggs at the Jewish parliamentarian Oona King during a war memorial service, and by 2006 the annual tally of anti-Semitic attacks in Britain had risen to 600, according to the London-based Community Security Trust. A synagogue was shot up in Oslo. Twenty Jewish shops were vandalized in Rome.

Europeans, like Americans, had developed a number of stereotypes about intolerance. Racism was something done by an unchanging class of perpetrators (rich, white Christians) to an unchanging class of victims (the poor, the dark skinned, the colonized, the down-trodden). It was assumed that anti-Semitic acts, should they ever reappear, would come neatly wrapped in the ideology of continental fascism as it had been practiced in the 1920s and 1930s. The change of dramatis personae left Europeans confused. So far was the new anti-Semitism from these usual stereotypes that the public—*especially* that part of the public trained to be vigilant against racism—was incapable even of recognizing it. A European Union study on anti-Semitism, set for release in 2003, found a heavy role for Muslim gangs. But it was suppressed, perhaps due to the incredulity of those who commissioned it. When it finally did appear, a year later, it came accompanied by a press release from the EU's UN delegation averring that "the largest group of the perpetrators of antisemitic activities appears to be young, disaffected white Europeans. A further source of anti-Semitism in some countries was young Muslims of North African or Asian extraction." But that was not what a tallying up of the incidents showed. Muslims were the primary, not the secondary, perpetrators.

Majorities in almost all European countries had an almost neuras-thenic sensitivity to anything in their own conduct or past that hinted at anti-Semitism, but no such self-scrutiny was demanded of Muslims—in fact, those who asked it of them were censured. When the Utrecht theologian Pieter W. van der Horst proposed to give his farewell lecture on the "The Islamization of European Antisemitism," it was quashed by the university administration.

Anti-Semitic incidents have returned as a standing problem in Euro-pean life. They tend to rise and fall along with events in the Middle East. Young Muslims around the world are easily whipped into a frenzy against Israel by urban myths, Internet rants and Arab satellite TV channels showing footage of various military and anti-terrorist operations. Increasingly segmented and targeted news media mean that television has exactly the opposite effect on immigrants and minorities that it had just a generation ago. Whereas the BBC once broke down barriers between communities, al-Jazeera erects them. The news shows immigrants get—increasingly sophisticated, exciting, and given to fast-cut MTV-style clips and music that makes your heart race—portray Israel as a perpetrator of spectacular, wanton atrocities. In the last decade, many young European Muslims decided to join (and, in the process, help discredit) the Palestinians' battle for an independent state, with vague notions of avenging themselves on Jews. The ones within their reach were their European neighbors.

Vicarious concern about conflicts in ancestral countries is pretty normal second- and third-generation immigrant behavior in the United States. Europe's pro-Palestinian Muslims can, in certain ways, be compared to Irish American supporters of the IRA. They have a rather incoherent relationship with their country of residence. They are simultaneously *bored* with it (since it seems to have solved many of the problems of everyday survival) and resentful of it (since its world-bestriding pretensions make the culture of their parents and grandparents look puny and marginal). Casting back to the ancestral community for some great drama to participate in can offer a wholeness to lives that feel fragmented.

But there are differences. Most European Muslims are not of Palestinian ancestry at all. And agitating on behalf of the Old Sod (a specific geographical space far away) is not the same as agitating on behalf of the ummah (the abstract community of the Muslim faith, whose laws are binding on Muslims wherever they may be). IRA fundraising had no effect on the political life of the United States, except, one hopes, to trouble its conscience. The ummah does have claims on Europe, not just the Middle East. "Two million Muslims live in the UK," notes the British historian David Cesarani, "and one thing that unites this diverse population is hostility towards Israel and its diaspora champions."

Like anti-Americanism and anti-racism, hatred of Israel is a means of joining a European culture without having to assimilate into it—of joining Europe on a footing of permanent opposition. For anti-Israel rhetoric not only unites Muslims with each other. It also unites them with an important segment of native Europeans, particularly on the political left. In an odd way, it is an avenue of integration. In 2002, Gretta Duisenberg, wife of Wim Duisenberg, then president of the European Central Bank, hung a Palestinian flag from their family home in Amsterdam. At the height of the Danish cartoon crisis in February 2006, in the very week when Palestinian groups explicitly threatened (through some process of free association) to kill any Norwegian found in Gaza, members of Norway's governing coalition threatened a consumer boycott—against *Israel*. In April 2006, Sweden refused to take part in military exercises in the Middle East because Israel was to be included in them. Europeans were prominent at the World Conference on Racism, held in Durban in the summer of 2001, which rallied the world's anti-globalization activists around an anti-Israel agenda.

These were not outrages or *faux pas*—much of the broader European population supported their politicians in such moves. In an infamous 2003 poll respondents in most European countries named Israel as the "biggest threat to world peace." Without quite realizing what they were doing, Europeans tended to blame Israel for the terrorist violence committed against it. The American essayist Paul Berman was the first to notice the peculiar effect that suicide bombings worked on European public opinion. They provoked "a philosophical crisis among everyone around the world who wanted to believe that a rational logic governs the world." Suicide bombing *had* to be about an unbearable injustice. If it was not, it was a mere homicidal cult. For a continent scarred by the homicidal cults of the twentieth century that was an unbearable thought. Europeans grew more interested in the "causes" of terrorism than in terrorism itself. The more Israelis the bombers killed, and the more ruthlessly they did it, the more public opinion shifted against Israel. Protests against Israel, Berman wrote, "rose and fell around the world in tandem with the suicide bomb attacks, and not in tandem with the suffering of the Palestinian people." Berman's view sounded eccentric when he first advanced it, but it has been vindicated. European hostility towards Israel has diminished since the building of a secure wall between Israel and the West Bank—which has not altered the justice or injustice of Israeli occupation, but which has dramatically reduced the level of suicide bombing.

Were Europeans using the outrage of their Arab minority over Israel to give Israel's "diaspora champions" a scare? The native born showed little active anti-Semitic comportment, but they showed even less alarm over Muslim anti-Semitism. It appeared to them like a legitimate gripe irresponsibly expressed. John Denham, chairman of the Home Affairs select committee, said in 2005: "It is no exaggeration to say that Israeli policy in the occupied territories is not simply a matter of foreign policy—it is a matter for British domestic security policy too." Denham, a man of principle who resigned from the Blair cabinet on the eve of the Iraq war, probably did not appreciate how this message would be understood, but it placed British Jews in an absolutely horrible position, one that differed little from the scapegoat position they occupied for centuries: If they did not renounce Israel and all its works, they would be blamed for any harm done, presumably through terrorism, to Britain's non-Jewish population.

Europeans now had two categories for understanding violence against Jews—there was anti-Semitism (inexcusable Jew hatred of the sort they had been thoroughly indoctrinated against) and there was "anti-Zionism" (opposition to Israel, which can take responsible and irresponsible forms). This is a perfectly valid distinction in theory. One can oppose the policies of Israel without being anti-Semitic; one can, in fact, oppose the existence of Israel without being anti-Semitic. But in practice, this distinction had the effect of laundering anti-Semitism back into the European political mainstream. The cause might advance in the name of anti-Zionism, but Europe's Jews were being attacked because they were Jews—they did not have to fill out a questionnaire first. In practice, anti-Zionism and anti-Semitism were approving and disapproving ways of describing the same thing.

"The Communism of the twenty-first century"

The Holocaust has in recent decades been the cornerstone of the European moral order. "Working through the past" (*Vergangenheitsbewältigung*, to use the German word) is a solemn moral undertaking, almost—for better and for worse—a religious one. This moral order was a success for decades, confining anti-Semitism to the outermost fringes of European life. Now it had somehow failed—spectacularly, suddenly, utterly. By 2005, 62 percent of French hate crimes had Jewish victims. This failure did not result from an abandonment of *Vergangenheitsbewältigung*. As Jews were defamed, attacked, and even killed, the Holocaust's standing as a moral lodestar continued to be loudly proclaimed. Europeans retained what Pierre-André Taguieff called a "hypermnesia" about totalitarian excesses in their past, albeit a selective one. A sincere repugnance for Nazi-style anti-Semitism and for the Holocaust remained part of the moral foundation of twenty-first-century Europe.

The moral order built on Holocaust remembrance failed not because it was abandoned but because it was applied indiscriminately. The European system of remembrance and repentance was a moral discipline—it was not a "chit" that Jews or other minorities could cash in for special consideration whenever they got embroiled in a communitarian political spat. There were few Jews left to claim such consideration, anyway. Under the pressure of mass immigration, however, post-Holocaust repentance became a template for regulating the affairs of any minority that could plausibly present itself as seriously aggrieved. Europe's Muslims were a living, thriving, confident European ethnic group with a lot of claims to press.

Once on the continent, Muslims took up a privileged position in any public debate on minority rights: they, too, were "victims." Laboring under socioeconomic disadvantage in Europe as well as occupation in Palestine (as they saw it, even if they weren't Palestinians), many Muslims felt their community offered native Europeans a more appropriate object than the Jews themselves for moral self-examination and moral self-flagellation. An increasing number of Muslims saw themselves, in fact, as the "new Jews." In December 2005, the leftist author Ziauddin Sardar published a cover story in the *New Statesman* called "The Next Holocaust." London mayor Ken Livingstone warned that Britons' discomfort over the veil "echoes very much the demonology of Nazi Germany." In 2006, Livingstone was suspended from office for four weeks for comparing a Jewish journalist to a concentration camp guard.

As the Jews accumulated "rivals" with an interest in dislodging them from their position as Europe's top victims, the system was suddenly turned inside out. The ideology of diversity and racial harmony, which had always been snickered at as well meaning and politically correct, now became the means through which anti-Jewish fury was reinjected into European life. Far from forgetting the lessons of the Holocaust, anti-Semites and anti-Zionists were obsessed with them. They were a rhetorical toolkit. If the Muslims were the new Jews, apparently, then the Jews were the new Nazis.

There were standup comedians who sneered at "the chosen people," most prominently the gifted half-Cameroonian Dieudonné Mbala-Mbala. There were black anti-Semitic street gangs, like Tribu Ka ("Tribe K"), which patrolled the Orthodox rue des Rosiers like a sort of postmodern Freikorps, trying to foment urban warfare on the hallucinatory logic that someone needed to stand up against the Jewish "*milices*." (The milices were the notorious collaborationist police under Nazi occupation.) Tribu Ka was finally banned in July 2006, shortly after disrupting a memorial service for Ilan Halimi, the Jewish cell-phone salesman mentioned in chapter 6, who was tortured to death over the course of three weeks by an African-led gang who called themselves "the barbarians."

In the wake of the Danish cartoon crisis, an Antwerp-based group called the Arab European League published a cartoon that portrayed Hitler naked in bed with Anne Frank, saying "Put this in your diary, Anne." The AEL's firebrand leader, Dyab Abou Jahjah, had aspirations that were less religious, and more nationalistic, than those of most European radicals from the Muslim world. He traveled with a detachment of bodyguards and backed Arab struggles everywhere, especially against Israel—but also against Europe, where he urged the creation of an Arab nation. His hope for the Anne Frank cartoon appeared to be that it would constitute some kind of "retaliation" for the ones published in *Jyllands-Posten*. "Europe, too, has its sacred cows," said Abou Jahjah triumphantly, "even if they are not religious sacred cows."

Abou Jahjah's remark was not just vicious but obtuse. He was quite right that Europe had taboos and sacred cows. What he ignored was that he and his followers were their primary beneficiaries. Was Abou Jahjah foolish enough to believe that Europe's Jews were the main winners in the postwar moral order? It was too late for most of them.

But the shock to Europe's conscience that followed their murder had made the continent safe for other minorities. An immigration of the sort that brought Muslims in such numbers to Europe would have been unthinkable without the anguished moral self-examination the Holocaust brought in its wake. Such an immigration would have provoked mistrust, xenophobia, and violence. It takes very little reflection to know how Europe—minus its guilt over the Holocaust—would have reacted to a radical Arab nationalist pressure group headquartered in Flanders.

"Working through the past" had kept Europe's intolerant impulses in check for half a century. It had done the job far too well. It had cleared not just a breathing space for immigrants, but a space of impunity for the worst among them. The new anti-Semitism was not simply a recrudescence of racism. It was an anti-Semitism that advanced under the protection of *anti*-racism, as the philosopher Alain Finkielkraut showed in a number of stirring books and essays. "I think that the lofty idea of 'the war on racism' is gradually turning into a hideously false ideology," Finkielkraut said in 2005. "And this anti-racism will be for the twenty-first century what communism was for the twentieth century: a source of violence."

10

Resistance and Jihad

Poverty, occupation, lost grandeur, and other grievances —Islam and violence—"Islam is peace"—Moderate Muslims—Tariq Ramadan and double language—Resistance and jihad

Islam was down for a very long time, but the world is taking notice of it now. The main thing people are taking notice of is the terrorism committed in its name, much of it in Europe. Long before September 11, the Arab world had been the main source of terrorist violence touching Europe, outside of England and Spain. But something changed between the late summer of 1972, when Palestinian terrorists murdered seventeen Israeli athletes at the Olympics in Munich, and Christmas Eve 1994. That night, French special forces at Marseille's airport overwhelmed and killed four members of Algeria's Armed Islamic Group who had hijacked Air France flight 8969, killing several passengers. The terrorists had planned to fly the plane into the Eiffel Tower.

In the interim, Islam had become not just the cultural sphere out of which terrorism came but the cause in the name of which it was committed. It was a cause that appealed to a growing number of European Muslims. Khaled Kelkal, a train bomber from Lyon, carried out a string of murderous attacks in 1995. Safir Bghouia, shouting that he was a "son of Allah" and firing machine guns and shoulder-launched rockets, made a deadly assault on police and the mayor's office in his hometown of Béziers, France, the week before the September 11 attacks. Swept up in the romance of Islamist rebellion,

European Muslims who had appeared fully assimilated—like Mohammed Bouyeri and Mohammed Sidique Khan—re-defected to their ancestral identities.

Such episodes pose an obvious problem for politicians. On one hand, citizens of every Western European country consistently put terrorism near the top of their lists of worries; on the other, Europe continues to grow more and more Muslim, both through immigration and natural increase. The consensus view was summed up by a senior politician in the summer of 2006: "The first thing that has to be done, is to keep migration separate from terrorism."

But this is a wish trying to pass itself off as an analysis. As the journalist Lawrence Wright wrote in his authoritative study of al-Qaeda:

What the recruits tended to have in common—besides their urbanity, their cosmopolitan backgrounds, their education, their facility with languages, and their computer skills—was displacement. Most who joined the jihad did so in a country other than the one in which they were reared. They were Algerians living in expatriate enclaves in France, Moroccans in Spain, or Yemenis in Saudi Arabia. . . . Islam provided the element of commonality. It was more than a faith—it was an identity.

Migration, in fact, has a lot to do with terrorism. That is part of what makes terrorism so difficult to fight.

Poverty, occupation, lost grandeur, and other grievances

What "causes" terrorism? It is natural to assume that terrorism, like war, is a continuation of politics by other means, that there must be some political grievance at the core of it. The bloody Madrid train bombings of March 2004, unleashed by al-Qaeda-linked Moroccans living in Spain, are the best piece of evidence for this Clausewitzian view, since: (1) Al-Qaeda opposed Spanish participation in the Anglo-American intervention in Iraq; (2) so did more than 90 percent of Spaniards; (3) the Socialist candidate José Luis Rodríguez Zapatero campaigned against the Iraq war; and (4) the bombings altered the result of an election that polls had shown him certain to lose.

The argument that Zapatero owed his victory not to the bombings but to the Popular Party's mishandling of public information in their wake is widespread in Spain. It is alleged that the Popular government of José María Aznar (not the Popular candidate Mariano Rajoy) tried to deceive the country into believing that Basque terrorists of the ETA, rather than al-Qaeda, had been behind the bombings. A full discussion of this argument is beyond the scope of this book, since it requires a precise timeline of the seventy-two hours between the bombing on March 11 and the election on March 14, and a detailed knowledge of Spanish political personalities, police bureaucracies, and military procedures.

But the explanation is not convincing. Surveillance of the ETA led Spanish intelligence officials to fear a bombing on the eve of the elections. The train bombers procured their explosives through ETA channels. And Socialist politicians were as "certain" as Popular ones that the ETA had authored the bombings well after they had taken place. This allegation of Popular Party mendacity probably owes its currency to the psychological requirements of Spain's fledgling democracy. Spaniards needed to believe, more than most Europeans would have, that their government was brought to power through domestic Spanish deliberations and not through the armed inter-cession of a foreign adversary. On taking power, Zapatero immedi-ately ordered his country's troops out of Iraq, repudiating Spain's alliance with the United States and launching in its place what he calls an "alliance of civilizations" with Islam.

Whether or not the Spanish bombings were a direct result of its Iraq policy, Spain's capitulation by referendum is likely to be the last of its kind for a long while, for pragmatic reasons. There is no longer a terrorist negotiating partner that can issue clear demands and credibly offer a quid pro quo—the quid being, invariably, a halt to terrorism. On September 11, 2001, Osama bin Laden was at least conceivably such a negotiating partner. That is, he enjoyed prestige in the Muslim world, commanded the largest and most effective body of terrorists, made demands, and threatened violence if those demands were not met.

But that command structure has been largely decapitated by the war on terror, and al-Qaeda is now less a command structure than an ideology aimed at wreaking a maximum of destruction on what Islamist propaganda calls the "alliance of Jews and crusaders." There is no course the West can follow to defuse terrorist grievances, because those grievances are numerous and protean. It is not even possible to say whether the basic gripe of al-Qaeda and kindred organizations is geostrategic, metaphysical, or sociological. Does it concern "occupation" in Muslim lands, whether in the form of U.S. military bases or of Muslim governments that European Muslims happen not to approve of? (If so, it is strange for Muslims to wish to bomb the European countries of which so many of their coreligionists are citizens.) Is it about something vaguer, such as the often-adduced "lament for past grandeur" diagnosed in the Muslim world? (If so, it is bizarre that the *European* lament for past grandeur should result in the exact opposite comportment—a tendency towards pacifism.)

It is much more difficult to pinpoint the political grievance behind the suicide bombings in London's transport network in July 2005. These were carried out by home-grown terrorists who may have been mere imitators of al-Qaeda but may have received al-Qaeda training. Certainly they disapproved of Britain's Iraq policy. But Iraq was only one of many Muslim grievances that were mentioned in Mohammed Sidique Khan's suicide video, and it was not the one mentioned most prominently. Polling numbers, as we have noted, suggest that Britain's involvement in the occupation of Afghanistan is sufficient to win considerable sympathy for terrorism among its Muslim population. So is any support for Israel. So, in many cases, is the sense that Muslims are second-class citizens in Europe. Germany's role as the founder and the standard bearer of the European anti-Iraq coalition did not spare it an attempt by three terrorists in the city of Ulm to set off a bomb made of three-quarters of a ton of highly concentrated hydrogen peroxide in September 2007. At that time, the state of Baden-Württemberg alone had identified hundreds of suspected potential terrorists.

Lacking a clear sense of what Islamist terrorists are so fired up about, countries have worked by wild guesses and preconceptions to preempt any complaint that might conceivably arise in any irate Muslim individual's head. A top-level interagency paper prepared for Tony Blair in early 2004 found that "less than 1 percent" of

British Muslims were engaged in terrorism in some way, at home or abroad. (One should hope so. One percent would be about 16,000 people.) An analysis from Britain's Department for Work and Pensions, part of the same package of studies, said: "The key to engaging this group [Muslims] in a positive way is, obviously, by reducing discrimination and promoting integration." That use of "obviously" is telling. Europeans almost instinctually reach for depraved-on-accounta-I'm-deprived explanations of terrorism and, for that matter, any shortcomings in Muslim communities. Even two of the most judicious observers of the situation of Muslims in France, Laurence and Vaïsse, have a ready-made disclaimer for the high rate of incarceration among French Muslims. "As a result of the alienation and desperation stemming from such socio-economic handicaps," they write, "persons of Muslim origin constitute a majority of the French prison population."

There is something condescending about assuming that the agenda of young Muslims will be determined by the actions of non-Muslims. If Muslims are like other people they will tend to build their ideologies out of their own values and aspirations, rather than other people's. Over recent decades Western attitudes towards the rest of the world have swung wildly, from colonial arrogance to hand-wringing self-detestation. Yet the animus of Muslim radicals against the West has been surprisingly constant. As noted earlier, the anti-Western rhetoric of today's "religious fanatics" is generally not distinguishable from that of yesterday's "godless nationalists." Terrorism is only one face of Muslim self-assertion in recent decades, the self-assertion not just of a religion but of a people.

The German social scientist and genocide researcher Gunnar Heinsohn argues that the violent acts of young men may have nothing to do with any ideological vision. Demography is a more likely spur to murder. Men between the ages of fifteen and thirty are the most violent part of any society. A society with an overload of young men due to rapid population growth—a "youth bulge," as Heinsohn calls it—is prone to trouble.

In a youth-bulge society there are not enough positions to provide the next generation of men with prestige and standing. Envy against older, inheriting brothers is unleashed. So is ambition. Military heroism presents itself as a time-honored way for a second or third or (as in Osama bin Laden's case) eighteenth son to wrest a position of respectability from an otherwise indifferent society. By Heinsohn's calculation, violence is almost inevitable when fifteen- to thirty-year-olds make up more than 30 percent of the male population—as they do in most of the Muslim world. There are sixty-seven countries with youth bulges now and sixty of them are undergoing some kind of civil war or mass killing. Heinsohn's theory does not describe the Muslim youth of Europe, necessarily, but it does describe a lot of the movements around the world that some European Muslims sympathize with.

Heinsohn noted that if Germany had had the same rate of population growth as Gaza (9 children per woman) since the 1960s, it would now have 550 million people, including 80 million young men aged fifteen to thirty. "Do you think these 80 million young Germans would be ten times as pacifist as the 7 million we have today?" he provocatively asked in a German-language newspaper. "Or is it not much more likely that they would be throwing bombs in Prague and Gdansk and Wroclaw and—just like the Palestinians—saying: 'This is our land, and it was taken from us for historical reasons that we had nothing to do with?'"

Islam and violence

If you followed this argument to its logical endpoint, then the "causes" in the name of which much Islamist violence is committed would be immaterial; the violence would simply be about itself. That is roughly what the Pakistani journalist Ahmed Rashid discovered when he studied the most hardened and dedicated jihadists, those who went to wage jihad in Afghanistan in the 1990s. "The young men who trained in these camps," Rashid wrote, "were not educated in the Islamic schools called madrassas and they were inspired less by extremist Islamic ideology than by their desires to see the world, handle weapons, and have a youthful adventure." The religion of Islam, the focus of so much contemporary strategic discussion, looks like a red herring in such cases, a convenient rationalization for violent people who want to think of themselves as something more than conventional criminals. While there is a clash of civilizations, it is not necessarily a civilizational clash.

Yet we should hesitate before discarding Islam as an explanation. Whatever terrorist violence is about, Islam is what terrorists say it is about. We can grant that customs, not Islam itself, create the biggest domestic problems in the Muslim confrontation with the West, from honor killing to female circumcision. But jihadist terrorism is different. Osama bin Laden is not fighting for Hadhrami folkways that risk being swept away in a wave of thoughtless globalization. He is fighting for Islam. Certainly there are other ways of living Islam than his. But we know enough now about Osama bin Laden's life—about his long hours of study in after-school programs, about his devotion to Islam not just as a loud terrorist leader but also as a shy young man—to know that he is living out the commands of Islam as he sincerely understands them. Muslims around the world, including thousands in Europe, have shown themselves willing to follow his path.

Of course, anyone can invoke religion when taking up arms. The question is whether the violence of Islam at this moment is something that comes from a passing conjuncture or from the very depths of Islam itself. Here, views differ. The British sociologist of religion David Martin, asked whether Islam was a religion of peace, replied, "Well, it seeks peace, but on its own terms." He cited similar observations made by the archbishop of Canterbury, Rowan Williams, who called Islam a fine religion, but one that places a high premium on victory. To some of those who see the Koran as a source of violence, this rivalrous strain in the Koran is what sets its incitements apart from those found in both Judaism and Christianity (from Deuteronomy 18:20 to Acts 3:22–23).

To others, there is a difference in the ethical *style* of Islam that makes its adherents quicker to resort to violence than the adherents of traditional Christianity. One often-adduced difference is Islam's lack of a concept of original sin. In sura 14:22 of the Koran, for instance, Satan allows he has no real power over man. The novelist Salman Rushdie has been a forceful proponent of this view: "The Western-Christian worldview deals with the issues of guilt and salvation, a conception that is completely unimportant in the East

because there is no original sin and no savior. Instead, great importance is given to 'honor.' I consider that to be problematic."

The Israeli diplomat Mordechay Lewy put the same point somewhat differently in a classic 2003 article on the subject in which he
distinguished between Christianity, which he called a "guilt culture,"
and Islam, which he called a "blame culture." According to Lewy, "In
the open or undeclared conflict between the two cultures, the West
cannot act freely, by reason of its self-imposed moral constraints. This
self-restraint is not honored by the blame-attributing culture of the
East, but is instead taken for weakness." Since such matters are decided
deep in the consciences of individual worshippers, they are beyond the
scope (or competence) of this book. They are mentioned here only to
lay out the contours of an ongoing argument, not to intervene in it.

Two peculiar things, however, should be noted about the way
Islam has historically interacted with politics, because they concern
Europeans' deepest political fears about Islam. First, Islam has sharia,
a code that regulates all areas of social conduct, varied and open to
interpretation though sharia may be. Second, Islamic cultures have
reliably produced authoritarian regimes—so reliably, in fact, that
when well-meaning scholars want to adduce evidence for Islam's
openness to reinterpretation and rational debate, they generally cast
back to the very short-lived innovations of the Mu'tazilites in the
ninth century. That non-Muslims think of Islam as the authoritarian
religion par excellence is the source of much misunderstanding with
Muslims, who argue—correctly—that it is a radically egalitarian
religion. In theory, it should be a radically *free* one. It envisions no
religious hierarchy and, strictly speaking, has no clergy. Perhaps,
since Islam recognizes no profane authority, it begets anarchy. And
governments that rest their legitimacy on an ability to bring order to
an anarchic situation are, almost by definition, authoritarian ones.

This paradox leapt out at the British adventurer Wilfred Thesiger
when he was traveling around the Empty Quarter of Arabia in the
years after World War II. He saw the Bedouins he met as the original
and archetypal Muslims, and wrote in his *Arabian Sands* (1959):

The society in which the Bedu live is tribal. . . . There is no security in the
desert for an individual outside the framework of his tribe. This makes it

possible for tribal law, which is based on consent, to work among the most individualistic race in the world . . . It is therefore a strange fact that tribal law can only work in conditions of anarchy and breaks down as soon as peace is imposed upon the desert, since under peaceful conditions a man who resents a judgement can refuse to be bound by it.

In the Muslim world, people will bind themselves more willingly to a government that speaks in Islam's name than to a government that speaks for a political party—which may be viewed as a rival tribe. Alternatives to theocracy have been tried over the last century, from Kemal Atatürk's Turkey to Saddam Hussein's Iraq, with varying degrees of success. But their era seems to have passed. The newest governments in Muslim lands—those of Iraq and Afghanistan, not to mention the post-Kemalist AK Party regime in Turkey—all envision a strong constitutional role for Islam.

"Islam is peace"

In 2006, after an inquest by the French interior ministry, forty-three baggage handlers at Charles de Gaulle airport were deprived of their security clearances. Interior minister Nicolas Sarkozy said it was important that those with access to runways have "no links, whether close or distant, to radical organizations." The radical organizations to which the baggage handlers were linked were, although Sarkozy did not say so, Muslim ones. French authorities bent over backwards to deny that devotion to Islam had had anything to do with the suspicions leveled at the baggage handlers, or any investigative value whatsoever. Sarkozy insisted that no one had been investigated for any reason having to do with group identity. "Being a practicing Muslim is not a criterion at all," said Jacques Lebrot, the subprefect of Roissy, where the airport is located. "But someone who goes to Pakistan several times on vacation—that raises questions for us." So in an attempt to exonerate itself from the suspicion of policing Islam, the government admitted to policing (for Pakistanis) visits home to one's family and (for others) tourism.

Faced with Islamist terrorism, Western politicians, including many who could not tell a *qadi* from a *wadi*, have reacted by making presumptuous claims to expertise in matters of Muslim theology. Some are anti-Muslim, like the Dutch rightist Geert Wilders, whose 2008 film *Fitna*, released over the Internet, presents the Koran as a kind of terrorist manual. Such politicians can win votes—the party Wilders founded held nine seats in the Dutch second chamber at the time his film came out. But they are held up in the news media as paranoid and sinister bumpkins, and either snickered at or hooted down. By far the majority of politicians, including Sarkozy and Lebrot, profess the opposite certitude: that terrorism never overlaps with the Muslim religion in any way. Those who hold the "nice" interpretation of Islam are spared ridicule, but it is by no means clear that their actual knowledge of Islam exceeds that of Wilders.

George W. Bush, days after September 11, set the tone for such interpretations, proclaiming that "Islam is peace." Therefore terrorism could, by definition, have nothing to do with Islam. Sarkozy tended to agree. "The attacks of September 11," he wrote in 2004, "were the act of a cult, a terrorist mafia, a clan of megalomaniacs who used religion as a pretext." In his televised address in the wake of the London bombings, Tony Blair said: "We know that these people act in the name of Islam but we also know that the vast and overwhelming majority of Muslims here and abroad are decent and law abiding people who abhor terrorism every bit as much as we do." Days later, he extolled "the moderate and true voice of Islam." Tory leader David Cameron concurs. He insists that Islamism is "driven by a wholly incorrect interpretation—an extreme distortion—of the Islamic faith."

In this view, no matter how theocratic its rhetoric and pretensions, Islamism is always a political, not a religious, movement. American commentators make this assumption when they speak, as they too often do, of "Islamofascism." The Islam expert Olivier Roy notes that al-Qaeda's "trials" of kidnap victims (who, in the early years of the Iraq war, were regularly decapitated on Internet videos for the delectation of stay-at-home jihadists) are "directly borrowed from the extreme left of the 1970s, particularly the staging of the Aldo Moro 'trial' by the Italian Red Brigades in 1978."

In its heyday, Communism was frequently compared to Islam—

not to Islamic radicalism, which did not then exist in the way it does today, but to Islam as normally practiced throughout history. The French sociologist Jules Monnerot made such comparisons in the 1940s. Since he wrote at a time when Islam was thought a spent political force, we can assume his observations had no polemical intent, at least not against Islam. For Monnerot, what made Communism like Islam was that it was simultaneously a religion (albeit a secular one) and a universal state (albeit an embryonic one). Like Communism, Islam has a detailed plan for social order, and an egalitarianism in theory that often becomes oppression in practice. "It draws on resentments, and organizes and streamlines the impulses that set men against the societies in which they are born," Monnerot wrote. In particular, Communists deployed a "historical myth apt to fanaticize men," as did the Fatimids of Egypt and Safavids of Persia. At the time Communism rose and spread, Monnerot wrote, such an ideology had been unknown "since Europe disengaged from the Mediterranean world"—i.e., since Europeans withdrew before Islam's advances.

For Monnerot, Stalin was a modern version of the Muslim "commander of the faithful" (*emir al-muminin*), and the Communist faithful were of a particularly commandable kind. In Communism as in Islam:

the believer does not think of himself as a "believer": He is in possession of the truth—or, better put, he takes the thing that *possesses him* for the truth. This truth inspires in him an active attachment that truth, in a scientific sense, doesn't inspire and never asks for.

Using the jargon of the time, Monnerot called Communism a "total social phenomenon" that breaks with the "autonomy of spheres of action" characteristic of modernity. Religious-type opposition, Monnerot thought, was precisely the kind that a liberal order is least capable of handling, because it "aggravates the real 'internal contradictions' of capitalism."

Comparing Communism to a 1,400-year-old religion that claims a billion-and-a-half worshippers is bound to result in oversimplifications that obscure as much as they reveal. But if we compare Communism to radical political Islam, Monnerot's idea of a "total social phenomenon" is useful. The greatest ideological asset of Islamism is the breadth of its appeal. Like Communism, it is an ideology capacious enough to accommodate a wide variety of grievances, and thereby to appeal to people of all different backgrounds and social classes. In 2005, the London *Times* reported on the results of a government study showing that "most young extremists fall into one of two groups: well educated—undergraduates or with degrees and technical professional qualifications in engineering or IT—or under-achievers with few or no qualifications and often a criminal background." Islamism can be understood by a university professor, as a highly elaborated intellectual structure; and by an illiterate kid with a baseball bat, as a battle cry.

How Islamism is related to Islam is beside the point. We can know that Islamism is a serious enemy of the modern liberal state before we have a clear sense of its religious logic, and before we know what, if anything, it has to do with "real" Islam. Proving that Islamism is not the same thing as Islam will not make it less dangerous.

But to say that Islam is peace is to protest a bit too much, particularly at a time when other time-honored affiliations and affinities (like "patriarchy") are rigorously examined for hidden structures of violence and coercion. Unlike Gunnar Heinsohn, who sets Islam aside because he thinks it is not the main cause of terrorism, Western politicians appear to be setting Islam aside because they fear, deep down, that it *is* the main cause. Never do politicians more loudly proclaim Islam a "religion of peace" than when bombs are set off in its name. If the terrorists' idea of religion is so evidently a perversion of the real thing, then why is it necessary for non-Muslims to lecture normal Muslims about it? If Islam has nothing to do with terrorism, then why do all European governments feel the need to reach out to Muslim groups in the aftermath of any terrorist attack?

Moderate Muslims

Reaching out to so-called "moderate Muslims" is the cornerstone of the European strategy against terrorism. Moderate Muslims are the people who can be trusted not to "distort Islam," or at least to distort it only in a positive way—by building a "European Islam" that can interact with the continent's political institutions without breaking them. Discussing Bernard Lewis's predictions that Islam will dominate Europe by end of this century, the Syrian-German sociologist Bassam Tibi said, "The problem is not whether the majority of Europeans are Islamic, but rather which Islam—sharia Islam or Euro-Islam—is to dominate in Europe." That kind of talk excites planners, visionaries, and politicians, but it does not exactly set ordinary Europeans' minds at ease. Euro-Islam wasn't in their college history textbooks, and they are not confident that it exists except as a figment of their leaders' politically correct imaginations.

What is more, the dynamic through which Euro-Islam would be promoted resembles that of Israeli–Arab peace negotiations, which center on the idea of "land for peace." The Western side gives up something (land) that is concrete, quantifiable, and irrevocable, once given. In exchange the Muslim side gives up something (peace) that is vague, subjective, and revocable by a change of mood. Europe can move to create a "Euro-Islam" only by altering its institutions. What it gets in return is an assurance from moderate Muslims that radical Muslims will be less ill disposed towards it.

No one has defined with any precision what a "moderate Muslim" is, or whether that term should be understood politically or religiously. If a "moderate Muslim" is a person who practices Islam in a moderate way, then by definition there exists another, immoderate alternative. This view is in line with European attitudes towards other religions—they're okay if you don't take them too seriously. But without an underlying belief that there is something especially dangerous about Islam, the term "moderate Muslim" makes no sense. Nobody speaks of former French prime minister Lionel Jospin as a "moderate Protestant."

A more optimistic (and reasonable) view is that a "moderate Muslim" is a political moderate, no matter what his view of religion —that what makes radical Islam "radical" is a certain attitude towards politics, not a certain attitude towards religion. This is the only use of the term "moderate Muslim" consistent with the traditional European idea of freedom of religion. Pushing Muslim identity in a more "fundamentalist" direction could mean more contemplation of God and less contemplation of grievance. Pushing Muslim identity in a more "mainstream," less pious direction could mean encouraging grandstanding and political ultimatums.

Conservative Muslims can be subversives or patriots or both. The Algerian-born, Saudi-educated conservative imam Hassan Moussa mentioned in the last chapter as an opponent of genital mutilation was among Sweden's firebrands at the turn of the century. But after the London bombings of 2005, he professed himself shocked, and called for the establishment of a council to combat extremism. At that point, he said, "I decided that I would leave the word 'but' out of my sermons." (He meant that he would no longer try to explain away terrorism as an overreaction to some just cause.) Moussa didn't gain much from going public. He lost influence within Stockholm's central mosque. But his articles in the tabloid press brought many moderate Swedish Muslim voices out of the woodwork.

Islam's compatibility with liberal institutions is hard to gauge. Like most religions, it is experienced by its believers as an accession to a higher kind of liberty, and extremism in defense of liberty is no vice. So once you favor sharia, you are unlikely to worry that people, institutions, or tactics are "too Islamic." Consider Lebanon. There, a majority (53 percent) of Christians consider Islamic extremism a threat to the country, while only 42 percent do not. But only 4 percent of Lebanese Muslims worry about Muslim extremism, versus 85 percent who do not. To add to the difficulty, many of the most sophisticated discussions of Islam's relation to democracy—by the Iranian intellectuals Akbar Ganji and Abdolkarim Soroush, for instance—are not accessible to many Westerners. In many cases they have not even been translated. This tends to de-democratize Western discussions of Islam, and place them in the hands of panels of experts. Experts condescend to European publics who doubt that Islam is compatible with democracy, scolding them, in essence, for not having a doctorate in theology and a reading knowledge of Farsi.

For now, the moderation of Islam is a hope, not a fact. Yet European leaders have wagered so much on it that they see evidence of it everywhere. For example, few Muslim leaders have as high a reputation for moderation as Mustafa Çeric, grand mufti of Bosnia-Herzegovina, largely on the strength of Koranic interpretations such as: "Religious tolerance is clearly commanded in our Holy Book: 'God does not forbid you to deal kindly and justly with those who have not declared war on your religion or driven you out of your homes. (60:8)'" To see moderation here is to leap to conclusions. While this Koranic passage is certainly open to a moderate interpretation, it invites other interpretations, too—not as a command to tolerance, but as permission not to be intolerant, if one chooses. "Declaration of war" and "driving out of one's home" can be construed in radical ways. They can mean "recognition of the state of Israel" or "failure to intervene militarily on the side of the Pakistanis in Kashmir" or something else no one has thought of. In fact, that is how they *tend* to be construed by the very radical muftis whom people like Çeric are supposed to coax into the liberal fold.

And not everyone is as inclined as Çeric to push in a liberal direction. In the immediate aftermath of the July 7 transport bombings, the British Muslim Massoud Shadjareh, chair of the Islamic Human Rights Commission, condemned the attacks—but with an astonishing qualification. "There needs to be a separation between those who are committing those atrocities and those who are passionate about injustice," he said. "We need to encourage that passion and give them avenues within the civil society to deal with injustices." While not explicitly supporting terrorism, this view holds al-Qaeda's analysis of the world to be essentially correct. It passes for "moderate," but all it really does is shift the ultimatum to the West to a different stage —from detonation to recruitment. Al-Qaeda says the West must do certain things or face terrorism. Moderates say the West must do certain things or moderates will join al-Qaeda. If this is the West's choice, then it is difficult to see what it gets out of cultivating moderate Muslims.

Voices like Shadjareh's are the kind that Western politicians—foolishly—want to hear. If the top priority is finding people with the street credibility to dissuade potential terrorists, then the ideal Muslim interlocutor is not just "moderate" but also "authentic." He is someone whose politics overlap a bit with the terrorists', but who renounces terrorism. This creates a trap for Muslims themselves. After September 11, Westerners expected loud and unambiguous denunciations of terrorism—because such denunciations were the only way of telling "moderate" Muslims from radical ones. As in the United States, the condemnation of terrorism by Muslims in Europe has never been frequent or full-throated enough to reassure their fellow citizens. There was a collective test of loyalty. Muslims, for the most part, failed it.

In theory, this was outrageously unfair. Why, after all, should Muslims who think of themselves as French or British feel any greater responsibility than their non-Muslim fellow citizens to vilify the perpetrators? The American journalist Kevin Cullen accurately captured the mood in London after the bombings of July 2005:

Muslims say that white Americans were not held responsible for the actions of Timothy McVeigh, convicted of the Oklahoma City bombing, and that white Britons were not accused of being complicit in the actions of Harold Shipman, an English doctor who was imprisoned five years ago for murdering more than 500 of his patients. So, why, they ask, are they not only being accused of being responsible for producing the bombers who struck last month, but also told to step back while the great and the good sort it out[?]

In practice there is a very big difference: There was no substantial body of white Americans who applauded McVeigh's act or said that, although his means were wrong, the injustices he named were real, and that to ignore his message was to invite retribution. There was no body of British whites who found Harold Shipman's serial killing anything less than repugnant.

Muslim repugnance was far from unanimous. In 2003, on the second anniversary of the bombings of September 11, 2001, the British radical Muslim group al-Muhajiroun posted handbills to publicize an event that would celebrate the 9/11 hijackers as "the Magnificent 19." The event was rightly seen as a tool for whipping up homicidal rage and recruiting fresh terrorists. Part of Britain's response to such threats—particularly after it had been devastated by four deadly bombings in July 2005—was to craft legislation mandating prison or deportation for those "attacking the values of the West." The home secretary at the time, Charles Clarke, suggested that saying "Terrorists go straight to paradise when they die" might be captured by the law. But what else might be captured under the rubric of "glorifying" terrorism? Some asked if an Irishman who celebrated the Easter Rising of 1916 would fall afoul of the statute. Authorities replied that obviously he would not. So "glorification of terrorism" wound up being like U.S. jurist Potter Stewart's definition of pornography: as something that people know when they see it. In the name of universalism, Britain was making law that could be reasonably enforced only through folk wisdom.

In April of 2007, almost two years after the London transport bombings, Scotland Yard's head of counterterrorism, Peter Clarke, said, "I firmly believe that there are other people who have knowledge of what lay behind the attacks in July 2005—knowledge that they have not shared with us. In fact, I don't only believe it. I know it for a fact." Urging those with knowledge of the terrorists to come forward, he added, "I do understand that some of you will have real concerns about the consequences of telling us what you know. I also know that some of you have been actively dissuaded from speaking to us. Surely this must stop."

Not every Muslim, then, was a "moderate Muslim." To say there were moderate and immoderate Muslims was simply a euphemistic way of expressing the view for which Europeans had heaped so much scorn on George W. Bush: "Either you are with us, or you are with the terrorists."

Tariq Ramadan and double language

After 2001, Muslim caginess in talking about terrorism unnerved Europeans, as it did Americans. Many who had a nodding acquaintance with Muslim terminology thought Muslims were using the ancient Shiite tactic of *taqiyyah*, self-protective dissimulation, and jumped to the conclusion that nothing Muslims said on the subject of religion, or of the clash between East and West, could be trusted. But in most instances, the troubling utterances of Muslim leaders were neither lying nor *taqiyyah*. They were what came to be called "double language."

Some Muslim leaders just flatly contradicted themselves, making one kind of speech in a European language and a very different kind in Arabic. A good example was the late Danish imam Abu Laban, who spoke in late 2005 about the new concept of Islam that his Copenhagen-based center, Islam Trossam, was working on. "It is a progressive vision, not built on fear of Western culture. There is no ghetto mentality. Women play an important role, parallel to men's role." As for terrorism, he added, "If we discovered Islam was a threat to the West, I would be the first to fight it."

Yet Abu Laban was at that very moment arranging to rile up certain radical religious leaders in the Middle East with sensational presentations of the Danish caricatures of Muhammad, which had been published a few weeks earlier. In the coming months, those leaders' broadcast denunciations would help spark violent protests around the world. And Abu Laban had given ample evidence of this less moderate side throughout his career. In 1995, he gave a talk about "ways to defend ourselves against Western contamination," before the Ninth Congress of the Islamic Cultural Institute of the viale Jenner in Milan. "They accept Muslims in their midst, they accept the chador and Islamic lifestyles," Abu Laban said. "We, therefore, must pretend that we accept their religion and their individual freedom. But this is impossible. Islam can accept no one who does not adore Allah."

Double language means something different. Double language is not saying two different things to two different audiences. It is preaching a consistent message that will be understood in different ways by two different audiences. A good example was community leaders' use of the word *respect* to describe the aspirations of France's ghetto dwellers. To social workers and politicians, respect sounded like a demand for equal rights. To those who lived in the ghetto, it had a retributive, intimidating, power-related connotation.

Tariq Ramadan—a charismatic political activist, prolific writer, freelance theologian, and motivational speaker based in Geneva—is, to his foes, the very embodiment of double language. Ramadan has denied using any kind of "double discourse". He told Andrew Hussey in the *New Statesman*, "To those who say it, I say: bring the evidence. I am quite clear in what I say." Ramadan tours university campuses in Europe promoting a reasonable-sounding society based on Islamic law, and demanding full recognition of Islam in all of Europe's institutions. Americans are used to well-read, highly politicized men of God of every political and theological leaning—Pat Robertson, William Sloane Coffin, Jeremiah Wright, John Shelby Spong, and Michael Lerner are among the varied examples. Contemporary Europeans are less well equipped to figure out Ramadan's role and views, which can be hard to pin down even after one has read most of his writings.

Ramadan is the grandson (on his mother's side) of Hassan al-Banna, who in 1928 founded the Egyptian Muslim Brotherhood, and with it the style of Islamism that has swept the world in the last few years. Ramadan's father, Said, was arguably more radical still. Although published accounts suggest he worked as a CIA informer, he was also close to Said Qutb, the anti-American Egyptian intellectual whose writings had a big influence on the founders of al-Qaeda, and he was implicated in the plot against the Egyptian government for which Qutb was hanged.

In an age of celebrity, all of this makes Tariq Ramadan, to any Muslim fundamentalist, a person to be reckoned with. The unapologetic radicalism of his brother Hani, with whom he works closely and who has publicly supported the stoning of adulterous women, increases his street credibility. Ramadan himself is given to remarks that leave fair-minded Europeans nervous. Even months after the September 11 attacks, he would go only so far as to say that there was a "very strong probability" that Muslim terrorists were involved. He insisted that there were other possibilities, including drug and arms dealers and unspecified gas and oil interests. He is given to looking for the "objective causes" of Islamist outrages, including the massacre of Christians in Nigeria, of which he has said, "We need to consider the situation objectively and bring a critical view as much to the causes—global homogenization and a sometimes savage Westernization—as to the consequences—ethnic and religious tension."

But in general he has made the case for Islam in a pluralistic enough way to reassure European political leaders that he can act as a bridge between Muslims and the broader European population. He has not ruled out Israel's right to exist. He is not a misogynist. His adversaries in Muslim countries are often arch-conservative clerics. And he has a gift for pithy formulas that offer something to both Muslims on the march and jittery Westerners: "Islam stands for the liberation of women," he says, "but not at the expense of children."

Not everyone is put at ease. Ramadan was barred from France in the 1990s, and was, as of this writing, still persona non grata in Tunisia, Egypt, and Saudi Arabia. In 2004, he was scheduled to take up a tenured professorship at Notre Dame in Indiana, but the State Department withdrew his visa, on grounds that were never made clear, although the USA Patriot Act was invoked vaguely. There has been a lot of published speculation about the reasons for Ramadan's exclusion: The Spanish judge Baltasar Garzón allegedly discovered contacts with an al-Qaeda operative. Ramadan reportedly told a U.S. embassy official in Bern that resistance in Iraq was justified. He made a €600 contribution to a French-based (and legal) Palestinian foundation that the United States has linked to Hamas.

Ramadan moved to Britain and spent the last months of Tony Blair's term in office teaching at Oxford and advising the British government. Since Ramadan is the most broadly listened to contemporary explainer—to both Muslims and non-Muslims—of Islam's most troubling doctrines, it is important to figure out whether his reflections on Muslims' role in the West are workable and sincere. Does he believe Muslims can be real European citizens or does he believe they will always remain somehow foreign?

Muslims have traditionally addressed such questions through a division of the world into two parts. There is *dar al-islam* (or the "house of Islam") on one hand and *dar al-harb* (or the "house of war") on the other. Ramadan starts by refusing this division altogether, on two grounds. First, the terms come from historians, not from the Koran. They are appropriate to the first three centuries of Muslim conquest, Ramadan believes, but not to a world altered by colonization and mass migration. Second, aside from a few frictions surrounding mosque construction, European laws give Muslims a liberty to practice their faith and vent their opinions that has no parallel elsewhere. "This could lead one to conclude," Ramadan insists, "that, in terms of security and peace, the name *dar al-islam* is applicable to almost all Western countries, but that it does not apply in the slightest to the great majority of contemporary Muslim ones." He refers to

Europe as *dar al-shahada*—which means something like the "domain of witness."

The problem, in Ramadan's view, is that Europe's core values are corrupt and sinful. He may not refer to the European geographical space as *dar al-harb*—but he reviles the "soulless capitalism that puts everything up for sale," and refers to the European-American system that underpins it as *alam al-harb*: the "abode of war." He has called for "resistance to the homogenizing international order" and declared himself "willing to do the impossible," he says, "to join and support any movement of consciousness-raising and resistance, such as the citizens' movement we saw [at the anti-World Trade Organization meetings in 1999] in Seattle." He is a regular at such anti-capitalist gatherings as the European Social Forum.

Ramadan is easily mistaken for a run-of-the-mill European Marxist or anti-globalization activist—a comrade-in-arms of a mostly secular movement who happens to be a Muslim, too. Since hard-line Islamists are known to hold Communism in low esteem, it is easy to assume that Ramadan is going out on a limb before his Muslim audiences, taking risks, speaking truth to power. To judge him this way—as a number of astute European and American thinkers, including Gilles Kepel and Ian Buruma, have done—is to understand his message as far more secular, and far less religious, than it actually is. According to Buruma: "Ramadan, as Kepel observes, is 'balanced on a tightrope,' for his socialism is not always congenial to devout Muslims. Marx (along with 'the Jew,' 'the Crusader' and 'the Secularist') is a demonic figure for the Muslim Brothers." But the thing about Ramadan's "socialism" is that there is no positive content—no political, material-ist, or economic theory—behind it at all. His leftism is purely a negative *spiritual* evaluation, from a strictly Islamic viewpoint, of the Western moral order, of which "capitalism" is just an outgrowth and a metonym. He is *anti-* the Western order without being *pro-* anything that would alienate the hardest of hard-line Muslims in the slightest.

The word *resistance* is the master key to Ramadan's thinking. It is the foundation of everything else about Ramadan that can be understood doubly. The word appears almost constantly in all of Ramadan's most important writings and speeches. He notes that "in my family, resistance was a key concept, resistance against dictatorship and colonialism." *Resist* is not a democratic verb, in the way that *reform* or *dissent* or *oppose* is. It is a revolutionary verb. Resistance is what one offers against a system that has no legitimacy whatsoever behind it. The French *reformed* their constitutional order in 1958; they *resisted* the Nazis after 1942.

In Ramadan's worldview, Muslims are a saving remnant. They are the last force capable of presenting a spiritual alternative, of saying no, to an anti-spiritual world order. If no major Western religion has seen fit, or been able, to stare down capitalism, that is not the fault of Muslims. "As far as this so-called 'progressive' order is concerned," Ramadan says, "the Catholic 'bastion' and the Jewish 'bastion' have both, it seems, surrendered. They've adapted, they have even at times supported and promoted the new economic order. The only ones left, it seems, are the implacable ones, the Muslims."

Contemporary Europeans, unable to conceive of themselves as thoroughly without legitimacy in anyone's eyes, have chosen to believe that when Ramadan speaks of "resistance," and calls on Muslims everywhere to wage it, he really means "reform." He does not. He means jihad.

Resistance and jihad

When Ramadan describes—quite movingly, it must be added—how we should struggle against the Western order, it is clear that he is not just talking about an economic system. He has bigger fish to fry. His point is metaphysical and even religious:

A human being who lives only by his superficial desires, and whose needs have for the most part been manufactured [by someone else] is no longer a human being. . . . He can become a mere beast, holding up the illusion of his humanity, a virtual monster whose excesses are sometimes restrained only by a strand of rationality that serves as a leash. If this rationality is a humane one, the monster is under control. But if the rationality should become no more than economic or financial, then the beast is unleashed and we can expect the worst, from slaughter to genocide, as we have seen all too often.

Our religion teaches us that the first resistance to these errors is an internal one.

That internal resistance is what Ramadan elsewhere calls *jihad*:

For the vast majority of Muslims, the concept of jihad refers to a spiritual effort and, more generally, to resistance.... I use the word daily in my relationship to myself. Jihad is primarily the effort one makes on oneself to resist the negative forces that inhabit us. It is a work of resistance against one's own anger, one's violence, one's greed.

Ramadan explicitly rejects the usage of *jihad* to mean holy war. This puts him in line with a couple dozen academic spokesmen for Islam in the West, who claim that the "greater jihad" is a struggle for self-mastery. But is it really accurate to say that a majority of Muslims think of a "spiritual effort" when they hear the word *jihad*? Why is it so desperately important to keep this word in common circulation, when it is understood by Muslims' western interlocutors, not to mention many ordinary Muslims, as a call to battle? Diffident modern Westerners tend to purge such words from their vocabulary altogether.

To be precise about how Ramadan is using the words *resistance* and *jihad*, it helps to go back to the writings of his grandfather. It would be unfair to use the writings of al-Banna as a means of elucidating Ramadan's thinking if Ramadan did not constantly claim al-Banna as an influence, touchstone, and source of pride. Ramadan's writings about his grandfather are more curatorial than critical, and we will confine ourselves to the writings of al-Banna that Ramadan himself has cited in his own work. In al-Banna, mental resistance (conscience) and political resistance (revolution) are simply different ways of describing the same coherent process. To al-Banna the worst thing about English economic and political colonization was that it produced a "colonization of the mind" (*colonisation des intimités*). It shaped and warped the private deliberations of Muslims, drawing them away from religious reflection. So for the Muslim Brotherhood in al-Banna's time, demanding the departure of the English from Egypt was an Islamic duty. You may agree or disagree with al-Banna's view of things, but it has its logic. There aren't two kinds of jihad— "real," spiritual jihad and its evil twin—even if pretending there are helps calm European nerves. Jihad means reconnecting with one's true, better self by struggling against harmful, foreign, un-Islamic elements, whether they are found in one's society or in one's own head.

The victory of this better self was inevitable, in al-Banna's view, because the West was spiritually bankrupt. Its materialist civilization was on the verge of collapse. "This is no illusion," al-Banna wrote. "It is rather a law of nature, and if it doesn't happen in our time, then 'Allah will bring a people whom He loveth and who love Him, humble toward believers, stern toward disbelievers, striving in the way of Allah, and fearing not the blame of any blamer.'"

Ramadan proclaims al-Banna a pluralist, on the grounds that he "never demonized the West." But this is an eccentric reading. At best, al-Banna is a pluralist of a selective and asymmetrical kind. What he admires about the West is its power, and what he admires about Islam is its wisdom. Islam has *sagesse*; the Occident has mere *savoir faire*. In a just society, power must serve wisdom, not vice versa. If Muslims possess a truth, and Europeans possess only a bag of practical tricks, then Europeans' system of ordering society—the European regime of rights—cannot be valuable for its own sake. It is valuable, but only for the opportunities it affords for the practice of Islam.

Let us be clear about what this means. As soon as the practice of Islam is constrained, the social contract is null and void. Muslims' acceptance of the European countries in which they live can only ever be provisional, contingent on Europe's willingness to give Islam free rein. The integration of Muslims into Europe will happen on Muslim terms. Or, as Ramadan puts it, "It will succeed when Muslims find in their tradition elements of agreement with the laws of the countries of which they are citizens, because that will resolve any questions of double allegiance." This is an extraordinary statement: Only when Europe's ways are understood as Islam's will Muslims obey them. And if not, not. "Islam is an element that needs to be taken into account, and will need to be in the future," Ramadan has said. "If this reality continues to be denied, it will inevitably produce radical resistance and clashes." Is this double language? While never threatening violence, Ramadan is warning the West that if it does not change in accordance with Muslim wishes, violence will somehow befall it.

When he discusses the world outside of the West, pluralism and rights seem hardly to enter the picture at all. "The future of Muslim countries," he says, "will evolve through a reappropriation of their [own] traditions, and through an endogenous evolution, according to the thinking and mindset internal to the civilization, albeit in relation to others." For Ramadan, the twentieth-century Islamists Muhammad Abduh and Jamal al-Din al-Afghani are exemplars. "They saw the need to resist the West, through Islam, while taking what was useful from it," he told Ian Buruma in 2007. Twentieth-century Islamists thought they could make cynical use of Western technological innovations while holding in contempt the culture out of which they sprang. Twenty-first-century Islamists such as Ramadan take the same attitude towards Western freedoms and rights. For Ramadan, freedom of religion is not a good in itself. It is a good because it allows the practice and consolidation of Islam.

Like al-Banna, Ramadan says what he says and does what he does in the confidence that the West is in eclipse. "Day-to-day life in Europe," he writes, "with its ways of thinking and consuming, its arrangements of work and free time, its movies and its music, winds up shaping, almost unconsciously, a second nature that seems like a prison." Under the circumstances, to raise the question of reciprocal obligations, or ask what Islam will "contribute" to Western society, is off the subject. To a thinker such as Ramadan, it is an impertinence. What Islam will contribute to the West is Islam.

I I

Liberalism and Diversity

Immigration, Islam, and the European Union—The project to bring Turkey into Europe—Pim Fortuyn and the weakness of the West—"Rightism" and "fascism" in the context of immigration and Islam— The Danish People's Party— Nicolas Sarkozy and the strength of the republic—Affirmative action

There is increasingly such a thing as "Europe." The growth of the European Union, global communications and the spread of English among the continent's elites have all brought Europeans closer together. And if Henri Pirenne was right that the movement of hostile Muslims northward was responsible for the founding of Europe 1,000 years ago, then the plantation of Islam in Europe and the hostility towards Europe that simmers in much of the Muslim world are likely to revive people's consciousness of themselves as "European," whether the EU proves a suitable expression of that allegiance or not.

The immigration problem and the Islam problem are similar in all Western European countries. There are, to be sure, variations. Britain remains, by far, the European country with the most serious dangers of violence and political extremism. Sweden is the country with the most intractable segregation. Spain, because of preexisting problems with national unity, is the country most at risk of being swamped by the sheer volume of immigration. Germany's Turkish population will succeed but will assimilate more slowly, largely because its own transplanted national culture is too rich and cohesive to give up.

France will have spectacular social problems, but its republican traditions give it the best chance of fully assimilating the children and
grandchildren of immigrants. It is the only country where a European
equivalent of the American dream is likely.

Still, the conditions unifying Europe culturally have not been better
for decades, and Islam is part of the reason why. Renewed acquaintance with Islam has given Europeans a stronger idea of what Europe
is, because it has given them a stronger idea of what Europe is not.

Immigration, Islam, and the European Union

As we noted earlier, the central political endeavor of almost all
Western European countries over the past half century has been the
creation of the European Union. The EU arose from a couple of
international cooperation agreements in the 1950s. First, the European Coal and Steel Community (1952) sought to bind French and
German industry together in a way that would not contribute to a
future war, as outright French rule over German industrial areas had
done after World War I. Second, the European Economic Community,
launched between France, Germany, Italy, Luxembourg, and the
Netherlands with the Treaty of Rome (1957), aimed at a more
ambitious harmonization of trade regimes. With the Treaty of Maas-
tricht in 1993, the community became the EU, expanding to fifteen
countries aiming at an "ever closer union." At this writing it has
twenty-seven.

From its start, the EU was a way of avoiding conflict by getting rid
of inefficient economic nationalisms. It has grown—in the minds of
its managers, at least—into a project for getting rid of nationalism
altogether. But "nationalism" is a thing too vague for bureaucrats to
root out. What they *can* root out is national sovereignty. This the EU
did in increasing measure. And that rendered the whole project less
and less popular.

The EU was not democratic in any sense in which a neutral observer
would use the word. It held elections for a legislature that sat in
Strasbourg, but it was not a duly constituted legislature. In 2005, a
proposed "constitutional treaty" was scheduled to make it one. It

would have formalized the role of the European parliament, and transferred other functions from nation-states to European authorities, under a process that was extremely (many said intentionally) confusing. The treaty was to have been submitted to about half the European voting publics for ratification by referendum. But French voters rejected it by a wide margin and the Dutch rejected it by almost two to one. This experiment in democracy having failed to produce the desired result, all of the other countries that had planned their own referenda (except Luxembourg) canceled them. The only country given a second crack at voting on the substance of ever closer union was Ireland, which happened to be one of the EU's greatest economic beneficiaries. But the Irish, too, rejected the constitution (repackaged as "the Lisbon treaty") by resounding margins in the spring of 2008.

It had always been assumed that the great potential obstacle to the European "project" would be the reemergence of ancient national rivalries. These might expose the contradictions and trade-offs in the EU project and undermine its most far-reaching ambitions. In the end immigration played as disruptive a role as nationalism did.

The EU stripped national governments of their capacity to carry out two immigration-related duties—defending borders and defending cultures—while failing to develop that capacity at the European level. Citizens of EU countries could settle, vote, work, pay taxes, and collect welfare in whatever other country they chose (although there were transitional regimes for the newest members). Under the various Schengen Agreements negotiated from the 1980s on, border checks between Western European countries (except Britain and Ireland) were abolished. But determining which foreigners would be allowed into the EU in the first place, whether to work or to seek asylum, was left up to the individual nations. At summit after summit, notably at Lisbon in 2000, even the most pro-EU national leaders resolutely refused to surrender their immigration policy to the EU. Their electorates would not permit it. As of this writing, another attempt has been made to harmonize immigration policies, and a common immigration policy is planned for 2010.

The situation that resulted from this mix of democratic self-rule and EU mandates was crazy. It meant that the immigration policy for the whole of Western Europe was set, at any given time, by whichever member state happened to be the most soft-hearted, lax, corrupt, or sanctimonious. At the start of this century, the problem country was Spain. In early 2005, on the eve of the Dutch and French referenda, Spain's Socialist prime minister José Luis Rodríguez Zapatero amnestied 700,000 undocumented immigrants. Such amnesties were not new in Spain. The government of Zapatero's conservative predecessor, José María Aznar, had passed five of them since the mid-1990s. But Zapatero's was simpler, and bigger than all previous amnesties combined. It was also more open to abuse. Announced many months in advance, it gave foreigners—particularly those who were already in other European countries—incentives to enter Spain to lay down a paper trail that would render them undeportable from any European country.

This only *looked* open-hearted. Ministers and editorial writers in other EU countries noted that Zapatero would reap the credit for his "generosity" but non-Spaniards would pay the bill. Once naturalized, non-Europeans could migrate to other EU countries, such as France, the Netherlands, and Germany, which have more generous welfare systems and better health-care services. (In some cases they were migrating *back* to these countries, where they had been living illegally, as "Spaniards.") A year later, when Spain was flooded with African boat people, Zapatero, in effect, admitted his critics were right. His government approached the EU to plead for financial and bureaucratic assistance in policing the flow of Africans. Zapatero complained that "regulating the conditions for entry cannot be the exclusive responsibility of those who are near the gate"—exactly the point that those who had condemned his amnesty had made.

So as a practical matter, EU member states were in a predicament. They had duties to immigrants but no control over how many of them they got. Immigrants had rights that could be claimed in all countries, but responsibilities that could be imposed only locally, and only for as long as they chose to stick around. In remedying this situation, Europeans faced an uncomfortable menu of options: cut welfare and other benefits for everyone, including natives, in order to make one's home country less attractive to newcomers; pull out of the Schengen agreements; hand over more power to Europe, in hopes that authorities in Brussels would limit unilateral amnesties; or take their distance from the entire project of building the EU. They chose the last option, and at the first possible opportunity—by pulling the plug on the constitutional referendum.

The project to bring Turkey into Europe

Nothing undermined popular support for the EU more than the decision of the European Commission to declare Turkey a model for the "moderate," "secular" Islam that Europe aspires to have within its borders, and to proceed with negotiations to admit Turkey to full EU membership. Big pluralities of French and Dutch "no" voters cited Turkey among their primary worries about the EU. Turkey is a fast-growing country. With a projected population of 100 million at mid-century, it would dominate the European parliament from the moment it was admitted. Since the country's per capita income is only 20 percent of the EU's, the inflow of laborers would dwarf anything Europe had previously seen. Turkey is European only in the sense that 5 percent of its landmass is west of the Bosporus. The rest of it runs deep into Asia and the Middle East, bordering on Syria, Iraq, and Iran. Its decades-old war against Kurdish separatists will not strike any Irishman or Dane as a patriotic duty to fight in. Turkey is distant culturally, too: 90 percent of Turks would not countenance living next door to a homosexual and 62 percent think it "perfectly acceptable" for a man to have more than one wife.

Cardinal Josef Ratzinger, shortly before he became Pope Benedict XVI, called EU negotiations a "grave error." They had an "anti-historical" goal, he said, since Turkey's Islamic roots place it in "permanent contrast to Europe." He seemed to have a point. Three-quarters (75 percent) of Turks say it is important for Islam to have an influential role in the world. They vote that way, too, as evidenced by their election of three Islamist governments—one radical, two led by today's more moderate AK party—since the 1990s. Since Kemal Atatürk founded the state in the 1920s, religious moderation has been enforced not by popular consensus but by an army that sees repressing political Islam as its main role. Europeans insisted that Turkey "democratize" in order to join the EU—starting with removing its army from politics. Turkey complied. As popular will has come more and more to the surface, the country has drifted further from the army-imposed "secularism" that was Europe's main rationale for recruiting it in the first place.

The worry of the European-in-the-street was that if his leaders will call *that* Europe, they'll call anything Europe. Continent-wide, only a third of Europeans supported Turkish accession. In not a single country did a democratic majority support Turkish admission to the EU, and in some countries the opposition ran almost five-to-one. The German Marshall Fund's Transatlantic Trends survey found that 46 percent of French people said Turkish accession was a "bad thing," versus just 10 percent who called it a "good thing." This wholesale public opposition seems to have given no one in the upper reaches of the EU bureaucracy a moment's pause.

The admission of Turkey turned out to be desperately important to Europe's Muslim leaders: It would mean not just that a Muslim nation was on good terms with its European neighbors but that Europe had accorded Islam a place as one of "its" religions. As Oguz Ücüncü, a leader of the German wing of the nationalistic religious group Milli Görüs, wrote during the accession negotiations: "If Turkey can't be a part of Europe, the next step is Muslims can't." This may also explain why, even as the EU has fallen to referendum-losing levels of popularity in Europe at large, its popularity among immigrants remains sky high, reaching 85 percent in some polls, according to the Iranian-Swedish immigration researcher Masoud Kamali. "You are not going to be a Swede," Kamali explained, "or, at least, it's not *you* who's going to decide if you are a Swede. But perhaps you can choose to be a European."

An almost inevitable result of heavy immigration is the growth of such legalistic conceptions of identity as Kamali's. A study on identity done by the Institute for Public Policy Research (IPPR), a Labour think tank, found that 51 percent of minorities in England considered themselves "British," versus 29 percent of whites. Meanwhile 52 percent of whites considered themselves "English," versus 11 percent of minorities. The late Sir Bernard Crick, an education expert and a designer of Britain's "citizenship curriculum," noted: "To the immigrant,

Britishness is essentially a legal and political structure. It doesn't mean the culture. When the immigrant says I am British, he is not saying he wants to be English or Scottish or Welsh."

This was the EU model of belonging: You are one person for your culture and another for the law. You can be an official (legal) European even if you are not a "real" (cultural) European. This disaggregation of the personal personality and the legal personality sounds tolerant and liberating, but it has its downside. Rights are attached to citizenship. As soon as your citizenship becomes a legal construction, so do your rights. They cease to be inalienable. The politics typified by the EU began to crumble when Pim Fortuyn—a flamboyant, gay, ex-Marxist ex-sociology professor—warned that Europe was throwing out the cultural baby along with the nationalist bathwater. There could be no European Union without a European identity.

Pim Fortuyn and the weakness of the West

For decades the Netherlands pursued a consciously multiculturalist policy, called "Integration with Maintenance of One's Own Identity." Those who offered even the meekest of warnings that this policy undermined the country's common culture were routinely censured. As noted earlier, when Frits Bolkestein, the center-right party leader, took the position in the 1990s that Muslim immigrants who had acquired multiple wives abroad should not be allowed to bring them all to the Netherlands, he was rebuked by the youth wing of his party. Any outright opposition to immigration, meanwhile, was held tantamount to inciting racial hatred. Hans Janmaat, who founded the tiny Centrum party in the 1980s on a program of halting immigration, was prosecuted for his views.

That climate of opinion changed all of a sudden. In November 2001, Pim Fortuyn was picked by the anti-establishment Livable Netherlands party to be its top candidate for national office. While he was never particularly pro-American, he had been shaken to the core by the attacks on the World Trade Center some weeks before. He saw the Dutch state's neutral tolerance of nonnative cultures, especially

Muslim cultures, as a mortal threat to the country. Fortuyn's remarks soon became too radical even for the radicals of Livable Netherlands, and he was forced to run as the candidate of a party he had started himself, the Pim Fortuyn List.

Fortuyn's view of multiculturalism was original, sophisticated, and confusing. In one sense, it is surprising that it raised any controversy at all. A great beneficiary of multiculturalism, first as a Dutch Catholic and later as a homosexual, he defended the Western system of liberties on precisely the same grounds that the multiculturalist establishment did. He shared their view of Dutch history's low points—colonialism, colonial war, collaboration with the Nazis. He also shared their view of its high points—increasingly equal treatment for women, nonwhites, Jews, and homosexuals.

But here they parted ways. Multiculturalists believed that the new system of rights made the West not just better but stronger. Fortuyn believed that such liberties made the West better but more vulnerable, unless novel arrangements were made to protect it. "We are," he said, "a lot less powerful than we think." This reassessment turned the whole Dutch immigration debate on its head. The main danger to the West, he felt, was the Islamic culture imported along with new immigrants and planted in the West by their children. "Our conception of our own culture is becoming dangerously relativistic," he wrote. "Fundamentalist Islam is not just a considerable cultural, political, economic and military force in the Middle East. It is also gaining ground in North Africa. Our cultural relativists have no response to it, and would rather stick their heads in the sand. There is no reason to doubt, over the long term, that this fundamentalism will grow stronger in our part of the world."

If the West could not withstand the influence of Islam, which Fortuyn called "a life-threatening culture," then the wisest course was to minimize exposure to it. This meant examining closely what imams were saying for evidence of subversion, in a way that Fortuyn explicitly compared to the surveillance of Communists during the Cold War. It also meant introducing sharp cultural distinctions into Western immigration policy. "The admission of someone from our own cultural sphere," he wrote, "is something totally different than the admission of someone from a cultural sphere far removed from ours. A quota policy for the acceptance of asylum-seekers looks inevitable to me."

In one way, such views made Fortuyn a perfect European. But it was a kind of European-ness incompatible with the treaties and institutions on which the EU was based. Fortuyn called for the Netherlands to withdraw from both the border-opening Schengen agreements and the 1951 UN convention on refugees. Fortuyn never ignored the Dutch constitution. "If you're born and raised here, you have citizen's rights, period," Fortuyn allowed. "Janmaat certainly went further than that. He wanted to give people [immigrants] a one-way ticket back. You won't see any of that with me." Fortuyn was not a racist, and his colorful repartee about the Moroccan men he had slept with was adequate to place him above the suspicion of being one. But, slice it any way you like, his argument was not different from Janmaat's. It was a different *style* of argument. It was the same argument in a multicultural idiom.

Fortuyn's idea of multiculturalism was idiosyncratic. "People use the term casually," he said, "but they're never able to define it, let alone provide it with a substantial content." His attempt to provide multiculturalism with such a content revealed a love–hate relationship with the whole constitutional order. Article I of the Dutch constitution forbids discrimination. Fortuyn vacillated between praise for it (as the bulwark of Western rights) and contempt for it (as an obstacle to their protection). He proposed to limit immigration to Holland in the name of openness. He proposed to destroy the global village in order to save it.

The Dutch, who harbored a similar ambivalence, could not get enough of Fortuyn's kind of talk. As he rose in the polls, it became clear that Holland's entire multicultural order was being propped up by taboos, not consent, and that most Dutch natives felt immigrants were using Dutch tolerance to take them for a ride. Fortuyn could well have become prime minister had he not been shot dead days before national elections in May 2002, by an animal rights activist who claimed to be acting to protect Dutch Muslims.

It is hard to say what would have come of Fortuyn's ideas had he lived. Alone among postwar politicians, he managed to start a debate about the very rationale of multiculturalism, about its costs and benefits, and this is a debate that few of its proponents wish to have even today. Essential to figuring Fortuyn out is understanding why he saw Islam as a *particular* menace for Europe.

Fortuyn's gripe does not appear to be a matter of doctrines, which he sought persistently to take off the table. He loved to speak of "Judeo-Christian culture," and of his own Catholic background, but almost never of Judeo-Christian religion. "I speak expressly in terms of culture," he wrote, "which is a far broader term than religion. Religions can be abandoned, as has happened on a large scale in our country, but a culture can't be left behind so easily." These premises are all highly debatable, even dubious. Was that really his problem with talking about religion? Or was it that *post*-religion—which Fortuyn calls "culture" but which others call "lifestyle"—was the only kind of religion he recognized?

For Fortuyn, multiculturalism was a kind of truce. "Church and religion belong to the private sphere of life, and must not determine the public sphere," he said. "At the very most they can influence it in a normative way." Culturally, everyone in a multicultural order is disarmed. Just as the classic nation-state was marked by a state monopoly on violence, the multicultural nation-state is marked by a state monopoly on moral order. *Any* fervently espoused religion threatens that monopoly, as surely as a private militia threatened the old nation-state. Christians and Jews may still worship God privately, but on normative matters, they have surrendered to the new, progressive order. Muslims are distinguished by their refusal to submit to this spiritual disarmament. They stand out as the only implacable source of resistance to multiculturalism in the public sphere. Should the multicultural order fall, Islam is the only value system waiting in the wings. Notice that Fortuyn's analysis of Islam's role as an identity of resistance is *exactly* the same as Tariq Ramadan's, even if the two have opposite views about whether this is a good thing or not.

Fortuyn saw Islam as Europe's biggest problem. But his rise revealed a broader problem that Europe would have even if not a single Muslim had ever immigrated there. It was not clear that Europe, as he saw it, was compatible with *any* religious worldview. He was willing to admit that the individualistic culture he adored arose from Europe's Christian past. But it was more important to Fortuyn that

that culture be past than that it be Christian. In large part, what made Islam intolerable to Fortuyn was that it was a living religion. To him, equal treatment of women, racial nondiscrimination, and (perhaps above all) freedom of sexual comportment are absolute rights. But freedom of religion is now a right whose claims have been rendered relative by the advance of history. Where it clashes with newer "cultural" rights, it must make way. This is to say that freedom of religion has ceased to be a right at all.

"Rightism" and "fascism" in the context of immigration and Islam

Pim Fortuyn was a battling kind of radical liberal. He was not a fascist, but he was murdered by someone who was under the impression that he was one. Such mislabeling, even when it is not fatal, always clouds discussion of immigration in Europe. The terms *fascist*, *xenophobe*, *extremist*, and *radical* are applied promiscuously to a wide range of anti-immigrant parties and tendencies, most of which are democratic. There are eccentric hobbyists whose members wouldn't harm a fly, like the UK Independence Party, which focuses on pulling Britain out of the EU, or the French hunters' rights party, which focuses on private property. There are also regionalist parties that, in America, would merely be considered conservative. Italy's Northern League, for instance, takes a hard line on immigration but only as part of the larger claim that the Italian welfare state loots middle-class taxpayers for the benefit of the politically favored. The favored include (but are by no means limited to) immigrants and asylum seekers.

The Flemish nationalist Vlaams Belang (VB) behaves similarly. It certainly opposes immigration, but such opposition is subordinated to the more pressing interest of carving an independent Flanders out of a Belgium that they perceive to be exploiting it. It is worth noting that the VB's political lineage can be traced back to World War II–era Belgian fascism. But many of Europe's historically fascist parties are now very much in the European mainstream on immigration matters. Italy's National Alliance (AN), descended from Benito Mussolini's party, is the best example. The party leader, Gianfranco Fini, is one of Italy's more *pro*-immigrant politicians (he has urged giving immigrants voting rights in local elections as soon as they arrive), and perhaps its most ardent defender of Israel. It was the Spanish Popular Party, which became the democratic home of conservative politicians after the death of Franco, that opened Spain up to mass immigration in the first place.

There have been episodes of serious anti-immigrant violence in Europe. "White riots" sometimes broke out in London between the 1950s and 1970s. Muslim graves were desecrated in Britain in 2005 by a group calling itself "The Black Nation." Areas in eastern Berlin, notably the Soviet-era housing developments of Hellersdorf and Marzahn, are considered no-go areas by many nonwhite Germans. Several Turks died when radicals burned their apartments in the cities of Solingen and Hoyerswerda in 1993. That is not to mention the hooliganism of football supporters and others, which often has a significant overlap with racism and fascism. In France, one Paris–St. Germain fan was convicted of setting the mosque of Annecy and a local Muslim prayer room on fire in 2004, in the company of a collector of Hitler paraphernalia. It is probable that we underestimate the gravity of anti-immigrant violence, since much of it is camouflaged as street violence. But the impact of anti-immigrant radicalism on day-to-day European politics can be exaggerated.

Although we should not be surprised if politics gets more radical in coming years, which look to be years of economic privation, it is unlikely that World War II-style fascistic movements are Europe's biggest worry. It is even less clear that the rightist parties that exist today are especially preoccupied with Islam. In France, the National Front (FN) founded by Jean-Marie Le Pen, made up largely of ex-Communists and whites stranded in heavily immigrant housing projects, is known for its anti-immigrant, anti-multiculturalist rhetoric. But its stance is more ambivalent than it looks. Le Pen has at times taken pains to *court* the votes of Muslims and other immigrants, mostly by trying to convince them that he shares Arab foreign policy views on Israel and (more recently) Iraq. Le Pen was Europe's most ardent defender of Saddam Hussein throughout the period between the two Iraq wars, both of which he strongly criticized. In the 2007 presidential election campaign, Le Pen, through his wife Jany, worked with the Franco-African comedian Dieudonné to promote the rights of pygmies in Cameroon.

The Freedom Party of Austria (FPÖ), which entered the Austrian government in 2000, did something similar. The main foreign policy interest of its late leader, Jörg Haider, during his time in the international spotlight, was to strengthen ties with the dictator Moammar Gaddafi in Libya, in return for which Gaddafi hectored Europe to get over its guilt about its Nazi past and to keep "its eyes on the interests of its people and not those of the Zionist system."

The European political landscape does include extremist parties that sow hatred and focus almost exclusively on immigrants, the most important of which is probably the British National Party. But it is a fringe party. The BNP controls a handful of local offices in northern England and southern neighborhoods such as Barking, a Labour stronghold in southeast London where the number of foreign born rose steeply over the last decade.

But even on the extremes, the link with opposition to immigration need not be crystal clear. The German National Party (NPD), which has overt neo-Nazi traits, is made up of intellectuals of the extreme right and habitués of the skinhead and Rammstein hard-rock movements of the 1990s. The NPD took a dozen seats in the parliament of (formerly East German) Saxony in 2004 on a program that mixes neo-Nazism and neo-Communism. (The NPD has sometimes campaigned in alliance with the similarly disposed German People's Union (DVU); the name it took sometimes depended on the state in which it ran.) Bavarian-born Karl Richter, the most eloquent of the NPD's members in the Saxon parliament, has expressed admiration for ex–Social Democrat Oskar Lafontaine, now a leader of the Left Party, which draws on the heritage and membership of the former East German state Communist party, the SED. The party communicates with its followers via rock music CDs featuring groups with names like "The Power of Capital." Sixteen percent of kids under eighteen said they would vote NPD if they could.

The NPD's importance is easily exaggerated. Saxony, the most geriatric of the German states, is projected to lose a sixth of its population by 2020. So a youth movement can grow in electoral weight even if it does not add members. Nor does it need a forward-looking agenda. The NPD, at least in Saxony, has stoked outrage for some of its members' "revisionist" views on World War II and the Holocaust. Richter called Cold War East Germany the more German of the two states, "a small-scale, less efficient copy of the Third Reich that awakens a certain nostalgia even in the West [of Germany]." But curiously, the NPD's rhetoric about immigration and Islam shows less animosity than one would expect. On the contrary, Richter expresses far more concern over what he calls American imperialism than over Muslim extremism. Of his party's foreign-policy vision, Richter stressed two pillars—to pursue a *rapprochement* with Russia and to restore the relations with the Muslim world that were "problem-free for centuries" until the postwar German alliance with the United States.

The Danish People's Party

The single most immigrant-obsessed party in Europe is rigorously law abiding and democratic. The Danish People's Party (DF) grew out of an anti-immigrant movement in Denmark that was started in 1986 by the Lutheran pastor, intellectual, and author Søren Krarup and by his cousin and fellow pastor Jesper Langballe. The two had come to despair over a 1983 refugee law that granted every asylum seeker the right to enter Denmark to have his case decided. "Such a rule is national suicide," Langballe recalled two decades later. "You cannot give the whole world such rights and guarantees without taking away Danish people's rights." Many Danes agreed, and some were even willing to say so. In 1996, the party itself, newly founded by the housewife Pia Kjaersgaard, entered Parliament. It took 13 percent of the vote in the 2001 elections and brought twenty-two members to Copenhagen, including Krarup and Langballe. While it did not enter the government, the ruling Venstre party was dependent on its support for the next half decade, and passed some of the most stringent restrictions on immigration and naturalization in Europe.

The DF combines a populist suspicion of high immigration with a determination to defend the Christian character of Danish life. It has little appeal among elites, who are quick to remark that it is "led by a housewife [Kjaersgaard] with only a ninth-grade education." Kjaersgaard has said that Islam is not a religion. Some DF parliamentarians have made remarks more objectionable still. One parliamentarian, Louise Frevert, suggested sending immigrant criminals to Russian prisons, "since our laws do not allow us to kill them." But the party is open and inclusive—Frevert, for instance, is a married lesbian and a former porn actress who once belly-danced for the Shah of Iran. And it is explicitly anti-authoritarian—many of its older members were ardent anti-Communists, according to Langballe. Tøger Seidenfaden, the editor of the daily *Politiken* and one of the DF's most prominent foes, says of the party, "There is nothing fascist at all about it, nothing anti-democratic or violent. They regularly eject extremists. They are not like the National Front. That said, they are xenophobic, intolerant and anti-Muslim."

The DF and movements like it owe their success not to any recrudescent European barbarism but to the silence of mainstream parties on issues that motivate voting publics. The big "people's parties" have been withering measurably in all countries for a couple of decades. Immigration is not the only issue on which the major parties have failed to find a voice, but it is the biggest. In the first round of the French presidential elections in 2002, Jacques Chirac managed to finish first with the support of just a fifth of the public. The rival socialists finished so poorly that they were passed for second place by the National Front. This does not mean, however, that people *want* the establishment parties to fail. When it became apparent that Chirac's challenger in the 2002 runoff would be Le Pen, 80 percent of France rallied behind Chirac.

The 2005 elections in Germany marked the first time since the Second World War that both major parties got under 40 percent, and the winning Christian Democrats were barely able to scrape their way to 35. The result of that election was a grand coalition, uniting the Social Democrats and Christian Democrats—a government that circled the wagons of the whole political establishment. It was the sealing of a similar establishment bargain in Holland—uniting the "red" laborites of the PvdA and the "blue" liberals of the VVD into a so-called "purple" coalition—that radicalized Pim Fortuyn.

Establishment parties had no incentive to respond to disquiet over immigration until the DF and the Pim Fortuyn List began to use it to draw votes. It is difficult to come up with a coherent policy for managing population flows in a complex global economy, and the cultural consequences that result from them. But it is easy to snigger at Pim Fortuyn and Søren Krarup and to say or imply that they are the second coming of Adolf Hitler. By the turn of the century, European politics was in stalemate. In the name of "protecting democracy," Europe's political system was growing steadily less democratically accountable. Protecting democracy meant silencing people who raised questions for which leaders had no answers. The stalemate was broken by Nicolas Sarkozy, who became president of France in May 2007.

Nicolas Sarkozy and the strength of the republic

During the riots in the heavily immigrant Paris suburb of Villiers-le-Bel in November 2007, six policemen were shot while using nonlethal crowd-control techniques to contain raging mobs of youths. "Some of them wore hoods, and didn't limit themselves to throwing projectiles and Molotov cocktails," one policeman said after the riots. "They used guns. And our response will not be limited indefinitely to firing flashballs and tear gas." One French judge expressed sympathy for the difficult living conditions endured by the rioters in Villiers-le-Bel, but insisted that there comes a time when assigning responsibility for violence is beside the point. "While it is clear," he wrote, "that the excesses of one part of the population should be understood as the direct result of social conditions, which are a shame to our society, that doesn't mean society has no right to defend itself."

Earlier that year, Xavier Lemoine, the mayor of one of the most violent of the Paris suburbs, Montfermeil, said of urban unrest: "France can tolerate neither the illness nor the cure." This "cure," one infers, meant getting tough with Europe's minorities, regardless of the constitutional and democratic niceties. And that was a grim diagnosis. The most important problem in Europe is the fallout from decades of mass immigration. The most important moral "value" in Europe is democracy. There is sometimes a striking lack of confidence in the latter's capacity to address the former.

Sarkozy is probably the representative figure of the politics that is replacing uncritical multiculturalism. He is a pure product of the French political establishment, of the various Gaullist parties of the 1980s and 1990s. But he is not from the elite branch of it, that part schooled at the country's specialized universities (especially the École Nationale d'Administration), and his rise was greeted with some of the same feigned horror with which the Dutch greeted Fortuyn.

In an important sense, Sarkozy was Fortuyn's opposite. Fortuyn's politics arose from the conviction that Western tolerance made the countries that practiced it weak. A country like the Netherlands was defendable only if it limited both immigration and the demands of multinational bodies. Sarkozy, by contrast, believed that "the republic and democracy are much stronger than we realize." They could handle immigration, even mass immigration of the sort that France had received over the decades. He urged patience with suburban troublemakers and the havoc they wrought. "They're young, they're new," he said in 2004. "That will fade. Give them time."

But if integration was inevitable, it was also non-negotiable. France could handle immigration because the French Republic was capable of being tough, and even ruthless. When the first riots of his presidency broke out in Villiers-le-Bel, Sarkozy told a roomful of police, "The response to riots is not spending more money and putting it on the back of the taxpayer. The response to riots is to arrest rioters." When asked why he had delayed an urban revitalization plan, he replied, "It's not up to delinquents shooting at the police to set the agenda of the Republic."

Toughness is the most memorable part of Sarkozy's agenda, because toughness is the most memorable thing about his character. As mayor of the city of Neuilly-sur-Seine in the 1980s, he walked into a building to negotiate personally with a man holding hostages at gunpoint. In 1999, taunted during a visit to a housing project outside of Paris by a hoodlum shouting "Sarko, go home!" he approached the young man and said, "*Mister* Sarkozy, if you don't mind." He later explained, "When they see you're not afraid, they respect you more."

Sarkozy was almost unique among French politicians in knowing what the inside of a housing project looked like. On the eve of the French banlieue riots of 2005, when the eleven-year-old son of an immigrant family was shot dead while washing his father's car as a Father's Day present in the Cité des Quatre Mille housing project outside of Paris, Sarkozy visited the family and promised to clean up the neighborhood *à karcher*—citing the trade name of a company that makes high-pressure hoses. We have already noted his promise to the residents of Aulnay-sous-Bois to take care of the "riff-raff" (*racaille*) who were terrorizing them.

Sarkozy thrived on the urban conflict that overwhelmed France in 2005. He was widely attacked for his *karcher* and *racaille* remarks, but he was the only major national politician whose popularity rose during the riots, not least among the voters who supported Jean-Marie Le Pen and the National Front. Polls during the 2007 election campaign that brought him the presidency even showed him doing better among Le Pen supporters than Le Pen himself. His best-known policy initiatives included trying sixteen-year-olds as adults, establishing a Ministry of Immigration and National Identity, and testing immigrants' DNA to prevent grants of citizenship and residence based on fraudulent claims of family relation. It was one of his proudest boasts as interior minister that the granting of first-time residency permits had fallen by 2.6 percent on his watch. Sarkozy was contemptuous of suggestions that he was pandering to fascists. "I always try to get as many votes as possible," he said in an interview at the Ministry of the Interior in the winter of 2006, "whether it's from the FN or anywhere else."

There was something in Sarkozy's program strongly reminiscent of Richard Nixon—not ethically, but in terms of both policy and political strategy. In 1968, after three years of race riots, Nixon won the U.S. presidency by nationalizing a crime issue that had until then overwhelmed local police chiefs and frightened national politicians into hand-wringing inaction. That part of Nixon's policy was overwhelmingly popular and has never been seriously challenged in the decades since. Sarkozy's imitation of Nixon may even have been a conscious one. Just as Nixon, in a Vietnam speech in November 1969, asked for the support of "the great silent majority of my fellow Americans," Sarkozy in his 2007 campaign invoked "*la France silencieuse, immensément majoritaire.*"

But there was another Nixonesque trait that is less appreciated. For all his get-tough talk, Sarkozy had absolutely no quarrel with the fundamental settlement the previous generation's political establishment had reached before he arrived on the scene. Just as Nixon was content to leave in place the welfare state built by Roosevelt and Johnson—and indeed, went to great lengths to protect and expand it—Sarkozy was not inclined to turn back the clock to a status quo before immigration. He did not think that France would be a better country without Muslims in it. "I think of myself," Sarkozy wrote in 2004, "as a demanding friend of the Muslims of France." Sarkozy's credibility with the French public may have rested on his promises of fewer immigrants and harsher punishment for those who broke the law. At the same time, Sarkozy warned the same public that their problems with immigration and the new, multiethnic society would abate only if they accepted that the newcomers who *had* come were in France to stay.

Like Fortuyn, Sarkozy meant to shore up, rather than overthrow, the attainments of postwar tolerance. To this end, he left no cliché unspoken. "To accept and to value a nation's diversity is to strengthen the nation," he wrote. But Sarkozy's tolerance was more a matter of principle than Fortuyn's. Fortuyn believed in protecting the beneficiaries of diversity—as they had been designated by the social movements of the 1960s and the decades of political consolidation that followed. Eliminating anti-Semitism, racism, and sexual moralism were an outright improvement in Dutch life, he thought. But no neutral principles flowed from these achievements and no analogies should be drawn from them. Newcomers were not automatically entitled to similar rights. Fortuyn's politics was a kind of tribalism, expressed in the language of diversity.

Sarkozy simply did not look at politics that way. For one thing, he did not fear religion (and particularly religious morals) the way Fortuyn did. Although Sarkozy was a firm defender of banning the headscarf in public school buildings, he did so not on the basis of progressive folklore about how the headscarf automatically means the subjection of women, but on the grounds of mutual respect. "When I enter a mosque, I take off my shoes," he said. "When you enter a school, take off your veil."

Of course, analogizing this way between a religious precept and a municipal building regulation is not exactly logical. The Sarkozy approach to a multiethnic society carried risks of its own. It required more of natives than they had so far proven inclined to give. It meant they had to mix with strangers to precisely the extent they were disinclined to. The biggest risk was that Fortuyn's assessment of the relative strength of the West might be right.

Affirmative action

Ultimately, Sarkozy's strategy rested on what he called "the remarkable experiment undertaken at Sciences-po." He meant affirmative action. In 2001, the Institut des études politiques, known as Sciences-po and frequently criticized as a stronghold of French elitism, launched a program that would allow students from "priority education zones" (Zeps) to bypass its notoriously grueling written examination and submit to an oral interview instead. These Zeps were not randomly chosen. They were all poor areas with heavily immigrant populations. Richard Descoings, director of Sciences-po, told a reporter, "We are not recruiting them because they are poor, Arab or black but because they are good." This was one of those white lies that are the mainstays of all affirmative action programs. Racial diversity was clearly the overarching goal. The program's defenders have in unguarded moments described it as a means of "integrating" Sciences-po.

A group of students brought suit against Sciences-po on the grounds that its unequal treatment of applicants violated the laws of French citizenship, which mandate equality of treatment. In 2003, an appeals court disagreed. While it faulted Sciences-po for extending the privilege in an arbitrary way (to some Zeps and not others), it held that variable criteria for entry were an acceptable means of reaching egalitarian goals. So France now has affirmative action, and the road is clear for similar programs to be launched in other sectors of public life.

Clamoring for diversity has become a private sector obsession, too, ranging from Arab and immigrant groups' successful agitation to get more nonwhite faces on French TV broadcasts to attempts in the editorial offices of *Le Monde* to get more Arab bylines. Official sources proclaim loudly that "diversity is an asset." Many in France saw the need for American-style diversity programs as too obvious to require justification. Rioting strengthened their hand. In the United States, at such times of racial unrest as the Rodney King riots of 1992 and the O.J. Simpson trial of 1995, authorities can consult and deploy influential black people as interlocutors. Affirmative action has played a key role in buying such people into the system —not just politicians but also high-ranking bureaucrats and corporate executives. When French-Arab violence against Jews turned into a national crisis in 2002, or when the suburbs erupted across the country in 2005, France could not ask its powerful Arab citizens to appeal for calm, because it did not have any.

Such interlocutors come at a high price, though. Affirmative action exacts a huge toll on the state's reputation for neutrality (because it must favor some groups over others) and probity (because if affirmative action is to do its work effectively, it cannot be admitted that its beneficiaries owe their positions to it). In Britain, the Policy Research Institute on Ageing and Ethnicity finds a third of businessmen say diversity contributes to performance—but many more disagree. We have already seen that the Harvard political scientist Robert Putnam has linked diversity to a decline of the trust-engendering social networks that he calls "social capital." A political leader who seeks diversity has to weigh whether pursuing it is worth the cost.

Sarkozy, as president, became his country's top defender of diversity. He appointed more Arabs and Berbers to high positions—including the justice minister Rachida Dati and the secretary for urban affairs Fadela Amara—than any of his predecessors. In his annual New Year's wishes in 2008, he demanded diversity at every level of society and even urged placing the word *diversity* in the preamble to the French constitution. And he has called insistently for more affirmative action programs. Sarkozy believes that the need for such programs will only be temporary. "Positive discrimination implies a limitation in time," he said in 2006. "Once the injustice is taken care of, there's no need to envision any specific discrimination." Asked whether it would take twenty years or more to take care of the specific injustice, he replied: "No, twenty years is too long."

This view is naive. It is heedless of the American experience. Affirmative action programs, though consistently unpopular, tend to be permanent. They do not fade away as the problems they solve fade away—because the constituency favored by such programs protects its privileges with its heightened power. Affirmative action programs have been overturned in several state referenda, only to be reimposed through court decisions and executive orders.

Nor do such programs evolve as the demographic balance of power evolves. California still has programs designed to foster the hiring of nonwhites even now that nonwhites are a majority in the state. One moves swiftly and imperceptibly from a world in which affirmative action can't be ended because its beneficiaries are too weak to a world in which it can't be ended because its beneficiaries are too strong. This logic is not lost on white people in the United States, and it will likely not be lost on European natives.

If some people are to be favored over others for diversity purposes, what is the criterion on which they are to be favored? American affirmative action programs, at least at the outset, had the advantage of conceptual clarity—they were to be based on race, in order to remedy a history of manifest de jure racial discrimination by whites against blacks. The European problem with minorities has no such clarity. It is *not* a legacy of slavery or Jim Crow, no equivalent of which existed in modern Europe. It is clearly not a legacy of colonialism, either—countries without an important colonial history, such as Sweden and Italy, have exactly the same problems with immigration and Islam that former colonial powers such as France and the Netherlands have.

But Europeans are attempting to solve their problem, whatever it is, as if it were a race problem, so it is taking on some of the dimensions of one. As affirmative action programs continue to spread, the racial logic behind them is expressed even more baldly than in the United States. The UK Home Office makes "race quality impact assessments" and sets ambitious "race employment targets" for new hires in police and immigration, as well as prison guards and employees, at its offices in London and Croydon (where this race-targeting program has lately accounted for 38 percent of new hires). Racism has not necessarily returned in Europe, but race, as a category of experience, has returned with a vengeance. The French writer Jean Birnbaum notes that intellectuals on the left have come to explain riots in the banlieues through the lens of race. "The revolt in the suburbs," writes Etienne Balibar, "testifies to the depths of a carefully repressed racial conflict at the heart of French society." Robert Castel called the same riots "a powerful revelation of the way the ethnic question is posed throughout French society."

Racism is a terrible problem, but at least it is a conceptually simple problem. Affirmative action was launched in the United States, whether wisely or unwisely, under the assumption that blacks want exactly the same things as whites, and that only racism stood in the way of their attaining them. The problem Europeans have is much more complicated. It is deeply held beliefs, not skin color, that present the main challenge. Europe's predicament involves population decline, aging, immigration, and the steady implantation of a foreign religion and culture in city after city. Europeans are not at all sure their minorities want the same things that they themselves do.

12

Survival and Culture

*Europe's duty to the world—European emancipation from
America—The American model of a multiethnic society,
and the Ottoman model—From "Islam is peace" to "Love
it or leave it"—Two types of utility*

For the first time in centuries, Europeans are living in a world they
did not, for the most part, shape. Mass immigration is part of a cluster
of social trends—including freer economies, more wealth, more
women in work, more income inequality, lower birthrates—that all
Western countries have experienced in the last generation or two.
Since there are no exceptions to these trends, it would seem Nicolas
Sarkozy is wrong to distinguish between immigration that is chosen
and immigration that is undergone. If immigration were really a
"choice," some countries would have chosen against it. And yet, over
the last half a century, not a single free Western country did.

Why didn't they? This is a mystery at first. Western countries are
supposed to be democracies, accountable to voter assessments and
preferences, and all Western publics believe they have too much immigration. Immigration, with all the cultural consequence it brings, is
an example of what the political philosopher David Singh Grewal
calls "network power"—individual choices, cumulatively, can add
up to societal "choices" that nobody consciously made, and outcomes
that nobody wanted. Certain influential Europeans believed after
World War II that it should be possible to bring immigrants from the
Third World to the First. But once immigration was possible in some
circumstances, it became irresistible in most circumstances. In

Mexico, 40 percent of people say they would move to the United States if they could. In Turkey, Gallup's polls have found that the top reason Turks favored their country's bid for EU membership is the ability to move to any country in Europe and work there.

The story of globalization is the story of the unintended collective consequences of individual choices freely made. There are many such consequences, but immigration is the one that poses the biggest challenge to democracies (and perhaps to democracy). It means importing not just factors of production but factors of social change. For decades, Europeans have been frustrated by the inability of their leaders either to regulate immigration or to take full economic advantage of it.

More often than not, globalization and republican self-rule, of the sort that Europe has enjoyed since the seventeenth century, are at odds. If you want to open your country up to the former, you must sacrifice elements of the latter. Europeans fear their individual countries are slowly escaping their political control, and they are right, although they can seldom spell out precisely how. They sense that Europe is being taken over culturally—whether by theocratic Islam or by a (market) liberalism that accords no particular value to Europe's most cherished traditions. The market's momentum has been stalled by the financial crisis that began in 2008, but it is not likely to remain stalled forever. Both forces, whether actively hostile or not, are spreading through acts and concessions, each of which is too small to protest, but all of which, taken cumulatively, spell a permanent and undesirable cultural alteration of their continent.

Europe's duty to the world

If Europe is getting more immigrants than its voters want, this is a good indication that its democracy is malfunctioning. European leaders have chosen to believe something different—that its immigration and asylum policies involve the sort of non-negotiable moral duties that you don't vote on. As one European cabinet minister put it in the summer of 2006, "We live in a borderless world in which our new mission is defending the border not of our countries but civility and human rights." If one is not careful with this kind of language, it can be taken to mean that Europe has no right to set any immigration policies at all.

Europeans are confused about whether they are citizens of the world or citizens of their own nations. In 2005, Spain and Morocco issued a joint call for a conference to discuss European and African differences over immigration. Morocco was a good negotiating partner for the EU, according to a news report in the *Financial Times*, because "Brussels considers Morocco one of the success stories of its 10 year programme to deepen ties with countries on the southern shore of the Mediterranean." Now, it is true that the EU *proclaims* Morocco a success story. But it is quite odd, as well, because just three years earlier, Morocco's armed forces had attacked EU territory, landing a force and raising their flag on the Spanish island of Perejil, hard by the African mainland—provoking Spain's largest military operation since 1939 and a diplomatic crisis that was defused only with strenuous behind-the-scenes negotiations led by the U.S. Department of State.

Power relations between Europe and the poor countries are more complicated than they look. The poor countries are not without trumps when it comes to immigration. The greatest of these is informational asymmetry. They know more about Europe than Europeans know about them, and they gain more from mutual contact. That is how it worked during the Roman Empire—where barbarians acquired (desirable) military tactics from the sophisticated Roman legions, and the legions brought the (undesirable) habits of frontier warfare back to Rome.

And that is how it works today. People can be swapped in and out of the Western economy, because Western society is a logical system that is fairly comprehensible to anyone who takes the time to study it. Consider the African immigrants arriving by flotilla in Spain, described in chapter 3. Television news has given them, even if they are scarcely literate, a knowledge of Spanish immigration law to rival that of most immigration bureaucrats. They understand that, until a newcomer confesses his national origin, the authorities cannot deport him, and that if his national origin is not discovered within forty days, he must be released into the general public. They know that

Spain has better extradition relations with certain countries than with others, and that it is therefore, as we noted earlier, better to claim to be from Ivory Coast than from Senegal.

Europeans, by contrast, have very little knowledge of the societies that send them immigrants. Any time there is a backlog of asylum applicants or boat people, immigrant source countries must be bribed to send "identification missions" to exert the kind of pressure that democratic authorities can exert only when they know where someone lives and who his family is. You can see what an enviable privilege it is not to have such things known about you. Compared with natives of Internet-age societies like those in Europe and the United States, who have been largely stripped of their anonymity, illegal immigrants positively luxuriate in it. They are princes of privacy.

Limiting immigration means accessing Third World expertise. This comes at a steep price—paid from rich countries to poor ones in the form of debt forgiveness, development aid, "co-development" (opening of Western businesses in which developing-country businessmen share an interest), and late-model four-wheel-drive vehicles for government officials. When the leaders of poor countries cooperate with the West in limiting immigration, it is generally described as a battle against "the mafia" or "human trafficking." These are very strange words for describing, let us say, a fisherman who charges for passage on his own boat, and who has more in common with a taxi driver than a crime syndicate. The word *mafia* is a necessary fig leaf for negotiators from poor countries, who cannot be seen to cooperate in closing the door on one of their natives' only exits from poverty. But it is a great comfort to European leaders, as well. It implies that if the continent can just manage to solve a crime problem, its immigration problem will disappear. Such talk disguises a problem of will as a problem of conscience. It implies that leaders are (selflessly) addressing a humanitarian crisis, not (selfishly) looking for ways to bar the door.

The asymmetry of knowledge between the West and the non-West may be the best weapon those at war with the West have. This is obviously the case where the war on terror pits Western arms against radical Islam. Compare the ease with which terrorists have operated in U.S. airports to the ease with which NATO troops operate in Pakistan's northwestern tribal areas. Muslims know a great deal about Western societies—starting with their languages—while Westerners know next to nothing about Muslim ones. Anything that evens the epistemological playing field can, in anti-Western eyes, seem a threat. Azar Nafisi's bestseller *Reading Lolita in Teheran,* for instance, has been praised by readers all over the West for its ability to humanize a people who have been little known for the past quarter-century, for providing social detail to a country that is looked on merely as a Western enemy. But that is exactly what Hamid Dabashi, a literary scholar at Columbia, doesn't like about it. In a revealing outburst of intolerance, he writes that Nafisi's book:

is reminiscent of the most pestiferous colonial projects of the British in India, when, for example, in 1835 a colonial officer like Thomas Macaulay decreed: "We must do our best to form a class who may be interpreters between us and the millions whom we govern, a class of persons Indian in blood and colour, but English in taste, in opinions, words and intellect." Azar Nafisi is the personification of that native informer and colonial agent, polishing her services for an American version of the very same project.

European emancipation from America

World War II, and the looming threat that something like it would be provoked by the Soviet Union, scared Europe into willing participation in an Atlantic alliance. The US role as occupier of the formerly fascist lands and defender of all the territory west of the Iron Curtain took a lot of the decisions about the direction of European societies out of European hands. It was the common experience of American occupation, American liberalism, and American legalism that homogenized Europeans to the point where they could contemplate European unity. The EU, although neither Americans nor Europeans are fond of admitting it, is the institutional expression of the Americanization of Europe.

Once the dangers of the Cold War had passed, Europeans sought emancipation from American tutelage. When Germany was reunified, 58 percent of its citizens wanted to withdraw from *both* alliances, NATO as well as the Warsaw Pact. Throughout the Clinton years, some European leaders sought pretexts—capital punishment, America's unwillingness to ratify the Kyoto global-warming accords, its opposition to an international criminal court—to make a show of their independence from the wishes of the United States. Europe was of two minds about America—other European leaders fought just as hard to preserve the continent's Atlanticist orientation. Of course, the link to the United States could not be broken as long as Europeans lacked the will for, or failed to see the logic in, paying for their own military defense. But the impatience with American tutelage is a constant. No doubt the Obama years, seen as a chance for a new beginning in Euro-American relations, will provide ample material for trans-Atlantic disagreements.

European impatience with American influences was powerful, and it was further strengthened by the al-Qaeda attacks on New York and Washington in September 2001. The opposition of France and Germany—and, later, Spain—to the U.S. invasion of Iraq in 2003 was an expression of Europe's preexisting wish for emancipation from American tutelage. The Iraq invasion was not the cause of that wish. Europeans commonly claim that their publics were in full solidarity with the United States after the attacks of 2001, and that it was only when legitimate self-defense drifted into George W. Bush's blundering military misadventure in Iraq that Europe had no choice but to resist. But this is not true. While the Bush administration expected that Europeans would have as much interest as Americans in shoring up a world system that had come under attack, Europeans were in a state of mind where their self-esteem meant more to them than their self-interest.

In many quarters, the attacks on the World Trade Center were met with indifference. In his diary of September 11, 2001, the former Labour MP Tony Benn recorded attending a monthly meeting of a group called Labour Action for Peace, where he was stunned by the behavior of his colleagues. "Although they all knew what had happened," he wrote, "they spent about an hour discussing who'd got the leaflets for the forthcoming conference, who was doing the collection, was the pamphlet ready, had the room been booked." Throughout Europe in the days after September 11, there were expressions of preemptive condemnation for an unjustified American overreaction that had not happened yet but which was seen as inevitable. Thousands marched in Paris against the invasion of Afghanistan under banners reading "No to the imperialist crusade!" On September 13, the leftist columnist Seumas Milne had written a lament on the *Guardian*'s website that could be mistaken for a parody of anti-Americanism from a satirical paper, such as *Private Eye* or *The Onion* or *Le Canard Enchaîné*:

Nearly two days after the horrific suicide attacks on civilian workers in New York and Washington, it has become painfully clear that most Americans simply don't get it.... Shock, rage and grief there has been aplenty. But any glimmer of recognition of why people might have been driven to carry out such atrocities, sacrificing their own lives in the process—or why the United States is hated with such bitterness, not only in Arab and Muslim countries, but across the developing world—seems almost entirely absent.

A more important question for our purposes is why America is hated with such bitterness in the columns of the *Guardian* and in other opinion forums in Europe. One reason is certainly that the U.S. eroded Europe's distinctive national traditions and replaced them with a homogenized, one-size-fits-all mass consumer culture. At least that is how it looked to Europeans. Europe had reached the point where it could not even generate its own fads. The United States had an ethnic women's fiction craze (Laura Esquivel, Louise Erdrich) around 1990; Britain got its own (Zadie Smith, Monica Ali) in the late 1990s. The United States had a mammoth and illogical row over reparations for the slave trade in the early 1990s; France blew up over the very same arguments (including their anti-Semitic formulations) in 2005. Affirmative action, which, as we noted in the last chapter, was formulated for a specifically American problem in the 1970s, swept Europe three decades later. Europe mocked America's anti-smoking laws for (a very few) years, before adopting them wholesale. Even if this dependence was not the result of any cultural-imperialist design on America's part, it was humiliating to Europeans.

America is ever present in the cultural laments of European intellectuals. It is seen as sapping the élan vital of these once-great civilizations. "A living heritage," wrote Matthias Politycki, is not least a storehouse of ways of thinking, building and behaving, a source of inspiration for all kinds of present-day duties. We in central Europe, however, are doing our utmost to surrender what is left of our millennial inheritance—the diversity of languages and the identities bound up with them—in favor of a rampant pseudo-Americanization.

In *The Elementary Particles*, Michel Houellebecq described a surgeon who kicked himself for having blown an opportunity because "he had completely missed the emerging market for silicone breast implants. He saw it as a passing fad that wouldn't sell outside America. That was clearly idiotic. There is no example of a fashion coming out of the United States that has failed to swamp Europe a few years later—none."

The American model of a multiethnic society, and the Ottoman model

Immigration *is* Americanization. They are two faces of the same disruptive system of economic relations that is supplanting traditional European ones. In an age of public atonement and rhetorical squeamishness, it has often not been possible to lament or condemn immigration, or the policies that summoned immigrants en masse. But it is possible to say that Europe's decision to welcome millions of foreigners was made at a time when it was not of sound mind and body, in a political landscape drawn up by Hitler and Stalin, and as the ward of a country—the United States—whose interests coincide less with those of Europe's now that the age of Hitler and Stalin has passed.

Enoch Powell (again), who was, not coincidentally, the most doggedly anti-American European politician of his time, warned in 1968, "With the lapse of a generation or so we shall at last have succeeded—to the benefit of nobody—in reproducing 'in England's green and pleasant land' the haunting tragedy of the United States." In the early 1990s, the Lombard League (later the Northern League) handed out leaflets in Italy reading, "If you like a *multiracial* society so much, you can move to New York."

Europe is thus in a funny predicament. It is an increasingly anti-American continent facing dire problems to which the only proven solution is to become more like America. Because the United States shows, at least, that one can receive great masses of immigrants from all over the world and retain a culture that is still open, free, and Western. American society appears to many Europeans, whether they like the United States or not, as their continent's consolation prize. It the kind of society Europe will have by default, if it musters the resolve (or makes the Faustian bargain) to keep its economy as free as the age's straitened financial circumstances permit.

Of course, "America," as it exists in the European mind is, now as ever, two-thirds myth. Europeans believe America equals European culture plus entropy. Perhaps the most cherished European myth about the United States is that Americans make no particular claims for their culture (to the extent they even have one) and don't particularly care whether newcomers hold on to theirs. This is quite wrong. America may be open in theory, but in practice it exerts Procrustean pressures on its immigrants to conform, and it is its pressures, not its openness, that have bound America's diverse citizens together as one people. Yes, you can have a "hyphenated identity" if you insist on it—but you had better know which side of the hyphen your bread is buttered on.

What confuses outsiders is that these pressures to Americanize are never stated. They are embedded in the social and (especially) economic system through which immigrants must move to survive. Immigrants to the United States, just like immigrants anyplace, seldom think of themselves as immigrants. They travel hoping to find scope for their ambitions that they cannot find in their own society. With the ease of modern travel, it is not unrealistic for an immigrant to aspire to reenter his society of birth at a higher socioeconomic level after a few years of work in a more advanced economy. But since, generally, the immigration years immediately precede the settling-down years, an immigrant can easily get trapped in a country he thinks he's just passing through. He may acquire a monoglot spouse and children. If employed, he will almost certainly get addicted to his level of income. It is true that an immigrant can maintain his ancestral culture. But if it is a culture that prevents him from speaking English well or showing up to work promptly, he will go hungry. Then he will go home. No one will miss him.

The American success with immigration is the product not just of brutal indifference and of government policies that are distasteful to most Europeans but also of historical conditions that are hard to replicate. First, America's nineteenth-century immigrants had a mostly empty continent to settle. Its late-twentieth-century immigrants had the mostly empty peripheries of the labor-starved cities of the American Sun Belt.

Second, the most recent mass immigration to America interacted with, and drew strength from, one of the great societal revolutions in American history—the rolling back of racial segregation. Just because blacks were no longer forced into the most menial jobs did not mean those menial jobs no longer had to be done. It may also be that the arrival of nonwhite immigrants served the white majority in the United States by providing a standing refutation of charges of white racism.

Third, another social revolution—not unrelated to desegregation— further simplified the assimilation of immigrants. Beginning with the Nixon administration and picking up steam thanks to the "war on drugs" of the 1980s, the U.S. penal system was reformed into a merciless, draconian machine, with offenses so numerous and prison sentences so severe that, as of this writing, a quarter of the prison inmates in the world are held in the United States. Despite occasional sensationalist magazine features about Salvadoran and Jamaican gangs, American cities and suburbs are extremely inhospitable places for immigrants who are criminally inclined. There has never in recent decades been the sentiment, as there is in Europe, that newcomers account for the bulk of the crime problem.

And even with all these advantages, in which Europe is totally lacking, the American public *still* does not like immigration. A 2006 poll by the Pew Research Center found that a majority of Americans (53 percent) think all 11 million illegals should be "required to go home."

In the present tormented context of the war on terror, it is hard to ignore one specific blessing America enjoys. It is that, despite having launched two wars in the Muslim world and stood steadfastly by the state of Israel in all its conflicts, the United States has had fewer rumblings of subversion from its first- and second-generation Muslims than Europe has. That has been the source of much self-congratulation among Americans, who rush to attribute the difference to a variety of real or imagined U.S. virtues, from lower taxes to less racism. Closer observers tend to see this self-congratulation as unfounded. "The real story of American Muslims is one of accelerating alienation from the mainstream of U.S. life," the journalist Geneive Abdo has written, "with Muslims in this country choosing their Islamic identity over their American one."

The United States has Muslims—but it has not yet had any *mass* immigration of Muslims. Scale matters. America has about 2 million Muslims (excluding black Muslims) scattered about the country. If its Muslim population were proportionate to that of France and similarly dispersed, it would have close to 40 million, concentrated in a handful of major cities and poised to take political control of them. All sorts of attitudes would change, including both Muslim deference to the wider society (which would wane) and the wider society's concern about Islam (which would wax). The jury is still out on whether the U.S. melting pot will work on Muslims as it has worked on other immigrants.

In a globalized world, where ancestral identities are no longer extinguished by long lack of contact with the mother country, a second immigration model may be much more relevant to the European situation than the U.S. melting pot: That is the millet system of the late Ottoman Empire. Ottoman cities of the time, like Sarajevo, Thessalonica, and Istanbul, may have been the most cosmopolitan places in the world. They included large minority populations of Greek Christians, Armenian Christians, Jews, and others, who were organized into ethnic communities, or *millets*, that enjoyed a certain amount of self-rule. But at the start of the nineteenth century, Turkey's European neighbors used the oppression of their "brethren" in Greece and other spots inside Ottoman borders as their pretext to tear the empire to pieces.

For decades the dominant strain of Turkish nationalist thinking has been that Ottoman tolerance was the most important weapon the empire's enemies used against it, and even that the empire *died* of its tolerance. It is easy to deplore nationalist myths. But this background should be understood by anyone wishing to comprehend the massacres of millions of Armenians during the First World War, or the idolatry of Kemal Atatürk, or what made Turkish nationalism so virulent and uncompromising that the Kurdishness of Kurdish-speaking Kurds has been officially denied by the central government for much of the last century.

What the Turks did, in reaction to the carving up of their multi-national empire, was to reconceive the rump of it as the birthright of one "people." They drew the lesson that to have any officially recognized minorities at *all* can, under certain circumstances, be a dangerous thing. It is striking that the European champions of Turkish admission to the EU, who are tireless in adducing commonalities between Turkish and European history, have paid not the slightest attention to the history of Turkish minority policy, except to deplore the country's modern-day persecution of the Kurds and pass retrospective condemnations of the slaughter of the Armenians.

The Danish cartoon crisis shows that Europeans and Ottomans have at least certain points in common. The worldwide violence and boycotts that followed on *Jyllands-Posten*'s publication of satirical cartoons about Muhammad did not require that the Danish Muslim community be badly integrated, or disgruntled—as indeed, they were not, particularly. All that was required was immigration, global media, radicalization of the Muslim world, extravagant claims for human rights, and a generalized fading of the sense that what goes on in someone else's country is none of your business. Under the circumstances, one traveling delegation of a few angry Danish imams was sufficient to rally violent people around the globe in defense of their allegedly beleaguered "brethren." Whether Europe's minority policies cause wider unrest will not depend solely on whether minority grievances are manageable.

From "Islam is peace" to "Love it or leave it"

Mass immigration into Europe and the consolidation of Islam there are changing European life permanently. As the intellectual historian Mark Lilla put it in 2007,

> It is an unfortunate situation, but we have made our bed, Muslims and non-Muslims alike. Accommodation and mutual respect can help ... Western countries have adopted different strategies for coping, some forbidding religious symbols like the head scarf in schools, others permitting them. But we need to recognize that coping is the order of the day, not defending high principle, and that our expectations should remain low.

Lilla captures perfectly the ambiguity of a Europe rueful about the legacy of immigration and disinclined (or too weak) to make a fuss about it. But his hopes for a strategy based on coping are unrealistic, at least in a democracy. Proud peoples are not content to "cope." And whether they are right or wrong, politicians who champion "low expectations"—from James Callaghan to Jimmy Carter—quickly wind up ex-politicians.

The deeper difficulty is that the "we" Lilla posits does not for the moment exist. Such a "we" existed 20 years ago when Europeans still lived under the minatory shadow of World War II, but it does not exist now. There is a generation of people born between 1930 and 1960 who drew not only economic benefit from immigration but moral prestige as well. Immigration allowed them to present themselves as people of high principle. That generation now shares power with a later one, which will pay for both the economic attainments and the moral pretensions of its predecessors. In this sense, Europeans have not grown "harder" or "less generous" towards immigrants. They are just in the bill-paying stage of a transaction that has already occasioned a good deal of buyer's remorse.

It is a brave thing to be an immigrant, to cast off from your old reference points and certitudes and set out in quest of a better life. But many native Europeans in our time are in a similar position. They live an *éxil à l'intérieur*—cut off by economic and cultural changes from the world they thought they would inhabit. In one respect they are in a worse position than immigrants—they didn't choose this disruption. And the economic downturn that began in 2008 has rendered European countries even less recognizable to their natives.

Contrary to widespread suspicions, the old, cushy social contract, the Europe of stable marriages, plentiful jobs, light policing, and frictionless social relations is not being sneakily withheld from Muslim and other newcomers by Europeans who have grown tired of offering it to them. Such a social contract is no longer available to Europeans themselves. For a good number of European natives, particularly working-class ones, expulsion from the culture of their parents is the story of their lives. That being the case, it no longer seems unreasonable to demand that immigrants who want to stay in Europe give up the ways of their own parents.

It is easier to make this demand in a globalized world. "I like the metaphor of a club," the Francophone intellectual and former Israeli diplomat Élie Barnavi told a journalist in 2007:

If you want to belong, there are rules. If you don't like them, you don't have to join. If you want to play by different rules, find another club. That's why, once again, the expression *"France—love it or leave it"* sounds fair to me. In a wide-open world, there's no reason you can't go elsewhere. Nobody is required to love his country or the values it proclaims. But if you choose a country, you have to accept it.

Barnavi was rejecting the idea that seeking a better life was reason enough to come and just obeying the law was reason enough to be allowed to stay. Others reject the idea that simply seeking a better life is reason enough to come in the first place. "Why should we welcome anyone who comes here only for the money?" asked the longtime newspaper editor Max Hastings. "If a newcomer is unwilling to defer to our values, flawed as these may seem, then surely no Western society has a moral obligation to admit him?"

Certain Europeans are resolved to defend their continent's values, particularly against Islam. But what does that mean? You cannot defend what you cannot define. There is no consensus, not even the beginning of a consensus, about what European values are. A united Europe would have nothing to fear from Islam, but Europe is not united. Its civilization is split in two, torn between the ideal of human rights and the ideal of patriotism, between fear of Europe's religious heritage and pride in it, between viewing Islam as a permanent new feature of Europe's religious landscape and as something that will dissolve on contact with hedonism and consumerism. Being true to Europe can mean getting tough (since the costs of battling Islam frontally will only rise as Muslims become more numerous) and being nice (since Islam will be powerful enough in Europe someday soon that Europeans will not wish to have crossed it).

Britain is a country that has moved back and forth between Islam is Peace and Love It or Leave It. It passed a tough Terrorism Act of 2000, a year before the attacks on the World Trade Center. After the London transport bombings of 2005, prime minister Tony Blair warned that those who do not "share and support the values that sustain the British way of life," or who incite hatred against Britain, "have no place here." A few months later, he added that Islamist preachers who condone terrorism "should not be in this country."

After the failed plot to blow up several airliners between Britain and the United States in the summer of 2006, this change become still more explicit. Global terrorism, Blair said, "means traditional civil-liberty arguments are not so much wrong, as just made for another age." Like George W. Bush, he made it easier to extradite terrorism suspects and to intercept suspicious communications. He extended the length of time that suspects could be held without trial. This was an astonishing reversal, for it was Blair who, shortly after his arrival in office in 1997, made British law subject to the European Convention on Human Rights, turning modern civil liberties into core British values. Suddenly he was arguing that they are no such thing—they are temporary adjustments that were useful under certain specific circumstances in part of Europe between World War II and the late twentieth century.

Tough approaches and nice ones are difficult to mix. Sometimes it is difficult even to determine what the tough and the nice options are. For instance, Souad Sbai, the longtime president of the Italian Moroccan women's association (Acmid-Donna) and now a deputy in the party of Silvio Berlusconi, has spent many years trying to bring Italian-style women's rights to Moroccan families. One of her main tasks has been agitating for custody on behalf of women whose husbands had kidnapped their children to North Africa. Typically, the cause of the kidnapping was that the mothers had shown some sort of untoward European comportment: resisting being locked in the house all day, resisting being joined by a second spouse in a polygamous relationship, or resisting wearing the veil. Just where a reasonable Westerner's sympathies ought to lie in this question is not easy to say. A victory for women's rights would most likely require reimporting the chauvinist father, who may be strong enough within the family to impose his Islamist worldview on all seven of his children. Asserting Italian law could mean working against Italian values.

The deportation of radical Islamist preachers, a centerpiece of both French and British domestic policy in the middle of this decade, provides another example. It is helpful only as a marginal component of immigration policy. It does nothing about the spread of Islamism among European citizens. Being tough on Muslim foreigners and nice to Muslim citizens will comfort Europeans only to the extent that they maintain the idea that immigration is something temporary and reversible.

Two types of utility

It no longer is. Europeans can only hope that newcomers, especially Muslim newcomers, will assimilate peaceably. Materially, immigrants *ought* to want to assimilate. In many cases, Europe's elevation of immigrants has been magnificent. At a magazine shop in a shopping mall in Copenhagen, it is not a surprise to meet a sneaker salesman with a run-of-the-mill state education who speaks four languages— say, Danish, English, Turkish and Kurmanji. This is an extraordinary attainment, whether you compare his education to that available in his parents' Anatolian village or to the education a member of the European working class would have got a century ago. From this perspective, it is hard to describe Europe as a civilization in decline. Yet it is a civilization in decline. It is missing some hard-to-define factor. Whether or not it can defend itself, it has lost sight of why it should.

Impressive though our Copenhagen sneaker salesman may be as a symbol of Europe, it is far from certain that his allegiance is with Europe. As the German jurist Udo Di Fabio has lamented:

The adherents of our well-intentioned politics of tolerance, which makes generous offers of integration in order to stave off the cultural fragmentation of society, are missing the basic problem: Why in God's name should a member of a vital world culture want to integrate into Western culture, when Western culture, which at least in his view is not producing enough offspring and no longer has any transcendental idea, is approaching its historical end? Why should he get caught up in a culture marked as much by self-doubt as by arrogance, which has squandered its religious and moral inheritance on a forced march to modernity, and which offers no higher ideal of the good life beyond travel, longevity and consumerism?

The Italian sociologist Vilfredo Pareto distinguished between two kinds of collective self-interest pursued in any community: utility *of* a community (survival value) and utility *for* a community (well-being). The conflict between these two utilities is sometimes clear, as in the rearing of children or the preparation for military defense, both of which require self-abnegation on the part of adults and divert resources away from present enjoyments. But such questions also come up when people are deciding whether to import immigrants to fix meals, make beds, and scrub floors for a pittance or to do the work themselves. As the American political intellectual James Burnham wrote in 1943:

In general, measures which provide more adequately for the strength of the community in the future, especially in a future some years or generations distant, diminish the satisfactions of the existing generation. Which, then, is better: a shorter historical life for the community, to end in its destruction, with more internal satisfactions as it goes along, or a longer life with fewer satisfactions? This seems to be frequently, perhaps always, the choice. The answer, needless to say, is never given by deliberate, logical decision.

For decades, European authorities pursued utility *for* themselves over utility *of* their society. Indeed, even to raise the question of whether immigration will promote or endanger European survival is considered vulgar and un-European at best, extremist at worst. Immigrant communities have felt under no such constraint.

Europe's basic problem with Islam, and with immigration more generally, is that the strongest communities in Europe are, culturally speaking, not European communities at all. This problem exists in all European countries, despite a broad variety of measures taken to solve it—multiculturalism in Holland, *laïcité* in France, benign neglect in Britain, constitutional punctiliousness in Germany. Clearly Europe's problem is with Islam and with immigration, and not with specific misapplications of specific means set up to manage them. Islam is a magnificent religion that has also been, at times over the centuries, a glorious and generous culture. But, all cant to the contrary, it is in no sense Europe's religion and it is in no sense Europe's culture.

It is certain that Europe will emerge changed from its confrontation with Islam. It is far less certain that Islam will prove assimilable. Europe finds itself in a contest with Islam for the allegiance of its newcomers. For now, Islam is the stronger party in that contest, in an obvious demographic way and in a less obvious philosophical way. In such circumstances, words like "majority" and "minority" mean little. When an insecure, malleable, relativistic culture meets a culture that is anchored, confident, and strengthened by common doctrines, it is generally the former that changes to suit the latter.

Bibliography

English titles of European works available in translation are given in square brackets.

Alesina, Alberto, and Edward Glaeser. *Fighting Poverty in the U.S. and Europe.* New York: Oxford University Press, 2005.

Allievi, Stefano. *Islam italiano.* Turin: Giulio Einaudi, 2003.

Aristotle. *Politics.* Edited by Ernest Barker. London: Oxford University Press, 1946.

Aron, Raymond. *Le Spectateur Engagé.* Paris: Éditions de Fallois, 2004.

———. *Une histoire du XXe siècle.* Paris: Plon, 1996.

Belloc, Hilaire. *The Great Heresies.* New York: Sheed & Ward, 1938.

Benn, Tony. *More Time for Politics.* London: Hutchinson, 2007.

Berman, Paul. *Terror and Liberalism.* New York: W.W. Norton, 2003.

Besançon, Alain. *Trois tentations dans l'église.* Paris: Perrin, 2002.

Blanchard, Pascal, Nicolas Bancel, and Sandrine Lemaire, eds. *La fracture coloniale.* Paris: Éditions La Découverte, 2005.

Bouzar, Dounia. *Monsieur Islam n'existe pas.* Paris: Hachette, 2004.

Brague, Rémi. *Europe: La voie romaine* [*Eccentric Culture*]. Paris: Gallimard (Folio), 1992.

Brauman, Rony, and Alain Finkielkraut. *La Discorde.* Paris: Mille et Une Nuits, 2006.

Brenner, Emmanuel. *Les territoires perdus de la République.* Paris: Mille et Une nuits, 2002.

Broder, Henryk M. *Hurra, wir kaputilieren! Von der Lust am Einknicken.* Berlin: Siedler, 2006.

Brubaker, Rogers. *Citizenship and Nationhood in France and Germany.* Cambridge, Massachusetts: Harvard University Press, 1998.

———. *Nationalism Reframed: Nationhood and the National Question in the New Europe.* Cambridge: Cambridge University Press, 1996.

Burnham, James. *The Machiavellians*. New York: John Day, 1941.

Buruma, Ian. *Murder in Amsterdam*. New York: Penguin, 2006.

Carlyle, Thomas. *On Heroes, Hero-Worship and the Heroic in History*. Berkeley: University of California Press, 1993.

Ceylan, Rauf. *Ethnische Kolonien: Entstehung, Funktion und Wandel am Beispiel türkischer Moscheen und Cafés*. Wiesbaden: Verlag für Sozialwissenschaften, 2006.

Chebel, Malek. *L'Islam et la raison*. Paris: Perrin, 2006.

Daun, Åke. *Swedish Mentality*. University Park: Penn State University Press, 1996.

Dench, Geoff. *Minorities in the Open Society*. New Brunswick, NJ: Transaction, 2003.

di Fabio, Udo. *Die Kultur der Freiheit*. Munich: C.H. Beck, 2005.

Dokumentationszentrum und Museum über die Migration aus der Türkei (DOMiT). *Zur Geschichte der Arbeitsmigration aus der Türkei: Materialsammlung*. Cologne: Ministerium für Arbeit [North Rhine–Westphalia], 2000.

Enzensberger, Hans Magnus. *Die Große Wanderung*. Frankfurt: Suhrkamp, 1992.

——. *Schreckens Männer*. Frankfurt: Suhrkamp, 2006. (Originally published as "Der radikale Verlierer," *Der Spiegel*, November 7, 2005.)

Evangelische Kirche in Deutschland (EKD). *Klarheit und gute Nachbarschaft: Christen und Muslime in Deutschland*. Hannover: Kirchenamt der EKD, 2006.

Fallaci, Oriana. *La Rage et l'Orgueil*. Paris: Plon, 2002.

——. *The Rage and the Pride*. New York: Rizzoli, 2002.

Florida, Richard. *The Flight of the Creative Class*. New York: HarperCollins, 2005.

Fortuyn, Pim. *De puinhopen van acht jaar Paars*. Rotterdam: Karakter Uitgevers, 2002.

——. *De verweesde samenleving*. Rotterdam: Karakter Uitgevers, 2002.

Fryer, Peter. *Staying Power*. London: Pluto Press, 1984.

Giudici, Cristina. *L'Italia di Allah*. Rome: Mondadori, 2005.

Goody, Jack. *Islam in Europe*. Cambridge: Polity Press, 2004.

Gresh, Alain, and Tariq Ramadan. *L'Islam en questions*. Arles: Actes Sud, 2002.

Grewal, David Singh. *Network Power*. New Haven: Yale University Press, 2008.

Groen, Janny, and Annieke Kranenberg. *Strijdsters van Allah*. Amsterdam: Volkskrant/Meulenhoff, 2006.

Hall, Peter. *Cities of Tomorrow* (3rd ed.). Malden, Massachusetts: Blackwell, 2002.

Handlin, Oscar. *Boston's Immigrants*. Cambridge, Massachusetts: Belknap/Harvard, 1969.

Heinsohn, Gunnar. *Söhne und Weltmacht: Terror im Aufstieg und Fall der Nationen*. Zurich: Orell Füssli Verlag, 2003.

Hirschman, Albert O. *The Rhetoric of Reaction*. Cambridge: Harvard University Press, 1991.

Hodgson, Marshall G. S. *The Venture of Islam*. Chicago: University of Chicago Press, 1977.

Hofmann, Corinne. *Die Weiße Massai* [*The White Masai*]. Munich: A1 Verlag, 1998.

Home Office (UK). *Report of the Official Account of the Bombings in London on 7th July 2005*. London: Home Office, May 11, 2006.

Houellebecq, Michel. *Les particules élémentaires* [*Atomised*]. Paris: Flammarion, 1998.

——. *Extension du domaine de la lutte* [*Whatever*]. Paris: J'ai Lu, 1997.

Huntington, Samuel. *The Clash of Civilizations and the Remaking of World Order*. New York: Simon & Schuster, 1996.

Kagan, Robert. *Of Paradise and Power*. New York: Knopf, 2003.

Khosrokhavar, Farhad. *L'islam dans les prisons*. Paris: Balland, 2004.

Laurence, Jonathan, and Justin Vaïsse. *Integrating Islam: Political and Religious Challenges in Contemporary France*. Washington, DC: Brookings, 2006.

Legrain, Philippe. *Immigrants: Your Country Needs Them*. London: Little, Brown, 2006.

Lemann, Nicholas. *The Promised Land*. New York: Knopf, 1991.

Leonard, Mark. *Why Europe Will Run the 21st Century*. New York: Public Affairs Press, 2006.

Lewis, Bernard. *What Went Wrong?* Oxford University Press, 2001.

Lewis, Philip. *Islamic Britain*. London: I.B. Tauris, 2002.

Lucassen, Jan, and Rinus Penninx. *Nieuwkomers, Nakomelingen, Nederlanders: Immigranten in Nederland, 1550–1993*. Amsterdam: Het Spinhuis, 1994.

Luft, Stefan *Abschied von Multikulti*. Gräfelfing: Resch-Verlag, 2006.

Mak, Geert. *Nagekomen flessenpost*. Amsterdam: Uitgeverij Atlas, 2005.

Malcolm X (with Alex Haley). *The Autobiography of Malcolm X*. New York: Ballantine Books, 1987.

Malik, Kenan. *The Meaning of Race*. New York: New York University Press, 1996.

Manent, Pierre. *La Raison des Nations* [*Democracy Without Nations*]. Paris: Gallimard, 2006.

Martin, Philip, Manolo Abella, and Christiane Kuptsch. *Managing Labor Migration in the Twenty-first Century*. New Haven: Yale University Press, 2006.

Meddeb, Abdelwahab. *La Maladie de l'Islam* [*Malady of Islam*]. Paris: Seuil, 2002.

Mirza, Munira, Abi Senthikumaran, and Zein Ja'far. *Living Apart Together*. London: Policy Exchange, 2007.

Monnerot, Jules. *Sociologie du Communisme*. Paris: Gallimard, 1949.

Pera, Marcello, and Joseph Cardinal Ratzinger. *Without Roots: The West, Relativism, Christianity, Islam*. New York: Basic Books, 2006.

Pirenne, Henri. *Mahomet et Charlemagne* [*Mohammed and Charlemagne*]. Brussels: Librairie Félix Alcan, 1937.

Powell, Enoch. *Reflections of a Statesman*. Edited by Rex Collings. London: Bellew Publishing, 1991.

Ramadan, Tariq. *Aux sources du renouveau musulman*. Lyon: Tawhid, 2002.

———. *Dar ash-shahada*. Lyon: Tawhid, 2002.

———. *La Foi, la Voie et la résistance*. Lyon: Tawhid, 2002.

———. *Les Musulmans de l'Occident et l'avenir de l'Islam* [*Western Muslims and the Future of Islam*]. Paris: Sindbad, 2003.

Renan, Ernest. *L'Islam et la science*. Paris: L'Archange Minotaure, 2005. (Lecture given at the Sorbonne, March 29, 1883.)

Rifkin, Jeremy. *The European Dream*. New York: Polity Press, 2004.

Roy, Olivier. *La Laïcité face à l'Islam* [*Secularism Confronts Islam*]. Paris: Stock, 2005.

Sanneh, Lamin. *Disciples of All Nations*. New Haven: Yale University Press, 2008.

Sarkozy, Nicolas. *La République, les religions, l'espérance*. Paris: Éditions du Cerf, 2004.

Sayad, Abdelmalek. *La double absence*. Paris: Seuil, 1999.

Sen, Faruk, and Hayrettin Aydin. *Islam in Deutschland*. Munich: C.H. Beck 2002.

Smith, Zadie. *White Teeth*. New York: Random House, 2000.

Sociaal en Cultureel Rapport 1998: "25 jaar sociale verandering." Rijswijk: Sociaal en Cultureel Planbureau/Elsevier, 1998.

Staud, Toralf. *Moderne Nazis: Die neuen Rechten und der Aufstieg der NPD*. Cologne: Kiepenheuer und Witsch, 2006.

Taguieff, Pierre-André. *Les contre-réactionnaires*. Paris: Denoël, 2007.

Thesiger, Wilfred. *Arabian Sands*. London: Penguin, 2007.

Thomas, Dominique. *Le Londonistan: Le djihad au cœur de l'Europe*. Paris: Michalon, 2005.

Tocqueville, Alexis de. *L'Ancien Régime et la Révolution*. Vol. 3, *Oeuvres*. Paris: Bibliothèque de La Pléïade, 2004.

Tranaes, Torben, and Klaus Zimmerman, eds. *Migrants, Work, and the Welfare State*. Odense: University Press of Southern Denmark, 2005.

Tribalat, Michèle. *Faire France*. Paris: La Découverte, 1995.

United Nations. *Replacement Migration: Is It a Solution to Declining and Ageing Populations?* New York: United Nations Population Division, 2001.

Walden, George. *Time to Emigrate?* London: Gibson Square Books, 2006.

Wansink, Hans. *De Erfenis van Fortuyn*. Amsterdam: Meulenhoff, 2004.

Weil, Patrick. *La France et ses étrangers*. Paris: Gallimard, 2004.

Winder, Robert. *Bloody Foreigners*. London: Abacus, 2004.

Wolfram, Herwig. *History of the Goths*. Berkeley: University of California Press, 1988.

Wright, Lawrence. *The Looming Tower*. New York: Vintage, 2006.

Notes

Chapter 1. Rivers of Blood

4. **Citing the poet Virgil:** Enoch Powell, speech to the Annual General Meeting of the West Midlands Area Conservative Political Centre, April 20, 1968, in Enoch Powell, *Reflections of a Statesman*, pp. 375, 379.

5. **the urban part of whole towns:** Enoch Powell, speech to the Annual Conference of the Rotary Club of London, Eastbourne, November 16, 1968, in Powell, *Reflections of a Statesman*, p 390.

5. **would rise to 4.5 million:** Ibid., p. 389. The nonwhite population of Britain at the time was 1.25 million.

5. **actual "ethnic minority" population:** Office for National Statistics, Census, April 2001.

6. **he told voters in Wolverhampton:** Enoch Powell, election speech, Wolverhampton, June 11, 1970, in Powell, *Reflections of a Statesman*, p. 403.

6. **according to the 2001 census:** Office for National Statistics, census indicators, http://www.statistics.gov.uk/census2001/profiles/00CW-A.asp; http://www.statistics.gov.uk/census2001/profiles/00CN-A.asp; http://www.statistics.gov.uk/census2001/profiles/1B-A.asp.

6. **literally vanloads of mail:** Sarfraz Manzoor, "Black Britain's darkest hour," *Observer,* February 24, 2008, Features, p. 6.

6. **"We are poor because you are rich":** Jay Rayner, "Drama out of Crisis," *Independent,* May 18, 1990, p. 16; Steve Clarke, "Stealing a march on the One World ideal," *The Times,* May 13, 1990.

7. **"encamped in certain areas of England":** Enoch Powell, speech to the Annual Conference of the Rotary Club of London, Eastbourne, November 16, 1968, in Powell, *Reflections of a Statesman*, p. 391.

7. **The free movement of capital:** Hans Magnus Enzensberger, *Die Große Wanderung*, p. 21.

8. **the 375 million people in Western Europe:** "Western Europe" is here defined as the so-called "EU-15," which includes all the major countries except Norway and Switzerland and excludes the remaining, mostly Eastern European countries admitted to the union this decade.

This is a good place for a note on statistics: The statistical offices of the individual European countries are the most comprehensive sources of migration data. Unfortunately, they collect very different kinds of data and judge it on very different criteria. So, for instance, you can get solid information on the ethnic background of Dutch citizens but not of French ones. Criteria change within countries, so you can get certain data on spousal migration from former British colonies *before* 1997 but not after. (See David A. Coleman, "Partner choice and the growth of ethnic minority populations," *Bevolking en Gezin,* vol. 33 (2004), pp. 2, 7–34.) And laws change in a way that makes long-term comparisons impossible. "Germans" and "Turkish" do not describe the same population before and after the country's citizenship reform of 1999.

Scholars, non-governmental organizations, and non-national govern-mental authorities (the European Union's Eurostat or the various United Nations departments, for instance) try to manage this data as best they can but seldom generate it themselves. It would take an entire book to sort these matters out, and that is not the book you hold in your hand. This book uses a lot of data sources, which will be identified in notes as they come up. Some are governmental, some academic or journalistic. An excellent collection of general and easy-to-digest population data is the *European Demographic Data Sheet* published by the Vienna Institute of Demography. The annual *International Migration Outlook* of the OECD is also useful. The most comprehensive and user-friendly source of statistics is the online "data hub" of the Washington-based think tank the Migration Policy Institute (MPI). The site usually offers links to the original study or census from which the figures are drawn.

8. **Between 2000 and 2005:** "World Migrant Stock: The 2005 Revision," population database, Population Division, UN Department of Economic and Social Affairs, http://esa.un.org/migration.

8. **The EU is not unanimously loved:** Anthony Browne, "Invasion of the New Europeans." *Spectator,* January 28, 2006, pp. 12–13.

9. **"like being like each other":** Author interview with Åke Daun, Stockholm, January 24, 2005.

9. **"undesirable expression of aggression":** Åke Daun, *Swedish Mentality,* p. 121.

10. **around 1.7 million new arrivals:** Edward Alden, Daniel Dombey, Chris

Giles, and Sarah Laitner, "The price of prosperity," *Financial Times*, May 18, 2006, p. 13.

10. **between 15 and 17 million Muslims:** This is the estimate Tariq Ramadan made in *Dar ash-shahada* (p. 13) in 2002.

12. **"too many Arabs":** Christopher Caldwell, "Allah Mode," *Weekly Standard*, July 15, 2002, p. 21.

12. **"is not—and does not wish to be—multicultural":** Christopher Caldwell, "Europe's Future," *Weekly Standard,* December 4, 2006, p. 25.

12. **"part of the Arabic west":** Wolfgang Schwanitz, "Europa wird am Ende des Jahrhunderts islamisch sein," *Die Welt*, July 28, 2004, p. 6.

12. **"authoritarian" countries and cultures:** Aldo Keel, "In Der Gewalt der Tradition", *Neue Zürcher Zeitung*, December 11, 2006, p. 25. Keel cites a 1999 article by P. C. Matthiessen in the Danish daily *Jyllands-Posten.*

13. **lowest levels ever recorded:** In Germany, in 2007, some early signs appeared that birthrates might be rising again. See Bertrand Benoit, "Baby boom times return for Germany," *Financial Times*, July 13, 2007.

14. **a society with total fertility of 1.3:** Wolfgang Lutz, Vegard Skirbekk, and Maria Rita Testa, "The Low Fertility Trap Hypothesis: Forces That May Lead to Further Postponement and Fewer Births in Europe," Vienna Institute of Demography, 2005. Cited by David Coleman in an address to the Hudson Institute, Washington, D.C., September 25, 2007.

14. **half its current size:** David Coleman, address to the Hudson Institute, Washington, D.C., September 25, 2007.

14. *la ville des vieux*: Alain Auffray and Prune Perromat, "A Montfermeil, le maire joue la carte antijeunes," *Libération*, April 26, 2006.

14. **close to a quarter of the Dutch population:** Caldwell, "Daughter of the Enlightenment," *New York Times Magazine*, April 3, 2005, p. 29. The article draws on "In 2050 ruim 1,6 miljoen meer allochtonen," *CBS Webmagazine,* January 8, 2007. A higher figure for the Dutch foreign origin population in 2050—32 percent—is given by David Coleman and Sergei Scherbov, "Immigration and Ethnic Change in Low-Fertility Countries—Towards a New Demographic Transition?" Paper presented at the annual meeting of Population Association of America, Philadelphia, April 1, 2005.

14. **Britain will have 7 million "non-whites":** Coleman and Scherbov, "Immigration and Ethnic Change."

15. **about 500,000 new immigrants:** Agence France-Presse, "2004 was record immigration year." *International Herald Tribune*, October, 21, 2005, p. 4.

15. **between 20 and 32 percent:** Coleman and Scherbov, "Immigration and Ethnic Change."

15. **immigrants account for 0.2 percent:** Author interview with Fr. Fredo Olivero, ASAI, Turin, March 23, 2006.

15. **A fifth of the children:** For Copenhagen: Jeffrey Fleishman, "A Mutual Suspicion Grows in Denmark," *Los Angeles Times*, November 12, 2005, p. A1. For Paris: Cour des comptes, "L'accueil des immigrants et l'intégration des populations issues de l'immigration," November 2004; in Jonathan Laurence and Justin Vaïsse, *Integrating Islam*, p. 23. For London: George Walden, *Time to Emigrate?* p. 45.

15. **foreign-born women in France:** Françoise Legros, "La fécondité des étrangères en France," *Insée Prémière 898*, May 2003.

15. **Pakistanis and Bangladeshis:** Nicholas Eberstadt, "A Union of a Certain Age," *Milken Institute Review,* Second Quarter 2005, p. 47.

16. **the "secret weapon":** Gunnar Heinsohn, *Söhne und Weltmacht*, p. 33.

16. **seven Polish-language newspapers:** Jörg Thomann, "Wenn Auswandern zum Volkssport wird," *Frankfurter Allgemeine Zeitung*, July 17, 2007, p. 38.

16. **six Chinese dailies:** Pal Nyiri, *2000* magazine, January 2005. Cited at www.perlentaucher.de/magazinrundschau/2005–04-05.html.

17. **"squeegee men":** Alexander Stille, "No blacks need apply; a nation of emigrants faces the challenge of immigration," *The Atlantic*, February 1992, p. 28.

17. **hydrogen peroxide and chapati flour:** "Court Hears of Horror Scenes on Tube," *Guardian* (on-line edition) January 23, 2007.

18. **continuation of colonialism:** See the essays in Pascal Blanchard, Nicolas Bancel, and Sandrine Lemaire, *La fracture coloniale*.

18. **a great policy error:** Geert Mak, *Nagekomen flessenpost*. Amsterdam/Antwerp: Uitgeverij Atlas. 2005: 34. The political scientist Carmen González Enríquez of the Universidad Nacional de Educación a Distancia (Uned), expressed similar views in an interview with the author (Madrid, October 28, 2006).

19. **easily assimilable high-tech geniuses:** Heinsohn, *Söhne und Weltmacht*, p. 150.

20. **radical imams from "Londonistan":** See, e.g., Dominique Thomas, *Le Londonistan: Le djihad au cœur de l'Europe* and Cristina Giudici, "Occhi chiusi a Cremonistan," *Il Foglio,* July 27, 2005, p. 6.

20. **Consciousness of inequality spreads:** Raymond Aron, "L'aube de l'histoire universelle," in *Une histoire du XXe siècle*, p. 805.

Chapter 2. The Immigrant Economy

24. The Nationalities Act made immigration easy: The Commonwealth Immigrants Act of 1962, which was tightened further by the Commonwealth Immigrants Act of 1968.

24. Britain had 55,000 Indians and Pakistanis: For West Indians, Peter Fryer, *Staying Power,* pp. 372–74; for South Asians, Philip Lewis, *Islamic Britain*, p. 54. The figure for national population of Indians and Pakistanis comes from Fryer, p. 372.

24. half are from the Caribbean: UK Census 2001, Population by Ethnic Group, http://www.statistics.gov.uk/cci/nugget.asp?id=273.

24. "main obstacle to our recovery": Patrick Weil, *La France et ses étrangers*, pp. 68–69.

25. rate of 70,000 a week: Weil, *La France et ses étrangers*, pp. 81–86.

25. a third had acquired French nationality: Institut National de la Statistique et des Études Économiques, *Les immigrés en France, édition 2005*, "Répartition de la population selon le lieu de naissance et la nationalité."

25. spreading to more distant lands: Christopher Caldwell, "Islam on the Outskirts of the Welfare State," *New York Times Magazine*, February 5, 2006, p. 56.

25. Thanks to guest worker agreements: Statistiska centralbyrån (Swedish central statistics office), *Statisk årsbok för Sverige 2007* (Statistical yearbook for Sweden 2007), p. 121, Table 99. We are talking about 1,463,358 people of a total population of around 9 million.

26. There were 329,000 Gastarbeiter: Philip Martin, Manolo Abella, and Christiane Kuptsch, *Managing Labor Migration in the Twenty-first Century*, pp. 88–89

The stages of the German Gastarbeiter program are laid out, country by country, in Thomas Bauer, Claus Larsen, and Poul Chr. Matthiessen, "Immigration Policy and Danish and German Immigration," in Torben Tranaes and Klaus Zimmerman, *Migrants, Work, and the Welfare State*, p. 36. After Italy, the program was extended to Spain and Greece in 1960, Turkey in 1961, Morocco in 1963, Portugal in 1964, Tunisia in 1965, and Yugoslavia in 1968.

26. Gastarbeiter program of its own: Exhibit, Kreuzberg Museum, Adalbertstraße, Berlin.

26. Turkish government petitioned for inclusion: See, for instance, Stefan Luft, *Abschied von Multikulti*, pp. 101–15.

26. **Three quarters of the 18.5 million**: Elmar Hönekopp, "Labor Migration from Central and Eastern Europe: Old and New Trends," IAB Labor Market Research Topics, no. 23. Cited in Martin, Abella, and Kuptsch, *Managing Labor Migration*, p. 86.

27. **Guest workers returned home**: Ibid., pp. 16–18.

27. **Germany had a "foreign population"**: Statistische Ämter des Bundes und der Länder, November 30, 2006, http://www.statistik-portal.de/Statistik-Portal/en/en_jb01_jahrtab2.asp.

27. **open labor market until 1973**: Author interview with Klaus Rothstein, Copenhagen, December 2005.

28. **"social causes for mass emigration"**: Oscar Handlin, *Boston's Immigrants*, p. 26.

28. **"long and steady movement of people"**: Robert Winder, *Bloody Foreigners*, pp. 1,472.

28. **DNA from people who arrived**: Nicholas Wade, "English, Irish, Scots: They're All One, Genes Suggest," *New York Times*, March 5, 2007, p. F1. Wade cites the geneticists Stephen Oppenheimer and Bryan Sykes, both of Oxford, and Daniel G. Bradley of Trinity College, Dublin, as well as the archaeologist Heinrich Haerke. Sykes's work is accessible at the website bloodoftheisles.net.

28. **Britain's 700,000 years**: Alok Jha, *The Guardian*, September 6, 2006, National News, p. 12.

29. **Slayn by the bloody *Piemontese***: In "On the Late Massacre in Piedmont."

29. **a third of all jobs in Germany**: Enzensberger, *Die Große Wanderung*, p. 49.

29. **Linen mills in the north**: Christopher Caldwell, "The Crescent and the Tricolor," *The Atlantic*, November 2000.

30. **coal mines are closing**: Christopher Caldwell, "Where Every Generation Is First-Generation," *New York Times Magazine*, May 27, 2007, p. 47.

30. **mechanization of Southern agriculture**: Nicholas Lemann, *The Promised Land*.

30. **unemployment reaching 40 percent**: Giovanni Di Lorenzo, "Drinnen vor der Tür," *Die Zeit* , September 30, 2004.

31. **Europe's citizens may once have accepted**: Christopher Caldwell, "Europe needs its immigrants" (*Financial Times*, May 2, 2004). A Eurobarometer poll showed that 56 percent of Europeans recognized the need for immigrant labor, while 80 percent wanted more stringent border controls.

31. **economic impact of immigration:** Scheherezade Daneshku, "Public do not see 'undoubted economic benefits' of migrants," *Financial Times*, February 19, 2007.

31. **"The uneasy cosmopolitan":** The article, by Stefan Wagstyl, appeared on p. 13 of the edition of September 21, 2006.

31. **challenged with increasing rigor:** See George J. Borjas, "The Labor Demand Curve *Is* Downward Sloping: Reexamining the Impact of Immigration on the Labor Market," *Quarterly Journal of Economics*, June 2003, pp. 1335–74; David Card, "Immigrant Inflows, Native Outflows, and the Local Labor Market Impacts of Higher Immigration," *Journal of Labor Economics*, vol. 19 (2001), pp. 22–64. Both papers take an occupation-specific rather than a location-specific approach, examining skill groups rather than geographic clusters of immigrants and better capturing the reality of the modern labor market. They find immigration has a negative net effect on native wages.

31. **Sober-minded economists reckon:** Philippe Legrain, *Immigrants: Your Country Needs Them*, p. 19.

32. **aggregate gross domestic product:** To be precise, $39,460,070,000,000.00. See the International Monetary Fund's World Economic Outlook database from April 2007: http://www.imf.org/external/pubs/ft/weo/2007/01/data/weorept.aspx.

32. **total costs of the integration process:** David Coleman, "Why Europe does not need a 'European' migration policy" (evidence submitted to the House of Lords, February 1, 2001).

33. **"raises the supply of labour":** Chris Giles, "British fears ignore boost foreign labour gives economy," *Financial Times*, February 20, 2007, p. 5.

33. **true in practice:** See Jonathan Portes and Simon French, "The impact of free movement of workers from central and eastern Europe on the UK labour market: early evidence." UK Department of Work and Pensions Working Paper No. 18, 2004, p. 33. The American experience is described in the Borjas and Card papers cited above.

34. **Kool Halal:** Jacqueline de Linares, "Quand ma cité sera la City," *Le Nouvel Observateur*, January 3–February 6, 2008, pp. 84–85.

34. **parallels between today's migrations:** Martin, Abella, and Kuptsch, *Managing Labor Migration*, pp. 11–12.

35. **Amendments to the Danish Aliens Act:** There is a list of these changes in Bauer, Larsen, and Matthiessen, "Immigration Policy," p. 35.

36. **less need for "labor saving":** Sarah Laitner, "Young Jobless," *Financial Times*, February 20, 2007, p. 5, notes that European productivity growth

was below 1 percent in 2005, as compared to the U.S. rate of 1.8 percent and the Japanese rate of 2.2.

38. **many preferred a life:** Alexander Stille, "No blacks need apply" (see chap. 1 Notes), p. 28.

39. **replicating the age structure:** United Nations, *Replacement Migration*.

40. **one must subtract the (high) cost:** Martin Feldstein, "Immigration is no way to fund an aging population," *Financial Times*, December 13, 2006.

40. **"migrants themselves will age":** Home Office, "The Economic and Fiscal Impact of Immigration," October 2007, p. 35.

40. **In the Netherlands:** Marlise Simons, "More Dutch Plan to Emigrate As Muslim Influx Tips Scales," *New York Times*, February 27, 2005, p. 16.

40. **pay out more in taxes:** Stefanie Rosenkranz, "Die deutschen Gesichter des Islam," *Stern*, October 12, 2006.

41. **German immigrants were in the work force:** Martin, Abella, and Kuptsch, *Managing Labor Migration*, pp. 19–20. They use a graph from the Bundesausländerbeauftragte, a federal office for immigrant matters.

41. **just 29 percent of all immigrants:** Information on both France and Britain is from Coleman, "Why Europe does not need a 'European' migration policy."

41. **an impressive work ethic:** "Wages and Productivity of Non-Western Immigrants in Denmark," Rockwool Foundation newsletter, November 2006, p. 10.

41. **"increased immigration from low income countries":** Torben M. Andersen and Lars Haagen Pedersen, "Financial Restraints in a Mature Welfare State—The Case of Denmark," *Oxford Review of Economic Policy* (22:3), May 2006, Vol. 22, Issue 3, pp. 313–329.

41. **"demographic bulimia":** Enzensberger, *Die Große Wanderung*, p. 31.

Chapter 3. Who Is Immigration For?

43. **"Mister I-Know-My-Rights":** Oriana Fallaci, *La Rage et l'Orgueil*, Paris: Plon, 2002, p. 142.

43. **"who is welcome on its territory":** "Au Mali, Sarkozy prône un 'partenariat rénové' et justifie sa loi sur l'immigration," *Le Figaro*, May 18, 2006.

44. **His name is Nicolas Sarkozy:** Translation mine. "Un Hongrois chez les Gaulois," http://www.youtube.com/watch?v=9k98p7wPABI. In French:

Il s'appelle Nicolas Sarkozy
Il a inventé l'immigration choisie
C'est l'histoire d'un fils d'hongrois
Qui veut se faire couronner chez les gaulois
Fini l'époque du nègre musclé —
Belles dents!
Aujourd'hui il veut du noir diplômé,
Intelligent
C'est ça le critère du nouveau négrier,
Il a le culot d'aller en Afrique pour l'expliquer
Nicolas Sarkozy,
Pourquoi ton père a fui la Hongrie?

44. Almost a fifth: "World Migrant Stock," http://esa.un.org/migration. The British, incidentally, sometimes referred to these policies as "Australian" rather than Canadian. See Alan Travis, "Migrants—The Verdict," *Guardian*, October 17, 2007, p. 3.

44. a 100-point scale: Citizenship and Immigration Canada, "Application for Permanent Residence," p. 4. Available online at http://www.cic.gc.ca/english/immigrate/skilled/application-regular.asp.

44. a third of its doctors: OECD, *International Migration Outlook, Annual Report* (2007 edition), p. 165.

45. percentages are rising: Ibid., p. 163.

45. didn't need low-skilled workers: Author interview with Wolfgang Schäuble, Interior Ministry, Berlin, February 5, 2007.

45. "We need 700,000": *Philosophisches Quartett* [television show], ZDF, October 29, 2006, "Radikalismus und Bevölkerungswachstum."

45. Seven of the new additions: Richard Florida, *The Flight of the Creative Class*, p. 108.

45. United States and Canada: Christiane Buck, "Schlechtausgebildete Einwanderer ziehen nach Europa," *Die Welt*, October 19, 2005, A1.

45. "green card" program: Bloomberg News, "German Cabinet Approves Plan to Allow More IT Workers," May 31, 2000. Starting in 2005, the program was broadened to admit anyone who could credibly promise to create twenty-five jobs.

45. It was a flop: Author interview with Green parliamentarian Omid Nouripour, Leipzig, September 15, 2005.

46. vowed to raise development aid: Associated Press, "Sarkozy calls for creation of international treaty on migration," *International Herald Tribune*, December 11, 2006.

46. **"Eating is a human right"**: "Mercosur condemns EU migrant law," BBC news release, July 2, 2008.

47. **"in Great Britain for the next 359 years"**: Caldwell, "Europe's Future" (see chap. 1 Notes), pp. 25–26. Jammeh's remarks were made in an interview with Mohamed Mboyo Ey'ekula that appeared in the Dakar-based daily *Walf Fadjri* on October 3, 2006.

47. **they account for more funds**: Sanket Mohapatra, Dilip Ratha, and Zhimei Xu, with K. M. Vijayalakshmi, 1"Migration and Development Brief 2: Remittance Trends 2006" [unofficial World Bank document].

47. **Transfers to El Salvador**: Heinsohn, *Söhne und Weltmacht*, p. 50.

47. **Moroccans, mostly in Europe**: Alden, Dombey, Giles, and Laitner, "Price of prosperity" (see chap. 1 Notes).

47. **opened its 300,000th agency**: Western Union Company: "Western Union Reaches 300,000th Agent Location Milestone" [press release], March 1, 2007.

48. **migration of doctors**: OECD, International Migration Outlook, Annual Report (2007 edition), p. 163.

48. **roughly half of Americans' antipathy**: Alberto Alesina and Edward Glaeser, *Fighting Poverty in the U.S. and Europe*, p. 146.

49. **This view is given strong support**: Robert D. Putnam, "*E Pluribus Unum*: Diversity and Community in the Twenty-first Century" (Johan Skytte Prize Lecture), *Scandinavian Political Studies*, vol. 30, no. 2 (2007), pp. 137–74.

49. **list of recent social science studies**: About three dozen are listed in Putnam, "*E Pluribus Unum*," pp. 142–43.

49. **"A State cannot be constituted"**: Aristotle, *Politics*, 1303a [V, III, 11].

49. **"Our mosques are largely tribal"**: Munira Mirza, Abi Senthikumaran, and Zein Ja'far, *Living Apart Together*, p. 40.

49. **Two-thirds of French imams**: Laurence and Vaïsse, *Integrating Islam*, p. 118.

49. **Migrations spark secondary migrations**: "Migrations of Ethnic Unmixing in the 'New Europe,'" *International Migration Review*, vol. 32, no. 4 (Winter 1998), pp. 1047–65. Also (regarding Poles and Germans) see Rogers Brubaker, *Nationalism Reframed*, p. 90.

50. **only half the descendants**: Handlin, *Boston's Immigrants*, p. 12.

50. ***Goodbye, Deutschland!***: Mark Landler, "Seeking Greener Pastures," *International Herald Tribune*, February 6, 2007, p. 1.

50. **Netherlands recorded more emigrants**: Oussama Cherribi and Pieter van Os, "Houd toch op Nederland vol te noemen," *NRC Handelsblad*, July 15, 2006, p. 7.

50. **swamped with inquiries:** Simons, "More Dutch Plan to Emigrate" (see chap. 2 Notes).

51. **a semifictional letter:** Walden, *Time to Emigrate?*

51. **white flight is happening:** Danny Dorling and Bethan Thomas, "A Short Report on Plurality and the cities of Britain," undated. Undated statistical analysis by two members of the SASI group, Department of Geography, University of Sheffield, released in 2008 by the Barrow Cadbury Trust as part of its initiative "Cities in Transition," http://www.barrow cadbury.org.uk/pdf/shortreportonplurality.pdf. Birmingham statistics are at p. 41, Table 6; Leicester statistics (from 70.1 percent white 1991 to 44.5 percent white 2026) are at p. 45, Table 17.

51. **"'Why should I pay'":** Caldwell, "Daughter of the Enlightenment" (see chap. 1 Notes), p. 31.

51. **gets only 20 percent:** Jason DeParle, "Spain, Like U.S., Grapples With Immigration," *New York Times*, June 10, 2008.

51. **"ethnic filtering":** Interview, Bernabé López-García, Madrid, April 20, 2004. See Bernabé López-García, "El Islam y la integración de la inmigración social," *Cuadernos de Trabajo Social*, vol. 15 (2002), pp. 129–43. Author interviews with Spanish government officials indicate he is correct.

52. **Britain braced itself:** Richard Ford, "30,400 new EU migrants will be looking for work in Britain," *The Times*, October 25, 2006, pp. 6–7.

52. **The economist Hans-Werner Sinn:** Sinn's calculations, from his essay "EU Enlargement, Migration and the New Constitution" (published by CESifo), are cited in Martin Wolf, "EU needs labour and welfare reform," *Financial Times*, April 5, 2005. Usrful on similar matters are Herbert Brücker and Tito Boeri, "The Impact of Eastern Enlargement on Employment and Labour Markets in the EU Member States," European Integration Consortium, 2000; Christian Dustmann, Maria Casanova, Michael Fertig, Ian Preston, and Christoph M. Schmidt, "The Impact of EU Enlargement on Migration Flows," Home Office Online Report 25/03, London, 2003 (has data on Spanish and Portuguese flows); John Kay, "How the migration estimates turned out so wrong," *Financial Times*, September 5, 2006, p. 17.

53. **The Baltic states:** United Nations, *Replacement Migration*.

53. **"the country will disappear":** Latvia details from Dan Bilefsky, "Migration's flip side: All roads lead out," *International Herald Tribune*, December 7, 2005, p. 1.

54. **European since the fifteenth century:** Immigration aside, Ceuta and Melilla are often described, most stridently by the Moroccan royal house, as symbols of European "occupation" and "colonialism" in the Islamic world. (See Ignacio Cembrero, "Mohamed VI aparca su reivindicación

territorial," *El País*, January 29, 2006, p. 26; "Rabat condiciona el diálogo con España a una negociación sobre el futuro de Ceuta y Melilla," *ABC*, November 8, 2007; and "La Liga Árabe da su 'apoyo total' a Marruecos en su reclamación de Ceuta y Melilla," *El Mundo*, November 9, 2007.) It is an odd claim. Melilla was conquered by Spain in 1497—before the high imperial age. Ceuta became Portuguese in 1415 and Spanish in 1580; it has been a continuously Christian city for longer than Istanbul has been a Muslim one. Spanish politicians have not been uniformly hostile to surrendering Ceuta and Melilla to Morocco. In fact, Spain's own desire to absorb Britain's Iberian outpost of Gibraltar creates a logic for such a renunciation. It is unlikely in the near term.

54. **Barbed wire was put up:** Martin Dahms, "Komm nicht, denn du könntest sterben," *Stuttgarter Zeitung*, November 8, 2005, p. 3.

55. **there were ten assaults:** Karin Finkenzeller, "Ansturm auf die Festung; Afrikas Flucht nach Europa," *Die Welt am Sonntag*, October 9, 2005, p. 9.

55. **they shot dead four people:** Nuria Tesón Martín, "Un año en el limbo de Melilla," *El País*, October 10, 2006, p. 28.

55. **Many accounts describe the migrants' assaults as "desperate":** See, e.g., Boubacar Boris Diop, "Die neue Verdammten dieser Erde," *Neue Zürcher Zeitung*, October 21, 2005; Diop calls the attack a "verzweifelten Sturm."

56. **secured with ditches:** Refugee aspirations: Mark Mulligan and Raphael Minder, "Spain and Morocco call for joint action over tide of migrants," *Financial Times*, October 12, 2005, p. 3.

56. **"Barcelona or Death":** Author interview with sociologist Malick Ndiaye, Dakar, October 16, 2006. See Caldwell, "Europe's Future," p. 24.

56. **estimated that 3,000 people:** Caldwell, "Europe's Future," p. 24.

56. **A rusty freighter:** Thierry Portes, "L'odyssée des clandestins du 'Marine 1,'" *Le Figaro*, March 10–11, 2007.

57. **Spanish patrol boat *Río Duero*:** Juan Manuel Pardellas, "Un cayuco ataca una patrullera española con 'cócteles molotov,'" *El País,* April 10, 2007. (A translation of the article, with some details different, appeared as Juan Manuel Pardellas, "African migrants trying to reach Spain in small boat throw Molotov cocktails at patrol," Associated Press, April 11, 2007.)

58. **international human rights incident:** Miguel González, "Alonso se opuso en el Gobierno a que la Armada interceptara barcas de inmigrantes," *El País*, October 9, 2006, p. 1.

60. **The guest is sacred:** Enzensberger, *Die Große Wanderung*, p. 14.

60. **they were given *hospitalitas*:** Henri Pirenne, *Mahomet et Charlemagne*, p. 37. See also Wolfram, *History of the Goths*, p. 133.

60. **almost dreamlike in its generosity:** Author interview with Fahmy Alma-jid, Copenhagen, December 12, 2005.

61. **had arrived after 1985:** Martin, Abella, and Kuptsch, *Managing Labor Migration.*

61. **"'noble' asylum-seeker":** Enzensberger, *Die Große Wanderung,* pp. 42–46.

62. **equality of white British citizens:** Both these quotes appear in Kenan Malik, *The Meaning of Race,* p. 24. The articles to which he refers both appeared on March 1, 1968.

62. **"ringlike pattern of political crises":** Christopher Caldwell, "Islam on the Outskirts of the Welfare State" (see chap. 2 Notes), p. 56.

63. **half of all residence permits:** Caldwell, "Islam on the Outskirts," p. 56.

63. **"legacy backlog":** Ben Leapman, "Asylum crisis getting worse, say officials," *Sunday Telegraph,* October 14, 2007, p. 12.

63. **half a million applications:** To be more precise, Germany got 438,000 applications in 1992. See Roger Zetter, David Griffiths, Silva Ferretti, and Martyn Pearl, "An assessment of the impact of asylum policies in Europe 1990–2000," *Findings 168* (publication of the UK Home Office), p. 3.

64. **only 9.2 million refugees:** *Guardian,* April 20, 2006, p. 34.

64. **approving only a tenth:** Jeffrey Fleishman, "A Mutual Suspicion Grows in Denmark," *Los Angeles Times,* November 12, 2005, p. A1.

64. **"a hell of a good story":** Author interview with staff of Centraalorgaan Opvang Asielzoekers, Leiden, November 16, 2005.

65. **know the best countries:** This information came from discussions with those who worked closely with immigrants at the COA, Leiden, November 16, 2005.

65. **camped in front of the office:** Michael Slackman, "Fleeing Sudan, Only to Languish in an Egyptian Limbo," *New York Times,* December 26, 2005, p. 3; Abeer Allam and Michael Slackman, "23 Sudanese Die in Raid in Egypt," *New York Times,* December 31, 2005, p. 1.

66. **rejected applicants who stay:** January 2002 ICMPD study on EU return policies and practices, cited in European Council on Refugees and Exiles, "The Return of Asylum Seekers Whose Applications Have Been Rejected in Europe," June 2005, p. 15.

66. **"I haven't got a clue":** Benedict Brogan, "Illegal migrants? I haven't a clue, says Blunkett," *Daily Telegraph,* September 22, 2003, p. 2.

66. **"futility thesis":** see Albert O. Hirschman, *The Rhetoric of Reaction,* pp. 43–80.

66. **"make-believe policy land":** Madeleine Bunting, "A modern-day

slavery is flourishing in Britain . . . ," *Guardian*, December 18, 2006, p. 25.

67. distrust of "left-wing intellectuals": Author interview with Jesper Lang-balle (DF parliamentarian), Copenhagen, December 12, 2005.

67. "stops being exclusively work immigration": Abdelmalek Sayad, *La double absence*, pp. 17–18.

Chapter 4. Fear Masquerading as Tolerance

68. "written in letters of blood": Aron wrote this at the end of his book *Clausewitz: Penser la guerre*. Quoted in Raymond Aron, *Le Spectateur Engagé*, p. 284.

69. credit for that peace: The way this question is dealt with and answered is one of the highlights of Robert Kagan's *Paradise and Power*.

69. Margot Wallström warned: David Rennie, "Vote for EU constitution or risk new Holocaust, says Brussels," *Daily Telegraph*, May 10, 2005.

69. "beckons us to a new age": Jeremy Rifkin, *The European Dream*, p. 385. Cited in Perry Anderson, "Depicting Europe," London Review of Books, September 20, 2007, p. 13. This estimable article includes lots of other hubristic citations.

69. "ability to attract others": Mark Leonard, *Why Europe Will Run the 21st Century*, p. 83.

70. "the debate over multi-culturality": From: *Sociaal en Cultureel Rapport 1998*, p. 266. Cited in Frits Bolkestein, "Vijftien jaar later," *De Volkskrant*, August 31, 2006, p. 10.

70. "not going to bother Turkish children": Paul Scheffer, "Het multicultu-rele drama," *NRC Handelsblad*, January 29, 2000. (English translation by Mr Scheffer.)

70. knowledge of the "Virolai": Jordi Barbeta, "Irrumpe la inmigración," *La Vanguardia*, October 21, 2006.

71. "hosh-kosh nonsense": Zadie Smith, *White Teeth*, p. 47.

71. "'their finest hour'": "Britain rediscovered" [symposium], *Prospect*, April 2005.

71. "Diversity is not about charity": Katrin Bennehold, "French minister urges collecting minority data," *International Herald Tribune*, December 16, 2005, p. 3.

72. "you can't have holidays": Stéphane Kovacs, "Saint Nicolas accusé d'esclavagisme," *Le Figaro*, December 5, 2005.

72. authorities in Derby: Mark Steyn, "Making a pig's ear of defending democracy," *Daily Telegraph*, April 10, 2005.

72. **voted to name their teddy bear:** "Teacher held for 'insulting Mohammed,'" *Irish Times*, November 26, 2007.

72. **such as *jihad* and *terrorism*:** Frits Bolkestein, "Vijftien jaar later," *De Volkskrant*, August 31, 2006, p. 10.

72. **"anti-Islamic activity":** "Tories attack Islamic terrorism 'rebranding,'" *Daily Telegraph*, January 19, 2008.

72. **"The term 'politically correct'":** Author interview with Melanie Phillips, London, April 13, 2006. See Christopher Caldwell, "Counterterrorism in the U.K.: After Londonistan," *New York Times Magazine*, June 25, 2006, p. 46.

73. **hundreds upon hundreds of letters:** Enoch Powell, speech to the Annual General Meeting of the West Midlands Area Conservative Political Centre (the "Rivers of Blood" speech), April 20, 1968, in Powell, *Reflections of a Statesman*, p. 377.

73. **"Those who kept the old faith":** Alexis de Tocqueville, *L'Ancien Régime et la Révolution*, p. 184.

73. **the "Macpherson inquiry":** Published in 1999, it is known as the Macpherson inquiry, after Sir William Macpherson, who led it. Cited in Mirza, Senthikumaran, and Ja'far, *Living Apart Together*, p. 25.

74. **"expanded list of the rights of man":** Pierre-André Taguieff, *Les contre-réactionnaires*, p. 562.

74. **"potentially homophobic attitudes":** Jonathan Freedland, "How police gay rights zealotry is threatening our freedom of speech," *Guardian*, January 18, 2006, p. 23.

74. **condemned to a month of prison:** Sweden's Supreme Court overturned the conviction in September, on the grounds that he had gone no further than the Bible in his condemnation. See Nina Larson, "Le pasteur suédois homophobe Aake Green disculpé par la Cour suprême," Agence France-Presse, November 29, 2005.

74. **first Frenchman convicted of homophobia:** Jean Valbay, "Le député Vanneste condamné," *Le Figaro*, January 25, 2006.

75. **renamed the Iqra School:** Mirza, Senthikumaran, and Ja'far, *Living Apart Together*, p. 24. The report cites P. West, *The Poverty of Multiculturalism* (London: Civitas, 2005).

75. **rolled back certain guarantees:** The "Gayssot Law" is Loi no 90–615 du 13 juillet 1990 (NOR: JUSX9010223L), available online at Legifrance.gouv.fr. The discussion that follows draws on Christopher Caldwell, "Historical truth speaks for itself," *Financial Times*, February 18–19, 2006, and Christopher Caldwell, "A question of expediency," *Financial Times*, October 14–15, 2006.

75. a celebrated family of *résistants*: Jean-Baptiste de Montvalon, "Les historiens pris sous le feu des mémoires," *Le Monde*, December 17, 2005.

75. historians who opposed the Gayssot law: In 2006, two petitions urging the repeal or gutting of all "memory laws" won the support of much of the intellectual world in Paris. The first, "Freedom for History," was signed by the historians Pierre Nora, Michel Winock, and Mona Ozouf, among others. The second, "Freedom to Debate," was authored by the anticolonialist philosopher Paul Thibaud and signed by several of the country's most distinguished historians and philosophers.

76. "other genocides and other assaults": Madeleine Rebérioux, "Contre la loi Gayssot," *Le Monde*, May 21, 1996. Cited (in part) in Jean-Baptiste de Montvalon, "Les historiens pris sous le feu des mémoires," *Le Monde*, December 17, 2005.

76. the "Yovodah": Stéphanie Binet and Blandine Grosjean, "La nébuleuse Dieudonné," *Libération*, November 10, 2005, pp. 38–39. The group was Coffad (Collectif des fils et filles d'Africains déportés), itself the echo of a memorial association for the Holocaust. According to Alain Finkielkraut (in Rony Brauman and Alain Finkielkraut, *La Discorde*, p. 245), *yovodah* is an invented word adapted from the Fon language, which is spoken in Benin. It means "white cruelty."

77. "Africans are forbidden": Binet and Grosjean, "La nébuleuse Dieudonné."

78. "something about Arab men": Oriana Fallaci, *La Rage et l'Orgueil*, Paris: Plon, 2002, p. 188.

78. "with their behinds in the air": Ibid., p. 92.

78. "multiplying like protozoa": Ibid., p. 29.

78. "the Koran authorizes lies": Ibid., p. 38.

78. "the most hardened of them": Ibid., p. 105

78. Many of the Shi'is: Marshall G. S. Hodgson, *The Venture of Islam*, vol. I, p. 381.

79. Syrian-born radical Omar Bakri: Ian Cobain, "Bakri pleads for UK visa to escape bombs," *Guardian*, July 22, 2006, p. 15. Note that Bakri was not expelled: he traveled to Lebanon and was refused permission to reenter Britain.

79. "transform the West into Dar Al-Islam": *Al-Hayat* (London), July 31, 2002. Cited in Middle East Media Research Institute, Special Dispatch 410, "Islamist Leaders in London Interviewed," August 9, 2002.

79. "Finkielkraut affair": Christopher Caldwell, "Politically correct intolerance," *Financial Times*, December 10–11, 2005.

79. The philosopher Alain Finkielkraut: Dror Mishani and Aurelia

Smotriez, "What Sort of Frenchmen Are They?" *Ha'aretz* (English-language edition), November 17, 2005.

80. **called him a "neo-reactionary":** *Nouvel Observateur*, December 1, 2005.

80. **"that very French tradition":** "Finkielkraut, réactions." *Libération*, November 30, 2005, p. 6.

80. **Another compared Finkielkraut:** Ibid., p. 6.

80. **MRAP dropped its threat:** "Le Mrap renonce à porter plainte contre Finkielkraut," Agence France-Presse, November 25, 2005.

81. **Institutions established to promote tolerance:** Christopher Caldwell, "What Will Become of Europe," Bradley Lectures in Political Philosophy, Boston College, February 10, 2006.

81. **can probably be managed:** Geoff Dench, *Minorities in the Open Society*, p. viii.

82. **coined the term *immigrationisme*:** Taguieff, *Les contre-réactionnaires*.

84. **young people's spending on fashion:** Sophie Péters, "Marques et banlieues, des liaisons dangereuses," *Les Echos*, November 24, 2005, p. 12.

84. *le look banlieue*: Ibid.

84. *Gringo*: Caldwell, "Islam on the Outskirts," pp. 56–57.

84. **Corinne Hofmann's erotic autobiography:** Corinne Hofmann, *Die Weiße Massai*.

85. **why Europeans like this sort of thing:** Kingsley Amis, *That Uncertain Feeling* (London: Victor Gollancz, 1955).

85. **What was a banker:** Michel Houellebecq, *Les particules élémentaires*, pp. 237–40.

85. **"White Man, What Now?":** Matthias Politycki, "Weißer Mann—was nun?" *Die Zeit*, September 1, 2005, pp. 39–40. The title is a play on Hans Fallada's novel of 1932, *Kleiner Mann, was nun?*

86. **The brutality of the raw life:** Ibid.

86. **the inhabitants' "unbridled energy":** Ibid.

86. **"What is troubling":** Ibid.

86. **"completely enlightened (read: godless)":** Ibid.

86. **"a moralizing flourish":** Enzensberger, *Die Große Wanderung*, p. 52.

87. **to remove her cross:** Both stories are in: Gina Thomas, "Religiöse Accessoires verboten," *Frankfurter Allgemeine Zeitung*, November 29, 2006, p. 39.

87. **"opens the gates":** Udo di Fabio, *Die Kultur der Freiheit*, p. 126. Cited in Christopher Caldwell, "Values and the German Debate," *Financial Times*, November 4–5, 2005.

87. **"White people are less likely":** Office of Communities and Local

Government, "Citizenship Survey April–September 2007, England & Wales." London, January 2008, p. 1.

88. "We no longer consider": Pierre Manent, *La Raison des Nations*, pp. 59–60.

88. "truly unforgivable human action": Ibid., p. 18.

88. solution lies in being explicit: "Britain rediscovered" [symposium], *Prospect*, April 2005).

Chapter 5. Ethnic Colonies

92. forgotten all about Islam: Hilaire Belloc, *The Great Heresies*, pp. 76, 92–93, 126–27.

92. defender of the Crusades: Ibid., p. 102.

92. "West was bottled up": Pirenne, *Mahomet et Charlemagne*, pp. 260–61.

92. "two different and hostile civilizations": Ibid., p. 132.

93. "Without the challenge of Islam": Bassam Tibi, "Europeanisation, not Islamisation," *Sign and Sight* [website], March 22, 2007, http://www.perlentaucher.de/artikel/3764.html; in (sort of) English at: http://www.signandsight.com/features/1258.html.

93. series of "encounters": see the long first chapter of Jack Goody, *Islam in Europe*.

93. liberals who defend Islam: Ernest Renan, *L'Islam et la science*, pp. 38–39.

94. clean-shaven men: See, for example, the beautiful collection of documents, photos, and news clippings assembled by the Dokumentationszentrum und Museum über die Migration aus der Türkei (DOMiT): *Zur Geschichte der Arbeitsmigration aus der Türkei: Materialsammlung*, Köln: [North Rhine–Westphalia] Ministerium für Arbeit, 2000 (especially pp. 39, 48, 56, 59). Also see Jan Lucassen and Rinus Penninx, *Nieuwkomers, Nakomelingen, Nederlanders*, p. 54.

95. More than half of respondents: Dominique Vidal, "Quand Jean-Christophe Rufin prône le délit d'opinion," *Le Monde Diplomatique*, October 21, 2004.

95. "oppression of women": Elisabeth Noelle, "Der Kampf der Kulturen," *Frankfurter Allgemeine Zeitung*, September 15, 2004, p. 5. This study is from the Institut für Demoskopie (Allensbach), which references it as Dokumentation 6614.

95. fully a sixth: All of the population statistics in this paragraph, on Paris, Behren-lès-Forbach, etc., come from the highly reliable Michelle Tribalat,

"Les Concentrations ethniques en France," *Agir*, no. 29 (January 2007), pp. 77–86. The figure of 40 percent of Parisian kids having at least one immigrant parent (Tribalat, p. 81) is for the *city* of Paris; but in the whole vast metropolitan area of Île-de-France, it is still over a third—33.5 percent.

96. "process of substitution": Tribalat, p. 81.

96. about 20 million Muslims: Number obtained by taking Tariq Ramadan's Western European estimate (see note to p. 10) and adding the Balkan Muslim population.

960. A million Muslims: Caldwell, "Counterterrorism in the U.K." (see chap. 4 Notes), p. 42.

96. Muslims account for more than a third: Of the 34 percent of Amsterdam residents who have a religion, according to the Amsterdam City Council research service (2006): 12 percent of the total population is Muslim, 10 percent Catholic, 7 percent Protestant (all denominations), 3 percent Buddhist, 1 percent Hindu, 1 percent Jewish. Cited in Simon Kuper, "Amsterdam's soft approach courts potential jihadists," *Financial Times,* September 11, 2007, p. 8.

96. U.S. National Intelligence Council: Michael Freund, "Say Goodbye to Europe," *Jerusalem Post,* January 10, 2007.

97. Caribbean and Eastern European immigrants: Eric Kaufmann, "Breeding for God," *Prospect,* November 2006.

According to Coleman and Scherbov, "Immigration and Ethnic Change" (see chap. 1 Notes), the total fertility of the Pakistani-born in Britain was 4.67 in 2001; that of the Bengali-born was 3.89. Coleman and Scherbov cite the Office of National Statistics, *International Migration: Migrants Entering or Leaving the United Kingdom and England and Wales 2002* (Series MN No. 29). London: The Stationery Office, 2004.

97. "this increase is likely": Barrow Cadbury Trust, "Cities in Transition" (a briefing document based on Dorling and Thomas, "A Short Report on Plurality"), p. 4.

97. According to four demographers: Anne Goujon, Vegard Skirbekk, Katrin Fliegenschnee, and Pawel Strzelecki, "New Times, Old Beliefs," Vienna Institute of Demography Working Papers, January 2006. (Cited in Kaufmann, "Breeding for God.")

97. Moroccan-Belgian community: Nicholas Eberstadt, "A Union of a Certain Age," *Milken Institute Review,* Second Quarter 2005, p. 47.

97. most common given boy's names: Hanspeter Born, "Belgien, adieu?" *Die Weltwoche* (Zürich), November 7, 2007.

98. "Commuters came no more": Kreuzberg Museum. Visited, autumn 2005.

100. **immigrants began arriving en masse:** The material on Sweden's Million Program draws on Caldwell, "Islam on the Outskirts," pp. 56–57.

100. **Seventy percent of the residents:** Ibid.

101. **bad environments for raising children:** See Peter Hall, *Cities of Tomorrow*, p. 247. Hall notes that Corbusierian high-density projects tended to work only when they were inhabited by middle-class professionals, as in the modest Unité project in Marseille. He cites a number of architectural critics who have marveled at the child-unfriendliness of modernist planning.

101. **a fifth of the women:** Caldwell, "Islam on the Outskirts," p. 57

101. **More than half of the country's North Africans:** Laurence and Vaïsse, *Integrating Islam*, p. 36.

101. **built in the 1960s:** Author interview with Ilda Curti, The Gate, Turin, March 23, 2006.

102. **Anyone who could control:** Christopher Caldwell, "Revolting High Rises," *New York Times Magazine*, November 27, 2005, p. 30.

102. **"lawless zones":** Robert Marquand, "Europe tightens immigration rules," *Christian Science Monitor*, October 17, 2007, p. 6.

103. **"the Bestiary":** Author interview with Pierre Cardo, Mayor of Chanteloup-les-Vignes, March 23, 2007.

103. **two-thirds of Chanteloup's residents:** From website of commune of Chanteloup-les-Vignes.

103. **grittily realistic exposé:** Sheila Johnston, "Why the prime minister had to see 'La Haine,'" *Independent* (London), October 19, 1995.

103. **In the days before** *La Haine*: Author interviews with Pierre Cardo, Mayor of Chanteloup-les-Vignes, Chanteloup, March 23, 2007.

103. **sixty hooded and armed youths:** Author interview with Françoise Nung, Chanteloup-les-Vignes, March 23, 2007; Julien Constant and Véronique Beaugrand, "Affrontements: Nouvelle nuit de violence dans les Yvelines," *Le Parisien*, February 4, 2007, p. 13; Agence France-Presse, "Violences à Chanteloup-les-Vignes," February 6, 2006.

104. **"hardening in its separateness":** Trevor Phillips, "After 7/7: Sleepwalking to segregation," speech delivered at the Manchester Council for Community Relations, September 22, 2005.

104. **was becoming** *less* **segregated:** Ken Livingstone, "Society is becoming more mixed in the UK" (letter), *Financial Times*, December 23–24, 2006, p. 6.

104. **"colour-laden value":** Ludi Simpson, "Speech for Anti-racist Priorities for the Labour Government fringe meeting," Labour Party Conference 2006.

105. "White Christians": Ibid.

105. "When I leave this meeting": *Community Cohesion* [The "Cantle Report"] (London: Home Office, 2001), p. 9.

105. apartments "open" for a Swede: Caldwell, "Islam on the Outskirts," p. 58.

106. "A lack of job qualifications": Di Lorenzo, "Drinnen vor der Tür."

106. "Mogadishu Avenue": Stéphane Kovacs, "Helsinki impose la mixité sociale par le logement," *Le Monde*, March 19, 2007, p 5.

107. "He was very pessimistic": Off-the-record discussion.

108. ghettoized on religious lines: Ian Johnson (with John Carreyrou), "Islam and Europe: A Volatile Mix," *Wall Street Journal*, July 11, 2005, p. A1. Also see Laurence and Vaïsse, *Integrating Islam*, p. 37.

108. "a string of towns and cities": Rod Liddle, "The Crescent of Fear," *Spectator*, November 12, 2005.

109. swimming hours at public pools: Johnson, "Islam and Europe."

109. serving of non-halal meat: Ahmed Taghza, "Des enfants musulmans refusent la viande non *hallal*," *L'Écho républicain*, November 25, 2004. Cited in Olivier Roy, *La Laïcité face à l'Islam*.

109. Ninety percent of the women: Author's estimate from a visit to Rosengård , January 2005.

109. sharply divided by political leanings: Rauf Ceylan, *Ethnische Kolonien*. Also based on author interviews with Ceylan in the March 2007. Ceylan's work may be the most rigorous, detailed, and empathetic account of any European immigrant community.

110. The mosque's request: Author interview with Zehra Yilmaz and Mustafa Kücük, Duisburg, March 12, 2007.

110. now had to speak Turkish: Cornelia Uebel, "Alles getürkt?" *Die Zeit*, October 20, 2005, p. 15.

111. sentences longer than five years: Caldwell, "Islam on the Outskirts," p. 58. The numbers come from the Swedish National Council for Crime Prevention (Brottsförebyggande rådet). It must be noted that, to a non-Swede, the scale of this problem is small. In 2004, there were only 329 people serving sentences of more than five years in all of Sweden.

111. "probably the first prison religion": Farhad Khosrokhavar, *L'islam dans les prisons*, p. 11.

111. forty-five percent of inmates: Author interview with Pietro Buffa, prison superintendent, Turin, March 24, 2006.

111. "'Sarà stato un marocchino'": Author interview with Franco Venturini, Rome, March 18, 2006.

111. "the natives are disengaging": Walden, *Time to Emigrate?*, p. 60.

112. **nine thousand police cars:** Michael Jeismann, "Neuntausend," *Frankfurter Allgemeine Zeitung*, October 26, 2005, p. 37.

112. **Unlike the American race riots:** Christopher Caldwell, "The Man Who Would Be *le Président*," *Weekly Standard*, February 27, 2006, p. 26.

113. **There were two basic explanations:** Katrin Bennhold, "In egalitarian Europe, a not-so-hidden world of squalor," *International Herald Tribune*, October 18, 2005, p. 1.

113. **You can't graft local police:** Jean de Maillard, "Le pire reste a venir," rue89.com (downloaded November 28, 2007).

113. **France had 4,244 crimes:** Christopher Caldwell, "Liberté, Egalité, Judeophobie," *Weekly Standard*, May 6, 2002, p. 20.

114. *Violence and Insecurity*: Laurent Mucchielli, *Violences et insécurité: fantasmes et réalités dans le débat français*; Loïc Wacquant, *Punir les pauvres: Le nouveau gouvernement de l'insécurité sociale*.

114. **Larousse:** *Larousse Standard French-English Dictionary*, 1994, p. 702.

114. **Robert:** HarperCollins/Robert French Unabridged Dictionary, 5th ed., 1998, p. 740.

115. **wave of Islamist killings:** Jean-Marie Pontaut, "Itinéraire d'un terroriste," *L'Express*, September 26, 1996.

115. **they were given a second wind:** Ivan Rioufol, "Cités: les non-dits d'une rébellion," *Le Figaro*, November 4, 2005.

115. **"exhaustion of political Islam":** International Crisis Group, *La France face à ses musulmans: Émeutes, jihadisme et dépolitisation* (Rapport Europe No. 172), March 9, 2006, p. ii.

116. **three urgent recommendations:** Ibid.

116. **an anchor of identity:** Mishani and Smotriez, "What sort of Frenchmen are they?"

117. **"we translate their appeals":** Alexis Lacroix, "Alain Finkielkraut: 'L'illégitimité de la haine,'" *Le Figaro*, November 15, 2005, p. 18.

117. **In early 2007, Angelo Hoekelet:** What follows draws on Christopher Caldwell, "Harsh policing goes transatlantic," *Financial Times*, March 31–April 1, 2007, p. 6.

117. **"the crowd doesn't try":** Jean-Marc Leclerc, "La banlieue, poudrière sous haute surveillance," *Le Figaro*, March 29, 2007.

118. **two nights of murderous violence:** This account follows Christopher Caldwell, "A bad sense of community," *Financial Times*, October 24–25, 2005.

118. **"Gang of 19 rape teen":** Stephen Brook, "Voice censured for Birmingham 'rape' reporting," *Guardian Unlimited*, February 21, 2006.

118. **emerged as tested paramilitary leaders:** Christopher Caldwell, "France must maintain ideals," *Financial Times*, November 11–12, 2005.

119. **"There are entire populations":** "Villiers-le-Bel: il faut des 'décisions politiques majeures' (Boutih, PS)", Agence France-Presse, November 28, 2007. (AFP was quoting remarks Boutih had made on the radio station RTL.)

119. **"It's war":** Yves Bordenaves, "'Ce sont eux les victimes et on les fait passer pour des voleurs et des criminels,'" *Le Monde*, November 28, 2007, p. 10.

119. **"I'd happily die":** Henri Haget and Marie Huret, "Le retour de flammes," *L'Express*, November 29, 2007, p. 98.

119. **were sent to Morocco and Senegal:** *Le Monde* (online edition), "Villiers-le-Bel : le dispositif sécuritaire maintenu 'tant que nécessaire,'" November 28, 2007.

Chapter 6. An Adversary Culture

120. **"was not rooted in this country":** BBC Panorama, December 2, 1968, in Powell, *Reflections of a Statesman*, p. 15.

121. **"howls of abuse":** Roger Cohen, "A European model for immigration falters," *International Herald Tribune*, October 17, 2005, p. 5.

121. **"To hold it against the French":** Pierre Marcelle, "Marseillaise," *Libération*, October 10, 2001.

121. **a loophole allowed entry:** See Enoch Powell, Sydney University lecture, "The UK and Immigration," September 1988, in Powell, *Reflections of a Statesman*, pp. 410, 412–13.

122. **not as illiberal as it looked:** A full history, along with a clear and sophisticated theoretical discussion of jus soli and jus sanguinis, can be found in Rogers Brubaker, *Citizenship and Nationhood in France and Germany*.

122. **he knew little of Turkey:** See "Fassungslos zwischen Döner und Knödel," *Süddeutsche Zeitung*, May 27, 1998; and Michael Mielke, "Eine unendliche Geschichte," *Die Welt*, March 4, 2005. As of this writing, a decade later, Ari remains in Germany, with a considerably longer criminal record than he had when he first entered the criminal justice system and the public eye.

123. **were suddenly more hostile:** "Europe's Muslims More Moderate," Washington, D.C.: The Pew Global Attitudes Project, June 22, 2006, pp. 1, 5. It is possible the Islamist terrorist attacks in Madrid in 2004 played a role in this distrust, but those happened a year before the amnesty.

124. **"I don't care if you respect"**: Author interview with Göran Johansson, Gothenburg city hall, December 7, 2005. Parts were printed in Caldwell, "Islam on the Outskirts."

124. **"My generation and the generation after"**: Sarfraz Manzoor, "It's about feeling you belong here," *The Guardian*, April 27, 2005, Comment & Features, p. 5

125. **"Integration is not assimilation"**: Luncheon meeting with Jürgen Rüttgers, German Marshall Fund of the United States, Washington, D.C., February 21, 2006.

125. **"You must learn the Dutch language"**: Author interview with Rita Verdonk, Den Haag, November 17, 2005.

125. **"The best form of integration"**: Otto Schily, "Ich möchte keine zweisprachigen Ortsschilder haben," *Süddeutsche Zeitung*, June 27, 2002.

125. **"They are no problem"**: Author interview with Jesper Langballe, Dansk Folkeparti, Folketinget, Copenhagen, December 12, 2005.

126. **"When Danes speak of immigrants"**: Author interview with Rikke Hvilshøj, Copenhagen, December 10, 2005.

126. **"want to remain distinct"**: Pew Research Center (Pew Global Attitudes Project), "Islamic Extremism: Common Concern for Muslim and Western Publics," July 14, 2005, p. 17.

126. **Punjabis and Mirpuris:** For a discussion of such divisions in the wake of the 2005 London Transport bombings, see Madeleine Bunting, "Orphans of Islam," *Guardian*, July 18, 2005.

126. **"What do you mean, 'Islam'?"**: Rosenkranz, "Die deutschen Gesichter des Islam."

127. ***"Mister Islam" Doesn't Exist***: Dounia Bouzar, *Monsieur Islam n'existe pas.*

127. **replacing Islam *in* France:** The authoritative Jonathan Laurence and Justin Vaïsse, in their *Integrating Islam* (p. 100), attribute the idea of creating a "Gallic Islam, just as there is an Islam of the Maghreb" to remarks of Berque in *Il reste un avenir: Entretiens avec Jean Sur* (Paris: Arlea, 1993), p. 203.

127. **"Islam in Italy is becoming Italian Islam"**: Stefano Allievi, *Islam italiano*, p. 216.

127. **about a third of Muslim students:** Vincent Geisser and Khadija Mohsen-Finan, "L'Islam à l'école," Institut des Hautes Etudes de la Sécurité Intérieure (IHESI), 2001. Cited in Laurence and Vaïsse, *Integrating Islam*, p. 75.

127. **the expression "second generation"**: Alain Gresh and Tariq Ramadan, *L'Islam en questions*, p. 299.

128. **had more in common with Muslims:** Mirza, Senthikumaran, and Ja'far, *Living Apart Together*. Discussed in Christopher Caldwell, "Graphic images of separateness," *Financial Times*, February 2–3, 2007.

128. **Britain's Muslims were joining the military:** Caldwell, "Graphic images of separateness."

128. **their own history of modernization:** Jörg Lau, "Französische Verhältnisse verhindern," *Die Zeit*, November 3, 2005.

128. **Muslim cemeteries in Europe:** Faruk Sen and Hayrettin Aydin, *Islam in Deutschland*, pp. 110–11.

129. **They are evenly split:** Rosenkranz, "Die deutschen Gesichter des Islam," citing FORSA poll of Turkish Muslims in Germany.

129. **"are no longer Berbers":** Ernest Renan, *L'Islam et la science*, pp. 22–23. Renan claimed that Persian Shia formed an exception to this rule.

129. **"utterly speechless and spellbound":** Malcolm X (with Alex Haley), *The Autobiography of Malcolm X*, pp. 346–48.

130. **"It was an amazing day":** Inayat Bunglawala, "I was wrong about Salman," *Guardian*, June 20, 2007.

131. **fatwa show on al-Jazeera:** Ian Johnson, Andrew Higgins, and Carrick Mollenkamp, "Bookstore Is a Focus of U.K. Probe," *Wall Street Journal*, July 19, 2005, p. A12.

131. **"'They send it to Denmark'":** Author interview with Fahmy Almajid, Copenhagen, December 12, 2005.

131. **do not believe Arabs committed the atrocities:** "Europe's Muslims More Moderate," p. 4.

132. **"we Muslims are suffering":** Ian Johnson and Carrick Mollenkamp, "U.K. Looks Hard at Muslim Community Dynamics," *Wall Street Journal*, July 15, 2005, p. A8. This article is part of an indispensable series. Also see: Ian Johnson, Carrick Mollenkamp, Glenn Simpson, and Jeanne Whalen, "Close Quarters," *Wall Street Journal* July 14, 2005, p. A1; and Johnson, Higgins, and Mollenkamp, "Bookstore Is a Focus of U.K. Probe."

132. **"We have far greater experience as victims":** Craig S. Smith, "At Mosque That Recruited Radicals, New Imam Calls for Help in Catching Bombers," *New York Times*, July 9, 2005, p. A6.

132. **Imagine that the West:** The nearest thing to such a migration came with the Mariel boatlift in the summer of 1980, when 125,000 left Cuba in a sudden migration provoked and facilitated by Cuban leader Fidel Castro. It was mostly an unstoppable flight of willing defectors. But it was composed, to a larger-than-normal extent, of violent nonpolitical criminals and inmates released from mental hospitals. The result was the construction

of an archipelago of holding camps, at which many of the *marielitos* were detained for several years. At the best known of these, in Fort Chaffee, Arkansas, serious riots in 1982 destroyed the reelection chances of the state's young and charismatic governor, Bill Clinton. (See David Maraniss, "Cuban Refugee Uprising Offers View of Clinton's Reaction to Crisis," *Washington Post*, October 22, 1992, p. A12.)

132. Islam's "bloody borders": Samuel Huntington, *The Clash of Civilizations and the Remaking of World Order*, pp. 254–58.

132. Two years into the Iraq war: French: Christophe Dubois, "Des groupes de combattants se constituent en France" *Le Parisien,* September 19, 2005. Britons: David Leppard, "British brigade of Islamists join Al-Qaeda foreign legion in Iraq," *Sunday Times*, June 4, 2006. Belgians: Stratfor.com, December 29, 2005.

133. clear and present danger: This account of Hanif and Sharif draws on Christopher Caldwell, "Treason returns to smoke out the enemy within," *Financial Times*, May 17, 2003, p. 13.

133. traveled to a Tel Aviv discotheque: Damien McElroy, "The British would-be suicide bombers stood out," *Sunday Telegraph* (London), May 11, 2003, p. 4.

133. "the soulless wastelands of modernity": Martin Bright and Fareena Alam, "Making of a Martyr," *Observer*, May 4, 2003, p. 18.

134. "being violated by America and Britain": McElroy, "British would-be suicide bombers stood out."

134. the largest mosque in Europe: Daniel Johnson, "Allah's England?" *Commentary*, November 2006, p. 46.

134. a quarter of its annual budget: Johnson, "Islam and Europe" (see chap. 5 Notes).

134. long financed by a sheikh: Caldwell, "Islam on the Outskirts."

135. most permit it to operate legally: Zeyno Baran, "Fighting the War of Ideas," *Foreign Affairs*, vol. 84, no. 6 (November/December 2005), pp. 68–78.

135. women of the Hofstad network: Private communication with Janny Groen, coauthor (with Annieke Kranenberg) of *Strijdsters van Allah*, a book about the women of the Hofstad network.

136. twelve hours of religion: Ian Johnson (with David Crawford), "Saudi Funds Tied to Extremism in Europe," *Wall Street Journal*, December 30, 2003, p. A8.

136. received a twelve-week sentence: Ian Buruma, *Murder in Amsterdam*, pp. 165, 167, 171.

136. to "milk the state": Buruma, *Murder in Amsterdam*, p. 168.

136. "homeland of tolerance": Author interview with Massoud Kamali, Stockholm, January 24, 2005.

136. "disappointable": Hans Magnus Enzensberger, "Der radikale Verlierer," *Der Spiegel*, no. 7 (November 2005), p. 174. Published in book form as *Schreckens Männer* (Frankfurt: Suhrkamp, 2006). The word he uses is *Enttäuschbarkeit* ("disappointability").

138. "higher sense of identity": Alberto Bisin, Eleonora Patacchini, Thierry Verdier, and Yves Zenou, "Are Muslim Immigrants Different in Terms of Cultural Integration?" Bonn: Forschungsinstitut zur Zukunft der Arbeit, Discussion Paper No. 3006, August 2007, p. 6. Since the study relied on British data, it should be added that this was not a reaction of political sour grapes against Britain's co-leadership in the war against Iraq, either. The data used were from the UK's Fourth National Survey of Ethnic Minorities, which antedated not just the Iraq war but also the September 11 attacks.

139. "that is impossible, because they're Muslims!": Jean-Pierre Obin, "Les Signes et manifestations d'appartenance religieuse dans les établissements scolaires" (report to the Minister of Education), Paris, 2004, p. 23.

139. "adversary culture": See Lionel Trilling, *Beyond Culture*, New York: Viking, 1968, pp. iii–vi. Trilling used the term in a different context. He applied it to a habit of mind common among U.S. intellectuals in the 1960s.

140. "Here it's called *Gastarbeiter*": Author interview with the rapper "Killa Hakan," Kreuzberg, October 20, 2005 (in the company of Taner, "Balina" [Tuncay], and Tarkan).

140. culture of the wretched: David Brooks, "Gangsta, in French," *New York Times*, November 10, 2005.

141. successes of Islamist proselytizers: As described by Farhad Khosrokhavar, *L'islam dans les prisons*, pp. 219–24.

141. cell-phone salesman Ilan Halimi: See Nidra Poller, "The Murder of Ilan Halimi," *Wall Street Journal*, February 26, 2006.

Chapter 7. Europe's Crisis of Faith

142. "We have a public debate": Author interview with Anders Jerichow, Copenhagen, December 13, 2005.

143. In France, 85 percent: Vincent Geisser and Khadija Mohsen-Finan, "L'Islam à l'école," Institut des Hautes Etudes de la Sécurité Intérieure (IHESI), 2001. Cited in Laurence and Vaïsse, *Integrating Islam*, p. 95.

143. just 6 percent of Germans: Olivier Hoischen, "Deutsche Jugend ohne

Gott," *Frankfurter Allgemeine Zeitung*, December 17, 2006, p. 1. Hoischen cites a study by Hans-Georg Ziebertz of Würzburg University.

143. **fast during Ramadan:** Ramadan, *Dar ash-shahada*, p. 15.

143. **group called the "Mullah Boys":** Shiv Malik, "My brother the bomber," *Prospect*, June 2007.

144. **there were 393 million:** Lamin Sanneh, *Disciples of All Nations*, p. xx.

145. **"It is 50–50":** Author interview with Pleun Reedijk, Rotterdam-Zuid, November 14, 2005.

145. **positive attitude toward Christians:** "Europe's Muslims More Moderate."

146. **"we would build them mosques":** "Schäuble wünscht sich 'deutsche Muslime,'" *Frankfurter Allgemeine Zeitung*, September 27, 2006.

146. **permission to build their mosques:** Georg Paul Hefty, "Was ist ein deutscher Muslim?" *Frankfurter Allgemeine Zeitung*, September 28, 2006.

146. **Central Council of Muslims:** in German, Zentralrat der Muslime.

146. **The loss of a church:** Evangelische Kirche in Deutschland (EKD), *Klarheit und gute Nachbarschaft: Christen und Muslime in Deutschland*, p. 69.

146. **"emphasizing their opposition to globalization":** Ian Johnson, Carrick Mollenkamp, Glenn Simpson, and Jeanne Whalen, "Close Quarters," *Wall Street Journal*, July 14, 2005, p. A1

147. **permit Saddam Hussein to pray:** Leo Wieland, "Jeder in seinem Haus—und Gott in allen," *Frankfurter Allgemeine Sonntagszeitung*, March 11, 2007, p. 10.

147. **"to go to Mecca":** Ibid.

147. **"the rights we ensure in Italy":** An interview with Cardinal Mario Pompedda published in *La Repubblica*, March 13, 2006.

148. **"announcing the end of religion":** Hans Jansen, *Een Hoorcollege over de islamitische godsdienst en cultuur* (The Hague: Home Academy, 2005).

148. **to say what Easter celebrates:** "Tu n'ignoreras point!" *Le Figaro Magazine*, December 27, 2003.

148. **"I don't believe in God":** The pastor was Thorkild Grosbøll, from the town of Taarbæk. Pernille Stensgaard, "Præsten tror ikke på Gud," *Weekendavisen*, May 23–27, 2003, p. 12.

148. **"framework of the church":** Bente Clausen, "Stort præsteflertal dømmer Grosbøll ude," *Kristelig Dagblad*, July 10, 2004. I thank Tøger Seidenfaden, editor of *Politiken*, for pointing out and explaining this article.

148. **"ties with England":** Handlin, *Boston's Immigrants*, pp. 177, 222.

149. **"alien to the spirit of progress":** Ibid., p. 131.

149. **"bright and beautiful sisterhood":** Ibid., p. 21.

149. **"members of culture B"**: Marcello Pera and Joseph Cardinal Ratzinger, *Without Roots*, p. 14.

150. **they do believe in "something"**: See Marjoleine de Vos, "Ietsisten voruit," *NRC Handelsblad*, June 30, 2003, p. 7.

150. **their crisis in "values"**: Its title, *Schluß mit lustig*, is almost untranslatable. The title of the Elvis Costello song "Clown Time Is Over" will give a good approximation.

150. **Crucifixes have been reintroduced**: These figures and observations come from Joshua Livestro, "Holland's Post-Secular Future," *Weekly Standard*, January 1, 2007, pp. 25–28. For his statistics about revivalism and a return to "orthodoxy," he cites Adjiedj Bakas and Minne Buwalda, *De Toekomst van God* (Schiedam: Scriptum, 2006).

150. **Britons who call themselves "Christian"**: Eric Kaufmann, "Breeding for God" (see chap. 5 Notes). Kaufmann cites a study by David Voas and Steve Bruce of the 2001 British census.

151. **"moral and spiritual vacuum"**: Stephen Fidler, "Christian soldier known for his honesty and directness." *Financial Times*, October 14–15, 2005, p. 2.

151. **Pope Benedict XVI**: What follows is adapted from points made in Christopher Caldwell, "Faith in power of reason," *Financial Times*, September 22, 2006.

152. **it was a reference point**: Pera and Ratzinger, *Without Roots*, pp. 121–22.

152. **"ultimate foundation of liberty"**: Christa Case, "Germans Reconsider Religion," *Christian Science Monitor*, September 15, 2006.

153. **"valid spiritual foundation"**: Pera and Ratzinger, *Without Roots*, p. 65.

153. **to hide your deep admiration**: Juan G. Bedoya, "Alá te ama, hermano Benedicto," *El País*, September 20, 2006, p. 10.

154. **Half of Arab youths polled**: These figures are from a UN press kit that summarizes: United Nations Development Programme, *Arab Human Development Report 2002*. New York: Oxford University Press, 2003.

154. **exports less than Finland**: Bernard Lewis, *What Went Wrong?*, p. 47.

154. **describe Islam in three words**: Sondage [poll] IFOP – Le Monde/Le Point/Europe, October 15, 2001.

154. **"positive influence on our culture"**: Author interview with Andreas Kinneging, The Hague, February 17, 2005. See Caldwell, "Daughter of the Enlightenment" (see chap. 1 Notes), p. 30.

155. **"living-out of one's faith"**: "Schäuble wünscht sich 'deutsche Muslime,'" *Frankfurter Allgemeine Zeitung*, September 27, 2006.

155. roughly 50,000 Italian converts: Author interview with Francesca Paci, Turin, March 22, 2006.

155. stop cooperating with the police: Caldwell, "Counterterrorism in the U.K." (see chap. 4 Notes), p. 75.

156. series of terrorist shootouts: Anne-Charlotte De Langhe, "Lionel Dumont, islamiste français en jugement," *Le Figaro*, December 5, 2005, p. 10.

156. story of Muriel Degauque: Craig S. Smith, "Raised as Catholic in Belgium, She Died as a Muslim Bomber," *New York Times*, December 6, 2005, p. 10.

156. formidably brainy young man: Lindsay's gifts are hinted at in the Home Office report *Report of the Official Account of the Bombings in London on 7th July 2005* (delivered May 11, 2006), p. 21: "At his local mosque and in Islamic groups around Huddersfield and Dewsbury, he was admired for the speed with which he achieved fluency in Arabic and memorised long passages of the Quran, showing unusual maturity and seriousness."

156. "Sincerity, in all senses": Thomas Carlyle, *On Heroes, Hero-Worship and the Heroic in History*, p. 58.

157. "la religion naturelle": Alain Besançon, *Trois tentations dans l'église*, p. 167.

157. Carlyle gave a lecture: Richard Garnett, *Life of Thomas Carlyle* (London, 1887), p. 171. Cited in: Carlyle, *On Heroes*, p. 278.

157. the first of all truths: Carlyle, *On Heroes*, p. 65.

157. "poorly trained, mostly foreign imams": Ian Johnson (with John Carreyrou), "French Muslims Face More Controls," *Wall Street Journal*, December 9, 2004, p. A15. The work of the *Wall Street Journal*, and particularly of Ian Johnson, on European Islam has been exemplary in its depth, originality, and range. If the writers make a mistake in emphasis here, it is one the author of this book has made many times: See Christopher Caldwell, "The Crescent and the Tricolor: Muslims in France," *The Atlantic Monthly*, November 1, 2000, p. 20, which refers to "poorly trained, fiery, self-appointed imams."

157. "poorly educated judges": Madeleine Bunting, "A Noble, Reckless Rebellion," *Guardian*, February 9, 2008.

159. an explicit concession: See Gaetano Quagliarello, *Il Foglio*, March 14, 2006.

159. "effusive 'anything goes' exterior": Leon De Winter, "Tolerating a Time Bomb," *New York Times*, Monday, July 16, 2005.

159. "Faith produces its effects": Rémi Brague, *Europe: La voie romaine*, p. 182.

160. *Moros y cristianos* festivals: The information that follows comes from Ezequiel Moltó, "'La mahoma' se cae de las fiestas de Moros y Cristianos," *El País*, October 7, 2006.

161. "is it *all* religion?": Roy, *La Laïcité*, p. 33.

162. veil was eliminated: Laurence and Vaïsse, *Integrating Islam*, p. 173.

162. "neutral" system of trade-offs: Christopher Caldwell, "In Europe, 'Secular' Doesn't Quite Translate," *New York Times*, December 21, 2003, p. 10; Christopher Caldwell, "Veiled Threat," *Weekly Standard*, January 19, 2004, pp. 22–25.

162. Tony Blair outlined: Discussed in Caldwell, "Counterterrorism in the U.K." (see chap. 4 Notes), p. 45.

163. "mediators in the daily life": Jean-Marc Ayrault, "Les cités, c'est la France!" *Le Figaro*, November 7, 2005.

163. pledged their loyalty only to the UOIF: Johnson, "Islam and Europe" (see chap. 5 Notes).

164. "unequal impact of formally neutral laws": Thomas Nagel (writing on Catharine MacKinnon), "Legal Violations," *Times Literary Supplement*, May 20, 2005, p. 8.

165. Salman Rushdie: This discussion follows some of the points made in Caldwell, "Bad sense of community" (see chap. 5 Notes) and "Counterterrorism in the U.K." (see chap. 4 Notes), p. 46.

166. insistence of the House of Lords: Racial and Religious Hatred Act 2006 (c1), Part III, 29J.

166. seeking the causes of terrorism: Geert Mak, *Nagekomen flessenpost* (Amsterdam/Antwerp: Uitgeverij Atlas, 2005), p. 26, cites Jessica Stern on explanations of terrorism.

167. "someone will slit my throat": Ben Hoyle, "Artists too frightened to tackle radical Islam," *The Times*, November 19, 2007.

168. a dozen cartoons of Muhammad: The account of the carton crisis that follows draws on Christopher Caldwell, "The reality of cartoon violence," *Financial Times*, February 3–4, 2006.

169. seventy-three-year-old Kurt Westergaard: Peter Popham, "Three arrested for plot to kill Mohamed cartoonist," *Independent*, January 13, 2008, p. 18.

169. Western Muslims blame "disrespect": "Europe's Muslims More Moderate," p. 21.

169. "a reality that already existed": Flemming Rose, "Wir waren vollkommen unschuldig," *Der Spiegel*, December 15, 2006.

170. "The issue at stake": Edgar M. Bronfman, "A free society must respect

all its religions" [letter to the editor], *The Times* (London), February 1, 2006, p. 16.

170. **"cartoons portraying Jesus"**: Jytte Klausen, "Rotten Judgment in the State of Denmark," *Salon*, February 8, 2006.

170. **"tough on the Catholic religion"**: Christopher Boltanski, *Libération*, March 23, 2006, p. 13.

171. **"No, there doesn't"**: Author interview with Flemming Rose, Copenhagen, December 13, 2005.

Chapter 8. Rules for Sex

170. **women outnumber men**: Esther van Kralingen, "Niet-westerse allochthonen in het voltijd hoger onderwijs," *Bevolkingstrends* (second quarter), Centraal Bureau voor de statistiek, 2003.

173. **children might be better off**: Nina Björk, "Det är barnen," *Dagens Nyheter*, October 30, 2005, p. C5. This paragraph picks up on points made in Caldwell, "What Will Become of Europe."

173. **"everyone works"**: Quoted in Eric Fassin, "Going Dutch," *Bidoun*, Spring 2007.

174. **In Great Britain ... if you ask Spanish non-Muslims**: Polling information in this paragraph is drawn from "Europe's Muslims More Moderate," p. 2, as is the author's judgment that, among European gender attitudes, it is those of the British that are closest to those of Muslim immigrants.

174. **"great number of Dutch Muslims"**: Nahed Selim, *De Trouw* (*Letter en Geest*), February 19, 2005.

174. **about 15 percent of men**: Michèle Tribalat, *Faire France*, pp. 93–94, 104.

175. **genital mutilation is widespread**: Anke van der Kwaak, Edien Bartels, Femke de Vries, and Stan Meuwese, "Strategieën ter voorkoming van besnijdenis bij meisjes" ["Strategies for preventing the circumcision of girls"]. Amsterdam: Vrije Universiteit Medisch Centrum, 2003, p. v.

175. **nationally supervised gynecological inspections**: Aldo Keel, "In der Gewalt der Tradition," *Neue Zürcher Zeitung*, December 11, 2006, p. 25.

176. **"certifications of virginity"**: See Johnson, "Islam and Europe."

176. **repair of broken hymens**: Caldwell, "Daughter of the Enlightenment," p. 30.

176. **"a membrane is constructed"**: James Chapman, "Women get 'virginity

fix' NHS operations in Muslim-driven trend," *Daily Mail,* November 15, 2007.

177. a category of "sluts": One young Turkish rap musician, engaged to be married, whom the author met in the Comenius Garden in the Neukölln neighborhood of Berlin in early 2007, used the word *Schlampen* ("sluts") to describe why he would not marry a woman raised in Germany.

177. Sohane Benziane, a young Berber woman: Charlotte Rotman, "Je pensais que si le feu allait partir je pourrais l'éteindre," *Libération,* April 4, 2006.

177. she had embarrassed the community: Pascal Ceaux, "Jamal Derrar a été condamné à vingt-cinq ans de réclusion criminelle pour avoir brûlé Sohane," *Le Monde,* April 9, 2006.

177. forty-five such murders: Caldwell, "Every Generation Is First-Generation," (see chap. 2 Notes), p. 44. Federal Criminal Investigation Agency is a translation of *Bundeskriminalamt.*

178. from a nice Kurdish girl into a slut: From the website of Fadimes Minnesfond (Fadime's Memorial Foundation): www.fadimesminne.nu.

178. "An authentic culture": Roger Cohen, "How to reconcile Islam, sexuality and liberty?" *International Herald Tribune,* October 22, 2005, p. 2.

179. Hassan Moussa: Annika Hamrud, "Könsstympning enar religiösa ledare," *Dagens Nyheter,* December 5, 2005, p. 1.

179. Turkish cousin marriage: Caldwell, "Every Generation Is First-Generation."

179. going to lessons in mosques: Private communication, Janny Groen, November 7, 2006. The book is Janny Groen and Annieke Kranenberg, *Strijdsters van Allah.*

180. "One of the biggest factors": Malik, "My brother the bomber" (see chap. 7 Notes).

180. "even on the woman question": Roy, *La Laïcité,* p. 66.

180. sharia-conforming stock funds: Rosenkranz, "Die deutschen Gesichter des Islam," p. 44.

181. outperformed the market: Deborah Brewster, "Amana stays ahead of faith-based funds," *Financial Times,* December 27–28, 2008.

181. "internal law of religious communities": Rowan Williamson, interview with Christopher Landau of the BBC Radio 4, *World at One,* February 7, 2008.

181. "delegation of certain legal functions": Rowan Williamson, Archbishop of Canterbury, "Civil and Religious Law in England: A Religious Perspective," Foundation lecture, Royal Courts of Justice, February 7, 2008.

181. **some of the headlines:** On February 8, 9, and 12 (respectively), 2008.

181. **rabbinical courts:** Information on the history of the London Beth Din is available on the website of the United Synagogue (theus.org.uk).

181. **decisions they ratify:** The journalist Madeleine Bunting pointed this out in an article that was generally sympathetic to the archbishop ("A Noble, Reckless Rebellion," *Guardian*, February 9, 2008).

182. **executing Muslims who renounce Islam:** Mirza, Senthikumaran, and Ja'far, *Living Apart Together*, p. 5.

182. **a majority of Muslims:** Undated poll for the *Irish Independent* and the RTE broadcast network, cited in Efraim Karsh and Rory Miller, "Europe's Persecuted Muslims?" *Commentary*, April 2007, pp. 49–53.

182. **"If two thirds of all Dutch people":** "Donner waarschuwt CDA tegen islamofobie," *Vrij Nederland*, September 12, 2006.

183. **rebuked by the JOVD:** Paul Lucardie, Ida Noomen, and Gerrit Voerman, "Kroniek 1992: Overzicht van de partijpolitieke gebeurtenissen van het jaar 1992," in Gerrit Voerman, ed., *Jaarboek 1992* (Groningen: Documentatiecentrum Nederlandse Politieke Partijen, 1993), p. 51.

183. **"a valid polygamous marriage":** Jonathan Wynne-Jones, "Multiple wives will mean multiple benefits," *Sunday Telegraph*, February 3, 2008, p. 1.

183. **tens of thousands of polygamous families:** Estimates range between 10,000–20,000 families (Axel Veiel, "Atemberaubende Krawalltheorien," *Neue Zürcher Zeitung*, November 20, 2005) and 15,000–30,000 (*Le Figaro*, December 16, 2005). The American anthropologist Stanley Kurtz ("Polygamy Versus Democracy," *Weekly Standard*, June 5, 2006, p. 23) estimates that 200,000 to 400,000 people in France live in polygamous families.

183. **sought to blame polygamy:** Veiel, "Atemberaubende Krawalltheorien." An interesting alternative explanation was given by the website www.stratfor.com on November 18, 2005. It was that polygamous marriages might be grounds for de-nationalizing certain new French citizens: "Most of the rioters are believed to be actual French citizens, a legal status that protects them from deportation—unless, of course, they are found to have violated French law in becoming citizens in the first place. If laws banning polygamy are enforced, it is possible that authorities might be able to deport not only a single person involved in the riots, but any family member who was allowed into the country on account of their ties with the family's root male. That would include any dependents or former dependents born of polygamous marriages or who entered France on the basis of any familial relation."

183. it *is* the immigration problem: The discussion that follows draws on Caldwell, "Every Generation Is First-Generation."

184. about 25,000 people a year: Unpublished report by Zehra Yilmaz, "Soziale und sprachliche Situation von türkischen Heiratsmigrantinnen." She cites as her source (in footnote) BMI [Bundesministerium des Innern = Interior Ministry] Zuwanderungsbericht 2004, p. 28. The range of immigrants cited is between 21,000 and 27,000 per year.

184. more than 60,000 in 2004: Laetitia van Eeckhout, "Immigration familiale: les faits," *Le Monde*, January 5, 2006, cited in Laurence and Vaïsse, *Integrating Islam*, p. 17.

184. family-related immigration now accounts: David A. Coleman, "Partner choice and the growth of ethnic minority populations," *Bevolking en Gezin*, vol. 33 (2004), pp. 2, 7–34. (He cites a 2003 OECD study.)

184. "an intake of new residents": Sir Herman (now Lord) Ouseley, "The Bradford District Race Review," 2001, p. 11.

184. Fully 60 percent: Migration Watch UK, "The impact of chain migration on English cities" (Briefing Paper 9.13). "Roughly 50 percent" means rates of growth for those three cities range between 45.8 and 52.8 percent.

184. three-quarters of Bengali children: Migration Watch UK, "Transnational marriage and the formation of ghettoes" (Briefing paper 10.12), September 22, 2005. They cite Lord Ouseley, "Race Relations in Bradford," for these statistics. Possibly because of outcry over such figures, the UK began keeping statistics on ethnicity with less precision in the 1990s.

184. "has increased *pro rata*": Coleman and Scherbov, "Immigration and Ethnic Change" (see chap. 1 Notes).

185. would not consider marrying a German: Both German figures are from Caldwell, "Every Generation Is First-Generation."

185. only 1 percent of British Bangladeshis: Tariq Modood, Richard Berthoud, et al., *Ethnic Minorities in Britain, Diversity and Disadvantage* (London: Policy Studies Institute, 1997), cited in Philip Lewis, *Islamic Britain*, p. 220n.

185. of the eighty-six women: Caldwell, "Every Generation Is First-Generation."

185. faces permanently marred: Sally Cope, *Yorkshire Post*, December 7, 2004.

186. "Forced marriages are illegal": Author interview with Wolfgang Schäuble, Berlin, February 5, 2007. Cited in Caldwell, "Every Generation Is First-Generation."

188. **The Danish experiment:** Aldo Keel, "In Der Gewalt der Tradition," *Neue Zürcher Zeitung,* December 11, 2006, p. 25. See also Migration Watch UK, "Transnational marriage and the formation of Ghettoes" (Briefing paper 10.12), September 22, 2005; it cites figures from the Year-book on Foreigners in Denmark, 2004, a later edition of which Keel was probably drawing on.

188. **"It has had bizarre consequences":** Author interview with Tøger Seidenfaden, Copenhagen, December 13, 2005.

188. **"The legislation is the same":** Author interview with Rikke Hvilshøj, Copenhagen, December 10, 2005.

189. **"It's necessary":** Ibid.

189. **use of the Muslim headscarf:** The section that follows draws in places on Caldwell, "Veiled Threat" and Caldwell, "'Secular' Doesn't Quite Translate" (see chap. 7 Notes).

190. **Even Bel Mooney:** Bel Mooney, "How can I turn a deep friendship with a fellow Muslim into marriage?" *The Times,* October 25, 2006, Times2, p. 6.

191. **a two-hundred-page book:** Emmanuel Brenner, *Les territoires perdus de la république.*

191. **laws against the wearing of masks:** Author interview with Ugo Cantone, Interior Ministry, Rome, March 16, 2006.

191. **forbids motorcycle messengers:** Editorial in La *Vanguardia* (Barcelona), October 21, 2006, p. 28.

191. **In 2006, Mustaf Jama:** Andrew Norfolk, "Police killer suspect fled Britain in a veil," *The Times,* December 20, 2006.

192. **Only 28 percent:** Mirza, Senthikumaran, and Ja'far, *Living Apart Together.*

192. **that breaks down to 19 percent:** Ibid.

192. **"It is a mark of separation":** Matthew Tempest, "Blair backs school in veil row," *Guardian,* October 17, 2006.

192. **98 percent of Britons:** Ibid.

192. **"visible statement of separation":** Dan Bilefsky and Ian Fisher, "Doubts on Muslim integration rise in Europe," *International Herald Tribune,* October 12, 2006, p. 2.

193. **"I'd be so alarmed":** Walden, *Time to Emigrate?* p. 120.

193. **"trial of one particular community":** "British official warns of riots over veils," *International Herald Tribune,* October 23, 2006, p. 3.

194. **"what is aimed at is Islam":** Farhad Khosrokhavar, "Une laïcité frileuse," *Le Monde,* November 20, 2003.

194. **they worked for the same reason:** A survey done for the tabloid *Le*

Parisien found that 69 percent favored a ban on religious signs. Dominique de Montvalon, "Un sondage choc," *Le Parisien*, December 17, 2003.

195. **only 12 students arrived veiled:** Laurence and Vaïsse, *Integrating Islam*, p. 171.

195. **the hundredth anniversary:** Michael Jeismann, "Neuntausend," *Frankfurter Allgemeine Zeitung*, October 26, 2005, p. 37.

195. **signs of family breakdown:** David Coleman in address to Hudson Institute, Washington, D.C., September 25, 2007.

196. **a patient's refusing on principle:** "Les principaux extraits du discours du Jacques Chirac," *Libération*, December 17, 2003.

196. **centered on a video:** Available online at http://www.naarnederland.nl/documentenservice/pagina.asp?pagkey=52133.]tb[

196. **has defended the Dutch film:** *La Repubblica*, March 18, 2006, p. 11 (*La Repubblica* cites the German tabloid *Bild*).

196. **"fathers make them cover themselves":** Tahar Ben Jelloun, "Marruecos y las razones del velo," *La Vanguardia*, October 21, 2006, p. 31.

196. **"I wanted to be like him":** Author interview with Zacarias Sayar, al-Quds school, Copenhagen, December 11, 2005.

197. **"repudiates core European principles":** Ian Buruma, "Tariq Ramadan Has an Identity Issue," *New York Times Magazine*, February 4, 2007, p. 36.

197. **a list of Florentine landmarks:** Fallaci, *La Rage et l'orgueil*, pp. 41–42.

197. **various erotic parades:** Henryk M. Broder, *Hurra, wir kaputilieren!*, pp. 30–35.

198. **"Divorce and easy re-marriage":** David Coleman, "Why We Don't Have to Believe Without Doubting in the 'Second Demographic Transition'—Some Agnostic Comments," in Vienna Yearbook of Population Research, 2004, pp. 11–24. (Contribution to a debate on the Second Demographic Transition, European Population Conference, Warsaw, August 2003.)

198. **divorces increased by 46 percent:** Marlise Simons, "Muslim Women in Europe Claim Rights and Keep Faith," *New York Times*, December 30, 2005, p. 3.

198. **hard-line mosque in Munich:** Author interview with Oguz Ücüncü, Cologne, October 25, 2005.

198. **out of fear that he would be ostracized:** Nicholas Kulish, "Gay Muslims Pack a Dance Floor of Their Own," *New York Times*, January 1, 2008, p. A4.

199. **Muslims are twice as likely:** Caldwell, "Man Who Would Be *le Président*" (see chap. 5 Notes). Article cites a Cevipof study from December 2005

that shows 39 percent of Muslim French disapproving, versus 21 percent of non-Muslim French.

Chapter 9. Tolerance and Impunity

203. **something ominous about the resolution:** Caldwell, "Veiled Threat." The Fadlallah letter was quoted on the now-defunct French website www.proche-orient.info.

204. **after the Irish first arrived:** Handlin, *Boston's Immigrants*, p. 55.

204. **most advanced democratic society:** This is the author's view, not Handlin's.

204. **Nativist fears failed to develop:** Handlin, *Boston's Immigrants*, p. 190.

205. **began to voice intolerant opinions:** Ibid., pp. 117, 192.

205. **immigrants first began protesting:** Christopher Caldwell, "Migration Debate out of control," *Financial Times*, March 3–April 1, 2006. For the role of politics in souring government on immigration in Germany and France, see Martin, Abella, and Kuptsch, *Managing Labor*, p. 90.

205. **many Muslims in Parliament:** Caldwell, "Counterterrorism in the U.K." (see chap. 4 Notes), p. 47.

206. **Greens were in the forefront:** Author interview with Özcan Mutlu, Berlin, October 19, 2005.

206. **after riots broke out:** Christophe Jakubyszyn, "L'inscription sur les listes électorales séduit les 'quartiers,'" *Le Monde*, December 29, 2005. Cited in Laurence and Vaïsse, *Integrating Islam*, p. 197.

207. **highest level of support:** Mirza, Senthikumaran, and Ja'far, *Living Apart Together*, pp. 5, 47.

208. **feature on Islamic converts:** Joshua Livestro, "Holland's Post-Secular Future," *Weekly Standard*, January 1, 2007, p. 28.

208. **"secret Christians":** Magdi Allam, *Corriere della Sera*, March 22, 2006. Allam was alluding to a book by Giorgio Paolucci and Camille Eid: *I cristiani venuti dall'Islam. Storie di musulmani convertiti* (Piemme, 2005).

208. **started receiving death threats:** Olga van Ditzhuijzen and Derk Stokmans, "Ik kan niet anders dan bezwijken onder de druk," *NRC Handelsblad*, October 3, 2005.

209. **"enemy of Islam":** Irene Hernández Velasco, "Italia pone escolta a una diputada tras las amenazas de un imam," *El Mundo*, October 25, 2006, p. 25.

209. **"The very first sura":** Interview with a European professor of Arabic, 2005.

210. **Celebrations were reported:** John Lloyd, "Poor whites," *Prospect*, May 2002.

210. **cheering on the streets:** Ian Buruma, *Murder in Amsterdam*, pp. 115, 134.

210. **"in complete sympathy":** Christopher Caldwell, "Holland Daze," *Weekly Standard*, December 27, 2004.

210. **A quarter of French Muslims:** "L'islam en France et les réactions aux attentats du 11 septembre 2001," *Le Monde*, October 5, 2001. The poll was carried out by IFOP. Cited in Laurence and Vaïsse, *Integrating Islam: Political and Religious Challenges in Contemporary France*. Washington: Brookings, 2006, p. 210.

210. **"They demand the elimination of Israel":** Christopher Caldwell, "Counterterrorism in the U.K.: After Londonistan," (see chap. 4 Notes), p. 74.

210. **"Go to Whitechapel":** Ibid.

210. **"The majority of Muslims":** Aatish Taseer, "A British jihadist," *Prospect*, August 2005.

211. **A sixth of British Muslims:** Mirza, Senthikumaran, and Ja'far, *Living Apart Together* p. 14.

211. **consider westerners "arrogant":** "Europe's Muslims More Moderate" (see chap. 5 Notes), p. 13.

211. **A Draft Report on Young Musims and Extremism:** Caldwell, "Counterterrorism in the U.K."

212. **"proud to be German":** Author conversation with Omid Nouripour, Green Party, Leipzig, September 15, 2005.

212. **"too much like an Italian":** Author interview with Francesca Paci, Turin, March 22, 2006.

213. **anything that was crummy:** Bernard Guetta, "Pourquoi est-ce aux Juifs de France de payer pour les échecs de l'intégration des immigrés?" *Le Temps*, August 7, 2004. See also Obin, "Signes et manifestations" (see chap. 6 Notes).

213. **Praise for the Nazis:** Obin, "Signes et manifestations."

213. **youths threw eggs:** Robert S. Wistrich, "Cruel Britannia: Anti-Semitism Among the Ruling Elites," *Azure*, Summer 2005, pp. 113, 116. See Richard Alleyne, "Jewish MP Pelted with Eggs at War Memorial," *Daily Telegraph*, April 11, 2005.

213. **tally of anti-Semitic attacks:** Karsh and Miller, "Europe's Persecuted Muslims?" (see chap. 8 Notes), p. 51.

214. **synagogue was shot up:** Aldo Keel, "In der Gewalt der Tradition," *Neue Zürcher Zeitung*, December 11, 2006, p. 25.

214. Twenty Jewish shops: Karsh and Miller, "Europe's Persecuted Muslims?," p. 52.

214. European Union study: The 2003 report was leaked to the *Jerusalem Post* by the French Council of Jewish Institutions (Conseil Représentatif des Institutions juives de France) and was accessible, as of this writing, at http://haganah.us/hmedia/euasr-00.html.

214. "Islamization of European Antisemitism": Broder, *Hurra, wir kaputilieren!*, p. 116.

215. "Two million Muslims": David Cesarani, "Community and disunity," *Jewish Chronicle*, October 24, 2003. Cited in Jenny Bourne, "Anti-Semitism or anti-criticism?" *Race and Class*, July 1, 2004.

216. threatened a consumer boycott: Caldwell, "Reality of cartoon violence." (see chap. 7 Notes)

216. Sweden refused to take part: Broder, *Hurra, wir kaputilieren!*, p. 60.

216. Protests against Israel: See the discussion in Paul Berman, *Terror and Liberalism*, p. 143. Cited in Christopher Caldwell, "Why Israel Is Gaining Friends," *Financial Times*, August 5, 2005.

217. "It is no exaggeration": Peter Oborne, *Spectator*, September 25, 2005, p. 14.

218. hate crimes had Jewish victims: Paul Berman, "Who's Afraid of Tariq Ramadan?" *New Republic*, June 4, 2007.

218. a "hypermnesia": French: *hypermnésie*. Pierre-André Taguieff, "La criminalisation des 'déclinologues,'" *Le Figaro*, July 3, 2006, p. 12. Taguieff also noticed an *am*nesia about the misdeeds of Communism, but that is outside the scope of this discussion.

218. "demonology of Nazi Germany": Sardar and Livingstone examples are from Karsh and Miller, "Europe's Persecuted Muslims?," p. 50.

219. standup comedians who sneered: In the "Mes Excuses" shows he did in late 2004.

219. Tribu Ka was finally banned: Mustapha Kessous, "Le conseil des ministres a décidé la dissolution du groupe extrémiste la Tribu Ka," *Le Monde*, July 28, 2006.

220. kept Europe's intolerant impulses: Caldwell, "What Will Become of Europe?", Bradley Lectures in Political Philosophy, Boston College, February 10, 2006.

220. "hideously false ideology": Dror Mishani and Aurelia Smotriez, "What sort of Frenchmen?" (see chap. 4 Notes).

Chapter 10. Resistance and Jihad

221. Armed Islamic Group: In French: Groupe Islamique Armé (GIA).

221. "son of Allah": Christopher Caldwell, "Liberté, Égalité, Judéophobie," *Weekly Standard*, May 6, 2002, p. 23.

222. "keep migration separate from terrorism": Off-the-record discussion.

222. tended to have in common: Lawrence Wright, *The Looming Tower*, p. 344.

224. home-grown terrorists: See: Intelligence and Security Committee (Chairman: The Rt. Hon. Paul Murphy, MP), "Report into the London Terrorist Attacks on 7 July 2005," London: HMSO, May 2006, p. 12.

224. state of Baden-Württemberg: Author telephone interview with Benno Koepfer, Verfassungsschutz, Landesamt Baden Württemberg (Research Group on Islamist Terrorism and Extremism), September 7, 2007.

225. "The key to engaging": David Leppard and Nick Fielding, "The Hate," *Sunday Times* (London), July 10, 2005.

225. "As a result of the alienation": Laurence and Vaïsse, *Integrating Islam*, p. 40.

225. violent acts of young men: Heinsohn, *Söhne und Weltmacht*. The discussion here is drawn from a lengthier treatment of Heinsohn's ideas at Christopher Caldwell, "Youth and war, a deadly duo," *Financial Times*, January 6, 2007.

226. "throwing bombs in Prague": Gunnar Heinsohn, "Wo es zu viele junge Männer gibt, wird getötet," *Neue Zürcher Zeitung*, November 19, 2006.

226. "The young men who trained": Ahmed Rashid, "Jihadi Suicide Bombers: The New Wave," *New York Review of Books*, June 12, 2008, p. 17.

227. Osama Bin Laden's life: See, for instance, Steve Coll, *The Bin Ladens* (New York: Penguin, 2008), pp. 138, 144–146.

227. Muslims around the world: In November 2007, MI5 knew of at least 2,000 people involved in terrorism in Britain, according to Jonathan Evans, the agency's director-general. See Stephen Fidler, "Down but dangerous," *Financial Times*, June 10, 2008.

227. called Islam a fine religion: Theo Hobson, "War and peace and Islam," *Spectator* 23, July 2005.

227. issues of guilt and salvation: Agence France-Presse, January 18, 2006. The version quoted appears to be a retranslation into English of remarks originally printed in German in *Der Stern*, "Sexuelle Angst der Männer vor

Frauen ist eine Ursache für islamistischen Terror" (interview with Salman Rushdie), January 17, 2006. Cited in Broder, *Hurra, wir kapitulieren!*, p. 152.

228. **"the West cannot act freely":** Mordechay Lewy, "Nimm meine Schuld auf dich," *Die Zeit*, no. 4 (January 2003) .

228. **they generally cast back:** See Abdelwahab Meddeb, *La Maladie de l'Islam*, pp. 24–30, or Malek Chebel, *L'Islam et la raison*, pp. 36–58.

228. **There is no security:** Wilfred Thesiger, *Arabian Sands*, p. 94.

229. **French authorities bent over backwards:** "Nicolas Sarkozy justifie, au nom de la sécurité, les mesures contre des bagagistes musulmans de Roissy," *Le Monde*, October 21, 2006. What he said was: "Il n'y avait là aucun délit de sale gueule." *Délit de sale gueule* might be translated as "the crime of I-don't-like-your-face."

230. **"were the act of a cult":** Nicolas Sarkozy, *La République, les religions, l'espérance*, p. 93.

230. **"the moderate and true voice":** Christopher Caldwell, "Sacred Cow of Religious Rights," *Financial Times*, July 15, 2005.

230. **"wholly incorrect interpretation":** Daniel Johnson, "Allah's England?" *Commentary*, November 2006, p. 45.

230. **"borrowed from the extreme left":** Roy, *La Laïcité*, p. 153.

230. **way of explaining Communism's rise:** Jules Monnerot, *Sociologie du Communisme*, pp. 9–25, esp. 20–25.

231. **"It draws on resentments":** Ibid., p. 21.

231. **"since Europe disengaged":** Ibid.

231. **the believer does not think of himself:** Ibid.

231. **"aggravates the real 'internal contradictions' ":** Jules Monnerot, *Sociologie du Communisme*, p. 23.

232. **"fall into one of two groups":** Leppard and Fielding, "The Hate."

233. **"which Islam—sharia Islam or Euro-Islam":** Bassam Tibi, "Grenzen der Toleranz," *Die Welt am Sonntag*, September 5, 2004.

233. **Pushing Muslim identity:** This discussion draws on Christopher Caldwell, "Counterterrorism in the U.K." (see chap. 4 Notes), p. 52.

234. **"I decided that I would leave":** Conversation with Hassan Moussa, Stockholm, December 7, 2005. In Caldwell, "Islam on the Outskirts," p. 58.

234. **But only 4 percent:** Pew Research Center, "Islamic Extremism," p. 1 (see chap. 6 Notes).

234. **"Religious tolerance is clearly commanded":** This was in a pamphlet published by Islamic Forum Europe called *Muslims in Europe*.

235. **"There needs to be a separation":** Craig S. Smith, "At Mosque That

Recruited Radicals, New Imam Calls for Help in Catching Bombers," *New York Times*, July 9, 2005, p. A6.

236. **Muslims say that white Americans:** Kevin Cullen, "Britain's Muslims take stock of a post-bombing backlash," *Boston Globe*, August 11, 2005, p. A10.

236. **"the Magnificent 19":** Caldwell, "Counterterrorism in the U.K.," p. 46.

236. **to craft legislation mandating prison:** Alan Cowell, "Britain planning tighter laws to fight terrorism," *International Herald Tribune*, July 18, 2005.

237. **something that people know:** Caldwell, "Counterterrorism in the U.K.," p. 46.

237. **real concerns about the consequences:** "Three are charged over July 7 bombings," *The Times* (on-line edition), April 5, 2007.

237. **"Either you are with us":** George W. Bush, speech to joint session of Congress, September 20, 2008.

238. **"It is a progressive vision":** Author interview with Ahmad Abu Laban, Norrebrø, Copenhagen, December 11, 2005.

238. **"ways to defend ourselves":** "Fanatismi incendiari contro ordinarie viltà," *Il Foglio*, February 7, 2006.

238. **"must pretend that we accept":** Ibid.

238. **"bring the evidence":** Andrew Hussey, "Not a fanatic after all?" *New Statesman*, September 12, 2005.

239. **Ramadan's role and views:** In 2007, a public debate—one could even say a battle—arose between the writers Ian Buruma and Paul Berman around the question of Ramadan's real political orientation in 2007. See Buruma, "Identity Issue" and Berman, "Who's Afraid of Tariq Ramadan?"

239. **worked as a CIA informer:** Johnson, "Islam and Europe" (see chap. 5 Notes).

239. **he was implicated in the plot:** Berman, "Who's Afraid of Tariq Ramadan?"

239. **there were other possibilities:** Gresh and Ramadan, *L'Islam en questions*, p. 139.

239. **looking for the "objective causes":** Ibid., p. 144.

239. **"consider the situation objectively":** Ibid., p. 151.

240. **Ramadan moved to Britain:** Christopher Caldwell, "At the Borders of Free Speech," *Financial Times*, September 30–October 1, 2007. Ramadan himself wrote an account of his exclusion from the U.S. See Tariq Ramadan, "Why I'm Banned in the USA," *Washington Post*, October 1, 2006, p. B1.

240. **appropriate to the first three centuries:** Ramadan, *Dar ash-shahada*, pp. 21–23.

240. "This could lead one to conclude": Ibid., pp. 29, 41.

240. "domain of witness": A *shahada* is a profession of faith. The expression and the concept are discussed by Tariq Ramadan throughout *Dar ash-shahada* and in *La Foi, la Voie et la résistance* (p. 14) and *Les Musulmans de l'Occident et l'avenir de l'Islam* (pp. 131–38).

241. he reviles the "soulless capitalism": Tariq Ramadan, "Les altermondialistes face aux défis du pluralisme," in *Quelles résistances pour une justice globale?*, pp. 75–76.

241. "abode of war": Buruma, "Identity Issue," p. 36.

241. "homogenizing international order": Gresh and Ramadan, *L'Islam en questions*, p. 156.

241. "to join and support any movement": Ibid., p. 178. His politics are basically anti-globalist.

241. "balanced on a tightrope'": Buruma, "Identity Issue," p. 36.

241. "resistance was a key concept": Ibid., p. 36.

242. "The only ones left": Ibid., p. 155.

242. who lives only by his superficial desires: Ramadan, *La Foi, la Voie*, pp. 68–69.

243. For the vast majority of Muslims: Gresh and Ramadan, *L'Islam en questions*, p. 162.

243. "colonization of the mind": Tariq Ramadan, *Aux sources du renouveau musulman*, pp. 360–61.

243. demanding the departure of the English: Ibid., p. 358.

244. victory of this better self: Ibid., p. 369.

244. Its materialist civilization: Ibid., p. 368.

244. "It is rather a law of nature": Ibid., p. 372. The quotation is from the Koran, S 5:54. Translation: Marmaduke Pickthall.

244. "never demonized the West": Ramadan, *Sources du renouveau*, p. 364.

244. Islam has *sagesse*: Ibid., pp. 367, 373.

244. "when Muslims find in their tradition": Gresh and Ramadan, *L'Islam en questions*, p. 327.

244. "radical resistance and clashes": Ibid., p. 156.

244. "future of Muslim countries": Ibid., p. 181.

245. "the need to resist the West": Buruma, "Identity Issue," p. 36. Ramadan is explicit about the anti-colonialist ways of appropriating colonists' knowledge in *Sources du renouveau*, p. 454.

245. "Day-to-day life in Europe": Ramadan, *La Foi, la Voie*, pp. 68–70.

Chapter 11. Liberalism and Diversity

250. **French and Dutch "no" voters:** Christopher Caldwell, "Why Did the French and Dutch Vote No?," *Weekly Standard*, June 13, 2005, p. 27.

250. **"permanent contrast to Europe":** Christopher Caldwell, "A partnership, if only in spirit," *Financial Times*, December 2–3, 2006.

250. **to have an influential role:** Pew Research Center, "Islamic Extremism," p. 27 (43 percent "very important" + 32 percent "somewhat important").

251. **only a third of Europeans supported Turkish accession:** Christopher Caldwell, "The East in the West," *New York Times Magazine*, September 25, 2005, p. 48: A Eurobarometer poll taken in 2005 showed 35 percent in favor.

251. **"If Turkey can't be a part":** Author interview with Oguz Ücüncü, Cologne, October 25, 2005.

251. **"choose to be a European":** Caldwell, "Swedish Dilemma" (see chap. 5 Notes).

252. **"When the immigrant says I am British":** Abul Taher, "Minorities feel more British than whites," *The Times*, December 18, 2006.

253. **"less powerful than we think":** Pim Fortuyn, *De verweesde samenleving*, p. 198.

253. **"fundamentalism will grow stronger":** Ibid., pp. 184–85.

253. **"a life-threatening culture":** Ibid., p. 191.

253. **surveillance of Communists:** "Grens dicht voor islamiet" (interview with Pim Fortuyn), *De Volkskrant*, 9 February 2002, p. 1; reproduced in Hans Wansink, *De Erfenis van Fortuyn*, p. 289.

254. **"A quota policy":** Fortuyn, *De verweesde samenleving*, p. 193.

254. **called for the Netherlands to withdraw:** "Grens dicht voor islamiet" (interview with Pim Fortuyn), Wansink, p. 288.

254. **"If you're born and raised here":** Ibid., pp. 285, 290.

254. **"they're never able to define it":** Fortuyn, *De verweesde samenleving*, p. 186.

254. **Fortuyn vacillated between praise for it:** Praise in Fortuyn, *De verweesde samenleving*, p. 181; contempt in "Grens dicht voor islamiet" (interview with Pim Fortuyn).

255. **"Judeo-Christian culture":** Fortuyn, *De verweesde samenleving*, p. 183.

255. **"must not determine the public sphere":** Ibid., p. 191.

256. **The party leader, Gianfranco Fini:** Christopher Caldwell, "Sensible extension of rights," *Financial Times*, November 22–23, 2003.

257. one Paris–St Germain fan: Accounts of hooliganism are from Christopher Caldwell, "No half measures for hooliganism," *Financial Times*, December 8, 2006.

258. rights of pygmies in Cameroon: Christopher Forcari, "Dieudonné vante les mérites de Jany Le Pen," *Libération*, March 16, 2007.

258. Gaddafi hectored Europe: Michael Leidig, "Gaddafi backs 'friend' Haider," *Daily Telegraph*, June 19, 2001.

258. Barking, a Labour stronghold: Katrin Bennhold, "In egalitarian Europe, a not-so-hidden world of squalor," *International Herald Tribune*, October 18, 2005, p. 1.

258. NPD took a dozen seats: I am grateful to Toralf Staud, reporter for *Die Zeit* and author of a study of the NPD, *Moderne Nazis*, for explaining the NPD to me in a series of e-mails and conversations in the autumn of 2005.

258. most eloquent of the NPD's members: Author interview with Karl Richter, Dresden, September 16, 2005.

258. Sixteen percent of kids: Author interview with Antje Hermenau, head of Green delegation in the Saxon Parliament, Leipzig, September 15, 2005.

258. Saxony, the most geriatric: Ibid.

259. "copy of the Third Reich": Author interview with Karl Richter, Dresden, September 16, 2005.

259. "Such a rule is national suicide": Author interview with Jesper Langballe, Copenhagen, December 12, 2005.

259. "led by a housewife": This is the formula used by the diversity consultant Fahmy Almajid (author interview, Copenhagen, December 2005).

260. "There is nothing fascist": Author interview with Tøger Seidenfaden, Copenhagen, December 13, 2005.

260. similar establishment bargain: As Fortuyn discusses in *De puinhopen van acht jaar Paars*.

261. "Some of them wore hoods": Zoé Cadiot, "Villiers-le-Bel reste sous haute tension," *L'Indépendant,* November 28, 2007.

261. One French judge expressed sympathy: Jean de Maillard, "Le pire reste à venir," rue89.com (downloaded November 28, 2007).

261. "neither the illness nor the cure": Telephone interview with Xavier Le Moine, mayor of Montfermeil, March 26, 2007.

262. "much stronger than we realize": Nicolas Sarkozy, *La République, les religions, l'espérance*, p. 88.

262. "They're young, they're new": Sarkozy, *La République, les religions*, p. 77.

262. "**The response to riots**": "Nicolas Sarkozy veut stopper la 'voyou-cratie,'" LExpress.fr, November 19, 2007.

262. "**It's not up to delinquents**": Didier Pourquery, "En touche," *Libéra-tion*, November 29, 2007, Événement, p. 2.

262. "**When they see you're not afraid**": Philippe Ridet, "La banlieue et ses électeurs, vus par Nicolas Sarkozy," *Le Monde*, October 7, 2005.

263. **one of his proudest boasts**: Associated Press, "Sarkozy calls for cre-ation of international treaty on migration," *International Herald Tribune*, December 11, 2006.

263. "**as many votes as possible**": Author interview with Nicolas Sarkozy, Ministry of the Interior, Paris, January 20, 2006. Cited in Caldwell, "Man Who Would Be *le Président*" (see chap. 5 Notes), p. 26.

263. **reminiscent of Richard Nixon**: Sarkozy's similarities to Nixon are dealt with in more detail in Caldwell, "Harsh Policing," *Financial Times*, March 31–April 1, 2007.

263. "*la France silencieuse*": Pascale Robert-Diard, "Les incidents de la gare du Nord relancent le duel Sarkozy-Royal," *Le Monde*, March 30, 2007.

264. "**as a demanding friend**": Sarkozy, *La République, les religions*, p. 75.

264. "**To accept and to value**": Ibid., p. 109.

264. "**When I enter a mosque**": Ibid., p. 78.

265. "**the remarkable experiment**": Ibid., p. 107.

265. **submit to an oral interview**: The program is described in more detail in Christopher Caldwell, "France takes a chance on a new ideal of equality," *Financial Times*, November 15–16, 2003, p. 15.

250. **Clamoring for diversity**: See Jeremy Harding, "Color Bind," *Columbia Journalism Review*, July/August 2006.

266. **diversity contributes to performance**: Jonathan Moules, "Benefits of ethnic diversity doubted," *Financial Times*, February 20, 2007, p. 4.

266. "**social capital**": Robert D. Putnam, "*E Pluribus Unum*" (see chap. 3 Notes).

266. **demanded diversity at every level**: Caroline Fourest, "La diversité contre l'égalité," *Le Monde*, January 18, 2008.

266. "**twenty years is too long**": Author interview with Nicolas Sarkozy, Ministry of the Interior, Paris, January 20, 2006. Cited in Caldwell, "Man Who Would Be *le Président*."

267. "**race quality impact assessments**": The Home Office Departmental Report 2006, p. 56.

268. "**a powerful revelation**": Birnbaum's observations and the quotations of Étienne Balibar and Robert Castel are from Jean Birnbaum, "Le spectre des origines," *Le Monde*, October 5, 2007.

Chapter 12. Survival and Culture

269. "network power": David Singh Grewal, *Network Power*.

270. they would move to the United States: David Rieff, "Migrant Worry," *New York Times Magazine*, November 6, 2005, pp. 15–16.

270. ability to move to any country: Christopher Caldwell, "Bordering on What?" *New York Times Magazine*, September 25, 2005, p. 46.

270. "We live in a borderless world": Off-the-record discussion.

271. "one of the success stories": Mark Mulligan and Raphael Minder, "Spain and Morocco call for joint action over tide of migrants," *Financial Times*, October 12, 2005, p. 3.

272. a battle against "the mafia": Caldwell, "Europe's Future" (see chap. 1 Notes), p. 26.

273. pestiferous colonial projects: Hamid Dabashi, "Native informers and the making of the American empire," *Al-Ahram Weekly*, June 1–7, 2006.

273. Germany was reunified: Stephen Sestanovich, "American Maximalism," *The National Interest*, Spring 2005.

274. "Although they all knew": Tony Benn, *More Time for Politics*, p. 5.

275. "No to the imperialist crusade!": Luuk van Middelaar, "Et voilà, de moderniteit," *De Trouw* (*Letter en Geest* section), December 1, 2001.

275. "most Americans simply don't get it": Seumas Milne, "They can't see why they are hated," *Guardian.co.uk*, September 13, 2001.

276. a storehouse of ways of thinking: Politycki, "Weißer Mann—was nun?" (see chap. 4 Notes).

276. "market for silicone breast implants": Michel Houellebecq, *Les Particules élémentaires*, p. 93.

276. "With the lapse of a generation": Enoch Powell, speech to the Annual Conference of the Rotary Club of London, Eastbourne, November 16, 1968. In Powell, *Reflections of a Statesman*, p. 393.

276. "you can move to New York": Alexander Stille, "No blacks need apply" (see chap. 1 Notes).

278. "required to go home": "The State of American Public Opinion on Immigration in Spring 2006," Pew Hispanic Center, May 17, 2006, p. 9.

279. "real story of American Muslims": Geneive Abdo, "America's Muslims Aren't as Assimilated as You Think," *Washington Post*, August 27, 2006, p. B3.

281. we have made our bed: Mark Lilla, "The Politics of God," *New York Times Magazine*, August 19, 2007, p. 50.

282. If you want to belong: Élie Barnavi, *La Tribune Juive* (cited in John

Thornhill, "Europe's holiday from its own history", *Financial Times*, February 19, 2007, p. 16).

282. **"Why should we welcome":** Max Hastings, "I confess, I have never had a Muslim to dinner in my house," *Weekly Telegraph* 732 (August 3–9, 2005).

283. **"should not be in this country":** Caldwell, "Counterterrorism in the U.K." (see chap. 4 Notes), p. 42.

283. **"traditional civil-liberty arguments":** Christopher Caldwell, "The Post-8/10 World," *New York Times Magazine*, August 20, 2006, p. 18.

283. **One of her main tasks:** Some of Sbai's stories are recounted in Cristina Giudici, "Gruppo di famiglia con Allah," *Il Foglio*, October 30, 2004, and in Giudici's book *L'Italia di Allah*.

285. **Why in God's name:** Udo di Fabio, *Die Kultur der Freiheit*, pp. 50–51.

285. **measures which provide more adequately:** My discussion of Pareto draws on this and surrounding passages in James Burnham, *The Machiavellians*, pp. 199–200.

Index

Acknowledgments

This would have been a duller book had not several editors—William Kristol, Fred Barnes, Richard Starr, and Claudia Anderson at the *Weekly Standard*; Gerald Marzorati and Alex Star at the *New York Times Magazine*; and Lionel Barber, Brian Groom, and Gwen Robinson at the *Financial Times*—let me write about some of the issues and places covered in it. I thank them. I am grateful to my brother-in-law, Jordi Galí, for reading chapter 2; to my European colleagues Paul Brill, Janny Groen, Blandine Grosjean, Michel Gurfinkiel, Lotte Folke Kaarsholm, Jörg and Mariam Lau, and Stuart Reid for generous advice and help; to my agent, Tina Bennett; and to my editors Kristine Puopolo and Helen Conford. Any mistakes or misjudgments in this book are mine.

Christopher Caldwell
Washington, D.C.,
February 18, 2009

Meet with Interesting People
Enjoy Stimulating Conversation
Discover Wonderful Books